Apple Pro Training Series

Encyclopedia of Visual Effects

Damian Allen / Brian Connor

Foreword by Ron Brinkmann

Apple
Certified

Apple Pro Training Series: Encyclopedia of Visual Effects
Damian Allen and Brian Connor
Copyright © 2007 by Damian Allen and Brian Connor

Published by Peachpit Press. For information on Peachpit Press books, contact:

Peachpit Press
1249 Eighth Street
Berkeley, CA 94710
(510) 524-2178
(800) 283-9444
Fax: (510) 524-2221
http://www.peachpit.com
To report errors, please send a note to errata@peachpit.com
Peachpit Press is a division of Pearson Education

This book has a companion website: www.vfxtechniques.com

Contributors: Tim Alexander, J Bills, Yanick Dusseault, Pablo Helman, Marshall Krasser, Tim MacMillan, Martin Rosenberg, Mike Seymour, Todd Vaziri
Editor: Serena Herr
Development Editors: Bob Lindstrom, Whitney Walker
Apple Series Editor: Nancy Peterson
Production Editor: Myrna Vladic
Technical Editor: Chris Parkinson
Technical Reviewers: Brendan Boykin, Mark Spencer
Copy Editors: Karen Seriguchi, Elissa Rabellino
Compositor: David Van Ness
Indexer: Valerie Perry
Cover and Interior Design: Mimi Heft
Cover Illustration: Kent Oberheu
Cover Production: Maureen Forys, Happenstance Type-o-rama

ISBN 0-321-30334-2

9 8 7 6 5 4 3 2 1
Printed and bound in the United States of America

Acknowledgments

Damian Allen To the Lord Jesus Christ, the original visual effects artist, whose work on the planet Earth is the definitive reference for realism.

To my beautiful wife Marne, for love, friendship, and uncommonly tasty chocolate chip cookies. To my little girl Makenzie, the most graceful ballerina/princess/puppy impersonator I'll ever know. And to our unborn child, can't wait to meet you, and please play nice with your sister when you arrive.

Thanks to Patty Montesion, a wonderful friend and the best agent I never had to pay for.

To Nancy, Bob, Karen, Erin, Elissa, Anita, Chris P, the whole Peachpit family, and all the editors we lost along the way, thanks for hanging in there. And especially to Serena; we'd still be somewhere between Alpha channel and Androgyny Simulation if you hadn't kept pushing.

Thanks to Marty Rosenberg for wrangling cameos from busy people with important jobs.

Thanks to J Bills, Mike Seymour, and all the unnamed compositors who passed on their techniques to me through the years.

Thanks to my mother for loving me regardless and keeping me alive long enough to reach adulthood, no small task.

And thank you, esteemed reader, for embarking on this great adventure into the world of visual effects. (Well, actually, I'm more excited that you purchased the book, but there you go.)

Brian Connor There are so many people to whom I am forever grateful. My wonderful, loving family; Darleen, Dan, Becky, Scott, and Michael Connor.

Friends past and present; Doug Paris, Mark Schoennagel, Ricardo Torres, Charles Migos, Anjenette Barad, Jean-Luc Bouchard, Christophe Garnier, Jessica Goce, and Sebastien Moreau.

And, of course, I ride on the back of the giants who came before: Bob Andrews, Tom Mahoney, Royce Steele, Jong Kang, Eric Hansen, Blaine Kennison, Dan Levitan, Masaki Mitchell, Peter Warner, Ron Brinkmann, Pat Tubach, Eddie Pasquerello, Kate Shaw, Sandra Karpman, Ben Snow, Lynwen Brennan, Marshal Krasser, Jon Alexander, Jeff Doran, Gretchen Libby, Pablo Helman, Kim Libreri, Tim Alexander, John Knoll, George Lucas, and all the very talented artists at ILM. Thank you for teaching me how to see. Special thanks to Miles Perkins and Megan Corbet for helping me get people to the important word, *Yes*.

This book owes a debt of gratitude to Patty Montesion and the fine folks at Apple. Special thanks for all the tireless work by my coauthor and patron saint, Damian Allen. And, of course, to Serena Herr and the many talented people at Peachpit. We literally couldn't have done it without you!

Finally, I want to thank all of the many students that I have had the pleasure of teaching. Thank you for always asking 'why' and for taking me to places that continue to inspire and fulfill me today.

Contributors

Tim Alexander is a visual effects supervisor at Lucasfilm's Industrial Light & Magic. His credits as VFX supervisor include *Harry Potter and the Goblet of Fire, Hidalgo, Want,* and *The Perfect Storm.* His credits as a digital compositor and digital effects artist include *Star Wars: Episode I, Titanic, Contact, The Lost World: Jurassic Park,* and *Star Trek: First Contract.*

Damian Allen is a commercial artist and president of Pixerati LLC, a Los Angeles-based visual effects design and consultancy corporation. He has designed and directed projects for British Airways, Coca-Cola, Amatil, Toshiba, Epson, Pfizer, and several multinational financial and telecommunications companies. Damian consults and lectures around the world on compositing theory and visual effects design.

John-Michael "J" Bills began his pursuit of visual effects first as a Graphic Designer for network TV affiliates in Kansas City, near his hometown. Trading KC for New York City in 2000, Bills made the rounds as a freelance compositor and 2D supervisor, eventually landing at artist collective Psyop by day while teaching compositing & VFX at the School of Visual Arts by night. 2003 marked Bills' first feature film work, when he found a home at Peter Jackson's Oscar-winning effects unit Weta Digital, working on the *Lord of the Rings* trilogy. Recent credits include *King Kong* and *X-Men 3: The Last Stand.*

Brian Connor is a Senior Compositor at Lucasfilm's Industrial Light & Magic and co-owner of Stimulate Productions LLC. His credits include *Jurassic Park III, Terminator 3, Star Wars: Episode II, Star Wars: Episode III, Pirates of the Caribbean: The Black Pearl, Pirates of the Caribbean: Dead Man's Chest, Poseidon,* and *War of the Worlds.* Brian also lectures on visual effects and compositing worldwide, and teaches at the Academy of Art University in San Francisco.

Yanick Dusseault is a lead matte painter at Lucasfilm's Industrial Light & Magic. Previously a senior matte painter at WETA Digital, Dusseault created some of the most memorable landscapes and backgrounds in *Star Wars: Episode III, The Lord of the Rings: The Two Towers,* and *The Lord of the Rings: The Fellowship of the Ring.* His other recent film credits include *War of the Worlds, Terminator III,* and *Pirates of the Caribbean: The Curse of the Black Pearl.* He has also worked extensively as a visual effects supervisor and 3D artist for commercial clients, including Adidas, United Airlines, and Nissan.

Pablo Helman, a native of Buenos Aires, Argentina, joined Lucasfilm's Industrial Light and Magic in 1996. As visual effects supervisor, his film credits include *War of the Worlds, Munich, Jarhead, The Bourne Supremacy, Master and Commander: The Far Side of the*

World, Terminator 3, and *Star Wars: Episode II.* As supervisor of ILM's Sabre department, Helman worked on numerous films including *Saving Private Ryan, Contact, Jurrasic Park,* and *Men in Black.* Previous to ILM, he was a compositing supervisor on *Independence Day* for Pacific Ocean Post, a digital compositor on *Apollo 13* and *Strange Days* for Digital Domain, and a Quantel Domino compositor on numerous projects for Digital Magic.

Marshall Krasser is a compositing supervisor at Industrial Light & Magic, where his credits include *War of the Worlds, Van Helsing, Rent, Lady in the Water, Hulk, Harry Potter and the Sorcerer's Stone,* and *Star Wars: Episode II.* He has also worked as a digital effects artist and digital compositor on numerous films, including *Titanic, Mission: Impossible, Snake Eyes,* and *The Perfect Storm.*

Tim MacMillan has been experimenting with the "frozen time" effect since the early 1980's when he developed his first time-slice camera system. He has worked as a lighting cameraman, visual effects supervisor, and director in films, TV, and commercials. He received Royal Television Society Craft awards for his ground-breaking work on the BBC Natural History series *Supernatural* and *Weird Nature.* His recent credits include BBC's *Miracles of Jesus.* He can be reached at (www.timeslicefilms.com).

Martin Rosenberg has been a Visual Effects Director of Photography since the film *The Right Stuff* in 1983. For over 20 years he has been a key member of Industrial Light and Magic and has shot effects for over 50 feature films. His credits include the recent *Star Wars* trilogy, several *Star Trek* films, *Mission Impossible, A.I. Artificial Intelligence,* and, most recently, *Lady in the Water.*

Mike Seymour is a visual effects supervisor and senior compositor. He is known for his work in the Discreet Flame community, which led to the formation of the very successful www.fxguide.com and the specialist VFX training site www.fxphd.com. Seymour lectures worldwide, and works and consults with clients in Spain, Australia, and China. He has won numerous visual effects awards, and was nominated for an Emmy in 2005.

Todd Vaziri is a sequence supervisor at Industrial Light & Magic, where he has contributed to such films as *Star Wars: Episode II* and *Episode III, War of the Worlds,* and *Mission: Impossible III.* Prior to ILM, Todd served as compositing supervisor on films including *Driven* and *Hart's War,* and as computer graphics supervisor on *American Pie.* Todd was the creator and author of Visual Effects Headquarters (www.vfxhq.com), the Web's foremost authority on feature film visual effects.

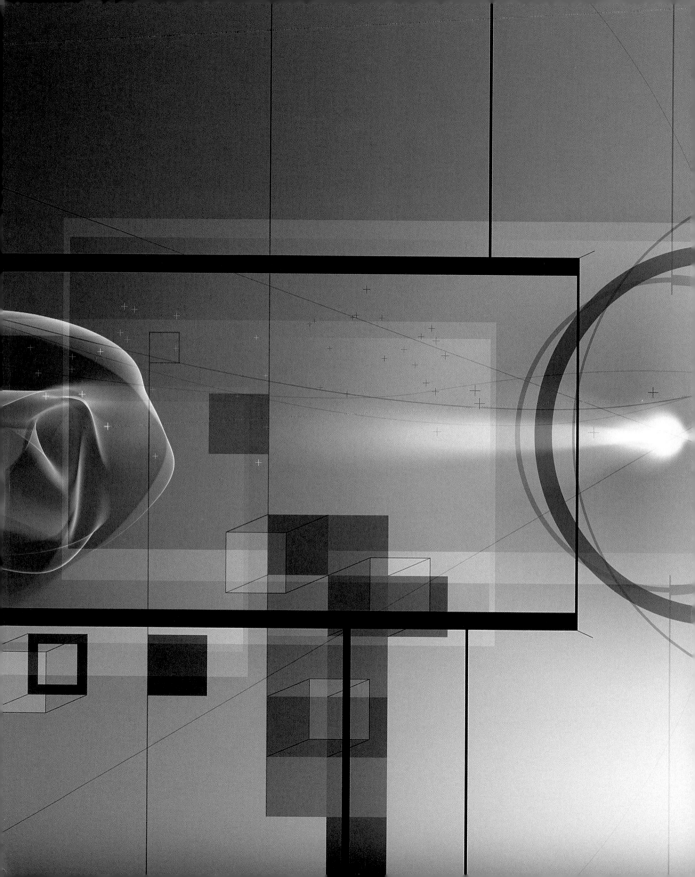

Contents at a Glance

Table of Contents

Encyclopedia of Visual Effects

Cameo   The Sands of *Jarhead*—Martin Rosenberg 389

Appendices

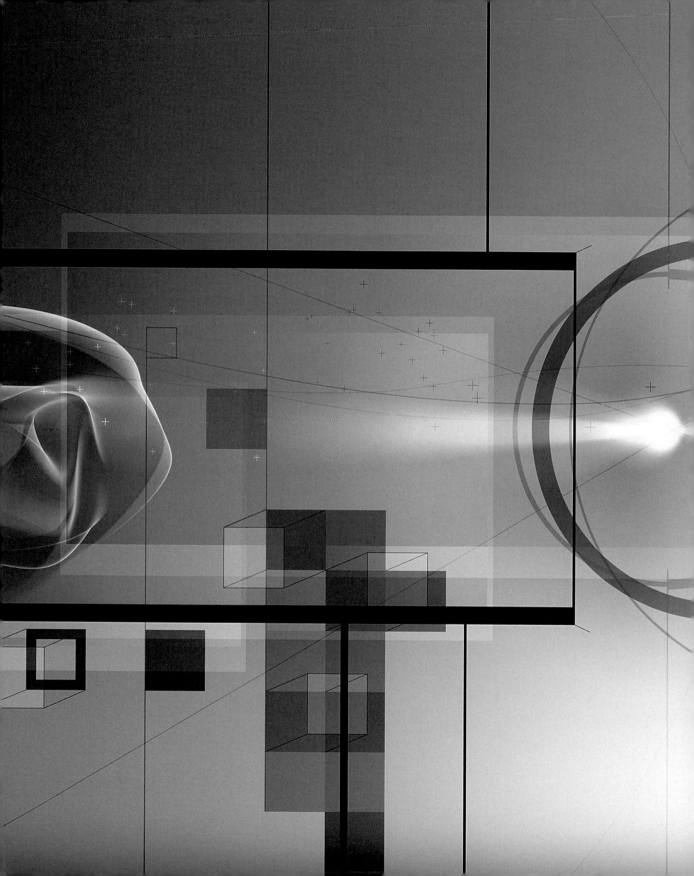

Foreword

For most people, their first exposure to visual effects will come while watching some magic unfold on the screen in a dark room—images telling stories of dramatic adventures and impossible landscapes. But one's first entry into *working* in visual effects can feel more like actually stepping into one of these worlds: bewildering and unfamiliar. The industry isn't intentionally obscure, but the combination of cutting-edge technology with a variety of different working methodologies can make it seem like you've entered a place of arcane rules and secret handshakes.

My personal entry into working in the visual effects industry happened to be at a facility that was also just getting started. There were only five or six of us at that point; some had a great deal of experience, but I certainly wasn't one of them! Instead, I was a classic case of someone who had a bit of knowledge about a few specific pieces of software but no "production experience." No real understanding of how to apply these tools in a real-world environment.

Things evolved rapidly, though, and Sony Imageworks (as we were eventually named) quickly went from being an "experiment" tucked into the corner of a building full of studio executives into a separate entity, growing to dozens, and later many hundreds, of people. I quickly went from some-one who knew how to navigate a particular piece of software to someone who, if nothing else, understood that the focus needed to be on *how* something could be done, not on what tools were used to do it.

The difficult thing about learning the techniques that make a skilled visual effects artist is that those techniques are almost always just "passed on" by someone else who has encoun-tered a similar situation. If you don't happen to have access to such a person, you'll often be left to your own devices. Although there are generally plenty of resources that describe the features and functions of any specific piece of software, the important stuff—how to apply these features in the real world—is a bit harder to come by.

More than a few years have passed since I started working in this industry, and right now I'm sitting in the midst of the SIGGRAPH 2006 conference, an annual gathering of people involved in all aspects of the computer graphics field. The topics of conversations around me range from scientific visualization to digital photography, from fine art to virtual reality, from video games to software engineering. But the star of the show (from my somewhat biased perspective) is the work being done in the world of visual effects: the behind-the-scenes tools and processes used to create the images that have such power to captivate us.

A great thing about this show—and the field in general—is that the experts still work alongside the novices, sharing knowledge and experience. The pioneers in digital visual special effects (and since it is a relatively young discipline, those experts are mostly still working) are approachable, accessible, and more than willing to share what they have learned. There's no benefit to keeping information secret in this business because every-body is focused on the same end result: to finish the production with the highest possible level of artistry. And the more people around you who know how to achieve those results, the easier everything becomes.

In this same collegial spirit, Damian and Brian have put down on paper an encyclope-dia of common scenarios that anybody working in the field of visual effects is likely to encounter at some point during a career. Having such an encyclopedia is a worthwhile thing, but providing practical methods for dealing with these situations is all too rare in the published literature. When combined with detailed case studies taken from actual productions and the wealth of companion information contained on the accompanying DVD, this encyclopedia becomes a truly invaluable resource. The people who have read this book will enjoy an almost unfair advantage over those who haven't!

Visual effects are usually a collaborative effort, and there are disciplines and subdisciplines within that broad category, including 3D and 2D, modeling, animation, rendering, compositing, rotoscoping, and keying. Not everything presented in this book will be directly applicable to your current work, but the best artists are aware of all aspects of their craft, even those they don't practice regularly.

I can guarantee that the longer you work in this business, the more you'll encounter the situations described here. You'll quickly find that every shot is different, presenting its own problems and requiring unique solutions. But fortunately there *are* a number of reasonably well-known techniques that address the most common situations, as well as a variety of more obscure processes that can save an incredible amount of time in certain circumstances. (I hesitate to call them "tricks," even though they can often feel like a bit of well-applied magic.) These are the things you'll find in the pages of this book.

Although I spend most of my time these days dealing with the design of tools used *for* visual effects, I'll still make the occasional foray back into the pain and joy of production. These experiences, coupled with feedback from all the people who *use* those tools, are humbling reminders that software is only as good as the people using it.

And while the ability to do something doesn't always translate into an ability to teach it (and more so for the converse), here we have a collection of material by people who have both taught *and* done visual effects, and have now proved to be equally adept at both.

These, then, are the tools of the trade: a grab bag of incredibly useful methodologies that are provided to you so that you don't have to hunt down *someone* who has already dealt with the issue, or even learn any secret handshakes. You might initially dip into it at random, but I think you'll quickly realize that the best course of action is to go through it at least once cover-to-cover, and then keep it on the shelf within easy reach. You'll be reaching for it often.

—Ron Brinkmann
August, 2006

Ron Brinkmann is an occasional supervisor in the world of visual effects and animation, the product designer of Shake compositing software, and the author of The Art and Science of Digital Compositing *(Morgan Kaufmann, 1999). He can be reached at www.digitalcompositing.com.*

Introduction

Getting Started

Welcome to the *Encyclopedia of Visual Effects*, a recipe book for creating some of the most important and useful effects in modern digital compositing.

Let's be clear from the outset: This book is not intended to teach you compositing theory. Rather, its practical goal is to show you how to accomplish specific techniques that you'll employ in the creation of visual effects. These techniques vary from the mundane but handy to the unusual and spectacular.

If you do need a more extensive introduction to the fundamentals of compositing, look at Ron Brinkmann's *The Art and Science of Digital Compositing* (Morgan Kaufmann). Ron's book does an excellent job of explaining compositing theory and the industry surrounding it.

The word *encyclopedia* implies a comprehensive coverage of subject matter. While we feel confident that this first edition comprehensively covers fundamental techniques and those techniques currently in popular use, it's by no means exhaustive, and in such a creative, rapidly changing field it never could be. The intention, then, is to continue to build on the knowledge base established in this edition, and make this an ongoing reference guide to the art of digital compositing.

The Methodology

There are two main sections in the book: the Fundamentals chapters and the alphabetized encyclopedia entries.

Compositing Fundamentals

The book includes three Fundamentals chapters: Keying, Tracking, and 3D Rendering. These chapters can be used as curricula for compositing courses or as a systematic approach for self-study. Each of the chapters provides a solid overview of the techniques and steps involved in producing an effect. The Keying Fundamentals chapter, in particular, presents a useful flow from the commencement to the completion of a green screen or blue screen shot, and could function as a checklist of tasks to perform during a compositing project.

The Fundamentals chapters refer to specific techniques that are listed in the alphabetized encyclopedia section of the book. They are, therefore, a good point of reference for working through some of the more foundational techniques.

Encyclopedia Techniques

Each entry in this section is a self-contained description or definition of a technique. As much as possible, we've tried to keep entries practical and tutorial; too many books talk *about* techniques without explaining how to implement them.

The level of detail in each entry varies depending on the technique. For very important or technically challenging techniques, you'll find precise procedures, tutorial footage, and exact parameters settings that guide you through the process. For other entries, the methods are described more generally, allowing you to easily adapt them to your specific situation.

One area of techniques not covered in great detail is color correction. That's because color correction deserves an encyclopedia of its own. You'll want to check out Alexis Van Hurkman and DigitalFilm Tree's *Apple Pro Training Series: Advanced Color Correction and Effects in Final Cut Pro 5* (Peachpit Press, 2005) to delve deeper into color-correction techniques.

NOTE ▶ While the Apple Pro Training Series book uses Final Cut Pro to demonstrate its techniques, the methods described can be applied using any software with capable color-correction tools, including Shake, Motion, and Adobe After Effects.

Which Software?

Since the encyclopedia focuses so heavily on technique, we've attempted to make it largely software independent. Nevertheless, where possible, we've included specific information for users of Apple's Shake, Apple's Motion, and Adobe After Effects. For your convenience, we've included trial versions of all three applications on the accompanying DVD.

The default application for most techniques is Shake. The reason is threefold: First, Shake is probably the most affordable pure compositing package on the market (at least at the time of publication). Second, it's been used prominently on most of the recent visual-effects-heavy motion pictures. Third, it clearly depicts the processes involved in each technique with its graphical, node-based structure.

In our opinion, node-based compositing more comfortably lends itself to the problem solving of visual effects work than do timeline-based systems like Motion and After Effects. That's not to say that these applications can't be used competently to create sophisticated visual effects—there's plenty of visual effects work out there that proves the effectiveness of these programs. However, the workflow for visual effects tends to be more cumbersome and restrictive in these timeline-based systems.

If you're new to Shake, you can use the trial version of Shake included on this book's DVD to work through Appendix B, "Shake in a Day," for a quick primer, or work through Marco Paolini's excellent book *Apple Pro Training Series: Shake 4*.

If you'd like to try node-based compositing but you're more comfortable in the world of Motion, try out the techniques in this book with dvGarage's Conduit (www.dvgarage.com), which adds a node-based interface to Motion. A trial version is included on the DVD.

Several of the techniques call for the use of Digital Film Work's Silhouette (www.digitalfilmworks.com), a very useful plug-in for Shake, After Effects, and Final Cut Pro. A trial version is also included on the DVD.

Copying the Lesson Files

Apple Pro Training Series: Encyclopedia of Visual Effects includes a DVD containing the files you'll need for working through some of the techniques. Each technique identifies the file-name and location of the relevant content.

Installing the Lesson Files

1   Insert the *Apple Pro Training Series: Encyclopedia of Visual Effects* DVD into your computer's DVD drive.

2   Double-click the DVD icon on the desktop, titled APTS_CycVFX, to open it.

3   Drag the APTS_CycVFX folder to your Macintosh HD icon.

Installing Trial Versions

Trial versions of Shake, Motion, dvGarage Conduit, and SilhouetteFX Silhouette are also available on the DVD. Find them in the Trial_Software folder, and follow the provided installation instructions as necessary.

Installing Macro Files

Shake macros are included for use with some of the techniques, as well as for your personal use. You'll find these in the Macros folder. Review Appendix A, "How to Install a Macro," to learn how to install these macros for use with Shake.

Text Conventions

A word about the text conventions used in the step-by-step techniques. Where practical, techniques are broken out with steps specific to the host compositing application:

SHAKE ▼

Shake steps are formatted in this style.

AFTER EFFECTS ▼

After Effects steps are formatted in this style.

MOTION ▼

Motion steps are formatted in this style.

When a technique step calls for the addition of a filter or node, a shorthand is used to describe the parameter adjustments for that filter or node.

For example, take the following wordy description:

SHAKE ▼

Select the DigitalFoundation node, and then, on the Filter tab, click a Blur node. In the parameters for the new Blur node, set xPixels to a value of 15.

We've chosen to describe such a step in the following concise style:

SHAKE ▼

Select the DigitalFoundation node. Apply a Filter > Blur (xPixels = 15).

As you can see, the following format is applied: First, the name of the filter or node group is presented (in this case, Filter). Next, the name of the filter or node is identified (in this case, the node Blur). Finally, any parameters that need to be changed from their defaults are listed in parentheses, along with the modified value.

In After Effects, the same step would look like this:

AFTER EFFECTS ▼

In the Timeline, select **DigitalFoundation.tif**. Apply an Effect > Blur & Sharpen > Gaussian Blur (Blurriness = 5) to **DigitalFoundation.tif**.

And in Motion, it would look like this:

MOTION ▼

Select the DigitalFoundation object. Choose Add Filter > Blur > Gaussian Blur (Amount = 2.2).

NOTE ▶ In the examples shown above, each application's parameter values differ because they measure blur intensity in their own ways.

Companion Website

This book has a companion website: www.vfxtechniques.com. From time to time, the authors may post additional content on this site. Please check the site for revised lessons, new content, or trial software.

About the Apple Pro Training Series

Apple Pro Training Series: Encyclopedia of Visual Effects is both a self-paced learning tool and part of the official training curriculum of the Apple Pro Training and Certification Program, developed by experts in the field and certified by Apple Computer. The series offers complete training in all Apple Pro products, and are the approved curriculum for Apple Certified Training Centers worldwide.

For a complete list of Apple Pro Training Series books, see the course catalog at the back of this book, or visit www.peachpit.com/applebooklet.

Apple Pro Certification Program

The Apple Pro Training and Certification Program is designed to keep you at the forefront of Apple's digital media technology while giving you a competitive edge in today's ever-changing job market. Whether you're an editor, graphic designer, sound designer, special effects artist, or teacher, these training tools are meant to help you expand your skills.

Certification is offered in Final Cut Pro, DVD Studio Pro, Logic, Motion, Shake, and Soundtrack Pro. Successful certification as an Apple Pro gives you official recognition of your knowledge of Apple's professional applications while allowing you to market yourself to employers and clients as a skilled, pro-level user of Apple products.

You can become a Certified Apple Pro by taking the online certification exam through an Apple Authorized Training Center. To prepare for the exam, self-paced learners can simply work through the lessons in the appropriate Apple Pro Training Series book.

For those who prefer to learn in an instructor-led setting, Apple offers training courses at Apple Authorized Training Centers worldwide. These courses, which use the Apple Pro Training Series books as their curriculum, are taught by Apple Certified Trainers. The courses balance concepts and lectures with hands-on labs and exercises. Apple Authorized Training Centers have been carefully selected and have met Apple's highest standards in all areas, including facilities, instructors, course delivery, and infrastructure.

To find an Authorized Training Center near you, go to www.apple.com/software/pro/training.

Contact the Authors

For direct correspondence with the authors of this book, you can reach Damian Allen at damian@vfxtechniques.com, or Brian Connor at brian@vfxtechniques.com.

Compositing
Fundamentals

1

Techniques

Chapter **1**
3D Fundamentals

3D rendering is a library of topics unto itself. This section describes how to manipulate 3D-rendered images in a compositing applica-

tion, rather than how to achieve photorealism with a 3D renderer. We'll explain the scene setup inside a 3D animation package when a technique requires it, but for the most part we'll focus on postrender compositing.

There are many ways to enhance and optimize 3D content during the compositing phase, but two common processes are worth looking at in detail: integrating 3D into live action, and multipass compositing.

NOTE ▶ In the past, the term *CGI* (computer-generated imagery) was commonly used to describe content generated by a computer, in contrast to content acquired by an image-capturing device such as a film or video camera. More recently, this abbreviation has been further shortened to *CG,* for "computer graphics," which helps avoid confusion with another IT computer term, *Common Gateway Interface.* Strictly speaking, CG encompasses any computer-generated content, which might include, for example, the two-dimensional rendering of a TV-screen insert. To help distinguish between generic CG and CG rendered by a 3D rendering package, this book will use the term *3D* to describe 3D-rendered CG.

Also note that *live action* describes content acquired with a real-world camera.

Integrating 3D into Live Action

In many ways, integrating 3D animation into live action is similar to compositing keyed screen elements into a background plate. The 3D element needs to be lit and color corrected to match the background, the shadows and reflections should be matched accurately, and grain must be added to match the grain density of the background footage.

Further, a 3D integration involves re-creating the pathway that real light takes on its way to the digital file you read into your compositing application. That is, to accurately match live action footage, the 3D elements must appear to have gone through identical processes, from lens distortion at the camera to artifacts like sharpening and chroma subsampling.

In this section, we'll step through some of the common processes involved in creating a convincing composite of 3D and live action.

Set Survey

Taking accurate measurements while filming the live action background can make it significantly easier to integrate a 3D element into a scene. Careful measurement of the distances between objects and the focal point of the camera, the orientation of the scene, and the use of tracking markers provide indispensable data for the 3D simulation. Light and reflective references are also very helpful, the most common of these being gray and reflective spheres (see gray ball).

3D Matchmoving

While 3D animation requires no keying (the 3D rendering package will automatically create a matte), almost all compositing of 3D into live action requires another significant step. To create a convincing composite, the 3D elements must appear to inhabit the same three-dimensional space as the objects in the live action scene. This is referred to as *3D matchmoving* (for a detailed discussion of matchmoving, see the Tracking Fundamentals chapter).

3D matchmoving involves creating a 3D model of the camera used to shoot the live action footage, and then placing virtual objects at the correct respective distances from that camera. For example, if a director wants a 3D character composited onto a live action counter-top, the character needs to be positioned in the virtual world at the same distance from the virtual camera as it would be from the real, live action camera.

You can achieve an accurate match either automatically by using a 3D matchmoving application, or manually by manipulating and aligning points (see matchmoving in perspective).

Once the live action scene has been replicated by the 3D animation package, the CG elements can be rendered and brought into the compositing application. The scene can be rendered using a multipass setup (see Multipass Compositing on page 8) for maximum flexibility, or rendered as a single beauty pass (in which the finished shot is contained within a single image).

Lighting

One of the most important tasks in any composite is creating the illusion that all the elements were lit by the same light sources. This is especially vital in "selling" 3D elements, since such elements are generated by simulations of real light and lack the subtle complexity of real-world illumination. Special attention must be paid to simulating the light sources that a real object would receive if it genuinely existed in the scene.

There are several useful techniques for matching the lighting of a 3D element to that of its live action background. Some of these, such as gray bias color matching (see color matching) and radiosity simulation (see radiosity, faux) can be adopted from keying methods. Other techniques are unique to 3D.

 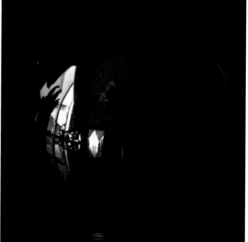

The same HDR image displayed at different exposure settings. Note the sky detail in the second image that was clipped by the exposure settings of the first image.

HDRI lighting is an emerging method for creating an accurate lighting match. This technique uses an HDR (high dynamic range) image captured from the live action scene to light the 3D object by means of a process called *global illumination*. Global illumination—also known as *image-based lighting*—attempts to simulate the interactive bounce lighting (known as radiosity) that produces the subtle shading detail of the physical world. Sophisticated techniques such as ambient occlusion passes can be used to create effects similar to radiosity at a fraction of the render time.

Shadow Passes

Whether or not you use multipass compositing for the overall render, it's essential to perform a *shadow pass* to realistically integrate the foreground and background of any 3D-in-live-action shot. In the 3D application, geometry matching the basic landscape of the live action scene (often just a basic plane) is created, and a shadow is rendered over this landscape based on the position of the 3D object to be integrated into the scene. The result is a matte of the shadow that can be used to color correct the background to simulate a real shadow (see shadows, faux).

Occlusion

Once the 3D element has been appropriately lit to match the live action scene, mattes need to be created for any elements of the live action plate that move in front of the element. For example, if an actor is supposed to be holding a 3D cat, you expect the actor's hands and fingers to hide parts of the cat from the camera. Rotoscoping is performed to isolate these live action elements and composite them over the 3D object, usually via a technique called *knockout compositing*.

Camera Simulation

The final step in creating a convincing composite of 3D and live action is to simulate the physical image capture. That is, the visual artifacts added to an image by the camera mechanics, and any subsequent processing, must be simulated in the rendered 3D image.

One of the telltale signs of 3D imagery is its purity, or "crispness." Because a 3D renderer works on a precise mathematical model, it produces images that lack the natural irregularities created by a film or video camera. Live action images undergo several degrading processes that should be replicated in the 3D imagery. These include changes arising from camera shake, chroma subsampling, depth-of-field (defocus), diffusion, grain, lens distortion, lens flares, motion blur, and sharpening. (See camera diffusion simulation; grain matching; lens flare; lens warping; matchmoving in perspective.)

Multipass Compositing

Multipass compositing is simply compositing with multiple render passes. Multipass rendering is the process of breaking up renders into separate passes—commonly the diffuse, specular, reflection, and shadow passes—to provide flexibility in the compositing stage (see multipass, basic passes).

Diffuse pass

Reflection pass

Specular pass

Shadow pass

The use of multiple passes solves a fundamental problem with 3D rendering: the inability to make changes to an image *after* it's been rendered. If you build enough flexibility into a multipass rendering setup, you can make extreme changes during the composite, such as relighting a scene or changing the surface properties of specific objects.

Scene relit during composite

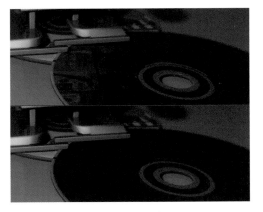

Reflectivity of DVD surface reduced during composite

NOTE ▶ Since multipass rendering and multipass compositing are two parts of the same process, the terms are sometimes used interchangeably.

It's important to understand that multipass rendering is *not* a technique reserved for high-end Hollywood production facilities. The technique is just as useful in short-form commercial postproduction work as it is in the feature film environment. In fact, the flexibility of multipass compositing may be *more* important in a commercial post environment, where last-minute client changes are the norm, and the opportunity and time to re-render are rare.

Multipass rendering does require some initial setup, so it's not something you perform on a whim. Once correctly established in a workflow, however, multipass rendering and compositing can be automatically applied to every project and render thereafter.

Good multipass rendering is a compromise between flexibility and efficiency. To borrow a mathematical term, multipass composites should be *elegant*, providing the greatest amount of postrender adaptability with the least amount of setup and adjustment.

In addition, the breakdown into multiple passes should not significantly increase rendering times over a traditional single "beauty" pass approach. In fact, most 3D renderers perform calculations (such as the evaluation of diffuse and specular lighting contributions) as discrete processes. In such cases, multipass compositing is a matter of intercepting the renderer before it "glues" the passes together. The only increase in rendering time is a slight I/O hit as the additional data is handled and the images are written to disk.

There are two fundamental approaches to multipass rendering and compositing: *per object* multipass and *per light* multipass. A third approach, in which each light is rendered as a grayscale render pass and then multiplied against a generic diffuse exposure, is used less frequently, so it won't be covered in detail here.

Per Object Multipass

When initially breaking down a 3D scene into passes, it would seem logical to render separate passes for each object. Then all of those passes could be brought together in the compositing application and assembled into the final scene.

In reality, so-called *per object multipass rendering* is appropriate only when the scene consists of no more than one or two objects, or when the live action integration dictates that the objects be handled separately. Beyond that, the scene becomes unmanageable, and the cumulative passes require an unjustifiable increase in time (since processes such as calculating reflections must account for all the objects in a scene, not just the object currently being rendered).

The toy robot scene, for example, has seven objects (including the floor) and three lights: a key light, a fill light, and a rim light. Breaking down the scene into the basic passes—diffuse, specular, reflection, and shadow—results in 7 objects × 3 lights × 4 basic pass types, for a total of 84 passes.

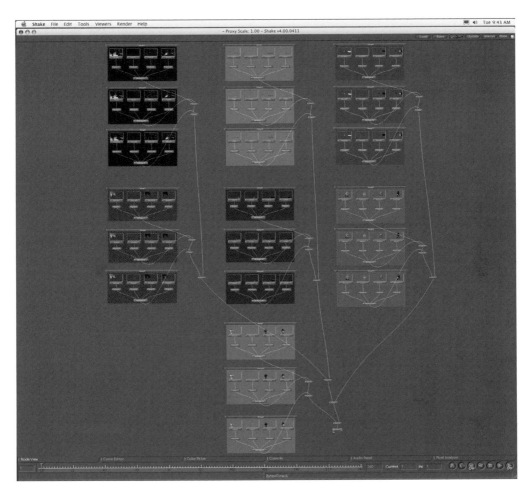

Per object breakdown of the toy robot scene: 84 individual nodes need to be combined for the final composite.

And that's just for a basic scene setup—if you were to include special passes (discussed on page 16 in Special Render Passes), this number would increase dramatically. As another typical example, a scene with 20 objects and 5 separate light sources undergoing a total of 10 render pass types would yield $20 \times 5 \times 10 = 1000$ separately rendered passes. These numbers are simply unmanageable for most situations, and the associated render times become prohibitive.

Per Light Multipass

A far more manageable method of multipass compositing is to break the scene down by light source (see multipass, per light). In this method, all the objects in the scene are included in each pass, and one pass is made for each light. In the toy robot test scene, instead of 84 individual passes we have 3 lights × 4 basic pass types, totaling 12 individual passes (along with 2 additional matte passes, discussed later). As you can see, this is a much more palatable compositing proposition:

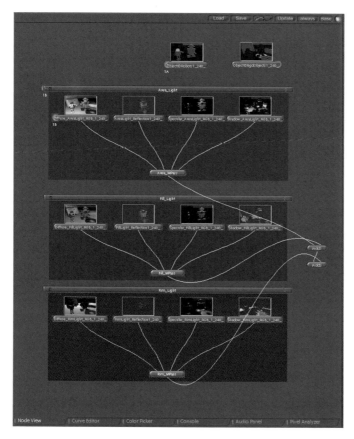

Per light breakdown of the toy robot scene: 12 individual nodes (plus 2 matte passes) need to be combined for the final composite.

Along with the basic lighting passes, per light multipass requires the additional rendering of matte passes. These are simply passes in which mattes for each object in the scene are rendered to separate the red, green, blue, and alpha channels of an image. In the example shown here, mattes have been rendered for the two toy robots, with the matte of the square robot rendered in the blue channel, and mattes for the helmet and body of the cylindrical robot rendered in the green and red channels, respectively.

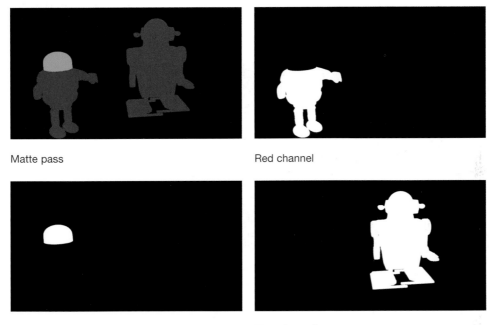

Matte pass

Red channel

Green channel

Blue channel

These mattes can be used to quickly isolate color corrections to specific elements in the scene (see multipass, per light), offering the same flexibility as the per object approach, but with a much more efficient compositing workflow.

A matte is used to isolate color correction to the diffuse channel of only one robot, turning it blue.

Matte passes require no shaders, no global illumination, and no ray tracing and are therefore extremely fast to render. They are also space efficient: Since standard images have red, green, blue, and alpha channels, up to four mattes can be stored in an image sequence. Many 3D rendering packages provide a simple toggle switch in an object's properties that set the program to render on one of the matte channels.

For even greater isolation of scene elements, *shader ID passes* (sometimes known as *object ID passes*) can be used. In this type of pass, specific ID color values are assigned to each textured element of a scene. A single object may be textured by multiple shaders, and a shader ID pass can isolate a specific part of an object for treatment during the composite. These ID mattes require some finessing, however, since they usually lack anti-aliasing.

Shader ID passes assign a different pixel brightness value
to each shader in the image.

A variant of per light multipass is to render different lights into the channels of RGB images as grayscale passes. A single fully colored and textured pass can then be rendered with high ambient lighting and subsequently multiplied against the grayscale light passes to produce the final image.

Disadvantages of Per Light Multipass

Per light multipass works best with multiple-object scenes. It can be inappropriate in other situations—most notably shots in which depth-of-field effects are introduced after the rendering is performed. Realistic defocusing of a background requires access to the portions of the background located *behind* foreground objects. If the entire scene is rendered in a single pass, the background pixels behind a foreground object will be unavailable;

they were not rendered because the foreground object occluded them. A work-around for this is to use the *background hole filling* techniques described in stereoscopy from 2D.

Other problematic situations include those that require refraction through transparent surfaces, and transparency in general.

> **TIP**▶ Even when problems arise in a per light multipass setup, it's sometimes most efficient to render out a segment of the shot to composite over the problem area, rather than re-render the entire frame.

Image Depth and File Format Choices

To take full advantage of multipass compositing, it's preferable to work with 32 bits-per-channel float renders of your 3D scene. Float images preserve subtle detail in areas such as highlights, allowing you to make extreme lighting changes and still produce acceptable results. Nonfloat images are simply unable to represent a comparable dynamic range of image data. Multipass compositing can be performed with 8 bpc (bits per channel) or 16 bpc renders, but the degree to which the scene can be relit without producing artifacts is significantly diminished.

This 8-bit image flattens after extreme relighting of the multipass composite.

This float image maintains contrast after extreme relighting of the multipass composite.

Most modern 3D renderers use floating-point calculations internally, so extracting a 32-bit float render is usually just a matter of choosing an export file format that can support float images. Common file formats that support float have the extensions iff, ct, ct16, mray, rla, rpf, and tif.

OpenEXR, a new file format developed by Industrial Light & Magic, is quickly becoming the de facto standard for storing float images due to its open-source nature, flexibility, and efficient file compression. OpenEXR plug-ins have been compiled for most of the major 3D rendering applications, so a quick search of the Web should locate a compatible OpenEXR exporter. Both Shake 4 and Adobe After Effects 7 include native OpenEXR support.

> **TIP** Targa files, also known as .tga files, have become a common format used by 3D animators. However, Targa is not a good file format choice in the modern computer graphics world. First, Targa does not support float image data. Second, due to variations in the way applications support Targa files, Targa files are often incompatible between applications. For those reasons, a modern file format such as OpenEXR, is recommended.

Special Render Passes

In addition to the four standard passes (diffuse, specular, reflection, and shadow), several other passes can assist in finessing the final composited image. These can be in the form of *render internals* or *additional render passes*.

Render Internals

When generating an image, a 3D rendering engine generates data or is fed specific data about a scene, which it then uses to calculate the final color of each pixel. Examples of this data include the distance each pixel in the final image is from the virtual camera, the angle at which the surface normal of a pixel faces the virtual camera, and the speed at which an object is moving (if at all). This information is already being generated by the rendering system and therefore requires no additional render time to harness.

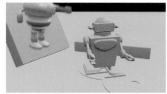

A surface normal pass (center) and a motion vector pass (right)

Most modern rendering systems provide ways to incorporate this information into separate image sequences while the standard RGB passes are performed. Additional passes are not required, and the only additional rendering hit is caused by the conversion of the data to an image-based file, and the associated increase in disk I/O. The result is useful data for compositing that is created with a near-negligible increase in render time.

Additional Render Passes

Dozens of possible passes can be generated by a 3D application for use in manipulating the final composited image. It's important to weigh the benefits of each pass against the additional render time. In a standard workflow, only those passes that will be used regularly should be performed. The exceptions to this rule are passes that can provide miraculous last-minute cures without the need to re-render.

Be careful not to overdo multipass compositing. Special passes can replace corresponding shading operations within the 3D application (for example, facing angles passes can be used to replace a Fresnel shader), but the additional flexibility may not warrant the additional complexity during the composite.

A Fresnel pass (facing angles pass) can be used to adjust the reflectivity of a surface based on its angle to the camera.

Special Render Types

Of the many render passes available, some of the most common are:

▶   ambient occlusion pass (also known simply as an occlusion pass)

▶   Fresnel shading pass (also known as a facing angles or incidence angles pass)

▶   grunge pass (sometimes called a dirt pass)

▶   surface normal lighting pass (also known simply as a normal pass, and occasionally a bump map pass)

▶   UV texture pass

▶   vector pass (also known as a velocity pass)

▶   *z* depth pass (also known as a depth matte, or *z* buffer; see depth keying)

An ambient occlusion pass

Time-Saving Techniques

A problem that will always plague 3D rendering is the time it takes. The faster processors become, the more realistic and complex the lighting simulations that are attempted. To reduce rendering times, it's possible to take advantage of 2D compositing gags to create faster simulations of otherwise render-intensive effects.

Original render

Rotoscoped matte used to drive the variable blur

Resulting variable penumbra effect

A perfect example of such an effect is a variable penumbra shadow (see shadows, faux), a shadow whose edges get softer as it moves away from the source object's point of contact with the ground. A 3D rendering of the shadow requires ray-traced area lights, which significantly add to the render time. A simpler solution is to use crisp shadow maps rendered from the 3D application (which are very fast to render), and then apply an image-based variable blur in the compositing stage to simulate the effect. What could become dozens of additional hours are reduced to a relatively simple one-hour rotoscoping exercise.

Other examples abound, but some of the more important time-saving techniques involve simulations of reflections, refractions, and transparency (see reflections, faux; radiosity, faux; and transparency, simulating).

A final technique worth mentioning when time is critical is rendering at 75 percent of the final frame size. The smaller image will render much faster, and *adaptive upsampling* to 100 percent may actually give a pleasing diffusion to the CG, making it unnecessary to simulate the diffusion by other means.

Image rendered at 75 percent of final scale

Image upsampled to 100 percent

Final Evaluation

CG content should be treated with the same scrutiny as live action imagery. Since the intent is often a simulation of reality, the many tweaks and fakes presented throughout this book for use with live action footage can also be applied to finishing CG.

As with keying, final shots should be subject to a gamma check and full-resolution play-back previewing. Due to the limited gamut of many 3D renders, dangerous mismatches can appear between CG and live action elements. Carefully previewing the content can save you significant embarrassment later on.

While this chapter offers suggested approaches to rendering and compositing, ultimately you should decide what solution is most appropriate for your needs. Always try to antici-pate how much flexibility you'll need during the composite and break out your rendering accordingly. If you have a solid, regular CG production pipeline, you owe it to yourself to implement some kind of multipass strategy, even if it involves only a few additional special passes.

2

Techniques

Chapter 2
Keying Fundamentals

One of the most fundamental processes for visual effects work is the combining (*compositing*) of isolated elements into a separately filmed background. In the case of live action elements, this requires the generation of a matte.

A **matte** is a grayscale image used by compositing software to select which parts of a foreground image are to be composited into the background image and which parts should be removed. Unlike computer-generated elements that are usually created with a pre-rendered matte, or **alpha channel,** live action elements do not inherently possess a matte. Therefore, the matte must be created, either by manual articulation (**rotoscoping**) or, more commonly, by the process of **keying** a green screen or blue screen.

> **NOTE ▶** Several technologies do exist for generating a matte during the filming of live action footage, but most of these work by estimating the distance from the camera to the subject on a per-pixel basis. The result is effectively a depth matte, and it suffers from the same shortcomings as computer-generated depth mattes (most notably, edge aliasing).

> An alternative method of generating a matte during filming is known as the *sodium vapor* method. Used to great effect in the '60s and '70s, this method generates a matte by utilizing a separate black-and-white film roll in addition to the color print. Although extremely effective, the temperamental dual-film setup is expensive and bulky, and it has not endured as a standard keying method. However, if you are the favorite nephew or niece of a rich, dying, childless, eccentric billionaire uncle, feel free to revive and economize the process for the rest of us.

Mattes, Alphas, and Keys

There is frequently a great deal of confusion when referring to mattes, alphas, and keys. The term *matte* comes from the film world, while the term *key* initially referred to a video-based process. In this book, the following distinctions are made:

A *matte* is a grayscale image used by graphics software to identify specific pixels in an image. Most commonly, mattes are used to **composite** only the relevant pixels of a foreground image over a background image. In such mattes, pure-white pixels indicate areas where the foreground image will completely obscure the background image, and black pixels indicate areas where only the background will be visible. Intermediate gray pixels indicate semitransparent areas where the foreground blends with the background.

A *key* is a matte that has been procedurally generated by the computer. An image is analyzed and—based on certain criteria such as color or luminance—a grayscale matte image is created. Commonly, a **green screen** or **blue screen** system is used. While these are currently the most used systems, emerging techniques such as *optical flow matte extraction* (using motion vectors to isolate elements in a scene based on their relative movement) and *edge contrast estimation* have the potential to revolutionize the keying process over the next decade.

Rotoscoping is the process of generating a matte by manual articulation. That is, instead of using a computer to determine which pixels should be transparent and which opaque, an artist uses points, curves, or paint to specify the opacity of pixels in the image. Other terms sometimes associated with rotoscoping are "excruciating pain" and "honest-to-goodness hard work."

A **mask** is an application of a matte. In the process of masking, a matte is used to determine where a certain effect will be applied and where the source image will remain unaffected.

An *alpha channel* is a matte that has been incorporated into the image data of an image file. Instead of the matte's having a separate computer file, its grayscale image is incorporated into a fourth channel of image data (the first three channels being red, green, and blue). When an image file is said to include an alpha channel, it simply means that the matte for that image is included in this fourth, hidden channel of the file format, ready for use in compositing operations.

The process of compositing a green screen or blue screen is almost an art unto itself, but there is a logical problem-solving workflow that can be followed. A description of that workflow follows, along with brief synopses of each section of the workflow.

> **NOTE** ► In this book, the terms *blue screening* and *green screening* refer to the process of generating a matte from footage filmed in front of a colored background. These are often used as umbrella terms to describe techniques applicable to green, blue, and even red backgrounds. Some other sources use the term **chroma keying** to describe such processes. However, since chroma keying is a specific keying methodology (and, in fact, inferior to other techniques), *blue screening* is used to maintain a distinction in the definition of terms.

The Blue Screening Process During Production

To create effective mattes, several issues must be considered and addressed during the production period (rather than in postproduction).

Selecting the Background Screen Color

Several factors can determine the most appropriate background screen color for a shot or series of shots. These can include the wardrobe requirements of the onscreen talent, their hair color, and the budget.

See screen color selection for more information.

Here, the blonde hair of the subject dictates the use of a blue screen for best luminance contrast.

Blue Screen/Green Screen Lighting

An evenly-lit background is essential to generating a clean key. How a background screen is lit will depend on the type of screen and the size of the studio used for the shoot. There are two primary methods of lighting screens: *studio lighting* and *camera ring lighting*.

When using studio lighting, try to use lights with an even distribution and as polarized a light path as possible. Companies like Kino Flo (www.kinoflo.com) make lights that are specifically formulated with frequency distributions sympathetic to green or blue lighting, enhancing the contrast of your final key.

It's also important to keep the backing screen lighting from illuminating your foreground subject. Wherever possible, keep your subject as far from the backing screen as possible to minimize spill (see spill suppression for more information). Use separate lights for achieving the lighting effects intended for the foreground.

There are many myths about lighting blue screens and green screens. One of these is to illuminate the foreground with the opposite color (on the color wheel) from the backing screen color. This is actually a bad idea, since it will be unlikely to improve the keying process and will almost certainly create a color-correction headache.

Be very careful to use the camera monitor to check the evenness of your backing screen lighting, especially when using the color blue. The human eye has a very high tolerance for variations in blue light intensity, so what may appear as an evenly lit screen to the naked eye often appears extremely patchy when seen through a camera's color monitor.

When using ring lighting such as the Reflecmedia system (www.reflecmedia.com), follow the manufacturer's lighting instructions. You'll most likely find that slightly underlighting your foreground will help promote a better key. Also beware of gray pixels toward the edge of the foreground subject.

Scene Setup for Blue Screens/Green Screens

It is essential to ensure continuity between the foreground element being shot against a blue screen and its final background. Perspective, lighting, and shadow placement must be accounted for ahead of time, since many of these elements are almost impossible to recover using only postproduction techniques.

Set surveillance is also essential. The use of LIDAR, grayscale reference cards, stand-in objects, tracking markers, a reference clean plate, and diffuse and reflective sphere leader shots can shave hours off the tweaking that may be required during the compositing stage.

Gray ball

Mirrored ball

Perspective mismatch is an extremely common mistake. If the camera shooting the background plate into which the blue screen is being composited is at shoulder level, make sure that the camera you are using to shoot the blue screen is at shoulder level, as well. If the blue screen element is supposed to appear 30 feet from the camera in the final composited image, make sure you film your element 30 feet from the camera. Perspective mismatch can be tweaked subtly in post, but serious misalignment can rarely be fixed.

Most importantly, make sure that the lighting contrast is coming from the same direction. If the lighting in the background plate appears to come from in front and to the left of the image, make sure you have a key light in the same position for your blue screen shoot. Facial shadows facing the opposite direction to the shadows in a background is another dead giveaway that a composite is a fake.

The Blue Screening Process During Postproduction

Once the blue screening process has been completed in production, several additional processes and possibilities face the effects artist.

Acquiring Blue Screen and Green Screen Footage

A high-quality keying setup can quickly be compromised by a poor choice of acquisition format or by mistakes made while acquiring the footage. Issues to watch out for include sharpening when you're scanning from film, and choosing the wrong digital video formats when performing the telecine transfer.

See footage acquisition, blue screen and green screen for more information.

Compensating for Problems in the Blue Screen or Green Screen

Invariably, significant blue screen or green screen problems are revealed after the footage has been acquired. Several preprocessing techniques can assist the keyer in generating a more accurate matte. These include the following:

- ▶ The correction of uneven lighting in the backing screen
- ▶ Grain treatment—grain removal via a median filter; signal processing; frame blending; and warping of problem grain areas
- ▶ Neutralizing black and white points
- ▶ 4:x:x (subsampled video space) compensation

Garbage Matting

Often a blue screen or green screen shot includes rigging, people, or other items outside the border of the colored screen. These unwanted areas and elements can be manually removed by rotoscoping a garbage matte in preparation for the key.

Generating a Key

The process of using a keyer to extract a reliable matte has its own methodology. An examination of the entries luma edge keying, 4:x:x simulation, and edge matte/core matte helps to elucidate the basic workflow. Invariably, there is also greater control and flexibility in the keying process when compositing outside the keyer itself.

Edge Matte and Core Matte Keying

The two most important elements of a good key are a solid *core matte*, also known as an interior matte (pure white in the foreground and pure black in the background), and a detailed soft edge matte (or exterior matte, the transition between the black and white areas). Unfortunately, these two create a fundamental compositing dilemma: The process of increasing contrast to make a matte solid necessarily hardens the edge of the matte. The solution is to generate two mattes: a core matte with solid black and white regions, and an edge matte that retains soft edge details. A variation on the core matte, the *inverse core matte*, can be used as an additional garbage matte. Also, in some cases, a luma key can be used as an edge matte.

Edge matte

Core matte

Choking the Matte

Regardless of the precision that goes into the keying process, the resulting matte often requires resizing to remove edge artifacts. These artifacts can be due to a sharpening filter applied to the video camera or film telecine, the subsampled color space of digital video, and so on. In many cases, unwanted edges can be *choked*, or eroded, to remove unwanted pixels at the border of the foreground image. Occasionally, reduced contrast around the edges of a keyed object can require that the matte be expanded, or dilated, prior to the composite.

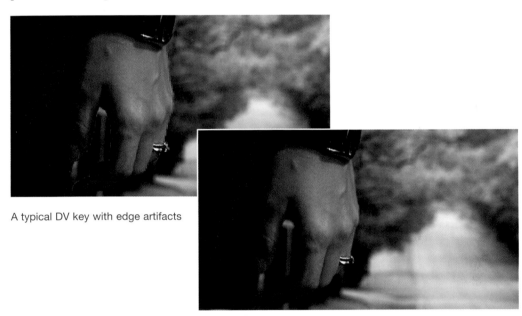

A typical DV key with edge artifacts

The same DV key with a choked (shrunken) matte (and a little chroma blur)

See mattes, shrinking and expanding for more information.

Rotoscoping Problem Areas

Once the edge of the matte has been correctly sized, final problem areas may exist in the matte where the keyer has failed to retain the opacity of the foreground or to correctly key out the background. These can be cleaned up by rotoscoping.

Suppressing Spill

Regardless of the attention to detail taken in preparing the blue screen or green screen shot, there will always be light-spill issues. *Spill* refers to the tinting of areas of the foreground toward the backing screen color. This happens when light reflects off the background screen and contaminates the foreground, and backing light diffuses into the foreground in the camera optics. Spill must be removed before a shot can be correctly color corrected (see spill suppression).

Matching the Background Color

Once the spill has been removed from the image, the color, brightness, and contrast of the foreground image must be matched to its new background. First, the black and white points must be matched, and then the overall image contrast and color bias of the background must be matched (see color matching).

Before color matching

After color matching

Matching Perspectives

As mentioned earlier, it is effectively impossible in postproduction to genuinely modify the perspective of a shot. However, when you have a mismatch it *is* possible to distort the foreground image so that it approximates the perspective of the background (see perspective match). Corner-pinning can be a simple and effective method for achieving this, although in some cases the more involved technique of camera mapping (also known as *sticky projection mapping*) may be required.

Background Light Wrap

If there are significant lighting sources present in the background that is being composited behind the blue screen or green screen, these sources must be factored into the final composite. Had the subject of the blue screen or green screen really been filmed on location in the background plate, those background light sources would have illuminated the subject. Using a modified edge matte, the background lighting can be added to the edges of the foreground subject to create the illusion that lighting from the background plate is wrapping over the foreground (see background wrap).

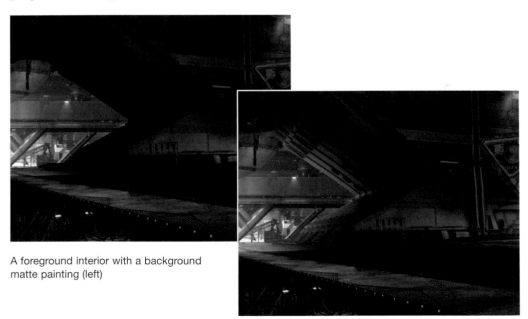

A foreground interior with a background matte painting (left)

The foreground with the background light wrap added

Matching Diffusion and Focus

Different exposure levels, camera optics, and acquisition systems will result in differing levels of softness across an image. Occasionally, blue screen or green screen elements need to be blurred slightly, or a more complex diffusion simulation must be added to an image (see **camera diffusion simulation**).

In addition, the width of the soft edge of the element may need to be expanded or choked to match the softness of equivalent edges in the background plate. For example, if a street sign in the foreground of an image has a soft edge transition of 5 pixels, the crisp edge of a blue screened actor's shirt should also have a 5-pixel-wide soft edge, assuming the actor is supposed to appear to be at the same relative distance from the camera.

Focus is also an issue. A composited element must match the focus of other objects that are at the same distance from the camera.

Without diffusion

With diffusion

Edge Blending

In situations where the edge of the matte has become unusually hard and the transition between the foreground element and the new background is obvious, it is sometimes useful to blend the edges of the composite. By blurring the edge pixels, you can disguise image aliasing and create a more convincing composite (see edge blend).

Matching Shadows

One of the key components when integrating a blue screen or green screen element into a new background is an accurate shadow. The element must cast a shadow on the background scene with properties that are similar to those of other shadows already in that scene. Techniques to achieve this include harvesting shadows from the blue screen or green screen, creating faux shadows (see shadows, faux), preparing a shadow displacement map, and using variable penumbra softening.

Without shadow

With CG shadow

Matching Reflections

Almost as important as matching shadows is adding reflected copies of the blue screen or green screen element to reflective surfaces in the background plate. Adding these reflections can make a vital difference in the believability of the composite (see reflections, faux).

Original image

Image with subtle reflection added beneath the feet

▶ **A Word on Believability**

The job of a visual effects artist is to combine several elements to create a single shot that looks as if it had been filmed live with one camera. This does not necessarily mean accurately simulating every physical reality of the scene. Rather, it is the process of simulating enough of reality to fool the human eye into *believing* that it's seeing a single shot. Due to the production constraints of time and money, it's necessary to focus on those tasks that are most important in achieving that believability.

Shadows are a perfect example. Human beings expect them to be in a scene and know something is wrong when they are absent. But it turns out that human perception is much more forgiving about exactly how shadows look. Techniques like adding faux shadows rely on the fact that the average observer doesn't care about the precise shape of a shadow, as long as it generally matches the properties of other shadows cast by similarly sized objects under the same lighting conditions.

Precision in physicality should be pursued only when a particular item is under severe scrutiny (such as in an extreme close-up), or when the client is throwing enough money and/or time at the project to justify such endeavors (although your lottery odds are better).

Matching Grain

Film stocks differ in the size and intensity of their grain. Even digital video content contains noise that is similar to grain, especially when shot in low-light, high-gain situations. In order to create the illusion that every part of an image was filmed by the same camera, the grain of all elements must match.

The grain of foreground elements is usually matched to the grain of the background. In certain situations, the foreground elements may have excessively large or intense grain. In such cases, either the background can be brought to the grain level of the foreground element, or the foreground element can be degrained using a degrain algorithm or a simple median filter (see grain matching).

Testing Blue Screen Integration

When a shot is nearing completion, a gamma check can be performed to test the integrity of the composite. This will reveal any problems hidden by the limited gamut of your display device, and will also provide feedback as to how well the composited elements blend with the contrast inherent in the background (see also black levels, checking/gamma slamming).

A final, essential test is full-screen animated playback. Since keys are typically adjusted and edited using a single still frame, the entire keyed sequence must be played back at speed to check for problems not visible at the single-frame level. For example, it's common to see hair strands disappear from one frame to the next during playback, something not evident when individual frames are viewed. You may also discover holes in mattes that show up only in specific frames and might otherwise have passed unnoticed.

When all else is done, show the shot to your nonindustry significant other. If they say, "What am I supposed to be looking at?" then you've done your job. If they say, "That looks fake to me," then it's time to go back and fix things.

3

Techniques

Chapter 3
Tracking Fundamentals

Tracking is a crucial component of visual effects work. While keying and color correction are used to make sure that the color and contrast match in foreground and background elements, tracking is required to ensure that the *movements* of those elements match.

Gate weave is a perfect example of a situation that calls for tracking in a composite. When frames of film are pulled onto the backing plate in a film camera, each frame may be slightly misaligned with other frames in the reel.

An example of extreme gate weave, which caused significant misalignment of the scene from one frame to the next

Cameras can vary in their degree of gate weave due to their pin registration (how many film sprocket pins hold the film in place) and their age. Gate weave also frequently occurs during telecine or film scanning.

A small amount of gate weave usually goes unnoticed by viewers; however, if stationary elements containing gate weave are introduced into a scene containing gate weave, those elements will look out of place because they lack the almost imperceptible movement of the rest of the background. The common solution is to remove the movement in the background plate—a process known as stabilization.

A more obvious example of the need for tracking would be the addition of a 3D character to the deck of a moored boat. If the character is to appear as if she's standing on the boat, she should move up and down with the boat as it bobs in the waves. The movement of the boat needs to be tracked and that movement must be applied to the 3D character. This process is known as matchmoving.

The Categories of Tracking

Tracking is the process of identifying and recording the movements of elements in a shot. If an object being tracked moves up and to the left, the new position will be recorded during the tracking operation. In the strictest sense of the word, tracking does not affect the image in any way; tracking is all about collecting data. What is *done* with that data is the subject of this chapter.

Stabilization

Stabilization uses tracking data to lock an object in place. For example, if an object is tracked as moving up and to the left by a certain amount, moving the footage down and to the right by the same amount will lock the object in its original position (see the example of the speed-limit sign in the figures below). This may introduce an edge border to the image, since the camera did not capture the scene beyond the borders of the unstabilized frame. In cases of minor movement—such as gate weave—this edge border can be removed by cropping and scaling the image. In cases of more extreme movement, such as in the figure, smoothing may be a more appropriate solution (see Smoothing, on facing page).

Frame 1

Frame 2

Frame 2 stablized to frame 1

Matchmoving

Matchmoving is the opposite of stabilization. It uses tracking data to create identical movement in elements added to a background plate. For example, if the background moves up and to the left, moving a composited element similarly up and to the left will create the illusion that the new element is moving *with* the background. That is, the element is *matching* the background *movement*. (Unlike other disciplines whose terms tend to be derived from Latin, the visual effects industry relies on more common English phrases such as *matchmoving*. This trend in nomenclature is sometimes attributed to the postproduction industry's distaste for the academic intelligentsia. Another, more probable, theory is that visual effects pioneers, for the most part, simply don't know any Latin.)

A new sign graphic is moved up and to the left to match the movement of the sign it's replacing in the background plate.

Smoothing

Smoothing is a variation on stabilization. It uses tracking data to remove only the *noise* in a movement, while preserving a smooth motion path for the tracked object. In this context, *noise* refers to unwanted movement, as opposed to a sound (like the agonized moans of a producer crying over wasted film). For example, if a handheld camera is panning from left to right across a scene, the shot may be rendered unusable by the shakiness resulting from holding the camera instead of mounting it on a tripod. If the shakiness can be removed while retaining the smooth movement of the pan, the shot might be salvageable.

In the figure below, the horizontal movement of an object in a scene has been tracked and plotted. It's clear that the movement is not smooth; the jaggy edge of the curve indicates that shake was introduced, possibly due to the camera's being handheld.

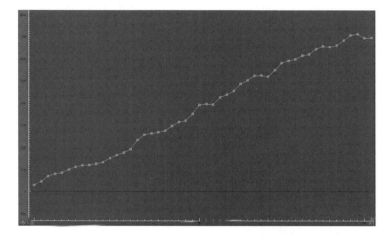

Through the averaging of tracking data (a process similar to blurring pixels in an image to make them more homogeneous), a smoothed curve is produced (see the figure below).

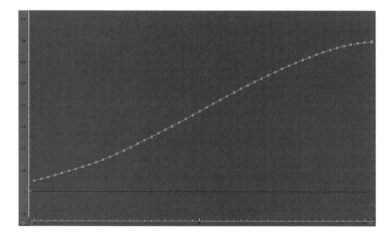

This new graph shows a smooth pan from left to right, albeit with some acceleration and deceleration at either end of the curve. A casual glance may suggest that the problem has been solved and that if this curve is used to stabilize the footage, all will be well. Unfortunately, the solution is not so simple.

If the smoothed curve data is applied to stabilize the original clip, the smooth pan will be eliminated, leaving the noisy shake as the *only* movement in the final clip. Remember that a stabilize operation works by applying the tracked data in the opposite direction. If the tracked object moves up and to the right, the stabilize will move the footage down and to the left to negate the movement. In the preceding example, if the clip moves up and to the right, the smooth data will move it back down and to the left, but *only* by the amount specified in the smoothed curve. Therefore, the smooth motion will be negated, but the shaky motion will remain.

The solution is to produce a curve that plots only the motion noise, and use *that* to stabilize the clip. This is simply a case of subtracting the smoothed curve from the original.

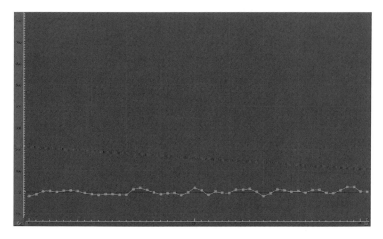

This leaves a curve that represents only the noise in the original movement. If this data is used to stabilize the footage, the noise will be negated and the smooth motion of the clip will be retained.

If this explanation seems intimidating, be reassured that the information is primarily useful for impressing fellow geeks at parties (although probably not the sort of parties you'd like to be invited to). Software packages include smoothing functions that will take care of the entire process for you. In fact, some software, including Apple's Shake, will automatically track and smooth footage without your having to manually identify and set tracking markers.

The Many Dimensions of Tracking

Until now, we've been working under the simplistic assumption that a single point is being tracked. If that point moves up and to the left, a stabilize operation can move it down and to the right by the same amount; or a matchmove operation can shift another element by an equal amount. In reality, some of the most useful tracking operations require tracking more than a single point.

A single tracked point can lock position but nothing else. For example, if the end of the pier in the figure below is tracked using a single point, the track detects no change from the first frame to the second. The camera has centered the end of the pier, so there's been no horizontal movement, even though the camera rotated counterclockwise while filming.

To detect rotation in an image, *two* points must be tracked. With two tracking points, basic trigonometry will provide the angle of rotation. (Again, thanks to software, this can be done for you behind the scenes.) Two points can also lock scale—if the points move closer together, the image must have been reduced in size; if the points move farther apart, the image must have been enlarged.

So, one tracked point can lock position, and two points can lock position, scale, and rotation. Three or more tracked points can lock perspective. Mathematically, at least three non-collinear points are required to define a plane (the mathematical equivalent of a sheet of paper), but life isn't always about mathematics. In the real world, surfaces requiring matchmoving are more often rectangular than triangular, including billboards, TV screens, cell phone displays, and so on. As a consequence, most compositing applications require that four points be tracked to stabilize or matchmove the perspective of an object.

Perspective matchmoving is fairly simple: four points on a surface (usually its corners) are tracked, and the element to be matchmoved is corner-pinned frame by frame to keep up with the change in position of the tracked points.

One-, two-, and four-point tracks are the common methods for stabilizing and match-moving footage. However, there's no reason to limit tracking to these numbers. In fact, even when locking position only, it's common to use more than one point. Several points can be tracked and their movements averaged to produce a more reliable result for the entire image. This is important in shots involving significant lens distortion. Due to the pincushion distortion of the lens, movement toward the outside of a frame will track at a different speed from movement at the center.

Lens warp is clearly visible in the inaccurate curvature of the beams in this image.

Manual and Automatic Tracking

There are two ways to perform a track: *manually* and *automatically* (also referred to as *user-assisted* or *computer-generated* tracking). In a manual track, the user identifies specific features in an image that make suitable tracking targets, then positions tracking markers over those features, adjusts the markers, and begins the track.

In an automatic track, the computer uses its own algorithms to identify trackable features and then proceeds to track them. An automatic track may track dozens or even hundreds of features with only the most reliable being used to calculate a final stabilization or matchmove. Automatic tracking takes a more significant role in 3D tracks (see Three-Dimensional Tracking, below).

The consensus among industry professionals is that manual tracking produces the most reliable results (and offers the most job security). Professional matchmovers generate the majority of their tracks manually.

Automatic tracks tend to be most useful for shots where consistent features prove elusive (that is, where few if any features remain unchanged and unobstructed over a period of several frames). Automated tracking is also better suited to smoothing operations, where tracking precision is less critical.

Three-Dimensional Tracking

The three modes of tracking discussed so far—one point (position), two point (position, scale, and rotation), and four point (perspective)—are effectively all two-dimensional operations. Even four-point perspective stabilization and matchmoving are two-dimensional planar operations. Compositing 3D into live action has become an everyday task in visual effects, and as a result, three-dimensional tracking is not only desirable but necessary.

3D trackers actually begin by tracking in two dimensions. The positions of multiple features in the source footage are tracked manually or automatically, as discussed. Once these operations have been performed, however, the position of each point in 3D space is computed.

The algorithms for these calculations are highly sophisticated, but the logic goes something like this: To travelers in a car, scenery close to the road (such as street signs) appears to move faster than scenery in the distance (like a mountain range). By calculating the relative speeds of tracked objects, their distances from the camera can be determined.

Unfortunately, the real calculations are far more advanced than this, but this simple car explanation should leave you with the pleasant illusion that you understand what's going on.

3D trackers produce a 3D scene, complete with virtual camera and null objects, for the various tracked points. Good 3D trackers will even calculate the correct focal length of the camera, although it's also possible to manually enter this information (if known) to improve the precision of the track.

The resulting 3D scene can then be exported to the 3D application of your choice, such as Autodesk Maya or 3ds Max, Softimage XSI, or NewTek's LightWave 3D. In the 3D host application, 3D objects can be inserted into the scene. Once the scene is rendered, the objects can then be composited over the footage used as a source for the track. These 3D objects should appear to maintain the same positions and perspective as other elements in the scene, even as the camera moves.

While a detailed examination of 3D tracking technique goes beyond the scope of the current discussion, a few major issues are worth noting. First, 3D trackers perform best with actual camera translation rather than simple pivots. That is, the camera should dolly (or truck) throughout the shot. A camera that simply pivots on a fixed tripod will not produce results that are as reliable, and it requires a different and usually inferior solution.

Second, current 3D trackers work best for shots with static scenery. For example, if a 3D character is to be composited into a scene, it will be much easier to composite onto a solid table than a moving vehicle. If possible, motion in the shot should be produced by the camera moving, and not the scenery. Most software offers the ability to mask off moving objects in a tracked scene, so as not to confuse the calculations.

NOTE ▶ Technologies are already emerging for solving scenes with moving elements. Therefore, this limitation should be less significant in the near future.

Third, the seemingly magical estimation abilities of this technology should not discourage the practice of detailed set surveying. Data collected during production invariably proves crucial to generating a solid solution.

TIP ▶ An excellent extended reference for 3D tracking technique is *Matchmoving: The Invisible Art of Camera Tracking,* by Tim Dobbert (Sybex, 2005).

The Process of Tracking

Trackers are reasonably straightforward tools. They don't sift through images to identify out-of-state license plates or facial characteristics. They use mathematical comparisons to find out where pixels have moved. This isn't to take away from the power of modern tracking systems. In the hands of trained professionals, they frequently turn motion-blurred sludge into well-behaved porridge. Nonetheless, it helps to understand what a tracker is doing in order to master the art of a fine track.

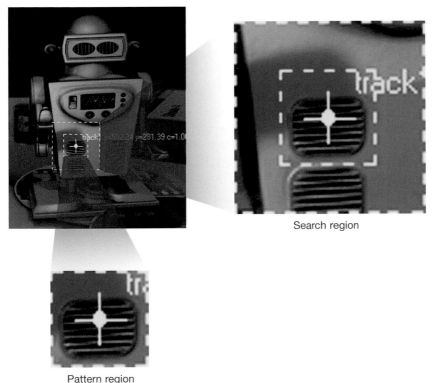

Search region

Pattern region

The user sets up two regions: a *pattern* region and a *search* region. At frame 1 (assuming you start the track at frame 1—most trackers can track forward or backward from any frame), the tracker takes a snapshot of the pixels in the pattern region. It then proceeds to frame 2. At frame 2, it begins scanning through each line of the search region, pixel by pixel (actually, subpixel by subpixel), comparing each position to the block of pixels it memorized at frame 1—the pattern region.

The pattern region is compared with different locations in the search region.

For each position, a correlation value is generated, a number that refers to how similar the pattern region is to the current position. Once the entire search region has been scanned, the position with the highest correlation is then considered to be the location where the pattern region has moved. (This is an oversimplified explanation. Optimized search algorithms usually search outward from the center to locate the pattern without needing to track the entire search area.)

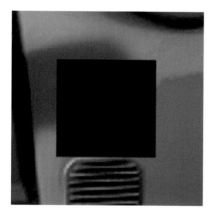

Each location compared is given a correlation value. The area with the highest correlation to the pattern region will be identified as the new location for the tracking target.

The tracker then re-centers the search area around this location and proceeds to frame 3. This course of events continues for each frame to the end of the tracked frame range. The tracker can also be set to stop on errors. If the correlation (that is, how similar the original pattern region is to the newly identified region) drops below a certain value—often called the *reference tolerance*—the tracker will stop, indicating that there is insufficient accuracy to continue.

Shake uses some sophisticated evaluation tools when tracking. For example, a reference behavior can be established so that if the correlation values drop below a certain level, a new pattern snapshot will be taken. The area in the last good frame that is determined to be the new location of the pattern region is taken as the new reference for all future frames. This is very useful when the original track point begins to look less and less like its original self. A book rotating from the camera's focal plane, for example, may originally have had its cover facing front. By the end of the sequence, only the spine is showing—a very different look.

Identifying and Establishing Tracking Points

While your proficiency in identifying good trackable features will always increase with experience, the following guidelines are useful for establishing tracks:

1. Track areas of high contrast, both horizontally and vertically.

    Trackers tend to lock best on pattern areas that possess a high contrast. This contrast should be in both the vertical and the horizontal axes. In the case of a flagpole, for example, the center of the flagpole might provide strong horizontal contrast but almost no vertical contrast, leaving the tracker free to slide up and down the pole from frame to frame. A better choice for a tracking point would be the top of the flagpole, where the sides and top of the pole are contrasted against the background sky.

2. Keep contrast changes *inside* the pattern area.

    For example, if you're tracking an oddly colored brick in a brick wall, include the transition to the surrounding mortar within the pattern area; don't set the pattern border right at the edge of the brick.

3. Avoid including moving background inside the pattern area.

    If you are attempting to track a moving car, do *not* include scenery behind the car inside the pattern area, even if it appears to be a neutral sky. Whenever possible, the only pixels that should be included in the pattern area are those that don't move relative to each other.

4. For rotation, scale, and perspective tracks, make sure that the tracked features belong to the same object.

    In the case of perspective tracks, the points must also lie along the same plane. Also, make sure the object is not changing shape.

5. Be sure the pattern region contains unique features.

    If tracking a pattern in wallpaper, be sure there is no recurrence of the pattern within the search area. If there is, expand the pattern region to include a unique feature.

6. Make the search region only as large as the greatest distance the tracked pattern will move from one frame to the next.

    Since the pattern location is reset after each tracked frame, you need be concerned only with movement between frames. Too small a search region will prevent the tracker from identifying the pattern if it moves beyond the region. Too large a search region will unnecessarily increase tracking times and the chance of a false positive (some other element being mistakenly identified as the tracked feature).

7. When tracking video, track only the Y channel in YIQ or YUV video space.

    The exception is when you are certain that the footage has remained 4:4:4 from the camera to your hard drive. The chroma subcarrier components in a subsampled 4:x:x video stream lack the resolution needed for an accurate track.

    NOTE ▶ Shake automatically uses a weighted luminance for tracking.

8. When tracking interlaced video, track only one field.

    The alternate field occurs at both a different time and a different space (1 pixel higher/lower). The resulting track data can then be applied to both fields.

Subpixel Resolution

Although the smallest picture element in a computer is a pixel, real life doesn't jump in convenient, quantized pixel increments. Instead, an onscreen object may move half a pixel. In order to accommodate this, trackers need to interpolate fractions of pixels. In fact, a good, solid track necessitates high-quality subpixel tracking.

In the recent past, tracking was a slow, CPU-intensive process. Lower subpixel resolution tracking was used to reduce calculation times. With modern desktop systems, tracking times are very reasonable—at least for standard 2D tracking tasks—and should not usually be a consideration in determining subpixel precision.

Subpixel resolution should be set to 1/256 or greater for reliable tracking; that is, tracks will be assessed to 1/256 of a pixel. This resolution will usually produce a very stable result, although 1/512 subpixel resolution may be necessary for critical tasks. Bear in mind that problems are more likely with tracks at these subpixel resolutions, due more to problems with the tracking targets than with the precision of the tracker.

Tracking Preprocessing

Several preprocessing operations can be performed to improve the quality of a track and avoid problems. A common problem is film grain. If film grain is pronounced, it may confuse the tracker, since the pattern region will look markedly different from one frame to the next due to the changing grain structure.

A potential solution to subduing grain noise in tracking is to apply a slight blur to the footage before feeding it to the tracker. This will reduce the clarity of the footage, but if the image contains good contrast detail, the tracker should still be able to lock efficiently.

A second preprocessing measure is to identify the best color channel to track. Look at the red, green, and blue channels to determine which channels have the most contrast. Then feed only those channels to the tracker. This tends to be useful only in the case of footage acquired from film; in the case of video footage, subsampling will make unusable all but the luminance channel of a YUV or YIQ image. Isolate color channels only if video footage has remained 4:4:4 from shooting right through to compositing.

Other color corrections can aid the tracker. Contrast adjustments can be applied to help tease out the contrast in an image prior to tracking. In cases of extreme motion blur, object hues may remain more consistent than luminance detail. In such cases, it may be preferable to change to an HSV color space, then feed a grayscale image to the tracker based on hue.

Occasionally, sharpening and edge detection are used to increase contrast for tracking purposes. While this may seem logical, there are potential dangers with such techniques.

Since these procedures rely on pixel convolution kernels, the results may be quantized to the pixel level, where the action in the footage is occurring at a finer subpixel resolution. This may not be an issue for coarser tracking scenarios, but it may prove unacceptable for achieving perfect lock.

Tracking with Concatenation

Any time footage is stabilized or matchmoved with subpixel accuracy, softening occurs to the resulting image. *Subpixel softening* is the result of neighboring pixels' being blended to simulate fractional pixel divisions. (That is, if an image moves 0.5 pixel to the left, a new pixel could simulate that movement by blending together 50 percent of the neighboring pixels to create a new pixel value.)

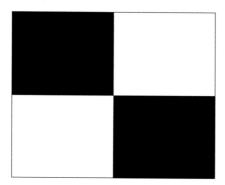

Sample black and white checkers magnified for effect

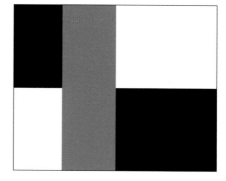

A 0.5-pixel move to the left creates a 50 percent gray at the border of the checkers, the result of blending the neighboring black and white pixels.

Once the softening has occurred, the damage is done. The new, blended pixel data is "baked" into the image. Performing the reverse operation—which should return the image to its original location—actually makes things worse, since more softening is required to perform the additional subpixel shift.

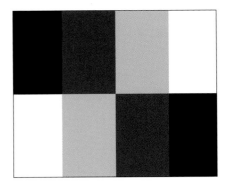

Moving 0.5 pixel back to the right increases the softening, since the gray pixel is now blended with the neighboring black and white pixels.

One solution is to make sure you perform all your transform operations in one step. That would include stabilizing or matchmoving, scaling, rotating, and general positioning. Another solution is to make sure all operations that don't require subpixel precision are performed only as full-pixel moves.

For example, if a tree needs to be composited into an image, but it doesn't really matter whether the tree is 20 pixels from the right of the screen or 21, make sure it's moved by an integer pixel value—20 or 21, for example, *not* something like 20.7.

There is, of course, a better way. It's called concatenation, and it's essentially the process of mathematically combining all the intended pans, rotations, shears, and scale operations into one master move. That is, instead of passing the pixels in an image through several different transform operations—each of which softens the image—a single transformation that meets all the requirements of the different operations is performed.

For example, if a pan operation moves an image 3.4 pixels to the right, and another pan operation moves the image 2.3 pixels to the left, a concatenation of the two operations would simply move the pixels 1.1 pixels to the right. Two operations become one, and instead of two occasions of subpixel softening, there is now only one.

Implementing Concatenation

The good news when working with Shake is that concatenation happens automatically. If two or more concatenating transform operators (denoted by a C in the top left corner of the node's tool icon) follow each other, Shake automatically combines them and applies them as a single transform.

For other applications—including Adobe After Effects—the process is not quite as simple. It *is* possible, though, as long as scripting is available in the application. To concatenate in this process, perform all the individual operations as required, then use an expression to link the individual transforms together.

For example, if a pan is performed (that is, the position of the image is changed), the image is then stabilized, and the image is finally matchmoved to another element, the position could be replaced by the following final expression:

```
Pan(x,y) + Stabilize(x,y) + Matchmove (x,y)
```

This is obviously not as neat as the Shake system, but it will perform the same basic function. The situation gets considerably more difficult when you move away from basic pans into the realm of rotation, perspective, and scale changes. These usually require the use of trigonometry in the expressions.

Concatenation Workflow

Concatenation opens up powerful alternate workflows for tracking. Since subpixel softening ceases to be an issue, compositors can perform multiple operations without the risk of degrading an image.

Progressive Refinement

When it's time to stabilize a news anchorman, a single track is all you need. If you need to stabilize spooky footage of kids holding flashlights to their faces in the middle of cursed woodlands, one track might not cut it.

The solution is multiple tracks. The workflow goes something like this: Track and stabilize a clip roughly (with a low subpixel resolution, if desired), using a generous pattern region and a large search area. This should remove the major shake from the footage. Take the resulting footage, and track and stabilize again. If the footage still needs refinement, continue to perform the operations until the footage is locked.

In Shake, the transforms will automatically concatenate, and only one transform will be performed. In After Effects or other compositing software, the results of each track can be concatenated into a final expression.

Manual Refinement

Sometimes you get a perfect track, except for an annoying jump at, say, frame 34. The solution is to manually keyframe a pan to correct the errant frame. By overlaying the previous frame with the current one, you can manually nudge the current frame into the appropriate position. Be sure to use a step-based keyframe structure to make sure your added manual movements don't unintentionally cause straying due to curve interpolation.

In some cases, automated tracking may be impossible due to the lack of high-contrast trackable features, extreme motion blur, or footage imperfections. In such situations, manual refinement is the only solution. By overlaying adjacent frames (also known as *onion-skinning*), you can manually align each frame to produce a stabilized clip. If a matchmove is required, the data can be inverted and used in an expression to matchmove another element.

Stabilize, Then Matchmove

Some situations require an element to be stabilized first, then matchmoved to another element. (See the face-element example in face replacement.) Thanks to concatenation, this process is relatively simple. Simply stabilize the element, then use the tracking data from a second element to reintroduce a matched movement. This can be done automatically using Shake, or using expressions in After Effects and other compositing software.

Stabilize, Comp, Destabilize

A common technique for matchmoving is to stabilize the background element first, then composite the foreground element, and finally destabilize the resulting composite back to the original element. To prevent subpixel softening, the following workflow is employed:

1. Stabilize the background.
2. Composite the foreground element.
3. Apply the background stabilization data to the foreground element as a matchmove (that is, reverse the direction of the data).
4. Remove the stabilize process from the background.

Using this method, the foreground is stabilized but the background remains unaffected. The foreground receives one iteration of subpixel softening, but the background is not modified at all.

Stabilize, Then Add New Motion

A very nice workflow for removing camera shake is to completely stabilize footage with one operation, then manually introduce a smooth version of the motion back into the clip. Bear in mind that any original motion blur will still be in the direction of the original motion, so dramatic changes to the original direction of the camera move will look unconvincing.

Offset Tracking

Finding good, high-contrast trackable targets can be an art unto itself. Even when identified, the little blighters have a nasty habit of disappearing offscreen right in the middle of a track. Fortunately, trackers usually have a method of dealing with such delinquency, namely *offset tracking*.

Offset tracking is—believe it or not—the process of offsetting a track. Think of the following example: Assume we're tracking the top of a street sign. If we know the top of the sign is exactly 250 pixels above its base, then by tracking its base we should also be able to calculate the position of its top—even if it has disappeared off camera.

250 pixels from base of
Stop sign to street sign

250 pixels from base of Stop sign to theoretical location of street sign

As long as the compositor switches to offset tracking while both points are on the screen, the pattern area can be moved to the feature remaining onscreen (in this case, the base of the Stop sign). This new feature is now tracked instead of the original track target (which is offscreen). However, simply adding the distance between the two points to the tracking data before recording will give the theoretical location of the offscreen feature. If the original track target returns to the screen, it can be reassigned as the pattern area. If it remains offscreen, the new feature can continue to be used until the end of the track. In many cases, the new feature will also disappear, requiring additional offset tracks using other trackable features in the shot.

Limitations to Tracking Operations

Tracking is a very powerful tool in the compositor's arsenal, but it has limitations. DPs and VFX supervisors can save much pain and overtime if they shoot source footage with an understanding of what best serves a tracker.

An archenemy of tracking is motion blur. A necessary by-product of camera movement, motion blur changes the appearance of tracking targets over time. In addition, complete stabilization is almost impossible with any significant level of motion blur, since the clip will exhibit the blur when the object is stationary.

Another important limitation is the fact that stabilizing a clip will always introduce blank spaces at the borders of the image. These must be addressed by scaling and cropping, or by reintroducing a more subtle movement over time to reduce their appearance.

Encyclopedia
of Visual Effects

3:2 Pull-Down Removal

DEFINITION ▶ A technique to convert video footage back to film footage. The practice involves removing the duplicate video frames that were inserted during pull-down, when the 24-frames-per-second film was converted to 30-frames-per-second video. *Related terms:* advanced pulldown; pull-down removal; reverse telecine.

SEE ALSO ▶ deinterlacing

What Is 3:2 Pull-Down?

3:2 pull-down is the somewhat inelegant postproduction technique used to compensate for the different frame rates of film and video. It enables converted film and HD footage to play accurately on standard televisions and other video devices. Here's a quick overview of 3:2 pull-down, followed by an explanation of why and how it must be removed for compositing.

NOTE ▶ Those of you living in the PAL/SECAM portion of the universe can skip this entry. Go back to your superior color space and slightly faster movie playback times, and leave this discussion to the rest of us whose electric current resonates at 60 Hz.

One of the most obvious differences between film and video is the frame rate at which they are displayed. Film is projected at 24 frames per second (fps) while video typically plays at 25 or 30 fps. (Standard NTSC video actually plays at 29.97 fps, but we'll round it off here.)

Another obvious difference is that, unlike film's full frames, standard video frames are *interlaced*. This means that each frame of video is comprised of two fields. One field contains the odd horizontal lines of pixels, the other field contains the even horizontal lines of pixels. For every frame of video, one set of lines is drawn to the screen first, then the other set is drawn, and the two fields are interlaced together to produce a single frame. So even though NTSC video plays back at 30 fps, each frame contains two fields, each of which is drawn to screen 1/60th of a second apart. In other words, NTSC video plays back at 60 fields per second.

It's worth noting that newer video formats (such as 24P and some high-definition formats) are not interlaced and can run at 24 full frames per second, just like film. But since the world's billion television sets can't play at 24 fps, and since it's not practical for video editors to edit at full film or HD resolutions, most film or HD video is *telecined*—or down-converted—to standard-definition video during postproduction—even if it will ultimately be output in a 24 fps format. That's where the 3:2 pull-down comes in.

To get 24 fps material to play on an NTSC device, our mission is to put 24 frames of film into 30 frames (60 interlaced fields) of video. Let's begin with the first four frames of the film sequence, which we'll label A, B, C, and D. If we were to put frame A into the first frame of the video sequence, frame B into the second frame, and so on, we'd get to frame 24 of the video sequence and we'd have six empty video frames (12 fields) to make a full second.

How do we fill up those 12 extra fields? The solution is to put in an extra copy of every other field: We alternate between copying each frame of film to two and then three fields of video, in the 2-3-2-3 pattern shown in the illustration. This means we put two fields of frame A into the first frame of video, two fields of frame B into the second frame of video, but an extra copy of frame B and the first field of frame C into the third frame of video.

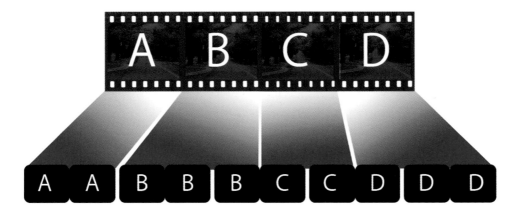

In the illustration, we've continued this pattern to successfully place four frames of film into five frames of video. Grammar school math tells us that $4 \times 6 = 24$ and $5 \times 6 = 30$. So if we repeat this sequence six times, we'll have fit 24 frames of film into 30 frames of video. That is 3:2 pull-down, though the name is slightly baffling. It should really be called 2:3 pull-down, since that's the order of the frame placement.

Now, you might think this is a messy, uneven way of converting the frame rate, since two of the frames of film have 50 percent more screen time than their counterparts. But it works quite well. If you've been watching prime-time NTSC for most of your life, you've been watching pull-down.

Removing the Pull-Down

To composite, however, we need to remove the pull-down. This is called a *reverse telecine*, because we are removing the extra video fields that were added during the telecine process.

You can use a number of tools to perform a reverse telecine. Final Cut Pro can do it during capture if it's used with video cards such as the Aurora IgniterX or the AJA Kona. You can also use Final Cut Pro with Cinema Tools to reverse-telecine clips in about four simple steps.

In Shake, you remove pull-down using parameters found in the FileIn node. In After Effects, you use the Interpret Footage dialog. In both instances, it's important to indicate the starting frame of the pull-down sequence in your footage. Is it an AA, BB, BC, CD, or DD frame? There are lots of clever ways to count this out. The easy way? Find a fast-moving portion of your footage and scrub through it with one of the start-frame options selected. If you see interlacing (a horizontal, comblike effect), try a different sequence order. There are only five possibilities, so it should take very little time to find the right one.

> **TIP** How do you know if your footage has 3:2 pull-down as opposed to plain old-fashioned interlacing? If the footage is interlaced at every single frame, then you've got yourself plain vanilla interlacing. If the footage is interlaced for two frames out of five (or one out of five for advanced pull-down—see below), then you've got yourself some pull-down.

2:3:3:2 Advanced Pull-Down

A host of newer video cameras, such as the Panasonic 24P cameras, shoot at 24 fps and use a scheme called *advanced*, or 2:3:3:2, pull-down to record directly to a regular 30 fps video tape. Instead of the AA BB BC CD DD sequence, these newer cameras use an AA BB BC CC DD sequence as they record, so that you end up with just one extra interlaced frame out of five.

But fear not: Traditional pull-down removal systems (such as the ones in Shake and After Effects) remove the pull-down just as easily from 2:3:3:2 footage.

4:x:x Simulation

DEFINITION ▶ A technique that simulates the subsampled color space of a given video format. Used when integrating computer-generated elements into video footage. *Related term:* DV artifacts

SEE ALSO ▶ blue and green screen; chroma keying; footage acquisition; grain matching

When CG elements are integrated into live action footage, all the artifacts, including those caused by camera limitations such as film grain, lens distortion, and lens diffusion, must also be simulated. That's also true for anything that happens to the footage *after* it's captured on film or a digital capture device. For video, this often means simulating the subsampled color space of the video format.

Simulating chroma subsampling is fairly simple. It's important to use an unpremultiplied image so that the alpha channel is unaffected by the operations. Since most 3D content is premultiplied, you may need to perform an MDiv procedure in Shake.

Begin by converting from an RGB color space to the native color space of the video format you're attempting to simulate. In the following example, we'll show you how to do this in Shake using NTSC DV, but the same methods will work with other formats. First use a Color > ColorSpace node, with the inSpace set to RGB and the outSpace set to the appropriate video space (YIQ for NTSC, YUV for PAL).

Next, pixelize (mosaic) the image by the appropriate amount. For 4:1:1, set the pixelation so that it creates basic blocks 4 pixels wide, but only 1 pixel tall. Apply a Filter > Pixelize node. For NTSC DV, set the xPixels to 4 and the yPixels to 1.

NOTE ▶ 4:2:0 is shorthand for a chroma subsampling that is both vertical and horizontal. Although this means you should pixelize vertically and horizontally by 2, be careful: Different implementations of 4:2:0 account for alternate fields differently. If in doubt, experiment.

Now copy the chroma components back into the original, "unpixelized" version, leaving the luminance component at full resolution. In Shake, the chroma components will be "living" on the G and B buffers after the color space conversion. Branch a Layer > Copy (channels = *gb*) after ColorSpace1.

You now have an image with correct video subsampling. As a final step, convert back to RGB color space and premultiply as necessary. Add a Color > ColorSpace node after Copy1, with the inSpace set to the appropriate video space and the outSpace set to RGB. Apply an MMult if necessary.

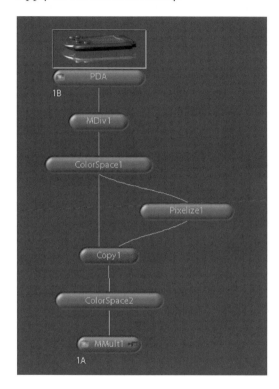

8 Bit

DEFINITION ▶ In video, a bit depth at which color is sampled. Eight-bit color is common with DV and other standard-definition digital formats. Some high-definition acquisition formats can also record in 8-bit, but they usually record in 10-bit. Refers to 8 bits per color channel, making a total of 24 bits in an RGB image and 32 bits in an RGB image with an alpha channel.

SEE ALSO ▶ bits per channel

Alpha Channel

DEFINITION ▶ In color images, the fourth channel after the red, green, and blue channels. In black-and-white images, the second channel after the luminance channel. Typically used to store transparency information for compositing: Instead of there being a completely separate file on the computer for a matte, the matte's grayscale image is incorporated into the alpha channel.

When an image file is said to include an alpha channel, it simply means that the matte for that image is included in this fourth hidden channel of the file format, ready for use in compositing operations.

SEE ALSO ▶ matte

Ambient Occlusion Passes, Using

DEFINITION ▶ A type of 3D render pass that simulates the shading produced by radiosity-based rendering solutions, but in a fraction of the rendering time. *Related term:* occlusion pass

SEE ALSO ▶ HDRI; HDR shop; light probe; light probe, lighting 3D scenes with; radiosity, faux

Ambient occlusion passes can be produced through a variety of methods, but essentially they measure the *accessibility* of geometry in a scene. That is, for a given surface point viewable by the rendering camera, an ambient occlusion pass estimates the degree to which that point can be accessed by ambient light. If other geometry in the scene prevents most light from illuminating that point, it will be shaded darker in the rendering. Or, put simply, if part of an object blocks indirect light from reaching part of the same object or another object, you get a shadow.

TIP ▶ A close cousin of ambient occlusion passes, dirt shaders use geometry accessibility to simulate the buildup of rust and mold where sunlight would fail to reach and evaporate grime-producing liquids. For more information, see **male academic, dorm-room of.**

Ambient occlusion passes have two key advantages over HDR radiosity: They render dramatically faster, and they're not as susceptible to frame-to-frame flickering. They are, however, an extremely simplistic simulation of global illumination, and as such they exhibit significant shortcomings: They fail to reproduce lighting variations in the surrounding scene, and they produce inaccurate, directionally nonbiased shadow detail.

Using Ambient Occlusion to Add Shading Detail

Typically, ambient occlusion passes are used to add ambient shading to 3D scenes that have been rendered with basic point lights, directional lights, and spotlights. In such cases, an ambient occlusion pass adds a sense of realism to the shading without your having to resort to more expensive (processor intensive) global illumination techniques.

To use an ambient occlusion pass in this fashion, take the final 3D scene, illuminated only by basic lighting (that is, no render-intensive global illumination), and mask it using an ambient occlusion pass. The simplest way to mask the render is by multiplying it with the ambient occlusion image.

A basic rendering, the ambient occlusion pass, and the resulting masked image. Note the soft shading detail around object edges and the subtle contact shadows where objects meet the floor.

The shadows of the ambient occlusion pass may prove too intense, in which case you may need to adjust the image's contrast before multiplying. Use the Compress node in Shake or the Levels filter in After Effects or Motion to make this contrast adjustment.

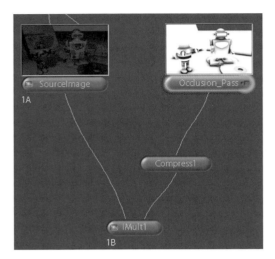

Using Ambient Occlusion as a Complete Radiosity Solution

While the method described above is useful for adding relatively realistic shading, it does not accurately reproduce the shading variations of a radiosity solution that is based on an HDR light probe. The following method attempts to produce similar results while still bypassing the limitations of conventional radiosity rendering—particularly the impractically long rendering times.

Production Considerations

Since this technique relies on a "fake" rather than a mathematical model of global illumination, it helps to have the "real thing" as a comparison.

To achieve this, use an HDR light probe image to generate a high-quality radiosity rendering of the scene. Choose a frame in the rendered sequence that best represents the scene's lighting, and then render that frame using a conventional radiosity render pass. Allow it to render with as much detail as is practical—if you can afford to wait a day, adjust the photon sampling in your radiosity calculations accordingly (or, better still, use an infinite refinement renderer, and stop when you're satisfied or mindlessly bored).

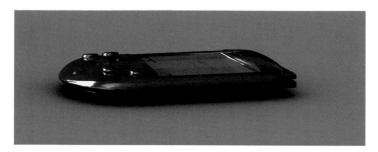

A conventional HDR radiosity render

In addition to the "comparison frame" radiosity render, a few other passes are necessary to complete the technique. All the passes detailed below render quickly and efficiently. For maximum flexibility, the passes are broken down to their most basic forms, but you may prefer to "bake together" some passes to simplify the process. Since 3D rendering software varies greatly, you may need to research the best way to achieve these passes in your specific package.

Environment Reflection Map

To create the appropriate reflections for the surrounding scene, render an environment reflection map. This is simply a map that wraps the background image around the geometry in the scene. It renders very quickly and produces equal reflections in all objects in the scene. Use the same light probe used for the high-quality radiosity render.

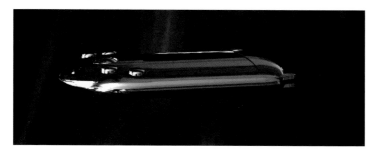

Reflection Matte

The reflection matte can be confusing at first glance. It simply describes the scene's reflectivity. More reflective objects appear brighter in the scene; less reflective objects appear darker.

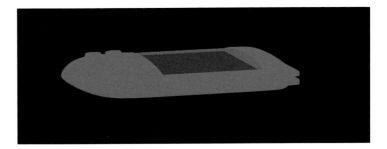

Diffuse Environment Map

To create a diffuse environment map, make a copy of the light probe image used for the background lighting and blur it heavily. The resulting image should keep the general sense of where lighting is coming from, without creating any reflective detail. You can then use the blurred version to produce an environment map in the same way the environment reflection map was created.

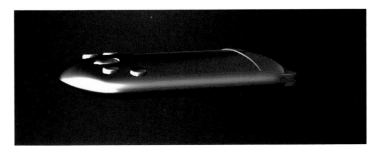

Diffuse Matte

Similar in principle to the reflection matte, the diffuse matte indicates the diffuse levels of objects in the scene.

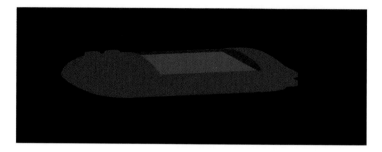

Luminosity Matte

This matte indicates any light-emitting surfaces in the scene.

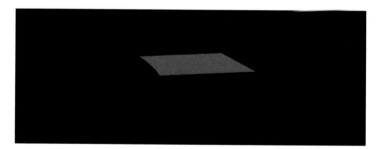

Raw RGB Pass

The raw RGB pass is an anti-aliased pass that displays only the color information in the scene—no shading, reflectivity, and so on.

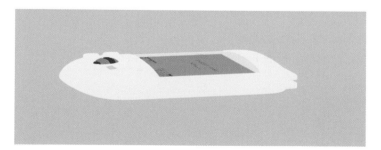

Ambient Occlusion Pass

The final piece to the puzzle is, of course, the ambient occlusion pass itself. Here's how to do it.

Poor Man's Version

S

This *is* the poor man's version. If you're richer in render time and/or money, you may want to shop in the more upmarket light probe, lighting 3D scenes with.

1   Mask the environment reflection map with the reflection matte. This will limit the environmental reflections to the reflective surfaces in the scene.

SHAKE ▼

Open **APTS_CycVFX/ProjectFiles/CG/AmbientOcclusion/ AmbientOcclusionStart.shk**. Combine ReflectionEnvMap with ReflectionMatte using an IMult.

Step-by-Step

2 Do the same with the environment diffuse map and the diffuse matte.

> **NOTE ▶** Since the model used in this demonstration is highly reflective, don't expect to see much after applying the diffuse matte.

SHAKE ▼

Combine DiffuseEnvMap with DiffuseMatte using an IMult.

3 Add the diffuse component and the specular component to create a single image. The resulting image represents only the reflections—both specular and diffuse—of the environment on the object, and therefore it doesn't provide much surface detail.

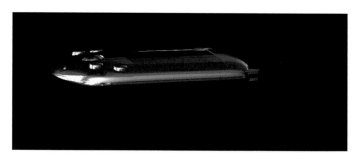

Combine IMult1 and IMult2 with an IAdd.

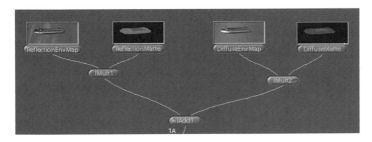

4   Use the luminosity matte to add brightness to the image to simulate illumination intrinsic to objects in the scene.

TIP ▶ You may wish to apply a blur to the luminosity matte to simulate light leaking to surrounding areas of the image.

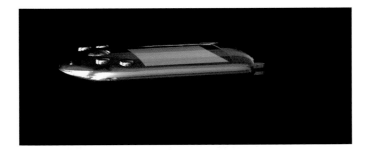

Apply an Add node (Color = 0.5, 0.5, 0.5) to IAdd1. Feed the Luminosity node into the mask input (side input) of Add1.

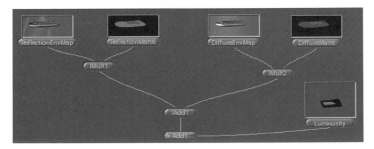

Step-by-Step

5   Combine the occlusion pass with the raw RGB pass to produce a shaded version of the object.

SHAKE ▼

Combine OcclusionPass with RawRGB using an IMult.

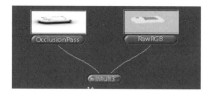

6   The environment maps can now be combined with the colored occlusion pass.

Combine Add1 and IMult3 using an IMult.

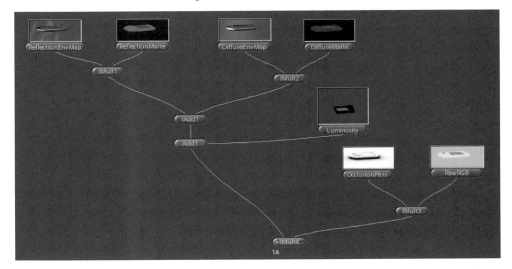

7 The resulting image should appear remarkably uninspiring. At this point the scene
has only been roughed into place. This is where the full-quality HDR radiosity render
of a single comparison frame comes into play. You can use the radiosity render as a
guide to color-correct the composite into a more realistic solution.

In the example comp, the environment maps need contrast adjustments, the brightness
of both the diffuse and reflection components needs to be increased, the saturation of the
combined reflection passes needs to be reduced, the occlusion pass needs to be tweaked to
reduce the contrast of the shadows, and the color of the added luminosity for the screen
needs to be adjusted.

> **NOTE ▶** There was nothing scientific in the way the above color corrections were
> determined. It was a matter of judging what was needed to match the comp to the
> radiosity render, and then of adding correctors by educated trial and error.

Note that the final result is by no means identical to the radiosity render, but ideally it will be close enough to satisfy. In fact, it's preferable to color-correct the final composite to match its intended background, rather than to rely solely on the radiosity render.

Also note the unpleasant jagged edges in the final occlusion comp. This is a result of inadequate anti-aliasing in the various render passes. Since so many passes are being combined, it's important to maintain high-quality anti-aliasing for each pass to avoid such a buildup of errors.

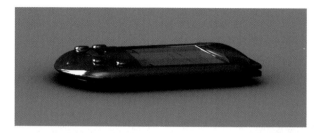

The radiosity render

The ambient occlusion comp

Final Touches

S

The following procedure simply provides a neutral background for comparison with the radiosity render.

SHAKE ▼

Add a Clamp node to IMult4 (to remove any non-normal color values from the float data). Composite Clamp1 over Background using an Over node.

The next steps perform the matching color correction.

SHAKE ▼

By loading RadiosityRender into buffer A, and Over1 into buffer B, you can adjust the color correctors until the two images match as closely as possible.

TIP ▶ You may want to use a horizontal or vertical compare in the Viewer to help you discern the differences between the radiosity image and the final composite.

SHAKE ▼

Add a ContrastLum (value = 0.7) after DiffuseEnvMap. Add a Brightness (value = 1.5) after IMult1. Add a Brightness (value = 2.9) after IMult2. Set the color of Add1 to 0.53, 0.55, 0.71. Add a Saturation (value = 0.5) after IAdd1. Add a Compress (Low Color = 0.2, 0.2, 0.2) after OcclusionPass.

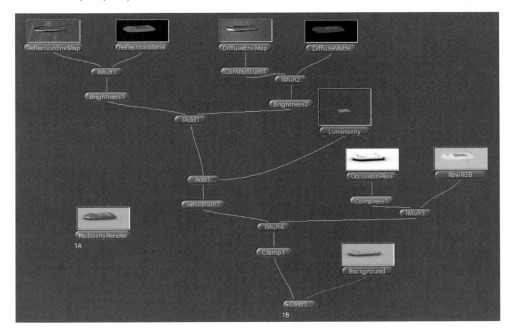

Anaglyphic Stereoscopy

SEE ▶ stereoscopy

Anamorphic

DEFINITION ▶ An image shot in a wide-screen format and then squeezed into a different frame size. A common example is 16:9 footage squeezed to a 4:3 aspect ratio.

SEE ALSO ▶ aspect ratio

Animation

DEFINITION ▶ The process of creating imagery on a frame-by-frame basis either by hand or digitally. Also, the process of changing any number of variables, such as color, audio levels, or other effects, over time using keyframes or behaviors.

Aspect Ratio

DEFINITION ▶ The ratio of the width of an image to its height on any viewing screen. Standard TV has an aspect ratio of 4:3; HDTV's is 16:9.

SEE ALSO ▶ pixel aspect ratio

Background Hole Filling

SEE ▶ stereoscopy from 2D

Background Plate

SEE ▶ plate

Background Wrap

DEFINITION ▶ A type of light wrap technique simulating the way lights in the background of an image wrap around objects in the foreground. Often used to integrate blue screen footage or computer-generated imagery into bright live-action plates. *Related terms:* edge wrap; light wrap.

SEE ALSO ▶ radiosity, faux; spill suppression

Computer-generated environment *without* background light wrap at the entrance (left)

In the real world, bright lights in the background of an image "wrap" around foreground objects because of the way

Computer-generated environment *with* background light wrap at the entrance

light bounces and reflects off of other surfaces. This wraparound effect, called *light wrap*, is influenced by the type of camera lens, as well as the exposure.

When you integrate computer-generated elements or keyed elements into a bright scene, you need to replicate the light wrap to create the illusion that everything in the scene was shot at the same time by the same camera.

▶ **The Light Wrap Cop**

Here's an extreme example you can use to visualize background light wrapping around a foreground object.

Picture, if you will, the infamous red and blue flashing lights you see in your rearview mirror when you get pulled over for not quite fully stopping at the stop sign (a maneuver called the California Roll). It's late at night; you find your license, registration, and proof of insurance, and ready your excuse.

Looking again in your rearview mirror, you see the police officer pass in front of his headlights. You astutely notice how the light appears to wrap around the officer—so much so that the officer appears only as a haloed silhouette, almost ghostlike. Unfortunately, he is all too real.

With wholly computer-generated virtual sets, background light wrap must also be added when layering, for example, interior CG passes over a bright exterior matte painting. The amount of background light wrap is proportional to the brightness and location of the source of the light in the shot.

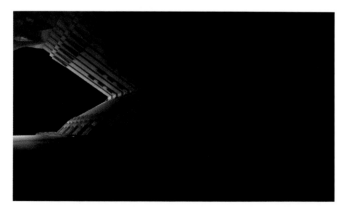

Background light wrap to be added to the computer-generated interior

Procedure

1   There are a few ways to create a background wrap effect from scratch. As with many image manipulation techniques in this book, you'll use the alpha channel or matte to do the work for you.

    SHAKE ▼

    Open **APTS_CycVFX/ProjectFiles/Keying/BackgroundLightWrap/ BackgroundLightWrap_start.shk.** Drag the noodle from the bottom of the Interior_CGenvironment_02 node into the Foreground input (left) of the Over1 node.

    A finished version of the script is always available for reference: **APTS_CycVFX/ ProjectFiles/Keying/BackgroundLightWrap/LightWrap_finished.shk.**

Background matte painting

Computer-generated foreground set

If you double-click the Over1 node, you should see the interior *over* the background.
Right now, the background looks as if it is literally from "a galaxy far, far away."
Creating and adding a light-wrap element will go a long way towards integrating the
foreground into the background.

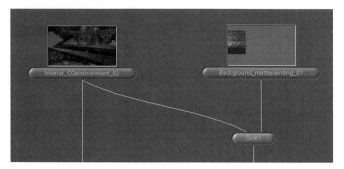

2   As stated earlier, using an element's alpha channel or attributes of the color channels
is an efficient way to procedurally create all sorts of wonderful things, light wrap
being just one of them. So, go back to the composite and do just that.

SHAKE ▼

Select the Interior_CGenvironment_02 node and add a Reorder node (channels =
aaaa). Change the channels parameter from rgba to aaaa. Next, add an Invert node
so that where there was black, there is now white, and vice versa.

TIP ▶ Reordering the alpha channel into the red, green, and blue color channels
allows you to view the grayscale alpha channel at all times and clearly designates it
as such.

NOTE ▶ Throughout this exercise, nodes have been renamed to clarify the
function they're performing. In this case, the Reorder node has been renamed
Reorder_alpha_to_RGB.

In the real world, the more descriptive you are in labeling your nodes, the better
off you'll be at 3 in the morning with a deadline looming.

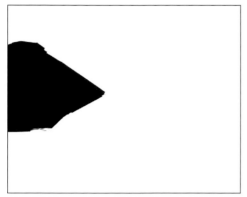

Alpha channel (matte) of the interior foreground

Inverted alpha channel (matte) of the interior foreground

3   You now have a stencil or pattern of sorts that you can use to constrain (cut out) the background matte painting. In this case, you want to dilate (expand) the matte so that more of the background painting can be placed *inside* the matte.

SHAKE ▼

Add an Expand_Alpha node. Adjust the x and y pixels parameter to be 21 and 11, respectively. In the Layers Tab, add an Inside node and place the matte painting into the Foreground (left side nub) input. Click and drag a noodle from the output (underside) of the Inverted alpha channel of the Interior_CGenvironment_02 matte into the Background (right side nub) input.

Background matte painting

Background matte painting inside the inverted interior matte

Step-by-Step

Note that the shape of the matte is retained. The importance of that fact will become obvious shortly.

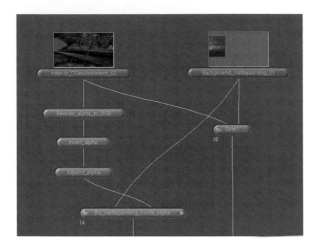

Now you have the piece of the background matte painting that happens to match the entrance of the interior. This is done so that you can attempt to mimic the effect of a bright background light spilling into (and wrapping around objects in) a darker interior foreground.

4   There are basically two important attributes to consider when adding background light wrap to a foreground object: how much the background light wraps around the foreground (the *amount*), and how intense or opaque is the wrap (the *density*).

You can dictate the amount of background light that wraps around the foreground by how much you blur the monster you have created. You can control the density of the wrap by brightening (Mult) or darkening the end result.

SHAKE ▼

Add a Blur: pixels = (x) 501 (y) 301. Adjust the x and y pixels parameter to the values 501 and 301, respectively.

Next, add a Mult: Color = (r) 1.1 (g) 1.1 (b) 1.1. (Adjust the Color parameter for RGB boxes to 1.1.)

Finally, place the resulting blurred image inside the original alpha channel of Interior_CGenvironment_02

Add an Inside node. Select the output of the Mult_Density_of_wrap node and feed it into the input (left nub) of the newly added Inside node (here renamed blurred_BG_Inside _interior_alpha). Select the output of the original interior_CGenvironment_02 node and feed it into the matte input (right nub) of the same Inside node.

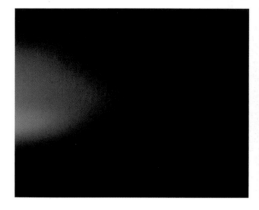

Blurred constrained background matte painting

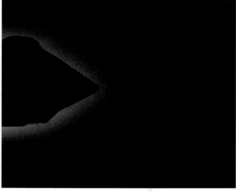

Blurred background matte painting inside the original alpha channel of Interior_CGenvironment_02

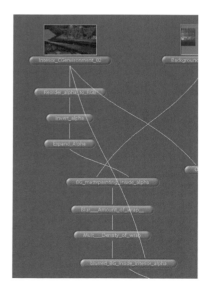

You have generated a background-light-wrap element by using a few layering techniques, color calls, and blurs, and the foreground interior's own alpha channel.

5 The background-light-wrap element is ready to be added to the earlier composite of the foreground interior and placed over the background matte painting.

SHAKE ▼

Use an IAdd. Layer the blurred_BG_Inside_interior_alpha node over the Over1 node (near the top right of the script), and use an IAdd to complete the composite.

The foreground interior *over* the background matte painting

The foreground *over* the background with the background-light-wrap element added to the composite

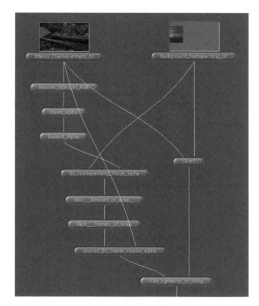

The final composite tree

Obi-Wan Kenobi dueling General Grievous in a computer-generated environment. Notice the characteristics of the light wrap around Grievous's arm caused by a lightsaber hit.

When balancing the multitude of computer-generated passes of a full CG environment, it can be useful to visualize yourself being there.

You might ask yourself, "If I were an Imbedded Imperial Newsperson shooting an epic lightsaber battle between General Grievous and Obi-Wan Kenobi and found myself on the tenth level of a sinkhole on the planet Utapau, what f-stop would I use? What kind of lens would be most appropriate? Which film stock would I use? What would the exposure settings be?"

It's questions like these—and, most important, having enough experience to answer them—that can steer one toward achieving apparent photorealism.

Beauty Pass

DEFINITION ▶ A render pass in which the finished shot is contained within a single image. The beauty pass is the equivalent of combining all other passes (such as diffuse, reflection, shadow, and specular).

Bits per Channel

DEFINITION ▶ The number of bits used to describe the range of values in a single color channel, be it red, green, blue, alpha, *z* depth, and so on.

Some confusion has been caused by reference to Adobe Photoshop images as 24-bit or 32-bit, the former being a standard RGB image, the latter being an RGB image with alpha. In such cases, the accounting method is bits per *pixel*, with 8 bits in each channel.

Always be careful to determine whether a bit depth reference is *bits per pixel* or *bits per channel*.

SEE ALSO ▶ bits per pixel

Bits per Pixel

DEFINITION ▶ The total number of bits used to describe color in a pixel. Rarely used in compositing, since it will vary with the number of extra channels included with the image file (*z* depth, shader information, alpha channels, and so on).

SEE ALSO ▶ bits per channel

Black Level

DEFINITION ▶ The measurement of the black portion of the video signal. This level is represented by 7.5 IRE in the United States; Japan (NTSC) and PAL measurements are represented by 0 IRE.

SEE ALSO ▶ NTSC; PAL

Black Levels, Checking/Gamma Slamming

DEFINITION ▶ Evaluating an image for irregularities hidden in blacks and mismatches in contrast, both of which may become visible when displayed via the broader gamut of film, or a video device with gamma settings different from those of your compositing display.

SEE ALSO ▶ contrast match, checking

During the compositing process, you've got to constantly check your black and overall contrast values by raising the gamma from a normalized value of 1 to a high value such as 2 or even 3. This is often referred to as *gamma slamming*, and if you do it at the end of the composite, it will reveal any mismatch in the black and contrast values of different elements.

As you adjust the gamma up or down, areas of similar intensity should wash out to white or fade to black at the same time. For example, if you composite someone wearing a white T-shirt over an image with a white paperboard in the background, the T-shirt and paperboard should have similar intensities. If during the gamma adjustment the T-shirt remains partially gray while the paperboard turns solid white, you know you have a mismatch in the scene contrast.

Most importantly, gamma slamming will also reveal any bad mattes that need special attention. Failure to do it will be painfully apparent on Grandma's old television.

To perform gamma slamming, apply a gamma filter to your final image. Then adjust the values greater than 1 and less than 1, watching for inconsistencies in the contrast of the image.

Before gamma slamming

After gamma slamming, revealing a harsh cutoff around the garbage matte of the foreground subject

Blanking

DEFINITION ▶ The black border around the edges of a raw video image. This is the image created by the video camera CCD scanners—the photosensitive receptors that translate the lens image into digital information. The very edge of the picture is usually worthless. These black pixels should be cropped out of your image if you plan to composite it over the top of other footage.

Bleach Bypass

DEFINITION ▶ The process of reducing or skipping the normal bleaching of the negative (or, more commonly, internegative) when developing color film to reduce the silver in the image. As described here, the term refers to the process of *simulating* the physical effect via color correction. *Related terms:* bleach fix; blix; skip bleach.

SEE ALSO ▶ Kodak Cineon

Recently gaining in popularity, the photochemical bleach bypass process has been featured with great effect in movies such as *Munich, Saving Private Ryan*, and *Traffic*. The process reduces or completely skips the normal bleaching that a negative undergoes—called *bleach-fix* or *blix*—which dissolves both the silver halides and the elemental silver.

Bleach bypass, also known as *skip bleach*, causes the negative's inherent silver to be retained throughout the rest of the developing process. In essence, a black-and-white image is superimposed over a color image. The result is a drastic color-correction effect that increases the contrast and reduces saturation, giving the film a gritty, '70s look. For many films, the effect has given a flashback or dream sequence an added dramatic impact.

Historically, the effect was risky, as it involved a laboratory technique performed directly on the negative. Fortunately, bleach bypass can now be achieved digitally by using third-party plug-ins from Digital Film Lab, Anvil, and DigiEffects, which achieve the same effect and have the added benefit of an undo button.

If the image source is film, it's sometimes best to push the image's contrast during transfer because the digital processing, if pushed too far, can amplify noise and other artifacts. If you're working with a flat transfer, you may consider reexposing the image using the

Kodak Cineon lookup table or EXR exposure controls to take advantage of a higher dynamic range.

The goal is to increase contrast and dip saturation, then follow it up with a slight cooling of the image by injecting a subtle bluish hue.

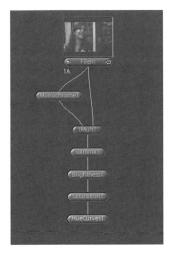

In Shake, after the FileIn, a monochrome version of the image is generated (with .33, .33, .33 as the respective RGB weights) and layered over the original with an IMult node. (A faster Reorder node set to *l* for luminance can be substituted for the monochrome node, but it will weight the channels differently and change the output colors slightly, so monochrome is recommended in this case.)

The monochrome is followed with a Gamma node set to 1.2 to recover some detail in the mids.

Then an overall contrast adjustment is performed using a Brightness node set to 2.

The Saturation node (set to .75) sucks out some overall color, and the HueCurves node pulls in a slight bit of cool blue by dipping the saturation in the reds around Hue value 0 to about .85.

Original image   Bleach bypassed

As this is an effect with its roots in film, it's best to use a film source or simulate a film look on your digital video to remove some of the digital edge. The basic recipe for a film look is to intelligently deinterlace, slightly desaturate, add contrast, and bloom the highlights a little.

As a final step, you can adjust the gamma to your liking, and if you weren't doing something chilly like a bleach bypass, you'd most likely warm the image with a slight bump toward red to give it the look of some film stocks.

Blemish Removal

DEFINITION ▶ The digital removal of minor imperfections from an image. *Related terms:* blur; median filter; synthetic grain

SEE ALSO ▶ grain matching; grain removal; skin repair (digital foundation)

A minor imperfection in an image can mar an otherwise exemplary shot. If the problem occurs in a fairly homogeneous area of the image (that is, one that lacks heavy or crisp edge detail), any dirt, scars, small tracking markers, and other unwanted detail usually can be removed with a fairly simple technique.

First, the problem area needs to be removed. A median filter (see grain removal) is the most subtle solution, but with larger problems a blur may be required.

Once the dirt is removed, add synthetic grain to match the original grain of the shot (see grain matching).

Finally, generate a matte (usually with a paint tool) to composite the filtered, regrained version over the top of the original, untouched image. The matte should be softened with a blur, or a soft brush should be used if the matte was generated via a paint tool. In Shake, you can use the QuickPaint node with the filtered, regrained image feeding into the original image, and then reveal input.

Blink Repair

DEFINITION ▶ A technique for removing unwanted blinks from live action footage, particularly when a time remap or ramping effect is employed.

Ramping, or varying a clip's speed throughout playback, can be a cool way to stylize footage. But when you speed up the action of live actors, they can end up looking like they're blinking incessantly. The following technique will remove the annoying blinks without turning your actor into a statue.

Begin by identifying and listing the problem frames. If the blink occurs over multiple frames, list them as a sequence.

TIP ▶ If you're fixing footage that will be sped up, make sure you edit the sequence after it's been retimed. Otherwise you'll be repairing more frames than necessary for the final piece.

Load each problem frame into the compositor. This is pretty much a one-frame-at-a-time thing, so charge by the hour (or, even better, by the frame).

1A

NOTE ▶ You can use an image editor like Photoshop for this technique as well.

For each frame, scan the source footage to find frames where all movement in the eyelid muscles has subsided. Find the first nonblinking frames before and after the problem frame, and import them into the compositor.

NOTE ▶ To follow along with this techique, use the images found in **APTS_CycVFX/ProjectFiles/Tracking/BlinkRepair**.

Determine which of the nonblinking frames is the best replacement in terms of scale and clarity. Always try to choose a replacement frame with the eyes at least as large as they are in the blink frame. At the same time, make sure the replacement frame is at least as crisp as the blink frame. You can always blur, but it's harder to convincingly sharpen.

Frame to be fixed

Source for eye replacement

Now subtract one image from the other. Once you have the resulting difference, scale, pan, and rotate the nonblinking image until it's mostly black. Before scaling, position the center of transformation (the anchor or pivot point) between the eyes, since the eye area is where we want the most precise transforms.

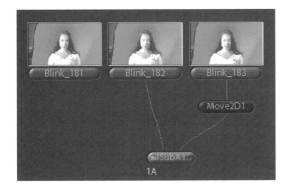

The eye area is the only place where you should have significant remaining detail. (For best results use an absolute subtraction: In Shake, ISubA provides that.)

TIP In Shake, position the mouse pointer over the parameters sliders and use Option–left arrow and Option–right arrow to nudge the values by 1/10 increments.

The final step is to remove the subtraction operator and use the nonblinking frame (now correctly aligned) as a clean plate for the blinking frame. Use a reveal brush or matte to uncover just the eye areas. If using a matte to perform the reveal, remember to blur the border of the matte to keep a soft transition between original and replacement pixels.

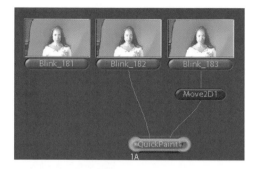

Blue Screen

DEFINITION ▶ An evenly lit, bright, pure blue background used behind images when they're filmed so that later the subject can be extracted and composited onto another image. The compositing process replaces all the blue in the picture with another image. Called *green screen* when the screen that is used is green.

SEE ALSO ▶ chroma keying; green screen; Keying Fundamentals chapter; keying generic elements; screen color selection

Blur

SEE ▶ camera diffusion simulation; screen blur composite

Cameo

Frankenstein's Third Dimension—Todd Vaziri

FRANKENSTEIN'S MONSTER STEPS to the edge of a burning windmill. Explosions and flame burst around him. The camera pushes in on him and then swoops around to reveal hundreds of mad villagers with torches who surround the windmill 100 feet below. That's Industrial Light & Magic (ILM) shot OPN72, from the Universal motion picture *Van Helsing,* that lead compositor Todd Vaziri (see Contributors, page v) was asked to complete. The only problem was that the plate was a partial set of the windmill, including the platform surrounding the top of the windmill, built ten feet off the ground, without a single angry villager in sight.

Original blue screen footage of Frankenstein's monster atop the windmill set

Multiple crowd passes composited in 3D space before color correction

Todd had some solid plates to work with that he ultimately combined into a breath-taking shot in the movie. The first plate was the windmill plate featuring Frankenstein's monster, shot against a black night sky. In addition, there were six plates of villagers, all shot from a large scaffolding at night against a fairly dark ground. Each group had approximately 35 extras holding torches. The extras were moved to different parts of the ground surrounding the windmill to create multiple plates.

Finally, Todd had the large ILM library of fire and explosions at his disposal. Using a Macintosh computer and After Effects, he worked for two months to shape these raw elements into the seamless black and white shot that is seen in the movie.

The key to this task was the ability to work with 3D compositing. 3D compositing is a hybrid technique in which you create 3D layers in the composite without the need to jump between several different applications. This allowed Todd to place elements, perform **rotoscoping**, and do **color correction** simultaneously without any rendering. The resulting workflow was much easier than what it would have been with more traditional methods.

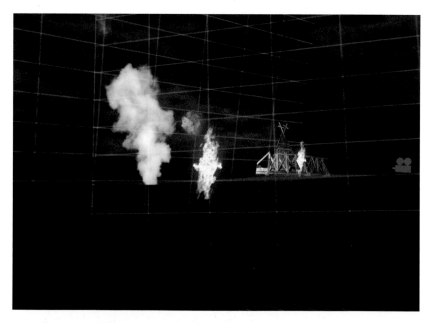

A 3D view of the different elements on simple planes, placed in 3D space. Note the virtual camera that contains the camera matchmoves data.

Among the several elements of the shot, creating the crowd became Todd's biggest challenge. There were six groups of villagers, and each group was used two to three times around the front of the windmill. But without further visual refinement, the crowd looked clumpy. The shot needed the organic feel of a mob of people, with a dense central core that tapered out toward the fringes.

Some of the original groups had a few stragglers—extras who looked as if they didn't hear the assistant director's commands and lingered listlessly around the edges of the group. These stragglers became the key. Four or five of them were extracted from the shot and placed throughout the frame numerous times to blend the separate groups together, something like organic, visual noise. These few stragglers accounted for the periphery of the crowd as well, leaving the impression that some people were just joining the party. The crowds were then placed on 2D cards in 3D space, as if they were in a bowl. As the camera moved across this bowl, pincushioning and perspective tricks were added to make the people in the crowd appear as if they had been photographed by the original camera.

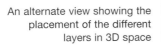

A 3D view of multiple crowd passes. Placement of different layers in 3D space allows for advanced camera effects like parallax.

An alternate view showing the placement of the different layers in 3D space

At the beginning of the shot, the burning sails of the windmill spin past the monster. The flame on the sails was the only pyro in the original plate. In the composite, several explosions and burning sections were added.

First, the timing and depth positions of the fire events were locked down. Second, interactive light was added to the windmill and the monster. Ultimately, the flaring and blooming of the lens during each eruption that were added into the composite really helped tie together all the pyro elements.

A sky was added to the shot that was more interesting than the blackness of the original plate. To do this, one of the movie lights in the frame had to be removed. In order to add the new sky and the pyro elements to the 3D composite process, the matchmove department performed a very accurate matchmove. The rotoscope department handled all of the rotoscoping of the windmill and the monster that appears at the head of the shot.

The original beginning of the shot

The enhanced final composite with added sky, explosions and interactive light

This shot was part of a black-and-white sequence that opened *Van Helsing* in the style of the Universal horror classics from the 1930s and '40s. However, the producers wanted the shot to be delivered in color, in case a color sequence played better for the foreign markets and for the video release. Unfortunately, when the shot worked in color—with delicate transitions from red to orange and from blue to green—it turned into a mushed-out black-and-white image. On film, the heat of fire is communicated entirely by the density of the image, so the balance between colors and densities was vital in achieving the visual intensity of the shot. In the end, Todd had to tweak the images in color to make them also work in black and white. It was almost like having to do the shot twice.

In all, the shot took two months to complete and contained 70 separate layers. A flawless matchmove was the essential building block that allowed the 3D composite process to proceed with ease. Todd laid out the shot very quickly with big brush strokes; there's a saying in visual effects that it takes 10 percent of the time to get 90 percent there, and the remaining 90 percent of your time is spent on the final 10 percent of the details. Polishing that final 10 percent required a very aggressive use of 3D compositing in After Effects. As Todd says, "I really banged on it, and it always worked flawlessly."

The final color-corrected crowd composite. Notice how far below the crowd seems.

Camera Diffusion Simulation

DEFINITION ► The digital simulation of the characteristic image softening that is caused by camera optics. *Related terms:* blur; camera softening; lens diffusion simulation; soft blur

SEE ALSO ► lens warping

These days, computer-generated (CG) 3D can look really good. A little too good, in fact, which can be a major problem for compositing.

The problem stems from the mathematical purity of 3D rendering. When an image is generated, the computer uses a precise mathematical model (be it Phong shading, ray tracing, radiosity, or final gathering) to simulate the way light behaves in the real world. The result is an all-too-pristine image, causing people to complain that CG images look too crisp.

The top image has no diffusion, but the bottom image has diffusion added.

What these perfect images need is a little diffusion. When light enters a camera, it gets banged about by the optics. Regardless of the German precision that may have gone into machining the lenses, imperfections in the glass always cause a small percentage of light photons to miss their target. As those photons expose parts of the film or camera CCD surrounding their intended target, the resulting image is softened. In order to blend CG elements into live action, that diffusion must be simulated.

Simulating Diffusion Using a Blur

A common practice for simulating lens diffusion is to blur the CG renders. This may seem like a good idea at first (but then so do those inebriated dalliances at the Christmas party), but the problem is that blurring removes detail from the image. Simple blurring would be appropriate only if *all* the photons passing through the camera optics were deflected by a certain amount. Blurring produces a more natural result than a pure render, but only at the expense of detail, and that's never good.

Render Down, Scale Up

Another solution is to render the image at 70 to 80 percent of its final size, then scale up, naturally softening the image. With modern intelligent scaling (like that found in Shake's FileIn node), this may produce acceptable results. The other big benefit: 70 to 80 percent of the intended scale means 70 to 80 percent of the rendering time.

> **NOTE** ▶ Be careful when working with 3D tracked content. You'll need to make sure when you scale up that the scale amounts are exactly the same.

Blurring Intelligently

The blur method is a good start, but instead of simulating that *every* photon goes astray, we want to simulate only *some* going astray.

We begin by once again blurring the image. Start by applying a blur at a very low value (around 5 to 7 in Shake), and then subtract the original image from the blurred version. The result is an image that displays only the portions of the blur that are distinct from the main image, as if you're seeing only the photons that went off course.

Now, if you're working with float renders, you'll need to clamp to zero to remove any sub-zero values (see clamping mattes).

Finally, add this image back to the original to produce the final composite. You should now have an image that appears more diffuse, but without the destruction of detail that you would have seen with a simple blur.

Adjust the blur strength to suit your taste. You may also need to reduce the brightness of the CG element to compensate for the addition of the stray photons. Oh, and keep the effect subtle. You're trying to simulate *real* camera diffusion, not *surreal*.

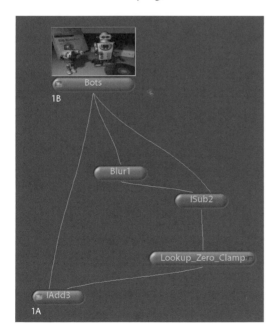

Camera Mapping

DEFINITION ▶ A technique for creating basic polygon primitives for features of a 2D image in order to more accurately simulate perspective shifts. *Related term:* sticky projection mapping

SEE ALSO ▶ Tracking Fundamentals chapter

Say you're creating a set of buildings using camera mapping, also known as *sticky projection mapping*. First, you start with a photograph of buildings to use as a background plate. Then you create rectangular prism primitives in a 3D application, match them to the positions of the buildings in the background plate, and "stick" your image onto the geometry of the 3D scene. Essentially, you're applying the original 2D image as a texture map to the 3D scene objects. You can then move a virtual camera, and the objects will appear to shift in perspective as if they were genuine 3D objects.

This technique is useful for subtle transformations. Since any translation of a real camera will reveal additional scene information, a virtual camera can only fake this perspective shift by stretching the existing pixels. Nonetheless, using this technique in postproduction can dramatically improve the believability of a slight camera movement. Even more useful is camera mapping for integration of 3D objects into a 2D scene. For more information, see the Tracking Fundamentals chapter.

Camera Shake, Smoothing and Removal

DEFINITION ▶ Tracking and stabilization techniques for smoothing and steadying undesired camera shake. *Related term:* motion smoothing

SEE ALSO ▶ stabilization

Camera operators used to get fired for extreme camera shake. These days they're liable to win an Academy Award. Nonetheless, compositors are often required to steady handheld shots to keep audience members from performing a motion-induced Technicolor yawn. The trick when treating camera shake is to remove the shake without removing desirable pans, tilts, and dolly moves. In this exercise, you'll learn how to lose the shake without locking down the camera altogether.

TIP For automated camera smoothing, try Shake's SmoothCam node. It will often produce excellent results with a single click (or two—no, maybe three). As a magic-bullet solution it can work miracles, but you'll still often need to resort to the manual method described below. Also, due to SmoothCam's super-incredible, ultrasophisticated, genius-level algorithms, it's molasses slow. (That's Golden Syrup slow for those of us who are still members of the Queen's Commonwealth. And yes, it's *colour* with a *u*—nice to get that out of my system once in a while.)

Procedure

S

1 The first step is to stabilize the shot. Decide whether you need to stabilize for position shake only, or also for rotation. In most cases you'll only be stabilizing position. Rotation shake typically occurs only under the influence of hallucinogenic drugs.

SHAKE ▼

Open **APTS_CycVFX/ProjectFiles/Tracking/HotNShaky/ShakyStart.shk**. To ShakyCam, add a Transform > Stabilize (subPixelResolution = 1/256) node. Position the tracking marker on the upper left corner of the picture frame, as shown in the figure below.

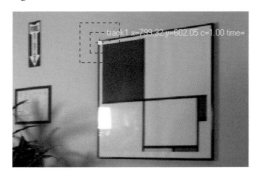

Under the Viewer, click the Track Forward button ![Track Forward] to begin tracking. You'll only get to around frame 16 before the track goes bad.

2   You now need to use offset tracking to complete the track.

SHAKE ▼

If the track is still running, stop the tracker (press the Escape key) and back up to the last good frame (around frame 16). Click the Offset Track button ▨. Reposition the tracking marker on the upper left corner of the rightmost picture frame, as shown in the figure below.

Click the Track Forward button again.

This time, you should make it to around frame 31.

3   Now you use offset tracking one more time.

SHAKE ▼

Since you're already in offset track mode, there's no need to click the Offset Track button. In fact, that would deactivate offset tracking and cause mess, pain, and confusion. (Something akin to the implementation of high-definition television in North America.)

Move back to the last good track. Reposition the tracking marker near the center of the leftmost picture, as shown in the figure below.

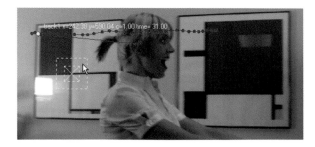

NOTE ▶ In "traditional" offset tracking, you should try to use the original point if it reemerges into the frame after being obscured. In this case, you're trying to eliminate camera shake rather than stabilize a specific object, so you actually want the tracker to be referencing pixels as close as possible to the center of the screen. That's why you should choose a new offset closer to center than the original target.

In fact, this tutorial was simplified to include only two additional offset tracks. In this kind of tracking situation, you'd ultimately be better served to create more offset tracks close to screen center.

When you track forward again, you should make it *almost* all the way to the end of the clip. Do one more offset to clean up the last couple of frames.

The view from frame 1

4   You can now apply the stabilize and see how you did.

SHAKE ▼

In Stabilize1, set the applyTransform to active. Render a flipbook to preview the results.

You should find that your shot is stabilized with two unwanted results. First, the background perspective distorts very strangely. Second, the action disappears off to stage right.

What you've done so far is remove *all* camera movement from the clip. You actually only want to remove the shake.

5 In this step, you will remove the shake from the tracking data.

SHAKE ▼

Copy and paste Stabilize1. Double-click the newly pasted Stabilize2 to select it and load its parameters. In Shake's Curve Editor, click the Current Autoload button to load the tracking data from Stabilize2. Make sure both curves are selected, then click the "Apply operation to curve" button 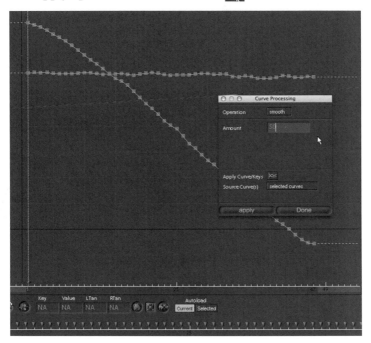.

Set the Operation to smooth and the Amount to *20*, click "apply," and then click Done.

You've effectively blurred the curve data, creating a smoother version of each curve. As a result, you've also removed the shake and left only the smooth motion of the camera's pan.

6   You can now apply the smoothed tracking data to the stabilized footage as a matchmove. That is, the first stabilize removes all movement from the clip (both the smooth camera move you want and the shake you don't), and your new smooth tracking data reintroduces only the smooth movement. Since you removed the shake by smoothing the curves, this movement is not reintroduced during the matchmove.

SHAKE ▼

Connect Stabilize2 to the output of Stabilize1. In the parameters for Stabilize2, set the inverseTransform to match. Stabilize1 and Stabilize2 concatenate to produce a single transform. Launch a flip-book to preview the results.

7   The shot now has a smooth motion without the shake. The final step is to remove the black borders that show up as a result of the removed shake. You can do this by scaling the final image. Begin by locating the frame containing the greatest amount of black space. (Hint for the lazy: It's frame 46.)

SHAKE ▼

In the Timeline, move to frame 46. Add a Transform > Move2D to Stabilize2. Increase the scale parameter until the black edge is no longer in the frame (around 1.07). Launch a flipbook to preview the results.

Cel Shade, Live Action

DEFINITION ▶ Simulating the look of hand-drawn animation using live action footage as the source. *Related terms:* anime simulation; cartoon look

SEE ALSO ▶ skin repair (digital foundation)

Sure, *A Scanner Darkly* is a cool flick, but who wants all that roto work? Cel shaders have been available in the 3D rendering world for many years, enabling 3D content to be rendered with a 2D cartoonlike appearance. A simple gag can do the same for video, and without a lick of roto.

Flattening the Image

One of the reasons cartoons look, well, cartoonlike is the lack of shading detail in surfaces. Where surfaces would normally appear graduated, cartoons are drawn in flat areas of color. To achieve a similar effect, we turn to the compositor's best friend, the blur. Blur the image until all of the main surfaces appear smooth, eliminating depth cues from the main elements in the scene.

Finding the Detail

Next, subtract the blurred version of the image from the original. The resulting image will display pixel values based on the difference between the original pixels and the average pixel color produced by the blur. In other words, you've isolated the contour detail in the image. Edge detail, which tends to be more uniform, will *not* be included, hence the dark lines in this image.

Losing the Detail

The final step is to simply subtract the "details" image from the original, essentially removing the unwanted detail.

> **NOTE** ▶ This technique relies on rounding values to 0 during the subtraction (something that doesn't occur naturally in float). If you want to flatten an image in float space, you must clamp subzero values after the first subtraction (see **clamping, subzero**).

Different shots will require different levels of blur, so be prepared to keyframe the blur amount.

A Final Touch of Animation

In order to complete the toon feel, you may want to try adjusting the frame rate of the image sequence. Cartoons are traditionally animated "on the 2s"—that is, every other frame, or 12 frames per second (fps). Why? Because somewhere, sometime, somebody looked at the numbers and said, "If we have to do 24 of these pictures for every second of the movie, we'll have repetitive stress injury lawsuits. If we only do half as many, we'll cut the lawsuits in half."

To simulate this frame rate change in Shake, apply a TimeX node with the expression floor(time/2)*2 for newTime.

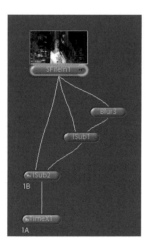

In After Effects, create three identical layers of the same image, apply a Gaussian blur to the center layer, and then for the top two layers set the transfer mode to Difference.

In Motion, apply the Gloom filter and play with the parameters.

Choking Mattes

SEE ▶ mattes, shrinking and expanding

Chroma

DEFINITION ▶ The color information contained in a video signal.

SEE ALSO ▶ YIQ; YUV

Chroma Blur

DEFINITION ▶ Smoothing edge detail in an image keyed from a subsampled video space (such as DV and HDV) by blurring the chrominance component of the image. *Related terms:* 4:x:x keying; DV keying

SEE ALSO ▶ footage acquisition, blue and green screen; mattes, shrinking and expanding

Blue screen and green screen keying methods generally work by comparing the red, green, and blue channels of an image. (How the comparison is performed can vary widely for different keyers, though.)

This can be problematic with digital video that has subsampled chrominance, since the color information is set at a lower resolution than the luminance information (see footage acquisition, blue screen and green screen for more information). So when a key is pulled, the edge of the key appears scaled or aliased. Reverse edge fall-off is one of the telltale signs of this problem. Edge pixels should get darker (becoming more transparent) toward the transparent background, but when reverse edge fall-off occurs, the edge pixels get lighter. This creates the staircase effect shown in the figures below.

Matte produced from standard keying of an NTSC DV image.

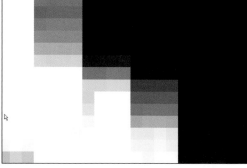

Close-up of pixels. Notice the pixels becoming lighter toward the edge (moving left to right).

In the case of the figures above, the pattern occurs in blocks of 4 pixels because the sample footage was shot on NTSC DV, a 4:1:1 format. In other words, it has one sample in the chroma components of the video signal for every four full samples in the luminance component.

There are some clever solutions on the market that attempt to reconstruct detail in the chrominance components by extrapolating from the luminance channel. While these can be very useful keyers, a simple compositing gag involving judicious amounts of blur can often provide a solution.

Changing Color Spaces

The common color space for compositing applications (including Shake) is RGB. Natively, however, digital video travels as a luminance signal with two chroma (color) subcarrier signals. These signals are converted to RGB space for convenience during the composite. You can use the ColorSpace node in Shake to revert to the native color space of the video signal.

Apply a ColorSpace node from the Color tab to the DV footage. Set the inSpace to RGB (since this is the current color space of the image) and the outSpace to either YIQ (the native color space of NTSC video) or YUV (the native color space of PAL video).

Original source image

NOTE ▶ The following image is used for the examples in this entry: **APTS_CycVFX/ProjectFiles/Keying/ChromaBlur/ChromaBlurSample.tif**.

If you view the red, green, and blue channels separately, you'll see that Shake has now placed the luminance (Y) component of the video into the green buffer, and the chrominance components (I and Q, or U and V, depending on your part of the global digital swamp) into the G and B channels.

   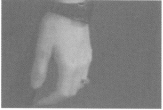   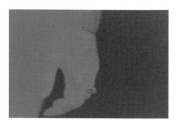

Y component   I component (U in PAL speak)   Q component (V in PAL speak)

Viewing the color channels together won't look pretty, but it's not meant to. This is purely a method of extracting the video signal information in order to manipulate it.

Blurring the Chroma

Add a Filter > Blur node after the ColorSpace node. Set the channels field to *gb* to apply the blur to just the green and blue chrominance components, while the red luminance signal remains unaffected.

Set the pixels amount to around 7.0 (you can review and change this later). By blurring the pixels in the G and B channels, you've created a blend and removed the 4-pixel staircasing we discussed earlier.

Back to RGB

Finally, apply a second ColorSpace after the Blur node. This time set the inSpace to YIQ or YUV (depending on which you chose in the first step) and the outSpace to RGB. You've now returned your image to standard RGB, but you've blurred the chrominance components using the blur sandwiched between your ColorSpace nodes.

Now attach your keyer and pull a key. You should be greeted by a much smoother edge. You can adjust the Blur node's pixels amount to suit.

Resulting matte after applying the smoothing operation

Chances are the blurring will enlarge the size of your matte edge and you'll need to choke (shrink) your matte to compensate. (See mattes, shrinking and expanding for more information.)

> **NOTE ►** Whenever you blur, you lose data precision in your image. It's important to understand that in blurring the chrominance components we've created a nicer-looking, but less accurate, key. Pay special attention to fine detail like hair, which doesn't usually fare so well in these little compositing gags.

Chroma Keying

DEFINITION ► A keying method that uses a chroma key to isolate a specific color value. Usually used to electronically matte or insert an image from one camera into an image produced by another.

The term refers to a specific process of keying based on a range of hue and saturation in the image. It is generally considered inferior to *color difference keying*, the most common method of extracting a matte from a color screen.

Chroma keying is often confused with *blue screening*, which is a more general term for generating a matte from footage filmed in front of a colored background. *Related term:* color keying

SEE ALSO ▶ Keying Fundamentals chapter; luma keying

Chroma keying is like fishing for colors, except you first cast a net to catch a certain color, and then you determine how wide your net should be. That is, you choose a color, and then you pick a range of hues most similar to that color's hue, a range of saturations most similar to that color's saturation, and a range of values most similar to that color's value.

It's very important not to confuse chroma keying with color difference keying, even though industry types will mistakenly interchange the two terms. Color keying is a superior method for keying blue and green screens. Chroma keying should be used only when you're keying an element that is not a primary red, green, or blue. So if you need to key a particularly vivid fuchsia, for example, you're going to be chroma keying.

TIP ▶ In Shake, Color > ColorReplace is often considered easier to work with as a chroma keyer than the actual Key > ChromaKey node. To use ColorReplace as a chroma keyer, activate affectAlpha in its parameters. Then set the Replace Color to a color other than the Source Color. It doesn't matter what color, just as long as it's different.

Chroma keying will invariably produce harsh edge detail, and it does not handle transparencies well. Chroma keys are usually just one part of the process, and will often be combined with rotoscoping and other matte-creation methods. When chroma keying, it's best to keep the value range low to preserve the shading detail in the resulting matte. If you increase the value range, most of the shading variation in the keyed color will be clipped to white in the matte, which is usually an undesirable effect.

Beyond standard HSV chroma keyers, there are 3D keyers that plot color space triplets (RGB, HSV, CMY, and so on) as three axes in a 3D coordinate space. Such mathematical models produce more sophisticated results and are therefore more useful for general keying.

Clamping Mattes

DEFINITION ▶ Removing unwanted float data using a Clamp or Lookup. *Related term:* removing float values

SEE ALSO ▶ clamping, subzero; float space

Conventional uses for mattes rely on the principle that the values of mattes lie between 0 and 1. Zero is pure black, 1 is pure white.

Float space permits numbers to have values greater than 1 or less than 0, which can cause composite problems with matte operations. So before you perform matte operations with float space, you must first clamp the mattes so that subzero values are clamped to 0 and greater-than-1 values are clamped to 1. In Shake, you can use the Clamp node, and in After Effects and Motion you can use the Levels filter to perform the same task. In fact, using any of the filters in After Effects that are not float compatible will automatically clamp pixel data to 8- or 16-bit linear.

> **TIP** ▶ The old 0–255 color value range refers to an 8-bits-per-channel system of color, and 8-bit images are on their way out as we move to an HDR world. You should retrain yourself to think of color levels as being from 0 to 1 (where 255 in the old scheme is equivalent to 1), since a good understanding of compositing and float space requires you to think in the 0–1 range.

Clamping, Subzero

DEFINITION ▶ Clamping subzero pixel values without affecting the upper range of pixel values. *Related term:* removing float values

SEE ALSO ▶ clamping mattes; float space

Float space is powerful because it permits users to work with high dynamic-range images, or HDRI. (See clamping mattes for an explanation of float space.) These images can contain highlight information several thousand times brighter than standard pixel values. That's incredibly useful for color correcting and for exporting to high dynamic-range formats such as projected 35 mm film.

Images in float can also have blacks "darker than dark." That is, if a numeric value of 0 represents true black, float images can have negative values below true black. That comes in handy when raising overall exposure or performing specific math calculations, but it often causes problems in other situations.

TIP ▶ If you're in float space and weird, unexpected things happen during a composite, chances are some hidden float values are causing the problem. In Shake, use the float viewer script (located at the base of the Viewer) to help identify the culprit.

In the following node tree, we have a white blob matte being added to a gradient ramp.

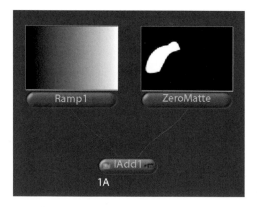

You would anticipate the following result:

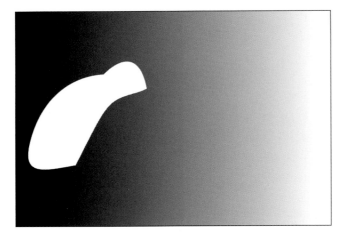

But what if there are negative values hiding in the black space of the blob matte on the right side? (For experimentation, go to **APTS_CycVFX/ProjectFiles/Color/ SubZeroClamping/ProblemDemo.shk**.) You might end up with something like this:

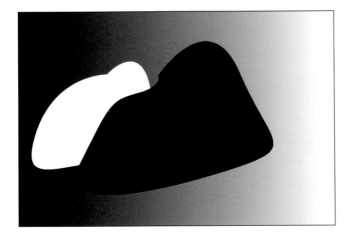

One solution in Shake is to apply a Color > Clamp node, which by default clips any subzero pixel values to 0 and any superwhite values greater than 1 to a value of 1. Clamping the superwhites is desirable for mattes, but it is very bad for regular images because it destroys all that high dynamic-range data that was your reason for working in float in the first place.

TIP In Shake 4, mattes inserted into the side mask input of a node are automatically clamped by default, making the addition of a Clamp node unnecessary.

You could always raise the high color values of the Clamp node above 1, but to make sure you didn't clip anything, you would first need to know exactly what the highest pixel value in your image sequence is.

The solution is to use a Color > Lookup node. If you thought Lookup was just a curves operator, you were gravely mistaken, my friend. Lookup is a very fast operator for performing color corrections via expressions.

TIP ColorX is more commonly used for creating color expressions in Shake, but Lookup is a better choice. Lookup performs scanline operations, while ColorX is a per-pixel operator. Use ColorX only if you need to compare and evaluate several color channels in one expression (such as comparing a pixel's red value to its green). Lookup cannot perform cross-channel evaluations.

Enter the following formula into the rExpr, gExpr, and bExpr parameters of a Color > Lookup node: x<0?0:x

This translates to: If x (a given pixel's color value) is less than 0, set x (the pixel's color value) to 0 or else set its value to x (keep the same value it started out with).

Now you'll have your blacks clipped to 0, but your superwhites will still be able to reach for the stratospheric values that made HDR images famous.

NOTE ▶ Be careful when clamping float values for film work. Just because you can't see them on your display doesn't mean they won't show up on film. Make sure you don't need those black values before throwing them away.

Clean Plate

DEFINITION ▶ An image of an effects shot with the foreground elements removed. A clean plate can be filmed in-camera by removing the foreground elements, or created in postproduction.

SEE ALSO ▶ clean plates, generating; subtraction matching

Clean plates are compositing gold. They enable the removal of wires and set rigging, the replacement of heads and limbs, and the introduction of computer-generated imagery where a stand-in had been.

The basic procedure for using a clean plate is simple (see clean plates, generating for a detailed procedure). The first step is to matchmove the clean plate to the original footage so that matching elements of the background overlap. Once the matchmove has been applied, subtraction matching is used to make sure the two plates are aligned. Most of the time, color correction (both primary and secondary) will still need to be applied to account for changes in lighting conditions between the original shot and the clean plate.

With the plates aligned, use a reveal paint operation (or a custom matte) to reveal the clean plate wherever foreground elements require erasing.

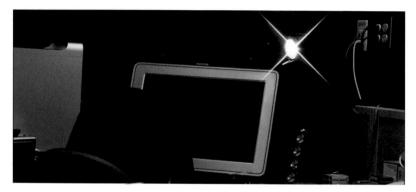

The clean plate is used to erase the actress's head, thanks to a Reveal brush in Shake's QuickPaint node.

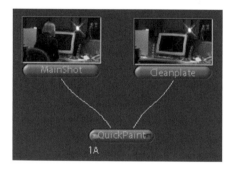

Clean plates are incredibly powerful but notoriously difficult to film. First of all, most clean plates require a locked-down camera. If the camera pans or dollies during the main shot, the clean plate movement must precisely match the original camera movement. This is usually only possible using an expensive motion-control camera rig.

It is sometimes possible to clean-plate a shot by approximating the movement on set and then matchmoving the clean plate shot to the original in postproduction, but motion-blur artifacts often compromise this solution.

Other Uses for Clean Plates

Clean plates are sometimes created to aid in the procedural extraction of objects shot in front of a blue or green screen. A plate of the blue screen or green screen without an actor, for example, enables the keyer to differentiate between what should be keyed out and what should remain when generating a matte procedurally (see also difference matte). This plate is very useful when dealing with unevenly lit blue and green screens, and greatly helps in generating usable mattes.

A clean plate can also be a shot of the background, without actors or blue or green screens. For the *Pirates of the Caribbean* films, for example, shots with computer-generated pirates were filmed first with the actors to capture their performances. A second clean plate pass was shot without the actors; the computer-generated pirates were composited into it.

Clean Plates, Generating

DEFINITION ▶ Creating clean plates to be used in other compositing operations. *Related terms:* cloning a clean plate; modified live action clean plate; offset clean plate; Shake's AutoAlign node; tracking in a still

SEE ALSO ▶ clean plate; subtraction matching

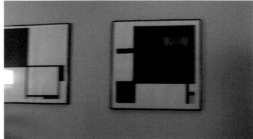

Short of locking down the camera, it's difficult to capture useful clean plates on the set. Very often it falls to the compositors to create their own clean plates, be it for wire removal or face replacement. There are several ways to generate a clean plate, and most situations call for a unique approach.

Modified Live Action Clean Plates

This is a hybrid technique, making use of a filmed clean plate but modifying it in post-production. Only a locked-down camera can produce a reliable clean plate on the set. (A motion-control rig can also do it, but they are touchy and expensive.) In this method, the original camera movement is approximated with a second live-action shoot (with unwanted foreground elements removed), and then the movement is adjusted to match the main shot in postproduction.

Motion blur will destroy the ability to usefully apply a clean plate, since mismatches in the speed and direction of the two camera movements will create incompatible blurring. The solution is to film the clean plate shot at one-half or even one-quarter of the main shot's speed. The footage can then be retimed in postproduction, but the slower camera movement will have eliminated or reduced the motion blur (which can always be added later).

Acquire the footage and retime it to match the original shot as closely as possible. Be careful *not* to use frame blending or optical flow retiming; you want the compositing application to discard extra frames rather than attempt to synthesize new ones.

Once the footage has been retimed, matchmove it to the main shot. You can also use the tracking data to introduce motion blur, although this requires a bit more processing than you might think. It's often better to use a directional blur, judiciously adjusted and keyframed.

Offset Clean Plates

In an offset clean plate, create duplicate copies of the main clip, then stagger them in time (set one clip so that it plays several frames ahead of, or behind, the original clip).

Then matchmove the clips so that the features in the background are aligned.

Finally, use a reveal tool to remove unwanted foreground elements from one clip, replacing them with vacant pixels from one of the other time-shifted clips. In many cases (as seen in the figure below), the process will need to be repeated with another offset copy of the clip to eliminate remaining overlap.

This offset technique works well only if the unwanted foreground elements move significantly relative to the background.

Cloning a Clean Plate

Another option is to paint out foreground elements with a clone brush, carefully reconstructing the background as completely as possible. Oftentimes, cloning is the only option when a foreground object never moves relative to the background. However, it tends to be difficult to perform over an animated group of frames. It's usually performed in conjunction with tracking in a still plate.

A clone tool is used to remove the unwanted foreground element.

Tracking in a Still Plate

If the background doesn't change significantly, often the best solution is to create a single still clean plate and use it for the entire shot. In this situation, the unwanted foreground elements are painted out (usually with a clone brush), leaving a convincing background in their place.

Once the unwanted elements in the background have been painted out, the still plate is matchmoved to the rest of the shot. That is, if the camera moves left, the still plate pans right along with the background in the shot.

The two most important things to add to a still plate are motion blur and grain (in that order). If there was significant grain to begin with, the clean plate will need to be degrained before being matchmoved to the shot.

Using Shake's AutoAlign Node

S

Shake's AutoAlign node is a clean plating tool masquerading as a stitcher. Simply offset a clip in time twice, then feed those clips into the AutoAlign's second and third inputs.

SHAKE ▼

For example, create three copies of a clip. Adjust the timeShift parameter on the second instance of the clip to +8, and adjust the timeShift of the third instance to –8.

Now you have three copies of the clip, each 8 frames from the next. Feed these into an AutoAlign node, setting the clipLayer to Input1, and the lockedPlate to Input1.

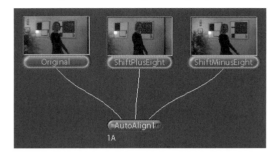

The AutoAlign will attempt to morph the three instances together so that they align. Once they're aligned, you can use the output to create a clean plate.

An offset image is warped by the AutoAlign node to match it to the original clip.

SHAKE ▼

Set the outputFrame parameter to Input2 or Input3, and use the resulting image as a reveal source against the original image. Duplicate the AutoAlign, if necessary, to use the other morphed plate to cover any background areas still obscured by foreground. (That is, if you originally used Input2 as the reveal source, use Input3 for a second reveal operation.)

NOTE ▶ This technique is only occasionally miraculous. Significant changes to the perspective of the background or large portions of foreground will render the results unusable.

Clipped Highlights, Fixing

DEFINITION ▶ Techniques for healing clipped areas of an image.

SEE ALSO ▶ clipping repair; luma keying; OpenEXR

Sometimes a shot is exposed for a specific object in a scene, which leaves other objects under- or overexposed. High dynamic-range file formats like Kodak Cineon or OpenEXR usually have the extra bandwidth to correct for these situations.

Elements that are commonly overexposed include highlights, explosions, and fire. An easy fix is to pull a key based on the luminance of the brightest areas (also called a *luma key*). Use this key as a matte and slip in a darker version of the same element to restore detail in the brightest areas. Because of the chaotic, random nature of explosions and fire, it is also possible to restore texture by using an entirely different element. Remember to blur the edges of the matte to smooth the transition.

To repair sections of images that will come under greater audience scrutiny, you can try a repair method based on channel replacement (see clipping repair).

Clipping Repair

DEFINITION ▶ Restoring contrast detail to pixel data in an image that has been otherwise irretrievably clipped. *Related terms:* highlight repair; restoring highlights

SEE ALSO ▶ clipped highlights, fixing

When you're looking through a camera viewfinder in the heat of the moment, it's often hard to see how much headroom you have left in the image exposure. You can see how much clipping has occurred only when you get the footage into your computer.

Clipping is data loss. As a result of clipping, detailed surface texturing that would be present at correct exposure levels has not been recorded. It's impossible to recover those details without reshooting the scene.

What you *can* do is substitute other information for the missing detail. And one of the easiest places to find replacement information is in the damaged image itself.

There are two options for replacing clipped areas of an image: cloning from an adjacent area, or borrowing and replacing data from an unclipped channel. Cloning works well for rigid surfaces without a lot of perspective shift. Channel replacement will work even if the surface is shifting, and it is often the only option. It relies on the fact that clipping probably did not occur in all three color channels—red, green, and blue—or that it occurred to a lesser extent on one of the channels.

In this exercise you'll perform a channel replacement, but be aware that the same basic color-correction steps still would be performed when cloning from a separate source.

Procedure

S

1   The first step in clipping repair is to determine whether all of the channels (red, green, and blue) have clipped. If not, you can use texture data from an unclipped channel for the repair.

> **TIP** Be wary of using the blue channel as a replacement, especially for footage originating on film. The blue channel contains the largest grain, and it may cause an unpleasant overaccentuation of grain in the resulting fix.

SHAKE ▼

Open **APTS_CycVFX/ProjectFiles/Color/ClipRepair/Start.shk**. Open ClipFix in the viewer, and examine the red, green, and blue channels by positioning the mouse over the Viewer and pressing the R, G, and B keys. Press the C key to return to full-color viewing.

The red channel   The green channel   The blue channel

After a quick viewing of the color channels, it's clear that the clipping is occurring primarily in the red channel. Although the blue channel is probably the least clipped, the contrast in the green channel is much closer to the contrast you would expect to find in an unclipped red channel. So, you'll use the green channel as your replacement.

2   With the channel-clipping situation sorted out, you can start making adjustments. First, the brightness of the image must be reduced to make room for the new, replacement highlights. After all, if the image had been filmed correctly, it would naturally be darker.

SHAKE ▼

To ClipFix, add a Color > Compress (High Color = 0.7, 0.7, 0.7).

TIP ▶ A Brightness node with the value set to 0.7 could have been used instead of the Compress. Using the Compress later gives you the option of adjusting the black level, if necessary.

3   Next, replace the red channel with the green channel.

SHAKE ▼

Add a Color > Reorder (channels = ggba) to Compress1.

Don't panic. Things do look a little weird right now, but that's because you've replaced the red channel for the entire image, not just for the clipped sections.

4   You'll need a matte for the areas that were clipped in the original image. You could use a luma key, but because you're concerned only with values that were clipped to 1, a threshold operation is actually easier. Because you're choosing only one pixel value (a value of 1), you'll have a hard matte. So you'll also need to blur the edge of the matte to smooth the transition between replacement pixels and original pixels.

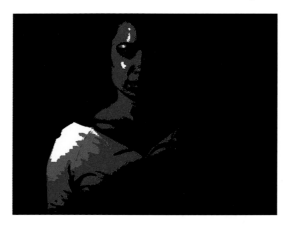

SHAKE ▼

Select ClipFix, and then Shift-click a Color > Threshold to branch. Set the R, G, and B Color values to *0.999999*. Add a Filter > Blur (pixels = 30).

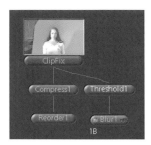

5   You can use the red channel of your new matte to isolate the channel replacement to include only those sections of the image where clipping occurred.

SHAKE ▼

Feed Blur1 into the mask input of Reorder1. Set the maskChannel of Reorder1 to R.

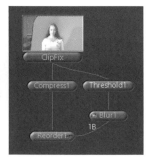

6   At this point, the face looks bruised. That's because skin is predominantly red, and the green replacement pixels we're using are not as bright as the surrounding original red pixels. The solution is to brighten the replacement pixels with a color correction.

SHAKE ▼

To Reorder1, add a Color > Mult. Feed Blur1 into the mask input of Mult1, and then set the maskChannel of Mult1 to R. While looking at only the red channel of the image, adjust up the red level in Mult1 until the replacement area matches the surrounding skin.

Before color correction   After color correction

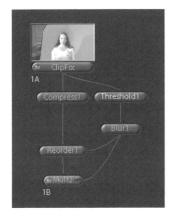

The treatment is complete.

Codec

DEFINITION ▶ Short for *compressor/decompressor*. A software scheme used to compress data to a smaller, more efficient storage format, and to decompress the data as needed.

Color Correction

DEFINITION ▶ Any process that alters the perceived color of an image.

SEE ALSO ▶ bleach bypass; chroma keying; color matching; depth keying; difference matte; neutralizing black and white points

Color Depth

DEFINITION ▶ The possible range of colors that can be used in a video, film, or image. Higher color depths provide a wider range of colors but also require more disk space for a given image size. Color depth is usually associated with the number of bits available to represent each channel of color.

SEE ALSO ▶ bits per channel; bits per pixel; float space

Color Matching

DEFINITION ▶ Making the color of one shot correspond with that of another by matching black and white points, midlevel grays, and color bias. Typically used to match the color of a foreground to a background, or to match the colors of disparate elements after they've been composited into a single shot.

SEE ALSO ▶ color correction; radiosity, faux

Before color matching   After color matching

Pulling a good matte is only part of the keying process. To really integrate a blue screen or green screen element into a scene, color correction is essential. If an audience is going to believe that the new foreground element is part of the background plate, both elements in the composite must appear to be lit by the same light sources.

There are three primary processes used for integrating the color of an object into a scene. These are black and white point match, contrast match, and hue and saturation match. While these are broken out as separate processes, in most situations they are performed out of order or even simultaneously.

Matching Black and White Points

Every shot has extremes in contrast. That is, some part of the shot is darker than the rest of the shot (usually shadows, although soul-sucking creatures from parallel universes may also fit the bill), and another part is brighter. It's essential that your introduced foreground element map to the same contrast range as the background.

The easiest way to perform the black and white point matching is to color-correct the foreground so that its black and white points are mapped to values of 0 and 1, respectively. Then, you can take the resulting image and compress it into the background's contrast range. Since this is a double correction, you should either use Shake's concatenation of color nodes, or work in 32-bit float (available in Shake, Motion, and After Effects).

The workflow in Shake is as follows:

In the Color tab, use an Expand node. Select the Low Color swatch and, using the minimum swatch, scrub through the blackest portions of the image. Be careful not to scrub any black areas in the frame border or in black areas resulting from a camera matte box.

Doing so will produce illegitimate readings. When you have your black point, scrub through a white portion of the image to select the High Color.

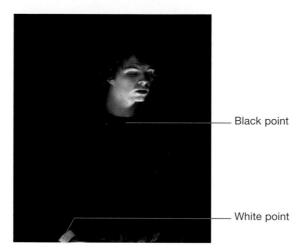

— Black point

— White point

NOTE ▶ When choosing the white point, be careful not to sample specular highlights (metallic glints). Good white-point matching will use a "diffuse" white surface—something that reflects light in all directions. This could be a shirt, or a matte white surface such as a billboard or piece of paper. Specular highlights represent areas of brightness that are often several orders of magnitude more intense than the diffuse white point of the scene.

The Expand node stretches the contrast of the image so that the black and white points you selected now have values of 0 and 1, respectively.

With the foreground image normalized, you can compress it to the background's black and white points. Identify black and white points of the background, and then, from the Color tab, use a Compress node to compress the foreground image into this range.

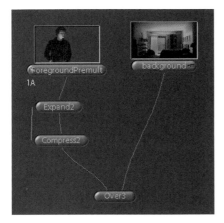

When using After Effects and Motion for color matching, the Levels filter alone can perform the same functions, though without the same ease and precision of sampling. Just adjust the Input Black and Input White until the black and white points are expanded to 0 and 1. Then adjust the Output Black and Output White until the black and white points map successfully with the background.

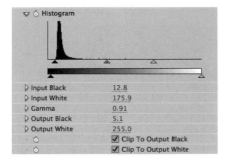

What do you do if you don't have a true white or black in your shot? Just take your best guess. Even using obvious black and white points, you still may need to adjust your initial settings to account for variations in the intensity of the selected blacks and whites.

Matching Contrast

With the black and white points set, it's time to match contrast. Contrast is the distribution of intensity between the black and white points in your image. Some scenes will have dramatic shadows and superbright whites; others will have a much more even distribution of intensities.

The first step in adjusting contrast will probably be a gamma color correction. Gamma operators adjust contrast in a way that appears very natural to the human eye. Gamma adjustments also are reasonably kind to the black and white points you may already have worked so hard to set. Gamma adjustments *will* affect your black and white points (unless for some unusual reason those values are exactly 0 and 1, respectively), but the effects won't be as dramatic as with other contrast adjustment methods. Nonetheless, there may be some push and pull as you're forced to go back and tweak your black and white points after adjusting the gamma.

If gamma doesn't cut it, then move on to something more dramatic: the ContrastLum node in Shake, or the Levels filter contrast adjustment in After Effects and Motion.

Matching Hue and Saturation

This is the toughest of the three processes. Once the contrast is set, it's essential that the hue of the lighting used to illuminate the background be matched in the introduced foreground element. While there is some scientific method to this (see "Grayscale Balancing," below), hue and saturation matching is often an arbitrary process. Use your favorite color-correction method to adjust the foreground until the coloration naturally matches that of the background.

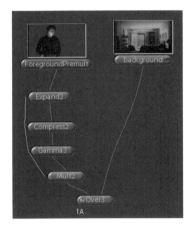

A useful technique to use when performing this match is faux radiosity (see radiosity, faux).

The final treated image

Grayscale Balancing

The technique of grayscale balancing involves using black, white, and gray objects in foreground and background images to accurately match the lighting color of the foreground to the background.

Judging color can be tricky. The essence of the problem is the way colors interact in the eyes of an observer.

First, an object has an intrinsic color. A blue ball absorbs most of the red and green portions of the visible spectrum, and reflects blue.

Second, light illuminating the object also possesses a tint. When a red light shines on a blue ball, the resulting visual is a combination of the two colors.

And then the radiosity bounce lighting (reflections from one surface to another) causes interactions of color between the objects in a scene. That creates complex and subtle color shading, which is always tricky to simulate in a composite.

As a result, it's essentially impossible to look at a photographed image and determine whether an object's color is intrinsic to its surface or the result of the scene lighting.

Gray Matters

Compositors love gray. Everyone else can keep their chartreuse, their pastels, and their moonbeam blue; we'll take gray. Gray is the one color that offers an objective insight into the lighting of a scene. Since the intrinsic color of gray objects has no tint, the final color of a gray object after being filmed is necessarily the color of the scene light.

Put another way, if a gray object and a red object are both illuminated with a red light, they may appear to an observer to be the same color. Without any other contextual clues, an observer would be unable to determine whether the object is truly red, or simply reflecting red light in the scene. But if the observer knows that one of the objects is gray, she can deduce the color of the scene lighting from the tint of the object in the photographed image.

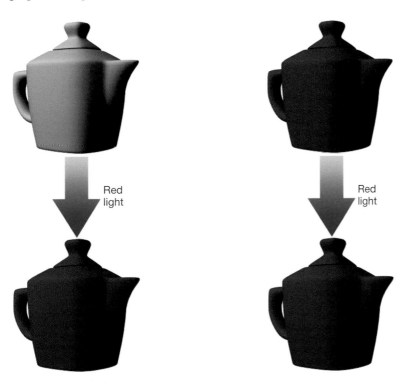

Red light

Red light

Color Correcting to Grays

In a perfect world, a compositor could match the tint of black, midlevel gray, and white points between a foreground image and a background image to produce the final color match. In fact, this is the principle behind Shake's ColorMatch node. Simply sample the black, mid, and white points for source and destination images, and the destination image's color will be adjusted to match the source.

> **NOTE** ▶ The same procedure can be performed in After Effects using the Curves filter. Shake's ColorMatch is similar, although it uses some extra math to prevent posterization of the resulting image.

In our imperfect world, it's often difficult to find pure blacks, grays, and whites in the shot you're working on. In fact, it's actually dangerous to assume too much. For example, assuming that a trashcan in the background plate is black when it's actually dark green could end up incorrectly tinting your color-corrected foreground.

This example also reinforces the importance of shooting reference cards on location. If a reference card with white, mid-gray, and black is shot during the green screen shoot and during the background shoot, color matching becomes a much simpler process. Professional test cards are available from many camera and video rental vendors, but even a makeshift card from an inkjet printer will be hugely beneficial (printed using only the black ink cartridge, and on matte paper stock).

Combining Mattes

> **SEE** ▶ mattes, combining

Component Video

> **DEFINITION** ▶ A type of analog video signal where the luminance and chrominance signals are recorded separately, thereby providing better video quality. The signal can be recorded in an analog form (Y, R-Y, B-Y), as in a Betacam SP, or in a digital form (Y, Cr, Cb), as in a Digital Betacam.

> **SEE ALSO** ▶ YIQ; YUV

Composite

DEFINITION ▶ The act of creating an image by combining two or more still or moving image elements. As a verb, *composite* refers to the process of combining these elements; as a noun, it refers to the final resulting image. In visual effects work, a finished composite gives the illusion that all the elements were captured by a single camera filming the scene. In motion graphics, the concern isn't so much to convince the audience that everything was shot in camera as it is to present a stylistic and coherent blend of elements.

Composite Video

DEFINITION ▶ A type of analog video signal that combines all chroma and luma information into a single waveform running through a single pair of wires. This can result in analog artifacts that affect the quality of the video signal.

Compositing Outside the Keyer

DEFINITION ▶ Compositing foreground and background elements without using the keying filter's built-in compositing. *Related term:* external compositing

SEE ALSO ▶ mattes, shrinking and expanding; spill suppression

Keyers (and especially third-party keyers) often attempt to be one-stop shops. They pull a key, spill suppress and color correct the foreground, garbage-matte out the background, hold out portions of the foreground, and glue together foreground and background elements. This is probably more than one tool should be doing.

Using a single keyer for all these operations can create several problems. It limits the available tools for correcting the foreground, forcing you to use only the keyer's color correction. It also prevents you from making adjustments to the blue screen or green screen that might improve the quality of the matte generated by the keyer. Finally, the keyer precludes adjustments to the matte, such as choking or dilating.

Compositing outside the keyer is a much more flexible choice. You can individually treat the foreground being fed to the keyer, the foreground being used for the composite, and the matte being used for the composite.

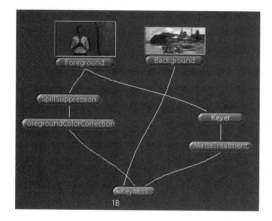

NOTE ▶ In Shake, KeyMix has the unusual distinction of setting the background as the first input to the node, the foreground as the second input, and the matte (or *key*) as the third input, resulting in the crossing "noodles" in the figure above). In other nodes, the foreground is always the first input and the background the second.

You may sometimes find that you like the spill suppression performed by the keyer. (For example, Keylight often does very capable spill suppression.) In that case, you can use the keyer to generate the matte *and* suppress the spill on the foreground. When you do, make sure that the keyer is set to output an unpremultiplied image.

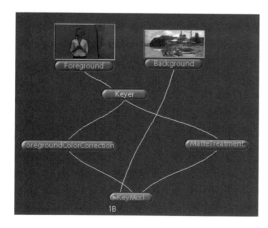

Using the keyer for generating the matte *and* performing spill suppression.

Alternatively, you can create two instances of the keyer: one for generating the matte, the other for applying spill suppression. This gives you total control, albeit with a little more mess.

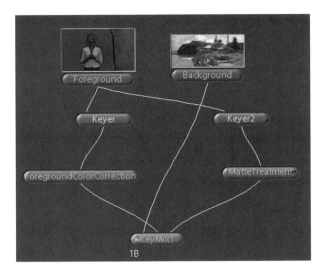

Using separate instances of the keyer, one for spill suppression (Keyer), the other for generating the matte (Keyer2)

Compression

DEFINITION ▶ The process by which video, graphics, and audio files are reduced in size. A *lossy* compression scheme refers to the reduction in the size of a video file through the removal of perceptually redundant image data. A *lossless* compression scheme uses a mathematical process to reduce the file size by consolidating redundant information without discarding it. Compare with decompression.

SEE ALSO ▶ codec

Concatenation

DEFINITION ▶ The process of mathematically combining multiple operations, such as color corrections, pans, rotations, shears, and scale operations, into one master operation. That is, instead of the pixels in an image passing through several different transform operations—each of which unavoidably softens the image at the subpixel level—a single transformation that meets all the requirements of the different operations is performed.

SEE ALSO ▶ Tracking Fundamentals chapter

Contrast

DEFINITION ▶ The difference between the lightest and darkest values in an image. High-contrast images have a wide range of values from the darkest shadow to the lightest highlight. Low-contrast images have a narrower range of values, resulting in a flatter look.

Contrast Match, Checking

SEE ▶ black levels, checking/gamma slamming; color matching

Core Matte

SEE ▶ edge matte/core matte; Keying Fundamentals chapter

Cameo

Anatomy of a Lightsaber Duel—Brian Connor

LIKE MOST SHOTS IN A MOVIE, UTC390 passes by quickly, one of many action sequences in the ultimate showdown between Jedi master Obi-Wan Kenobi and the biomechanical General

Grievous in *Star Wars: Episode III*. Nonetheless, it is an elaborate mix of green screen photography with more than 65 layers of a wholly computer-generated environment.

Original Obi-Wan green screen with a General Grievous stand-in wearing fashionable spandex

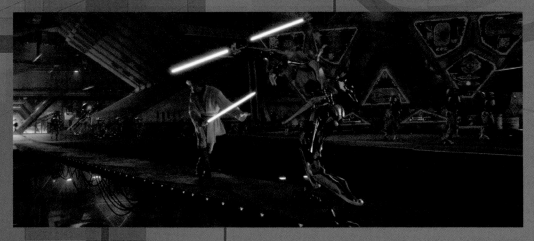

Obi-Wan locked in a duel to the death with General Grievous in an all-CG environment

The planet Utapau is the stage for this duel to the death inside the tenth level of an enormous sinkhole.

Obi-Wan brazenly drops in on the unsuspecting leaders of the separatist movement. After dispatching some bodyguard droids, Obi-Wan turns his attention to the chancellor's second-in-command. General Grievous, skilled in the ways of the Jedi and their lightsaber, attacks Obi-Wan with not one arm but four, each with its own lightsaber gathered from Jedi that he has killed. Shot utc390 joins the fight after Obi-Wan has skillfully hacked off two of Grievous's four hands, and features both warriors on a catwalk while Grievous prepares another attack.

The Level 10 interior is a very complex 3D-rendered environment—so complicated, in fact, that each lighting pass was rendered separately to prevent any re-renders. The multiple lighting passes also enabled a significant amount of control in the assembly of the final composite. This is where Brian Connor (see Contributors, page iv) and company come in.

TIP "John [Knoll] wanted the interior to look like it was being lit mostly by external daylight. Using the different lighting passes allowed us to get the look he wanted with minimal re-rendering."

—Brian Connor, Compositor, ILM

The exterior matte painting

The ambient light pass

The diffuse light pass

The spotlight pass

The reflection pass

The animated light
panels and runway
lights pass

The spotlight and
atmosphere pass
using practical
elements

The Talent

No *Star Wars* motion picture would be complete without the huge ensemble of droids, super battle droids, crab droids, and octuptarra droids. Each was rendered out in its own layer and color corrected.

Several passes of good and bad laser fire, muzzle flashes, and explosions were also added to the shot as story points.

The combined background droids pass

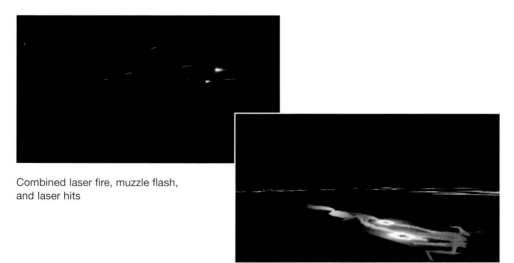

Combined laser fire, muzzle flash,
and laser hits

Combined shadows of all droids, Grievous,
and Obi-Wan

"You're my only hope..."

Like most of the live-action elements, Obi-Wan starts his life where the grass (and the wall) is always green. Using procedural keying techniques coupled with multiple roto-scoped mattes, Obi-Wan was extracted, color corrected, and integrated into the CG environment. Interactive lightsaber glows were added to finish off the element.

The Obi-Wan green screen element

Obi-Wan extracted and color corrected

Obi-Wan extracted and color corrected with interactive lightsaber light

The General

General Grievous is one of many complicated characters that inhabit the *Star Wars* universe. Countless hours went into developing, texturing, animating, and lighting him. As with the Level 10 interior, multiple passes were rendered, color corrected, and combined in the composite. Interactive lightsaber glows were placed to help integrate the lightsabers that were added next.

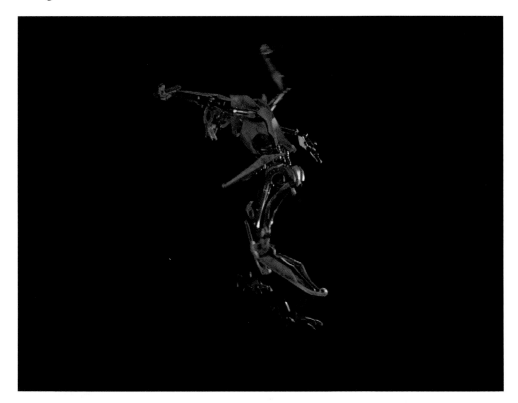

The color-corrected General Grievous element

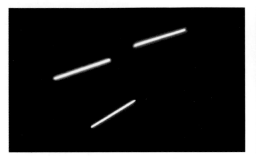

Lightsaber cores

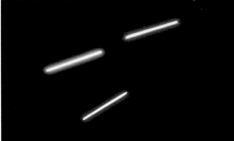

Combined lightsaber cores and glows

No duel would be complete without the requisite lightsaber. Obi-Wan's lightsaber was made the traditional way using multiple rotoscoped mattes animated by hand (see **lightsaber, creating**).

The effort and painstaking attention to detail that constituted the work on this shot was typical. utc390 is only one of hundreds of complicated shots that came together in *Episode III* to complete the Star Wars saga that George Lucas started over 20 years ago.

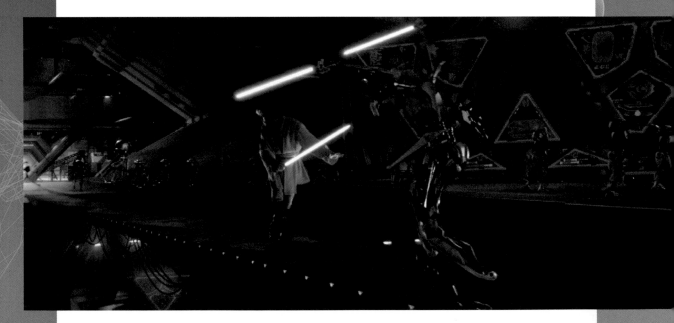

The final composite

Dailies

DEFINITION ▶ Term used to describe unedited footage from a film shoot. Usually developed and delivered to the director for review the morning following a day of shooting.

In the era of digital media, no development is necessary and review of recorded footage is instantaneous. The term *dailies* is still sometimes used to refer to a daily period of review of captured footage. In the postproduction world, it can also refer to the daily review of CG work in progress. Typically, the effects are rendered at HD resolution and reviewed using an HD projector.

Data Rate

DEFINITION ▶ The speed at which data can be transferred, often described in megabytes per second (MBps). The higher a video file's data rate, the higher its quality will be, but the more system resources (processor speed, hard-disk space, and performance) it will require to render. Some codecs allow you to specify a maximum data rate for a movie during render.

Day for Night

DEFINITION ▶ Converting a scene that was shot in daylight into one that appears to be shot at night.

SEE ALSO ▶ color correction; luminance, weighted

There are almost as many reasons for shooting in daylight as there are for shooting blue screen. Shooting day for night is often desirable because of the availability of talent, the use of a location, cast and crew safety, and the limitations of the camera.

Like the human eye, the camera is not adept at gathering detail in low-light situations, and most cameras will exhibit a lot of video noise or film grain in low light, which can degrade the final image quality. Shooting during the day, and then manipulating the image to appear as if it had been shot at night, can overcome this.

There are in-camera photographic techniques to create a day-for-night look, such as using a blue filter and underexposing by a few stops. Unfortunately, you are stuck with the in-camera results if that day-for-night look is not right. It is always better to start with the higher quality available in a daytime shot and darken the shot than it is to try to brighten an already noisy, darker image.

An image actually shot during the daytime

> **TIP** ▶ "Generally, with day for night you want to fool the audience into buying that it was a nighttime shot—and that's where it is tough to find the fine line. Like in *The Perfect Storm*, realistically you would have seen very little at night and in a rainstorm; but in order to tell the story, you have to alter realism."
>
> —Marshall Krasser, Compositing Supervisor, Industrial Light & Magic

Color correction is the primary tool used for changing a daytime shot into a nighttime shot. Bringing down the highlights using a Mult node (Brightness) and reducing midtones using a Gamma node are pretty obvious methods. Not so obvious is using a luminance matte to protect and retain the brightest light sources in both hue and saturation. The saturation of the entire image should be brought down at least 20 percent, depending on the shot. Adding a slight blue tint to the image gives the moonlit look we all know and love.

The process becomes problematic when color correcting a daytime shot containing harsh shadows. At night, light is more diffused and less contrasty, and produces soft shadows. To imitate reality, most day-for-night color correction attempts to flatten the image by reducing the contrast range. However, those sharp shadows can be a dead giveaway that something is not quite right with the shot. To minimize fixing in post, you should shoot a day-for-night shot when the daytime skies are slightly overcast.

Specific light sources in a shot need to be processed differently than the general light source. You can use a combination of blurred luminance mattes and rotoscoped splines to prevent light sources like lamps and illuminated items around them from being too darkened or desaturated. These same mattes can be reused to add more bloom, atmosphere, and glows to the light sources.

A final element to attend to is sharpness, or the lack thereof. In low-light situations, less image detail is perceived by the naked eye (or captured by film or video), and therefore the image appears less sharp than it would in brighter light. A nice touch is to blur all of a color-corrected day-for-night shot, and then add about 1 or 2 percent of the blurred image back into the original nighttime shot. This technique slightly softens the image without blurring it, thereby mimicking the scattered look of light at night.

The color-corrected "night" image.

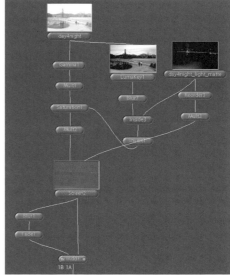

A day-for-night tree in Shake

Decompression

DEFINITION ▶ The process of creating a viewable image for playback from a compressed video, graphics, or audio file. Compare with compression.

Deinterlacing

DEFINITION ▶ Method for removing the interlacing of video frames so that the sequence can be manipulated in postproduction. *Related term:* removing fields

SEE ALSO ▶ 3:2 pull-down removal

Interlacing is one of a compositor's many archenemies. When footage is interlaced, it can't be scaled, rotated, filtered, or panned vertically without causing extremely unpleasant artifacts. There are several methods for removing interlacing; some are better than others.

Identifying Interlacing

Interlacing was introduced with the advent of television in the 1930s, when the phosphors used in the CRT screens were less efficient than they are today. The idea was to reduce the sensation of flicker on the TV screen by increasing the frame rate from 30 *frames* per second (NTSC) to 60 *fields* per second.

Interlacing is the process of recording two distinct moments in time in a single frame of video. For the NTSC video standard, the video camera will take a snapshot of the scene at each 1/60th of a second. Instead of creating a sequence of 60 frames per second (fps), pairs of these fields (the snapshots taken at 1/60th of a second) are combined into a single frame, creating a 30 fps sequence. (In PAL, the pairs of snapshots are taken at 1/50th of a second, amounting to a 25 fps sequence.)

These fields are combined by placing one of the fields into the odd lines of the frame and the other into the even lines. When looking at a video frame as a still, you see a comblike effect representing two moments in time: The odd fields are a snapshot at 1/60th of a second, while the even lines are the same snapshot 1/60th of a second later.

NOTE ▶ Interestingly enough, even though film is only 24 fps, each frame is actually presented at the projector twice—for a display frame count of 48 fps—to accommodate the "persistence of vision" in human perception.

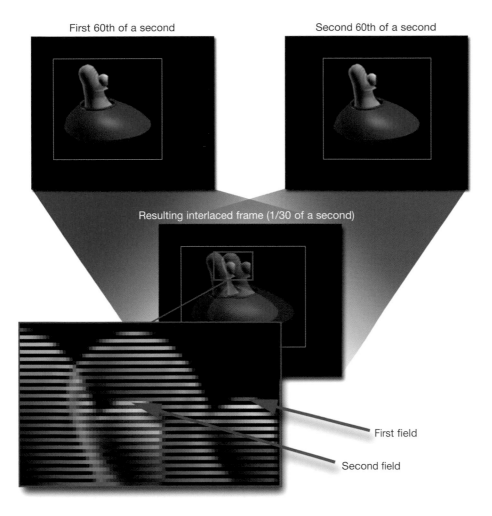

First 60th of a second

Second 60th of a second

Resulting interlaced frame (1/30 of a second)

First field

Second field

Unfortunately, interlacing and compositing don't mix. Take a simple case in Shake: You want to move your interlaced image up by 1 pixel, so you apply a Move2D node and choose a yPan value of 1. Now the odd field lines are in the position of the even field lines and vice versa. Essentially, the two fields have time traveled: The first 60th of a second captured on camera is being played back during the second 60th of a second, and vice versa. This is not good.

It gets even worse if you try to rotate the footage, because the field lines rotate as well, so that they're no longer horizontal. But when you play back the resulting footage as video, the video monitor displays the odd horizontal lines of the image first, then the even. The result: a video display of a rotated image with weirdly striped lines.

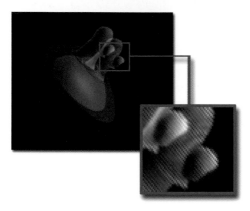

In fact, most common compositing operations, with the exception of color corrections, will negatively affect fields. What we need to do, therefore, is remove the fields before we begin the composite.

Unlacing the Interlace

There are four primary ways to remove fields, called *deinterlacing*.

Discard and Double

The first technique simply involves throwing away one set of fields and doubling up the other so that you have only one moment in time recorded at each frame. Unfortunately, that also means you lose half the vertical resolution.

Average the Fields

A second technique is to average adjacent fields together. So, you take line 1 and line 2 of the image, average them together, and replace line 1 with the result. Then take the average of line 2 and line 3, and replace line 2 with the result. This has the advantage of blending the two moments of time contained in the original frame into one, but it still ultimately degrades the image.

> **TIP** These methods are available in Shake via the Other > Deinterlace node.

Separate the Fields

Usually the best technique is to separate the two fields into different frames and double their height, resulting in a 60 fps sequence instead of 30 fps (or, for PAL, 50 fps instead of 25 fps). Shake, Motion, and After Effects perform this in very similar ways, so let's take a look at Shake's handling here, for simplicity.

Shake stores the second field at the 0.5 points on the Timeline. So, if frame 3 contains two fields, the first in the odd lines and the second in the even, then two new frames would be created during the deinterlacing process. The odd lines would be doubled to become the new frame 3, and the even lines would be doubled to become frame 3.5.

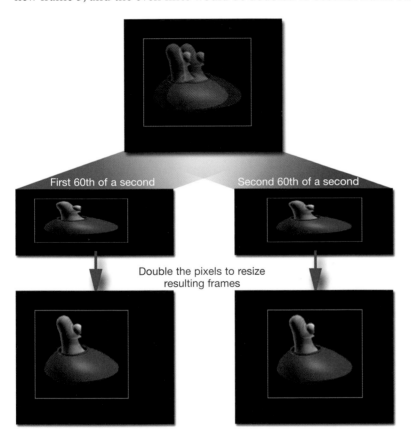

Once all the compositing has taken place, Shake simply recombines the frames occurring at whole numbers on the Timeline and those occurring at the 0.5 positions back into a single frame with two fields. Any panning, rotation, scaling, or blurring done along the way is sandwiched in between the deinterlacing and the reinterlacing.

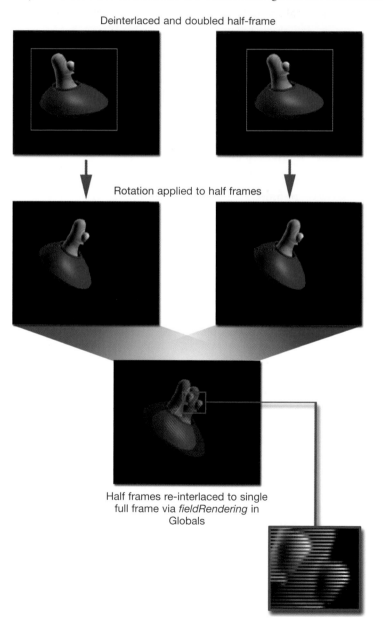

Deinterlaced and doubled half-frame

Rotation applied to half frames

Half frames re-interlaced to single full frame via *fieldRendering* in Globals

Oh, and one more thing: You might be tempted to assume that the first 1/60th moment in time would appear in the odd scan lines of the image, and the second 1/60th in the even. Unfortunately, there's never been a global standard, so different video systems use different conventions. As a result, you need to choose the appropriate field order, or *dominance*, when deinterlacing.

To manually check the order of a file's fields in Shake, set the Inc (located to the right of the Timeline) to 0.5, and then use the right arrow on the keyboard to step through the footage. If you see a "Canadian three-step"-like behavior, where the footage seems to move forward in one frame and then back a little in the next, you know you have the field order wrong. Remember, you need to be on a whole frame and set the increment back to 1 when you're done.

As if all the previous information weren't difficult enough, different video software and hardware manufacturers refer to these fields with different nomenclature. Some talk about odd and even fields, some about first and second, and some about upper and lower. A quick rule of thumb (which, unfortunately isn't always the case, but should steer you right most of the time) is that the terms *upper*, *odd*, and *first* mean the same thing, and then, conversely, *lower*, *even*, and *second* match, as well.

Interface Specifics

In Shake, deinterlacing is performed in the FileIn node's parameters. Reinterlacing is performed in the Globals tab via the fieldRendering parameter.

In After Effects, deinterlacing is performed in the Interpret Footage dialog. Reinterlacing is performed in the Render presets section.

In Motion, deinterlacing is performed in the Media Inspector tab. Reinterlacing is performed in the Export output options.

Optical Flow Retiming

The final deinterlacing method uses an optical flow algorithm to interpolate new, integrated frames. The algorithm will essentially warp the two fields into a single cohesive frame representing one slice of time, instead of two competing moments. Optical flow retiming may be the best choice if you plan to stay at the resulting progressive frame rate. However, it is not recommended if you plan to return to the original interlaced format for output, since it will degrade the final quality.

Depth Keying

DEFINITION ▶ Using a Z channel to generate a matte for masking purposes (but not depth compositing). *Related terms:* depth matte; *z* matte

SEE ALSO ▶ clamping mattes

If you've spent any time around rendered 3D images, you've probably come across a depth matte, aka *z* buffer. If you've tried to make sense of such images for compositing, you may have ended up confused and frustrated. Read on, friend, for in these very pages we unlock the ancient secrets of *z* space.

A depth matte represents how far an image's pixels are from the camera. Pixels closer to the camera will appear lighter than pixels farther from the camera, or vice versa, depending on which scheme is employed.

The problem with depth is that it can be, well, very deep. In one 3D scene, the distance of the farthest object from the camera may be 30 feet. In another scene involving planets and galaxies, that distance might be light-years.

To attempt to represent both those extremes with a simple 256-tone, 8-bit grayscale image buffer would be a bit silly. Instead, at least 16 bits of linear data are usually required, and most decent implementations use 32-bit float space. (See clamping mattes and float space for more information.) For the rest of this discussion, we assume you're working with a float-based depth matte.

NOTE ▶ If you're working with Maya renders, you may be confused by the default depth pass. Maya renders its depth pass as 1/z in an effort to normalize the depth values to fit into a linear 16-bit render. Now that Maya ships with the mental ray shader, there's no excuse not to render your own depth pass in float space, but if you're determined to make a go of the traditional Maya depth matte, you may want to download the Maya Shake macros found at www.highend2d.com.

Uses for Depth Mattes

Depth mattes are incredibly useful, just not in the way you'd initially think. Most people get excited about the idea that you can use a depth matte to composite elements so that the objects closest to the camera are automatically layered in front of other objects.

That would be very cool. Unfortunately, it creates fundamental problems with edges. As you should know now from reading this book, good, soft edge detail is the holy grail of compositing. Depth mattes have completely hard edges because each pixel in a depth matte represents the distance of the corresponding RGB pixel from the camera, so only one depth value can be recorded. At an edge pixel, where there is a blend between a foreground object and the object behind it, only one object's distance value can be recorded, either the foreground object's distance *or* the distance of the object behind it. That means hard edges, which makes for an ugly composite. Sorry.

And the problem is not only with edges. You'll experience similar difficulties anywhere you have transparent objects in your scene. If you have a glass vase you want to composite over a background, the depth matte will not provide transparency information. Some 3D applications include an option to anti-alias the depth matte, but that simply creates an object that tapers from one depth to another.

Wait! Don't throw away your depth mattes just yet. You're going to need them for color corrections and depth-of-field effects.

Color Correction

As things move into the distance, their appearance is affected by the particles in the air between them and the observer. They tend to lose saturation and pick up a blue hue due to the lower attenuation of blue light passing through the air. (Here in Los Angeles, they pick up a slightly brown hue, thanks to the delightful smog.) Depth mattes can be used to apply a matching color correction to computer graphic elements so that they appear to lose saturation moving into the distance.

Depth of Field

Depth-of-field effects are very expensive to render in 3D applications, and performing them there means that they're baked into the images. Want to create a rack-focus effect in postproduction? Too late—go back four squares and re-render.

Using a depth matte to create depth of field involves selectively applying a blur, or defocus, effect based on an element's position in the depth matte. A rack focus can be achieved by varying which portions of the matte will be blurred and which portions will remain in focus, untouched.

There are two problems with depth-of-field fakes like this. First, they are fakes. True depth of field means the camera lens samples the scene from different perspectives. 3D rendering applications achieve this by performing multiple passes, slightly offsetting the lens angle each time, then blending the passes together. That's why these renders take so long. The good news is that the 2D fake can be a pretty good one and save a lot of rendering time.

Second, image-based blur operations (like IBlur in Shake) lack the ability to "blur around corners." When the blur reaches one of those nice depth matte edges, it stops. A true defocus would mushroom beyond the borders of an object. The solution? Either render your objects with separate passes for each element, so that no object is occluded by another (this takes more rendering time and is quite fiddly), or use a cool plug-in that handles these border issues for you.

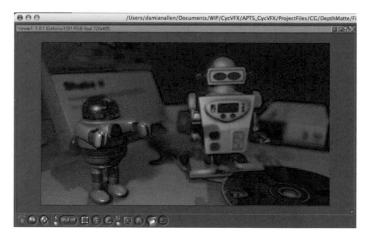

Standard defocus with edge problem

Correct defocus, using Depth of Field Generator Pro (www.dofpro.com)

Depth Matte Setup

One of the most confusing moments in a young compositor's life is the first encounter with a float-based depth matte. It often looks something like this:

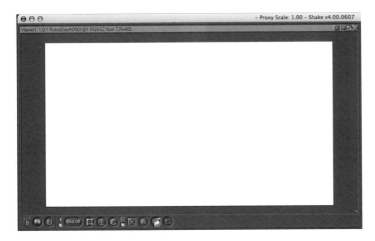

NOTE ▶ To follow the discussion for this example, use the images found in **APTS_CycVFX/ProjectFiles/CG/DepthMatte**. If working in Shake, open **start.shk**.

That big white rectangle you see there? That's your depth matte. Float images can have any kind of value they like; you could have a float map with a pixel value of 5,345,234 or –0.5. Any float value higher than 1.0 will display onscreen as white, so your first look at a float-depth image will rarely give useful results.

TIP ▶ A really nice way of rendering depth mattes is to embed the distance units in the pixel values. So if you're measuring your 3D geometry in meters, a pixel that's 30 meters from the camera would have a depth matte value of 30.

To get a useful matte, use an "expanded" color correction and set a new 0 black point and a new 1 white point. That means that the value you choose for your lower color gets mapped to 0, while the value you choose for your high color gets mapped to 1. Although it's called an expand operation, with depth mattes you're actually *compressing* float values into the 0-to-1 range.

By sampling pixel values for the closest and most distant parts of our depth matte, you end up with the following image:

To produce the new image, the values used were 8.2 for the low color and 20 for the high color. So when you popped those values into the expand operation, any pixels with a value of 8.2 became 0, any pixels with a value of 20 and higher became 1, and all the pixels in between those values distributed themselves between 0 and 1. You'll see that the background remains white, since those pixels had values greater than 20.

You can refine your matte to include different pixels simply by changing the values for your expand operation. Using a low color of 12 and a high color of 16 effectively isolates the matte contrast to the robot on the right.

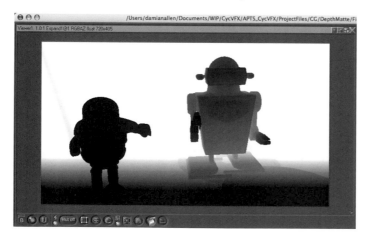

Obviously, the useful values will vary depending on how the depth matte was rendered. So the trick is to identify from the RGB image which part of the image should be closest to the camera, and then sample your low color from there (sampling from the raw depth matte, not the RGB image). Then decide how far back your matte should extend, and sample from an appropriate location at that distance.

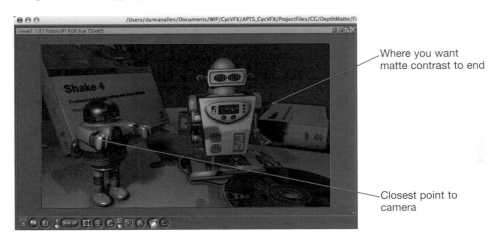

Where you want
matte contrast to end

Closest point to
camera

Using a Depth Matte for Color Correction

Assuming your matte is set up to be white in the distance and dark in the foreground (you can always invert it if it's the opposite), you can color correct the entire image to the way you want distant objects to appear, then apply the depth matte as a mask for the color correction.

It is simple, really. First, be sure that you've clamped the matte to remove any values greater than 1 or less than 0, since those will produce unpredictable results in your masking operation. (See clamping mattes for more information.) Note that as of Shake 4.0, mask inputs are automatically clamped for you. Nice.

Add the color correction; make your color changes, then add the mask, being sure to set the mask operation to the appropriate channel. So if your modified depth matte is on the RGB channels, choose R, G, or B as the masking channel.

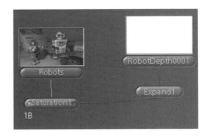

As an extreme example, let's say the background area of the image has been completely desaturated with the color correction masked by our depth matte. The distance from the camera to the back of the sample scene is obviously fairly short, so we would expect an extremely subtle change (if any) in the real scenario.

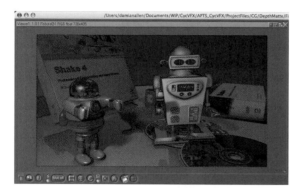

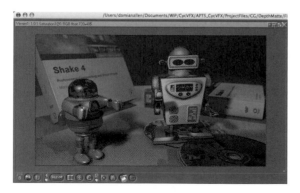

The image on top is affected by the depth matte in the middle to produce the image at bottom.

Using a Depth Matte for Defocusing

The following tree can be used to generate a defocus based on the depth matte. But remember, it'll suffer from the edge problems discussed earlier. For a more natural solution, you'll need to render the objects separately, or use a dedicated plug-in designed for defocus magic.

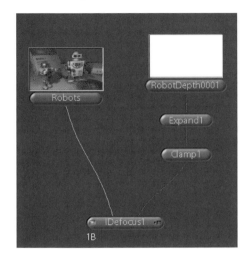

Depth Matte

SEE ▶ depth keying

Desaturate

DEFINITION ▶ To remove color intensity from a clip. Desaturation of 100 percent results in a grayscale image.

Difference Matte

DEFINITION ▶ A matte created by comparing two images and generating the matte based on pixels that aren't the same in both images.

SEE ALSO ▶ Keying Fundamentals chapter

Typically, an image containing an element that needs to be isolated or removed is compared with a *clean plate* of the same image that does not contain the element. When the difference between the pixels is computed, you theoretically are left with a matte of just that element.

But in practice, difference mattes are rarely usable because of camera gate weave, film grain and video noise, subtle time-of-day or lighting changes, motion-control camera-rig anomalies, and so on. Subtle differences between the grain structures of two frames within the same locked-off shot can introduce enough noise to blow the whole operation. Many times, the difference matte is just the first step toward a more usable matte, but only after much refinement.

NOTE ▶ The difference matte generally can be finessed with the tolerance settings in the difference matte node to allow for deviation from one image to the other.

Typically, difference mattes are used only for quick garbage masks of an element. Depending on the purpose, that garbage matte may be all a compositor needs for a rough comp or for a general color correction that doesn't require precision matte edges. So a difference matte is always worth a quick try—just in case!

For example, examine this locked-off shot of a basketball player driving toward the camera.

The player eventually exits the frame, which gives you a clean plate.

However, even with a strong clean plate, the resulting difference matte and rough comp are hardly usable for any purpose other than garbage masking because of the intense motion blur on the player as he streaks through the frame. Also, it's likely that the ball's bouncing off the floor has caused minor bumps to the camera/tripod position.

A rough comp is just that—pretty rough.

Generating a Difference Matte

You can create a simple difference matte by subtracting the original element from its clean plate.

A sample foreground image

A sample clean plate

Use an absolute subtraction to ensure that the resulting matte contains all results of the subtraction, not just the positive ones.

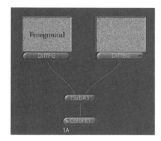

If your compositing application lacks an absolute subtraction, you can add the results of two separate subtractions: Foreground—CleanPlate and CleanPlate—Foreground.

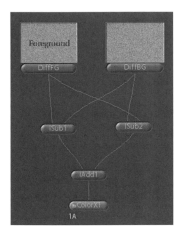

NOTE ▶ This double subtraction requires clamping prior to the IAdd if you're working in float space.

After the subtraction is completed, the red, green, and blue pixels are added to produce a grayscale image. In the two trees above, a ColorX node with the expression r+g+b in the aExpr field produces the desired matte on the alpha channel of the resulting image.

Notice that the difference matte is not a pure, solid matte. It contains holes where foreground and background pixels approach the same color values. You can sometimes produce a more useful, but hard-edged, matte by applying a threshold operation after summing the matte channels. If you set a threshold of 0, all of the nonzero pixel values can be forced to 1. (In Shake, set the crush to 1 and the alpha threshold value to 0.)

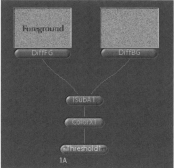

Masking Paint Work

A typical and more successful use of difference matting is to mask off paint work for the purpose of degraining and regraining it to match the original plate. For example, in this frame from the short film *Coupled*, the couple embarrassedly walk into the locksmith shop to get their handcuffs removed (it's a long story . . .). Let's assume the director wants to remove an unwanted sign in the frame right, "Guns & Ammo."

A paint artist is brought in to replace the sign.

The objective is to composite in a sign more appealing to the director and story.

Let's say the paint work was done in a dedicated paint package. The new sign will stick out like a sore thumb if not matched to the original grain of the plate from frame to frame. To separate out the newly painted pixels from the shot's original pixels, use Shake's Common node (Shake-speak for difference keyer).

If you set the Common node to mode 3 (black) and leave the tolerances set to 0, you will have the changed pixel set in white, which looks a lot like your average alpha channel.

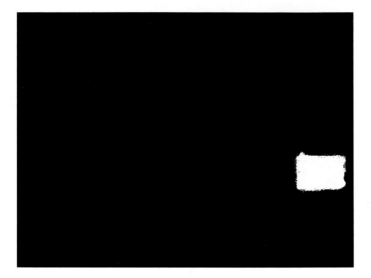

Finally, use that alpha channel to matte off the Degrain and Regrain nodes so that they perform grain operations only on the paint strokes and not on the original pixels of the shot.

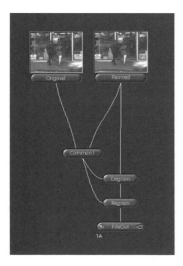

Diffuse Pass

SEE ▶ multipass, basic passes

Diffusion Simulation

SEE ▶ camera diffusion simulation

Digital Foundation

SEE ▶ skin repair, digital foundation

Dolly

DEFINITION ▶ To physically move the position of a camera while filming.

SEE ALSO ▶ pan

Dust Busting

DEFINITION ▶ The removal of dust and dirt artifacts from digital footage. *Related terms:* dust removal; scratch removal

SEE ALSO ▶ clean plate

If you've watched a few movies at the local multiplex, you've probably noticed just how much dirt and hair appear on each frame as it flies through the projector. One of the tedious but essential tasks of visual effects work is the removal of dust from film prints after they've been scanned.

Film doesn't start out dirty. Most of the artifacts you see at the theater occur when the movie was optically printed from intermediate copies of the master reel. The dust you see on a scanned image was most likely trapped on the master as it was being scanned. The original source film can always be wiped clean, but if we don't remove the dust from our scans, it'll be "baked" into the final image.

There are four basic approaches to dust busting: cloning, performing a reveal, performing an adjacent frame reveal, and generating a defect map.

> **TIP** A popular method for removing dust from plates is to draw a box separated into four quadrants on a piece of paper. Then scrub through a shot and record where the dust is in the relevant quadrant. You can usually record the dust by just drawing a dot and writing in the frame number below it. After this is done for the whole shot (if it was a particularly dirty plate, you'll have a box with lots of dots and numbers on it), you can systematically proceed with your dust busting.

Cloning Away the Dirt

This is the most common method of dust busting. A clone brush (or the Rubber Stamp tool in Adobe Photoshop) is used to replace affected pixels with adjacent areas of the image that possess identical (or extremely similar) textures.

> **TIP** Now that Photoshop supports 32-bit float images, it makes a great dust-busting tool, especially since dust busting is all about treating individual frames. Unfortunately, to take full advantage of Photoshop's Pattern Stamp and Healing Brush tools, you'll have to work in 16 bits per channel or lower (for version CS2), but that's still a reasonable dynamic range, given the power of these tools. You may also want to try performing the operations on the original Cineon log plate, which is only a 10-bit image anyway.

Performing a Reveal

Occasionally you get lucky. If a particular shot calls for a matching clean plate to be filmed, you can use the clean plate as a reveal source and use it to replace dust-affected portions of your image. Be careful to correctly align the clean plate first.

NOTE ▶ For a working example of this, refer to Marco Paolini's excellent *Shake 4: Professional Compositing and Visual Effects*, part of the Apple Pro Training Series (Peachpit Press, 2005).

TIP ▶ Be careful to correctly align the clean plate before making use of it. See clean plate.

Performing an Adjacent Frame Reveal

In the absence of a clean plate, it's often possible to use an adjustment frame. Since dust usually varies from frame to frame, chances are the frame ahead or behind the current frame will not have dust in the same location. On a fairly static shot you can often combine two or three frames to create a single clean plate and use it for the majority of the sequence. Or you can use a stitching utility like Shake's AutoAlign tool to force the alignment of adjacent frames, giving you a reliable clean plate even when there's a substantial camera move to the clip.

Generating a Defect Map

Sometimes the source of dust artifacts isn't the film itself but the optics used to generate the image. When the camera lens has dust, it will appear in an identical location on every recorded frame. The easiest way to remove it is to generate a defect map, a matte that isolates only the dust artifacts in an image. In a best-case situation, you can use a luma key to generate a matte from a reference gray-card or white-card frame. Otherwise, you can use frame blending to isolate the defects.

Once you've generated a defect map, use the map as a mask to isolate the color correction only to the defective portions of the original image. Because dust appearing on the lens of a camera is extremely out of focus, the artifacts should be subtle enough to allow for moderate correction with acceptable results. Be sure to correct the red, green, and blue channels separately.

Edge Blend

DEFINITION ▶ Blurring a composited edge to smooth the visual transition between foreground and background elements. *Related terms:* edge blur; edge smear; edge soften

SEE ALSO ▶ chroma blur; edge matte

No matter how carefully you work on creating the perfect matte, an obvious separation sometimes shows at the border between foreground and background. The problem commonly occurs in subsampled video content in which the edge detail has been quantized by the chroma limitations (see chroma blur). As with all good compositing gags, the solution lies in a blur.

By blurring just the edge area of the composite, you can "smear" together the foreground and background pixels, better integrating the seam between those elements.

The technique is simple. Apply a blur to the final composited image; then mask the blurred section just to the edge. You can use an edge-detection filter to generate the edge matte, or generate your own (see edge matte).

 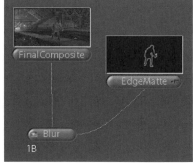

Edge Matte

DEFINITION ▶ A matte describing only the outline of a given subject. *Related terms:* outline matte; ring matte

SEE ALSO ▶ background wrap; edge blend; edge matte/core matte; grain removal; skin repair (digital foundation)

Edge mattes are infinitely useful and essential for such important techniques as background wrapping and edge blending. Most applications contain an edge-detection filter, but those filters are render intensive and often don't provide the flexibility to create a good edge matte. There is a better way.

To create a quick, flexible edge matte in Shake, create a blurred copy of an object's original matte.

Then, composite the blurred matte over the original using an Exclusive Or (Xor) function. In Shake, this is done using an Xor node.

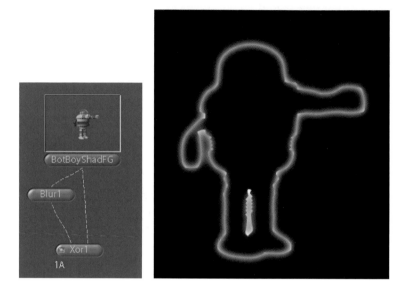

In After Effects and Motion, the matte must be placed on the visible channels before blurring. In After Effects, use the Channels > Set Channels filter. In Motion, use the Channel Swap filter.

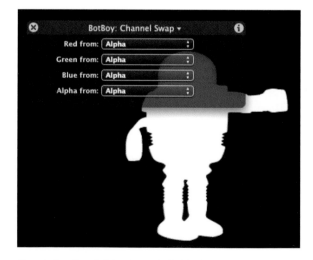

Reordering the visible channels in Motion

Once the channels are set, duplicate the object and apply a blur to the duplicate. Then set the blend mode to Exclusion.

Setting the blend mode to Exclusion in After Effects

You may find that the resulting matte is a little too dim. If so, color correct the matte until the intensity is set to the appropriate brightness.

For a gentler slope on the edge, you can also apply a second blur to the final edge matte, brightening the intensity if necessary.

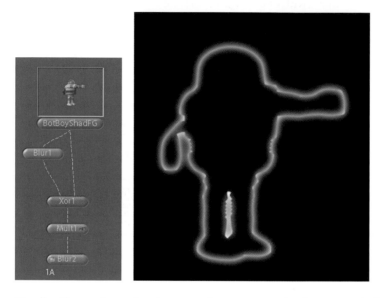

Finally, if your intention is to use the matte on the foreground object only (unlike edge blending, in which foreground and background pixels are both affected), composite the resulting edge matte inside the original matte.

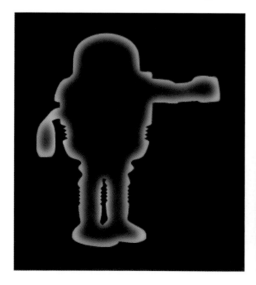
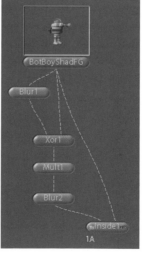

Edge Matte/Core Matte

DEFINITION ▶ A technique that involves generating two mattes: one to create a detailed, soft edge; the other to create a solid center. *Related terms:* hard/soft mattes; inner/outer mattes; inside/outside mattes

SEE ALSO ▶ edge matte

Original Obi-Wan green screen with blue man cameo

Obi-Wan composited into computer-generated environment

The process of extracting a foreground object from a continuous colored background has been around for some time. Using the difference between the red, green, and blue channels can go a long way toward generating a matte, or key (see the Keying Fundamentals chapter for more information). Using color-difference algorithms from keying software like Ultimatte, Keylight, and Primatte makes the process somewhat easier and relatively quick compared with traditional methods.

Unfortunately, those who do not create effects sometimes take it for granted that you can "fix it in post" and fail to properly set up a blue screen shoot. To be fair, there are many legitimate reasons for thinking this way, including the fact that most times it actually is cheaper to fix things in postproduction.

At the end of the day, it is up to the visual effects artist to put on his or her analytical, problem-solving hat and figure out how to extract an object from a background. More often than not, this requires taking specific areas from multiple mattes and combining them to form the final matte. The final matte is then used to extract the foreground objects from the background. A common means of extracting fine edge detail coupled with the requisite solid core is an edge matte/core matte.

A common mistake made by beginners is to try to obtain a perfect matte with only a single key. It is possible to get what appears to be a decent-looking matte with one key. However, a closer inspection usually shows that a trade-off has been made, especially when the extracted matte is compared with the original blue screen. By brightening or adding contrast to make the inner core of the matte fully opaque, the subtle details on the edges are sacrificed.

A better method is to pull two keys: a soft edge key with all the detail, and a hard core key to fill in the areas the initial edge key missed. You get the best of both worlds when two, three, or even more mattes are combined into the final matte.

A soft edge matte. Notice that Obi-Wan's hair and the motion blur of the blue man's lightsaber are retained. This is a good thing!

A hard core matte. Notice that the core of Obi-Wan is solid.

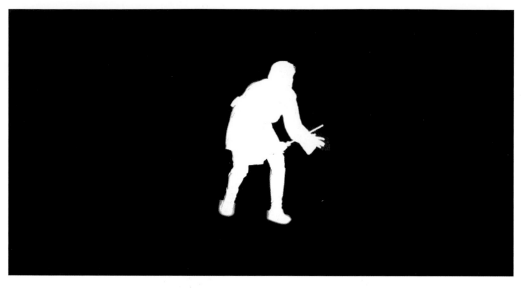

Combined edge matte and core matte, plus a garbage matte to get rid of the catwalk set and blue man who just will not go away nicely

> **TIP ▶** When naming your scripts, mattes, elements, composites, or whatever, never name anything "final." Ignore this advice at your peril. As soon as you name an element *myshot.final*, someone, somewhere, will want to change it—and make it un-final.

Closer to the Edge...Matte   ⬛S

1   First, generate a highly detailed edge matte. This should be done with a soft touch, including just enough opacity, or density, to ensure that wispy details as small as individual strands of hair are gathered for the final extraction.

SHAKE ▼

Open **APTS_CycVFX/ProjectFiles/Keying/EdgeMatteCoreMatte/ EdgeMatteCoreMatte_start_v2.shk**. Select the obiwan_gs (for *green screen*) node. In the Key tab, add a Keylight node.

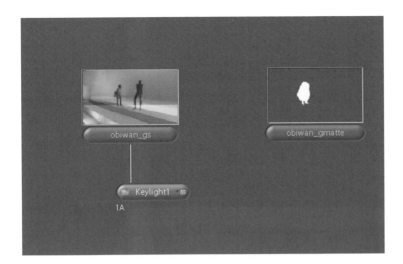

Select the right side of the Keylight1 node to expose the parameters. Select the screenColor color swatch. This should link and launch the Color Picker.

In the Viewer, scrub the cursor next to Obi-wan's hand on the green screen. Now double-click the Keylight1 node, and press the A key to view the alpha channel.

NOTE ▶ A finished version of the script, **APTS_CycVFX/ProjectFiles/Keying/ EdgeMatteCoreMatte/ EdgeMatteCoreMatte_finished_v2.shk** is available for reference.

A soft edge matte in all its glory

A rotoscoped garbage matte used to take out the "garbage" and help with the extraction

2   Notice how soft the edge matte is. Indeed, so soft that there is still visible noise and grain outside the edge matte. Believe it or not, in small doses this is perfectly acceptable and can usually be remedied with simple garbage matting or an inverted hold-out matte. The primary concern is to retain the edge detail.

SHAKE ▼

Select the obiwan_gmatte (for garbage matte) node. In the Color tab, add an Invert node.

Drag the noodle from the bottom of the Invert1 node into the input (right side) of the Keylight1 > GarbageMatte node.

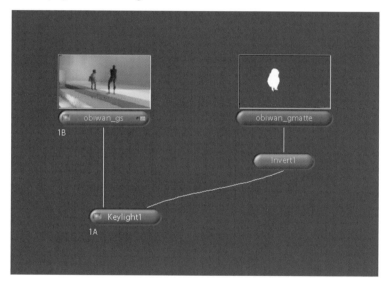

The obiwan_gmatte is telling the Keylight keyer that the white areas of the gmatte are garbage and should be removed (see garbage matting). Though Anakin—soon to become Darth Vader—may disagree, Obi-Wan is not garbage and should *not* be matted out. This means you need to invert the obiwan_gmatte before feeding the result into the Keylight1 node.

Details, Details, Details

Another way to generate a detailed edge matte is by using individual color channels. Each color channel, or *register*, is a grayscale image that produces a color image when combined with the other grayscale channel images. It is no mistake that a blue screen is blue. Human flesh, in particular, has very little blue, large amounts of green, and, of course, a great deal of red. So, if you view the red channel, you will see the beginnings of a nicely detailed edge matte. This edge matte based on luminance can be color corrected and combined with a garbage matte to add further detail to the final matte (see luma edge keying).

NOTE ▶ Color film negatives for major motion pictures were sometimes split into three separate pieces of black-and-white film. This was done because black-and-white film is much more stable than color film and does not deteriorate nearly as fast. Film restorations performed today sometimes are created by digitally combining three black-and-white elements.

SHAKE ▼

Place the cursor over the main Viewer. Press the R, G, and B keys individually to view each grayscale channel image.

The red channel. Notice the nice highlights on the tips of Obi-Wan's fingers and the side of his face.

The red channel reordered into the alpha channel, then expanded to be used to add in any lost detail, especially in the highlights

The green channel. Notice the absence of contrasty edges.

The blue channel. Notice that there is very little blue in the image. Also notice the visual "noise" in the image.

For obvious reasons, individual color channel mattes are usually coupled with garbage mattes and holdout mattes. Once again, using one matte to constrain yet another matte is very common practice in visual effects.

Creating a Core Matte

A soft edge matte obviously leaves something to be desired when it comes to opacity. Another inner core matte is needed specifically to fill in the edge matte. When combined, the two are a match made in matte heaven.

When creating a core matte, it is perfectly acceptable to brighten and add contrast to make the matte as opaque as possible. In fact, a common practice is to manipulate the blue screen using color correction and blur *before* keying.

1   First, add a Blur node.

SHAKE ▼

With the obiwan_gs node selected, go to the Filter tab and add a Blur node while holding down the Shift key. This will spawn another branch and add a Blur1 node for the inside core matte that you're going to create. Set the xPixels and yPixels values to 9.

Select Blur1 and add another Keylight node (Keylight2). Choose the key color as you did on Keylight1. Drag the noodle from the bottom of the Invert1 node into the Keylight2 > GarbageMatte input (right side) of the Keylight2 node.

The core matte with tweaked keyer parameters

The inverted garbage matte used to remove unwanted images.

2   As you may have noticed, your core matte is not fully opaque and needs a little help. Using the inverted obiwan_gmatte will help Keylight or any other keyer produce a better matte.

SHAKE ▼

A few tweaks in the Keylight2 fineControl parameters, and you'll get a nice dense core matte.

Select the Keylight2 node. In the fineControl parameter, change the midtoneGain and highlightGain to –.21 and –.2, respectively. Adjust the screenRange to approximately .34 (your results will vary depending upon what color you sampled on the green screen).

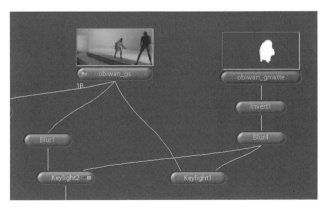

Before you layer the dense core matte (Keylight2 node) over the soft edge matte (Keylight1 node), you need to make a few adjustments to compensate for the blur you added earlier.

If you layered the core matte over the edge matte at this point, the core matte would be larger than the edge matte. Of course, this would kill all of the detail and produce a blurred matte.

3   To compensate, you can erode (shrink) the matte and add a small blur so that the core matte blends with the edge matte seamlessly.

SHAKE ▼

Add a Dilate/Erode node. Adjust the xPixels and yPixels values to −1. Toggle on the soften parameter and set the sharpness to .95.

Next, select the Keylight2 node and add another Blur node. In the Blur2 node, set the xPixels and yPixels values to 7.

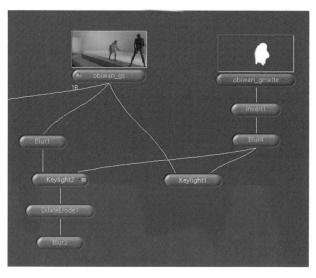

It's a Matte, Matte World

Now you have two, three, or as many as ten mattes to combine into one final matte. This a relatively simple task using standard layering techniques such as Max, Screen, Xor, Subtract, and Over, among others.

SHAKE ▼

Select the Blur2 node and add an Over node. Click and drag the noodle from the output of the Keylight1 node into the background (right nub) of the Over1 node. Your results will vary depending upon how much you shrunk and blurred the inner core matte. You may need to adjust the size of your inner core matte or change your blur settings to match the results shown here.

Edge matte with help from a garbage matte

Core matte with help from a garbage matte

Combined edge matte. Notice that Obi-Wan's hair and soft edges are retained. This is still a good thing!

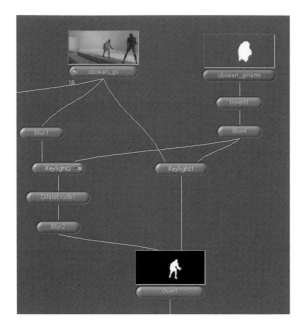

The combined core and edge mattes

Always keep in mind my own adage, "Once you have a matte, you're golden." Simply put, once you generate a matte, it can be used in many different ways by itself or in conjunction with other mattes. And those new mattes can be used in a myriad of additional ways, and on, and on, and on.

As noted in the background light wrap instructions, mattes can be reused for a variety of purposes. This is also true for an inner core matte. Once generated, a core matte can be dilated (expanded), inverted, and turned into a decent holdout matte. Likewise, even an outer edge matte can be color corrected until it is opaque. Add a slight eroding (shrinking) and a touch of blur and, presto, you have an instant core matte.

This process is not always additive. Mattes can cut out other mattes that are used to drive, say, a blur on yet another matte.

When it comes to keying, or extracting the foreground from the background, there are few hard and fast rules. In some situations a few mattes are sufficient. Even more situations require numerous, very specific keys coupled with good old-fashioned rotoscoped mattes.

There are about as many ways to generate keys as there are keys on your keyboard. Suffice it to say, we live in a world of color constantly manipulated by black-and-white mattes (and every variation in between).

But Wait, There's More

The preceding leads up to a matte that you can use to place Obi-Wan in an environment. There are several methods for creating this matte as well. One way is to treat the matte and color information separately, similar to the way you treated the edge and core matte separately and then combined them.

The same method can be applied to color information. In the example below, the green screen spill was suppressed and the image color corrected to match the color of the cg_background. Finally, the color information was multiplied by the combined matte to produce a premultiplied image that could be placed *over* the cg_background. This technique is covered more fully in keying generic elements.

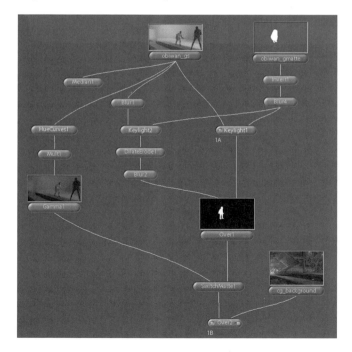

A sample script

The composite before edge blending or grain is added

Effects

DEFINITION ▶ A general term used to describe filters and behaviors that are added to objects in a film or video image.

Cameo

Duran Duran in 3D— Pixerati

PRODUCING STEREOSCOPIC MOVIES is an art in itself. The rigs alone—consisting of two cameras perfectly aligned, with their focus and zoom equally matched—are a technical achievement worthy of an Oscar. But what happens when the movie is shot with a regular *2D* camera rig, and the production company wants to convert it to 3D?

That was exactly the situation facing Pixerati (see Contributors: Damian Allen, page iv) when creating special content for the *Duran Duran— Live from London* (2005) DVD. After the entire project was filmed in high-definition video, the band chose one of the concert songs to be converted to 3D. No forethought was given during production to the composition of the future 3D video, so *everything* had to be performed in postproduction.

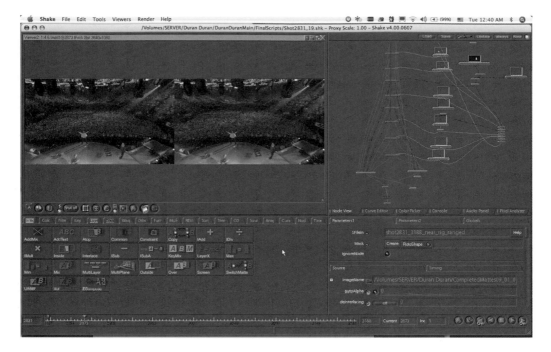

The first step was to decide on a delivery mechanism for the stereoscopic effect. Mass distribution of the video via DVD precluded the use of expensive technologies like LCD shutter glasses or polarized glasses. The only common solution for 3D viewing on standard television is red/cyan anaglyphic **stereoscopy.**

Anaglyphs have the advantage of being affordable, but they also come with major disadvantages. They limit the saturation of color and the separation of the left and right video channels. We quickly consulted with the production company, Coming Home Studios, and received approval to reduce the concert footage to black and white, thus eliminating any cross talk the original colors would have caused to the red/cyan anaglyphic effect. Rock concerts use liberal amounts of red and blue lighting, making it especially difficult for anaglyphic work. Due to that lighting bias, a custom-weighted luminance was used to derive the black-and-white version of the footage.

NOTE: ▶ A major issue when creating stereo anaglyphs for DVD is MPEG-2's poor compression of red. You may have noticed this in the blocky appearance of pure red titles encoded to DVD. Unfortunately, it's largely an unavoidable problem. If you can control the distribution method for an anaglyphic 3D project, you should avoid color compression whenever possible.

In our case, we also had issues with gamma shifts when the online edit of the final composite was sent for MPEG-2 encoding. The online editor was forced to bump the gamma of the red channel to maintain parity with the green and blue channels.

Sample stereoscopic views. To preview freestyle, cross your eyes gradually until the two images resolve into one. (Don't try this without a full night's sleep.)

The same image rendered as a red/cyan anaglyph.

With the delivery mechanism established, it was time to go to work. Since everything was filmed in two dimensions, elements intended to stand out in three dimensions needed to be isolated from the rest of the footage. That meant **rotoscoping**. In fact, to get the job done in the two weeks allotted, it meant rotoscoping in three time zones.

We had artists working in the United States, Australia, and India to complete the work. Every band member, amplifier stack, microphone stand, and stomp box that needed to stand out in 3D was rotoscoped for all 7793 frames of the HD footage.

The intention was to cut each element out of the footage, then place it on a plane in a 3D space—they would be like cardboard cutouts standing at various distances from a virtual camera. This quickly presented two problems: scale versus distance, and foot placement.

The scale versus distance problem was simple. Something small and close to the camera might have the same apparent height as something large and distant. We needed to identify the distance of each object from the camera.

The foot-placement problem involved the question of where to position an object relative to the floor. If a band member is standing on the stage, that part of the stage might be 3 feet from the camera or 30 feet from the camera. If we used only 2D cutouts, how could we make objects like the stage floor recede into the distance, and keep band members grounded rather than appearing to float in the air?

In every good compositing project, you're allowed at least one big break. Ours was the solution to these problems. We found that creating displacement gradients was an incredibly simple and incredibly effective way to generate convincing 3D spaces. For every space, whether it was a stage or the entire stadium, we used Shake's RotoShape tool to generate mattes that started dark near the camera and became pure white at their greatest distance from the camera. We used these mattes to displace pixels in

opposite directions in the virtual left and right cameras to create the stereo effect.

Wherever pixels are black in the matte, there is no displacement, and both camera views share the same pixel positions for the objects in those areas. Wherever pixels are white, there is maximum displacement, creating the most marked difference in the stereo pixel placement between the two virtual camera views. As pixels in the matte move from white to black, a decreasing shift is created, generating a genuine sense that parts of the scene are deeper than others.

In fact, this displacement technique worked so well that we decided in some shots to use the technique for *all* the stereoscopy—not just the backgrounds. We fed each of the rotoscoped mattes into the displacement node to shift them with the background. We tracked the color of our custom-made gradients at the point of contact of each foreground object (using Shake's PixelAnalyzer node). We then colored the mattes of each object (well, shaded, since they're grayscale), based on the tracked color. So, if the background vocalist was standing on a portion of the stage that had a gradient value of 0.5, her entire matte was shaded to 0.5 before being fed into the displacement node. This ensured that her feet would contact the ground at the correct relative location. It also created something of an automatic z-depth detection for our cardboard cutouts.

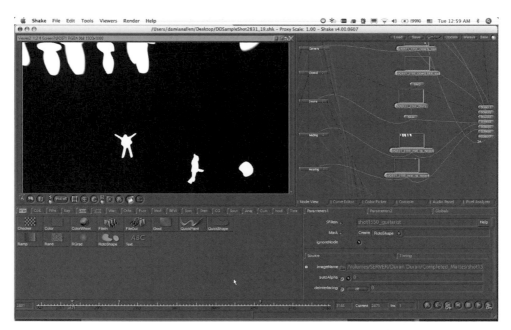

After the foreground mattes were composited over the background gradient, the entire scene was displaced to produce a stereo separation. Problem solved? Unfortunately, not quite.

As the background was separated from the foreground cutouts, black holes appeared around the edges of those cutouts. In real stereoscopic footage, the two cameras in the rig would be able to "see around" foreground objects, each camera photographing a part of the background unseen by the other. Since our original shoot was purely 2D, no additional "hidden" background was recorded. We had to invent background to fill the black spaces.

One solution was the Foundry's (www.thefoundry.co.uk) Furnace plug-ins suite. One of those plug-ins, SmartFill, attempts to texture missing information based on surrounding pixel data. While the plug-in performed admirably, it was slow. Yes, it had a lot of very intelligent design choices to consider, so the execution time was reasonable. However, under the constraints of our production deadlines and available CPU horsepower, SmartFill just wasn't going to finish in time.

The solution? Build a Shake macro. A little fella by the name of SideSmear, to be precise. SideSmear works by inwardly displacing pixels that are outside of a given matte, creating a smearing of the pixels inward to cover the gap produced by the matte. It wasn't the most articulate re-creation of the missing background, but as it turns out, it was quite sufficient for the majority of cases. (Occasionally, more drastic cloning methods were required.)

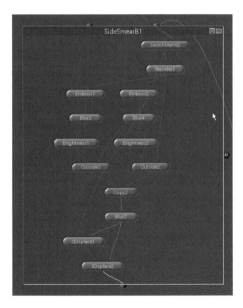

Background before SideSmear

Background after SideSmear

When all the hard work was done, the red channel was copied from one camera view into the other, and the anaglyph was complete. A multiplier variable called OcDist (for *ocular distance*) was used to scale the separation of the two cameras until one of two things happened: The stereoscopic sensation of the anaglyph broke, or the SideSmear failed to adequately cover the background behind cutout objects.

Upon reflection, now that we've massaged the RSI out of our fingers and seen therapists for our "rotophobia," the 2D-to-3D workflow was actually kind of cool. In fact, it gave us more control over the stereo separation of the scene, and the cardboard-cutout effect produces a more dramatic stereo image in many ways than you would see in a genuine production-filmed 3D movie. But before you go out and pitch the concept to your favorite music video producer, take a little time to roto a test shot, then budget accordingly.

Face Replacement

DEFINITION ▶ A procedure for replacing one face or head with another in live action footage. *Related term:* head replacement

Face replacement—along with its close cousin, head replacement—is one of the most spectacular techniques in visual effects work. Despite the apparent wizardry, the workflow is fairly straightforward. The technique involves tracking the movements of the source and target faces, and using that data to matchmove the source face to the target face. After the movement and position are matched, skin tones are color corrected to blend accurately.

Common uses of face replacement include the insertion of an actor into historical footage, *twins shots* (in which a single actor is shown as identical twins), and dramatic clone scenes.

Production Considerations

When filming the replacement face, there are two important considerations. First, the actor should practice replicating the timing and positioning of the head movements in the original footage as accurately as possible. The more closely the movements and positions match, the less work there is to perform in postproduction.

> **NOTE** ▶ This is not the case for the media used in the following exercise. In order to demonstrate some of the difficulties of face-replacement techniques, the source and target faces have been created with completely different movements.

Second, the face should fill the frame as much as possible, so that there is plenty of resolution to play with. Scaling down a replacement face is much preferred to increasing its scale to match the original face.

When framing the face, be careful to match the perspective of the original shot. That is, the camera should be positioned at the same distance from the replacement face as the original camera was positioned from the original face (or at least as closely as can be estimated from the source footage). Once the camera position is established, the camera can be zoomed in so that the face fills the frame.

If the replacement face footage is filmed with the specific intention of face replacement, the following considerations should be observed:

▶ Radical changes in the orientation should be avoided (such as turning the head from front-facing to profile).

▶ Hair should be kept in a uniform position as much as possible.

▶ The distance of the original face from the camera should be noted and used for the filming of the replacement face.

▶ Facial tracking markers should be used—at least on the destination footage.

Procedure

1   The first step in the process is to track and stabilize the source face (the face to be composited into the replacement shot, also known as the *target face*). When tracking faces, it's important to observe which features of the face move relative to the overall bone structure, and which features stay locked.

In the image below, the contrast of the eyebrows suggests that they would track well, but the fact that people expressively raise and lower their eyebrows usually puts eyebrows into the category of unlocked features. The overall position of the eyes doesn't change (because they remain fixed in the eye sockets), but the movement of the pupils

Eyebrows—Track well but may move with facial expressions

Eye corners—Maintain position but can be difficult to track during blinking

Base of nose—May move downward during a smile; does not take jaw movement into account

Body piercings—Fashion's gift to the visual effects industry

Base of chin—Accounts for jawbone movements but can be difficult to track, due to relatively horizontal contour

and the propensity of actors to blink prevents them from providing a satisfactory track target. In fact, in the upper region of the face, the corners of the eyes usually provide the most solid track, since their positions stay fixed even as the eyes open and close. (Nonetheless, offset tracking is recommended when blinking occurs.)

In the lower portion of the face, the two best candidates for tracking are the base of the nose (just above the philtrum) and the base of the chin. The nose can sometimes cause problems, since it lowers slightly during a smile. In addition, since the jaw moves downward independent of the rest of the face, the base of the nose will not reflect changes in the jaw position. As a result, when replacing an entire face (including the mouth), the base of the chin is a preferable choice, even though its shape doesn't naturally lend itself to tracking.

In the source face in this example, a body piercing on the chin provides the perfect tracking marker.

To lock perspective in a shot, four corner points usually are required. In this exercise, the eyes provide two tracking points, but the chin (or the stud on the chin of the source face) offers only one. The solution is to do a three-point track and use the third point as a substitute for both base points.

SHAKE ▼

Open **FaceReplaceStart.shk**. To SourceFace, add a Transform > Stabilize node (trackType = 4 pt, subPixelResolution = 1/256, limitProcessing set to on). At the bottom of the Stabilize parameters tab, deselect the visibility LED for track2Name. Make sure that the Timeline is positioned at frame 1. Position the trackers as indicated in the image below.

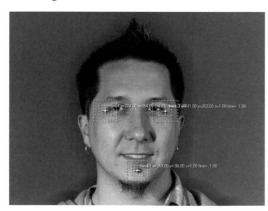

2 You should have no problem tracking the facial features for most of the sequence. However, the actor blinks on two occasions, which will cause errors in the tracking data. To solve this, you can use offset tracking and temporarily track the eyebrows through these problem sections.

> **TIP** ▶ It's a good idea to run the tracker twice: once for the eye points and once for the chin point. That way, the chin point can track completely without being interrupted by the offset tracking required for the eyes.

SHAKE ▼

At the bottom of the parameters for Stabilize1, deselect the visibility LEDs for track3Name and track4Name. track1Name should be the only tracker with an active visibility LED and, as a result, should be the only tracker visible in the Viewer.

Track forward through the entire Timeline. Move back to frame 1 and turn on track3Name and track4Name, turning off track1name (to prevent the new tracking data from being overwritten in the next track).

Track forward and press the Escape key as soon as the actor blinks to stop the track from continuing. Back up to a frame in the Timeline before the blink (around frame 35), and use offset tracking to track the outer edges of the eyebrow.

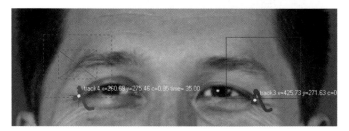

Resume tracking, and then press the Escape key as soon as the tracker has moved past the blink. Back up to a point in the Timeline just after the blink (about frame 53), pause your pointer over the left tracker to select it, and then click the Reset Search Area button ![icon] at the base of the Viewer. This will set the trackers back to the corners of the eyes. Place the mouse pointer over the right tracker, and click the Reset Search Area button again.

Repeat the process to track past the second blink.

3 It's now time to generate two tracking points from the one chin point.

SHAKE ▼

In the Stabilize1 parameters, pause your mouse pointer over the track1Name label, then click and drag it onto the track2Name label to copy the tracking data.

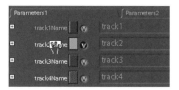

Click the disclosure Plus button to the left of track1Name, and open the track1X section. Click to the far right of the enclosed curve expression (that is, click once to select the entire expression, and then press the right arrow key to move the pointer to the end of the expression), and enter –15. This offsets all the tracking data for track1Name 15 pixels to the left.

Repeat the process for track2Name, entering *+15* to move track2Name 15 pixels to the right.

4 The two lower trackers have now been offset horizontally by a total of 30 pixels. It's time to test the tracks and see if they correctly stabilize the perspective of the image. The main facial features should be locked into place, with the outer parts of the head forced to distort to accommodate the pinning.

SHAKE ▼

In Stabilize1, set applyTransform to active. Launch a flipbook to preview.

5 Now that the foreground is stabilized, you can stabilize the background. The woman whose face is to be replaced does not move her eyebrows throughout the sequence, so the outer edges of her brow can be used to stabilize the shot. Additionally, the hair near her left eye does not move significantly, so the tracker can safely be placed at that border.

In the absence of body piercings, the base of the chin will be used for the lower track.

SHAKE ▼

Repeat steps 1–4 for the TargetFace image, this time using the tracking areas indicated below.

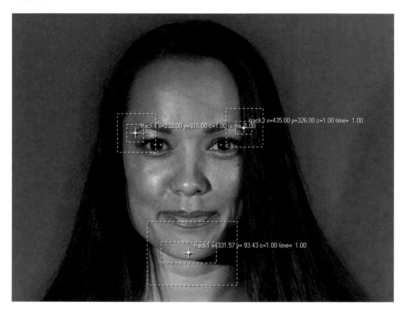

6 With both faces stabilized, you can perform the composite. This first requires drawing a matte of the area in which the replacement will occur. The matte needs to cover the facial features, but leave room to blend the skin around the features using a soft-edge matte. Be careful to leave a fairly tight edge around the hairline at the left of the face, since the facial features run up against the hair there.

Add an Image > RotoShape node (then load Stabilize2 into the Viewer). Making sure that you're at frame 1, draw a shape around the edge of the facial features. Use the Edge Points feature to create a soft edge to the matte, but be careful to leave a fairly clean edge where the facial features meet the hairline.

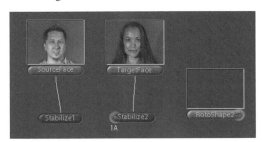

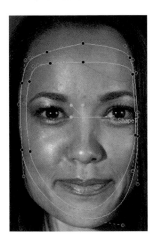

7   With the matte created, the two images can be composited.

> **NOTE ▶** It may be necessary to animate the matte over time if there is a significant change to the replacement area, such as hair or a foreground object obstructing facial features.

SHAKE ▼

Add a Layer > KeyMix node with the background input connected to TargetFace's Stabilize node, the foreground input connected to SourceFace's Stabilize node, and RotoShape1 connected to the Key input.

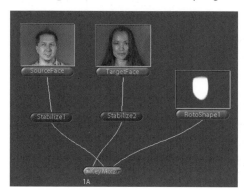 

8   At this point, the two faces are composited together, but the source face is in the wrong position and the skin tones don't match. First you'll move the face into position, and then you'll apply a color correction to blend the skin tones.

SHAKE ▼

Add a Transform > Move2D node after the Stabilize connected to SourceFace. Position and scale it into place (scale up to around 1.1).

9 To complete the integration, you need to color correct the skin tones. This is best done by separately adjusting the red, green, and blue channels, looking at each channel as an individual grayscale while adjusting. It may help to squint as you make the adjustment.

Be aware that this is a simplistic color correction of the shot; in color correcting the skin tone, we've also adversely affected the color of the eyes and teeth (and possibly lips). Separate mattes may need to be created for these areas of the face to prevent them from being color corrected, or to apply a different color correction.

SHAKE ▼

Connect a Color > Mult node directly after SourceFace. Looking at the KeyMix node, position your pointer over the Viewer and press the R key to display a grayscale image of the red channel. In the Parameters tab, position your pointer directly over the center of the Color swatch. Press R, then click and drag to the left to reduce the intensity of the red in the source face. If necessary, lift the mouse and repeat the process. When you're satisfied that the skin tones of the two faces match, release the mouse button.

Repeat the process for the other color channels, using the G and B keys, respectively. When finished, position your pointer over the Viewer and press the C key to return to full color viewing. (The values should be close to 0.84, 0.84, 0.71.)

The precorrected views of the red, green, and blue channels

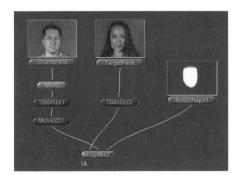

10 The integration is complete, but there's a problem with the motion. Both faces are stabilized; however, what you really need to do is keep the motion of the original clip and matchmove the new face to the movement. This is achieved simply by applying the stabilization data of TargetFace as matchmove data for SourceFace. That is, the SourceFace movement is stabilized first, and then the movement of TargetFace is introduced by TargetFace's tracking data.

NOTE ▶ Since the matte was created using the stabilized version of TargetFace, it also must be matchmoved.

SHAKE ▼

Extract Stabilize2 (the Stabilize node connected to TargetFace) and reconnect it between the Move2D and KeyMix nodes. In the parameters for Stabilize2, change the inverseTransform from stabilize to match.

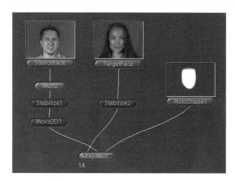

Copy and paste Stabilize2, and connect the pasted version directly after RotoShape1 to matchmove the matte. Launch a flipbook to preview the result.

11 This is one of those techniques in which the procedure will usually get you 90 percent of the way there. To complete the shot, you'll need to make slight changes in face shape. A warp tool could be applied now to smooth inaccuracies occurring in the face over time.

Fade

DEFINITION ▶ The process of transitioning an object from fully transparent to fully opaque, or vice versa.

Faux Shadows

SEE ▶ shadows, faux

Filmic Fade

DEFINITION ▶ The digital simulation of a characteristic analog film cross-dissolve, or fade to black. *Related terms:* cross-fade; dissolve

Have you ever noticed how dissolve transitions performed by nonlinear editing (NLE) systems lack the warmth of feature film fades? That's because filmic fades are performed on clip negatives, while NLEs use positives for their transitions.

In traditional filmic fades, the A roll is first fed through the system, exposing the new master. The aperture starts in an open position, then closes, fading the new master to black.

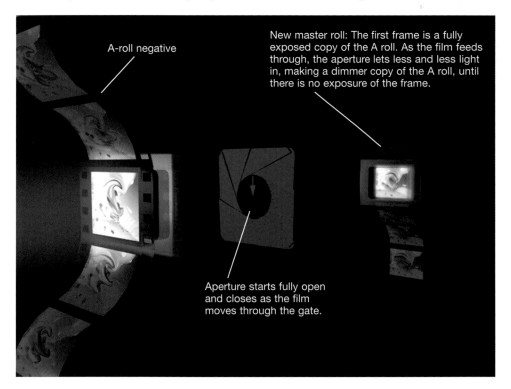

A-roll negative

New master roll: The first frame is a fully exposed copy of the A roll. As the film feeds through, the aperture lets less and less light in, making a dimmer copy of the A roll, until there is no exposure of the frame.

Aperture starts fully open and closes as the film moves through the gate.

The master is then rewound and the B roll is fed through the system—this time with the aperture starting in a closed position, then opening—exposing over the top of the previous A-roll exposure.

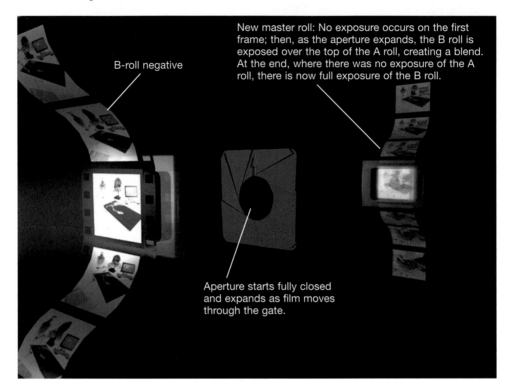

B-roll negative

New master roll: No exposure occurs on the first frame; then, as the aperture expands, the B roll is exposed over the top of the A roll, creating a blend. At the end, where there was no exposure of the A roll, there is now full exposure of the B roll.

Aperture starts fully closed and expands as film moves through the gate.

The new master negative is converted to a positive. In other words, filmic fades take the negatives of two scenes and optically blend them to create a master negative. This new negative is then converted into a positive print, ready for projection.

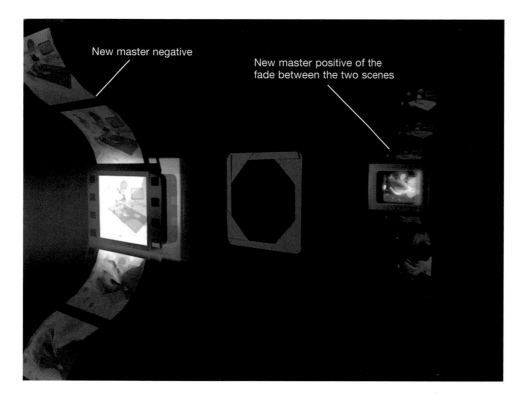

This process is simulated by a Screen operator. The Screen starts by creating negatives of the two source images. It then multiplies them together, simulating the optical mix of exposures seen in the filmic fade above. Finally, it inverts the result back to a positive.

If you were to "grow your own" Screen, it would look like this:

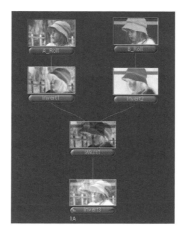

One of the most important aspects of a Screen is its ability to combine very bright images without clipping. When images with pixel values close to 1 (very bright) get inverted inside the Screen, those values become close to 0. (The equation for the inversion is simply Output = 1 − Input.) Now, when you multiply any number by another number less than 1, it becomes closer to 0. So values that became close to 0 when inverted become even closer to 0 during the multiplication of the images inside the Screen. Once they're inverted back to a positive, they become close to 1. Really bright values screened together will become even closer to pure white, but will never clip.

Screening is a nice way to combine specular highlights over an image for the very reason stated above—no clipping. Beware of using a Screen in float space; a Screen does what it does because values of the source pixels don't exceed 0 or 1. Float values outside this range will produce unusual results.

Implementing a Filmic Cross-Fade

Implementing a filmic fade is simple. Begin with your A-roll image at 100 percent brightness, then reduce the brightness to 0. At the same time, take the B-roll image and fade it up from 0 to 100 percent. Then screen the two images together.

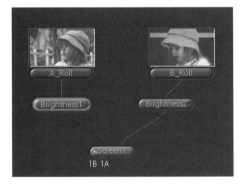

To automate the fade, create a linking expression for the level of the brightness filter attached to the B-roll image. In the Shake tree above, the expression for Brightness2's value would be 1−Brightness1.value.

Filter

DEFINITION ▶ A function that transforms an image in some manner, such as a blur filter. Most commonly used to refer to processes based on convolution kernels.

Flipbook

DEFINITION ▶ A RAM-based image player that loads a clip into memory so that it can be played back in real time.

Float Image

DEFINITION ▶ A 3D image that has been rendered at 32 bits per channel. Float images preserve subtle detail in areas such as highlights, allowing you to make extreme lighting changes and still produce acceptable results. Nonfloat images are unable to represent a comparable dynamic range of image data.

SEE ALSO ▶ float space

Float Space

DEFINITION ▶ Using image data capable of possessing pixel color values beyond the standard range of 0 to 1. Float images preserve subtle detail in areas such as highlights, allowing you to make extreme lighting changes while maintaining the dynamic range of the original image.

SEE ALSO ▶ 3D Fundamentals chapter; HDRI; OpenEXR

Float space is important for a number of reasons. First, it's essential when working with content destined for output to film. Second, when you output to 8-bit video, it can protect the hours invested in perfecting your visual effects from disappearing down the proverbial gurgler. Finally, it enables you to make dramatic changes to 3D renders without flattening the contrast. Just what is float space, and how is it able to perform these miraculous feats?

Float Demystified

Float space can seem quite confusing at first, but we've enlisted the help of the Stay Puft Marshmallow Man from *Ghostbusters* to help clear things up. Before he goes to work, let's recap the way modern compositing apps represent color values. For every pixel in an image, there are separate red, green, and blue values that specify the amounts of red, green, and blue in the color of that pixel. Compositing applications allow each of these channels of color to have data values from 0 to 1. A value of 0 is "soul-sucking black." You can't get any darker than 0. A value of 1 is "visitation from God" bright. That is, 1 is the brightest a pixel can be displayed on a computer monitor. So, a value of 1 in a pixel's red channel would mean that the pixel is as red as it can get; a value of 0 would mean that there is absolutely *no* red in that pixel.

> **NOTE** ▶ Some applications reference color values between 0 and 255, referring to the 8 bits of data used to store color values in those programs. For the purpose of the current discussion, know that a value of 255 in those applications is equivalent to a standard compositing app's value of 1.

So what happens when you try to brighten pixels that already have color data close to a value of 1? The answer is that the values clip to 1. If you try to brighten a pixel beyond a value of 1, its value will be limited to 1. This results in flat image areas that lack any contrast detail. You may have seen this effect in digital video that was overexposed during filming. Once data in an image has been clipped, you can't recover it. If you try to reduce the brightness of the image, you end up with flat gray patches where the clipping occurred, instead of flat white patches.

Clipped image

Clipped image with brightness reduced   Unclipped image with brightness reduced

So how does float space help avoid this clipping, and what does it all have to do with the Stay Puft Marshmallow Man? Imagine that the Stay Puft Marshmallow Man stands up in a large auditorium with a concrete roof. Our puffy friend is taller than the auditorium roof. As he stands, his head is squished by that concrete roof. If he crouches back down, his head remains squished and looks horribly flat and deformed (what the marshmallow community refers to as a "bad s'mores day"). This is what happens to normal color data when it's brightened to clipping.

Now, imagine that the auditorium has a suspended ceiling (like the ones in corporate offices with tiles made of some carcinogenic substance or other). As our puffy buddy stands up, his head goes through the suspended ceiling, but it isn't squished.

To an audience member this may look just like the first situation with the concrete roof, but instead of being squished, the top part of his marshmallow noggin is simply hidden from view. When he stoops back down, the part of his head that was hidden above the suspended ceiling is again revealed exactly as it was (perhaps with the unfortunate addition of carcinogens from the tiles).

The second scenario is analogous to what happens in a float color space. In float, image data can have values bigger than 1 and less than 0. Even though a pixel will never be displayed onscreen with a value greater than 1 (we've already said that 1 is the brightest that a pixel will display on your monitor), the pixels can retain values above 1 to preserve their original appearance if a color correction ever brings their values back below 1. So, instead of the marshmallow man having his cranium permanently flattened, his head is allowed to live above the suspended ceiling (the ceiling representing a value of 1 on our color scale) so that its shape will be retained if his head returns below the roof level.

Float Space and Film

Float space is especially important in film work. Film images have a very wide dynamic range of colors—much wider than the range that can be displayed on a computer. When film images are brought into a computer, the black and white points of the film are clipped to fit the most important parts of the image onto the computer's display. In normal color spaces, that means that some of the subtle shadow detail is clipped to 0 and some of the fine detail in the super-bright parts of an image (such as a cloudy sky) is clipped to 1. In float space, this extra detail is retained unclipped, and it can be recovered when the footage is converted back out to film.

Float Space and Video

Even though video is traditionally stored in 8-bit or 10-bit non-float formats (the number 8 or 10 refers to the number of bits per channel, a standard image including red, green, blue, and possibly alpha channels), video composites can still benefit from float space. Although a computer works in an RGB color space, video is stored in a different color space. Video pixel values are broken into a luminance component and one or two chrominance components. The luminance component stores the basic contrast information of an image, while the chrominance components carry the color information. The two common video formats are YIQ, for NTSC, and YUV, for PAL.

If an 8-bit RGB image is converted into an 8-bit YIQ or YUV image, rounding errors in the conversion can often result in *banding*, which is especially common in finely graduated backgrounds. After hours of tweaking your particle system, you may find that the beautiful collage of yellow and purple looks like a topographical map of the Himalayas, instead of the smooth psychedelia you had intended.

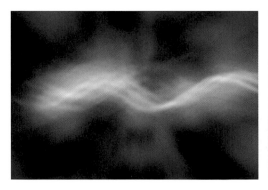

Original image

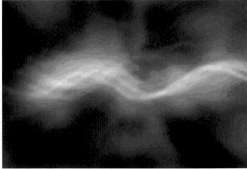

Image with banding after conversion to video space

The solution? You may have guessed it: float space. Simply put, float space provides sufficient data headroom to perform the conversion to video space without causing banding.

Importing Float Space Images

Several image file formats support float images, but the emerging hero of the float world is OpenEXR. This open source file format was developed by Industrial Light & Magic, and it has quickly been adopted as the standard for storing float data. If you want to import images already in float space, make sure the exporting application has saved the images in OpenEXR format. (If your application doesn't natively support OpenEXR, do a quick search of the Web. Chances are someone's already written a free—or cheap—plug-in to do just that.)

Some film-scanning bureaus now offer the option of receiving linear OpenEXR scans instead of log Cineon files. However, these bureaus usually scan to Cineon, then convert to OpenEXR; so if you're comfortable with converting Cineon files, you may prefer to receive the Cineons and avoid the arbitrary assignments of black and white point made by the engineer overseeing the conversion process.

Fog

SEE ▶ keying generic elements

Footage Acquisition, Blue Screen and Green Screen

DEFINITION ▶ Techniques for acquiring footage from video and film sources to optimize keying during postproduction, including turning off sharpening. *Related terms:* film scanning; sharpening; telecine; video capture

The acquisition format is critical to generating a good matte from green screen or blue screen footage. While certain digital compression schemes can dramatically reduce storage space without compromising the quality of ordinary footage, those same schemes can cripple footage intended for keying. Problems may also arise from processes applied to the footage during acquisition.

Sharpening

Due to sharpening, the green screen at the border of the steering wheel has a distinct ring of light green. This hardens the edge and creates a potential halo around the matted subject.

Sharpening is one of the archenemies of a good key. Keying is all about preserving detail in a matte's soft edges, and sharpening destroys that softness. Sharpening is a convolution filter that finds neighboring pixels with high contrast between them and increases that contrast. The result in blue and green screens is a light halo area at the border of dark objects set against a key background.

Most footage benefits from sharpening as it's acquired; the sharpening creates a sense of crispness and focus that may have been lost due to diffusion in the footage. As a result, sharpening is usually applied by default during acquisition. It's important to plan ahead and ensure that sharpening is deactivated for blue and green screen footage. Sharpening can always be applied in postproduction after the composite if necessary.

Film: Scanning and Telecine

Most film scanners and telecine machines have a sharpening option. Make sure that it is deactivated when capturing blue and green screens. In fact, for most effects work the sharpening should be turned off, since it could cause other issues with tracking, degraining, and the like.

Video: Camera Acquisition

Even though video footage doesn't pass through an official "acquisition stage" like film, sharpening is usually applied by the camera electronics before the video signal is recorded on tape. Again, it's important to turn the sharpening off. The filter may go by a different name, such as "softness."

An unfortunate side effect of low-budget shooting is that "prosumer" video cameras—those selling for less than $10,000—frequently offer no option for deactivating sharpening. (Sharpening can help to disguise some of the focus problems of cheaper optics, which is presumably one reason these cameras don't offer the ability to deactivate the filtering.)

You should also try to deactivate sharpening when shooting with a digital still camera.

Digital Acquisition Formats: The 4:x:x Factor

Intermediate storage formats have produced a great deal of confusion about compression. Many formats that claim to be "uncompressed" still have compressed color spaces and, as a result, compromise the keying process.

The trouble arises from techniques used by video engineers to take advantage of the limitations of the human perceptual system. Video signals are encoded with a luminance component and two color components. (See luminance, weighted for more information.) Since the detail is primarily contained in the luminance channel, the two color component channels can be *subsampled* to reduce the data space without noticeably affecting the quality of the image as it's perceived by the final audience.

Original NTSC DV image

Y luminance component

I chrominance component

Q chrominance component

When footage is captured using the NTSC DV format, for every four samples of the luminance channel (denoted as Y), only one sample is recorded for each of the two chrominance channels. This can be clearly seen in the images below—a zoomed portion of the pixel data from the figure of blocks printed above. Notice that while the Y (luminance) channel pixels are square (at least in this illustration), the I and Q channels have "brick-like" pixels, four times wider than they are tall. This is the result of the subsampling.

> **NOTE** ▶ YIQ is the standard signal division for NTSC video. A similar scheme for PAL broadcast video is referred to as YUV.

Y component zoomed in

I component zoomed in

Q component zoomed in

This particular form of subsampling is referred to as *4:1:1* because there are four luminance samples for every sample in each of the chrominance channels. Another common format is *4:2:2*, in which there are four samples in the luminance channel and two samples for each chrominance channel. Examples of this form of subsampling are D1, Digital Betacam (Digibeta), DVCPro50, and DVCProHD. (A variation of this is 4:2:0, which subsamples by two horizontally and vertically. It's the method used for PAL DV and MPEG-2.)

This subsampling causes very few problems for the final audience, since the human perceptual system draws its sense of detail primarily from the Y (luminance) component of the signal.

On the other hand, the subsampling causes serious problems for visual effects work. Since compositing occurs via the mathematical processing of pixel data, low-resolution data in the source images will result in low-resolution aberrations in the final image. While this subsampling causes problems with many compositing tasks, such as stabilization and matchmoving, it is most debilitating to the keying process.

Acquisition Recommendations

Whenever possible, request scanned and telecined footage as an uncompressed image sequence at the highest bit depth at which the material was scanned (usually 10-bit for log film footage, and 8-bit or 10-bit for direct linear conversions). Be wary of files in older image formats such as tga (Targa) that do not support depths beyond 8 bits per channel. Importing as an image sequence avoids the additional hassle of removing *pull-down* from a video stream.

An acceptable alternative is to acquire image data using an uncompressed QuickTime codec. Again, be sure to use a 10-bit codec if the source was acquired at that quality.

Avoid at all costs transferring to an intermediate format such as Digibeta for delivery. While formats like Digibeta *are* digital formats, they use 4:2:2 or worse color compression and therefore compromise your footage. Check with the scanning facility to see if it will accept a FireWire drive or similar storage device for direct transfer of your acquired media, rather than relying on inferior tape formats for delivery.

Four-Point Tracking

DEFINITION ▶ A process traditionally used to match the perspective of one shot and apply it to another—for example, tracking the four corners of a sign and replacing it with a new billboard.

Frame

DEFINITION ▶ A single still image from either video or film. For video, each frame is usually made up of two interlaced fields.

SEE ALSO ▶ interlaced video

Frame Blending

DEFINITION ▶ In clips with slow motion, the process of blending adjacent frames to create new in-between frames.

SEE ALSO ▶ grain removal

Frame Rate

DEFINITION ▶ The playback speed of individual images that make up a moving sequence; stated in frames per second (fps). For example, 16 mm or 35 mm film is usually shot at 24 fps; NTSC video is 29.97 fps; PAL video is 25 fps. HD video can have several different frame rates.

Fresnel Shading Pass

DEFINITION ▶ A technique that uses a Fresnel pass to attenuate reflections based on camera angle, commonly used to simulate realistic reflectivity in 3D objects. *Related terms:* facing angle pass; incidence angle pass; reflections, attenuating

SEE ALSO ▶ reflections, faux

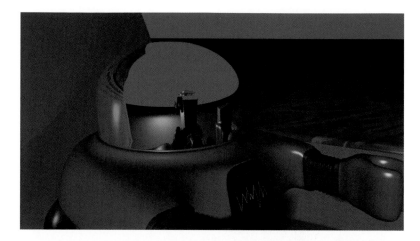

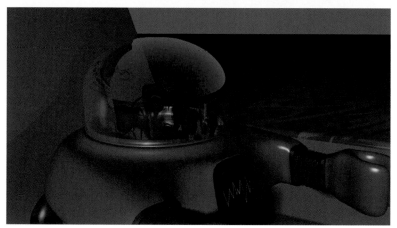

The reflectivity of many surfaces varies according to the angle from which the observer views them. The most obvious example of this is a body of water such as a lake or stream. Viewed at an angle, the surface appears reflective, mirrorlike; viewed from directly above, the water surface is transparent, revealing the fish and rusting auto parts beneath.

This variation of reflectivity is known as the Fresnel (pronounced "freh-NEL") effect, named after 19th-century French physicist Augustin Fresnel, who is credited with having observed many of the diffractive properties of light. The effect can be simulated in 3D renders by using what is often referred to as a Fresnel, or *facing angles,* pass—a shader that generates brighter pixel values as surface normals point farther and farther away from the camera.

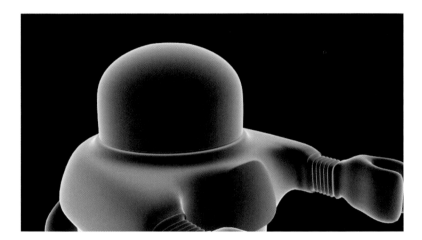

The result is an image that is akin to an electron microscope scan (and that can, in fact be used to simulate an electron microscope effect). Using the render as a matte, the surface reflections of an object can be reduced or eliminated in dark areas and preserved in the light areas, creating a realistic simulation of variations in reflectivity.

Production Considerations

When rendering for this effect, you'll need to create two passes in addition to the Fresnel pass. First, you need a pass with the reflections fully active—it's often worth setting the surface reflection value to 100 percent, since it will be attenuated by the Fresnel pass during the composite. Second, you need to render a pass with the surface completely transparent, revealing whatever is behind the reflective surface. Be sure to include any refractive effects needed in the transparency pass. (For example, a glass surface would refract the background visible in the nonreflective portions of the surface.)

The extra render passes required for this effect can be expensive, so it's important to consider whether postrender control of reflectivity is essential to the shot. Most 3D applications have a Fresnel shader that can be used during the render. These shaders fix the effect, preventing modification during the composite, but they usually speed up the render.

Procedure

1   The first step is to matte the reflection pass with the Fresnel, or facing angles, pass.

SHAKE ▼

Open **APTS_CycVFX/ProjectFiles/CG/Fresnel/Start.
shk**. Add a Layer > SwitchMatte node to MirrorShot. Connect Fresnel to the second input knot. Set matteChannel in
SwitchMatte1 to R. (The Fresnel pass is on the visible channels, while SwitchMatte defaults to using the alpha channel.)

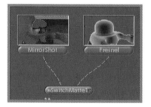

AFTER EFFECTS ▼

Open **APTS_CycVFX/ProjectFiles/CG/Fresnel/Start.aep**. Drag **Fresnel.tif**
above **MirrorShot.tif** in the MirrorShot Comp 1 Timeline. Set its transfer mode to
Stencil Luma.

MOTION ▼

Open **APTS_CycVFX/ProjectFiles/CG/
Fresnel/Start.motn**. Navigate in the File
Browser to APTS_CycVFX/CG/Fresnel and drag
Fresnel.tif above **MirrorShot.tif** in the Layers
tab of the Project pane. In the Dashboard, set its
blend mode to Stencil Luma.

2   Rather than create the effect for the entire object, the effect should be isolated to the transparent surfaces in the shot. In this case, we'll use a matte to isolate the helmet.

SHAKE ▼

Add a Layer > Inside node to SwitchMatte1, then connect the Matte node to the second input.

AFTER EFFECTS ▼

Add **Matte.tif** above **Fresnel.tif** in the Timeline, and set its transfer mode to Stencil Alpha.

MOTION ▼

Add **Matte.tif** above **Fresnel.tif** in the Layers tab, and set its blend mode to Stencil Alpha.

3   It's now a simple matter of compositing the treated reflective surface over the shot with the transparent surface.

SHAKE ▼

Add a Layer > Over node directly after Inside1 and connect InsideShot to the second (background) input knot.

AFTER EFFECTS ▼

Select **Matte.tif**, **Fresnel.tif**, and **MirrorShot.tif**, and choose Layer > Pre-compose. Give the new composition the name *HelmetReflection* and click OK. Add **InsideShot. tif** below HelmetReflection in the Timeline.

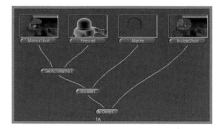

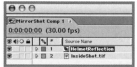

MOTION ▼

In the Layers tab, insert **InsideShot.tif** as a new layer below MirrorShot. Select InsideShot and press Shift-F to display the media Inspector. Set the Alpha Type of InsideShot to None/Ignore. Click back to the Layers tab.

Select the original layer (containing Matte, Fresnel, and MirrorShot) and set its blend mode to Normal in the Dashboard.

4 Finally, to modify the intensity of the effect, color correct the contrast of the Fresnel pass.

SHAKE ▼

Select the Fresnel node and add Color > MDiv, Color > Add mode, and then Color > MMult nodes. Set the red, green, and blue values of the Add1 node to 0.2. This brightens all the pixels in the image, enhancing the intensity of the reflections.

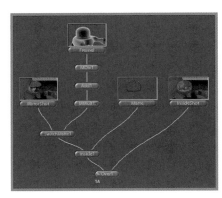

AFTER EFFECTS ▼

Open the HelmetReflection composition. Select **Fresnel.tif** and choose Effect > Adjust > Levels. Set the Output Black to a value of around 45, then return to viewing the MirrorShot comp.

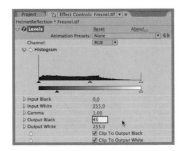

MOTION ▼

Select the Fresnel object and choose Add Filter > Color Correction > Levels. In the Inspector, set RGB Black Out to a value of around 0.18.

Gain

DEFINITION ► In video, the level of white in a video picture; in audio, the increased loudness of an audio signal passing through a given stage of processing.

Gamma

DEFINITION ► A curve contrast adjustment principally affecting the middle tones of an image. Gamma is a nonlinear function often confused with brightness or contrast. Changing the value of the gamma affects midtones while mostly leaving the whites and blacks of the image unaltered.

Gamma adjustment is often used to compensate for differences between footage acquisition formats. The gamma curve also resembles the nonlinear response of the human eye. As a result, gamma adjustments often appear more natural to the human observer.

SEE ALSO ► black levels, checking/gamma slamming; Keying Fundamentals chapter

Gamma Slamming

SEE ► black levels, checking/gamma slamming; Keying Fundamentals chapter

Garbage Matte

DEFINITION ► A common technique used to rapidly remove unwanted portions of a clip by creating a rough matte around the object or area to be keyed. Often the first step in the keying process.

SEE ALSO ► clamping mattes; edge matte; edge matte/core matte; holdout matte

Before you start keying, it's always a good idea to use a garbage matte to remove any unnecessary portions from the edges of the subject area of the image, so that you and the computer don't have to do more work than is necessary.

There are obvious elements that must be garbage matted, like set rigging at the edge of a frame. You should also remove anything that is easy to remove quickly. Due to the circular shape of a camera's iris, the corners of a frame will be dimmer than the rest of the image, making these harder to key. If these areas don't contain any foreground, why bother keying them? Removing portions of an image can also optimize computer processing if the application is capable of computing a subframe domain of definition.

You could try to key the entire green screen. You could also attempt to scale Mount Everest in board shorts and a tank top.

Creating a Garbage Matte

Garbage mattes are easy to create. The trick is to determine how much effort should be expended. A good rule of thumb is that a garbage matte should initially contain around 4 to 12 edge points. Any greater complexity and you're working too hard. But this shouldn't be confused with fine rotoscoping: In areas where the keyer fails or the subject moves beyond the green screen rig, you'll definitely need to tune your roto mattes to great degrees of precision.

Be careful to estimate where things will move in later frames. Give a lot of grace to things like hair, which have a tendency to expand far beyond the borders of your mattes, thanks to the wind.

Applying the Garbage Matte

The simplest way to apply a garbage matte is to feed it into a keyer that accepts a garbage matte input. Consider using a blur to soften the transition at the borders of the garbage matte, especially with heavy grain.

A more flexible option is to combine it with the keyer's output.

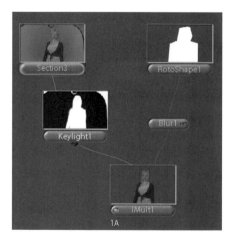

You might be tempted to apply the garbage matte before feeding to the keyer.

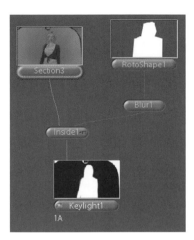

While this may seem like a good idea, it will usually produce an unwanted border during the keying process.

Gate Weave, Correcting

SEE ► stabilization; Tracking Fundamentals chapter

Gradient

DEFINITION ▶ A generated image that changes smoothly from one color to another across the image.

Grading

DEFINITION ▶ The process of color correcting footage to achieve a desired look.

Grain Matching

DEFINITION ▶ The process of adding simulated grain to CGI or composited elements in order to match the grain structure found in the original footage or background plate. Achieved either through automated grain analysis tools or manual grain matching. *Related terms:* film grain; grain simulation; noise; regrain; synthetic grain

SEE ALSO ▶ grain removal; grain removal via warp

Film grain and video noise are often "felt" but not seen. In film, grain is essentially the individual silver halide crystals that are the by-product of the photochemical development process. In video, noise is the result of an impure video signal, which you can track using a luminance signal-to-noise ratio.

Grain and noise must be scrutinized and matched just like any other attribute (such as the hues in color matching) in order to ensure the proper blending of the elements added to a still or frame sequence. When adding a still or computer-generated imagery, it is especially important to zoom in and pepper it with grain or noise to match the background as closely as possible. Nothing gives away a fake composite faster than a background plate with moving grain or noise and an added element with none.

Different film stocks and video shutter settings affect the quality of the grain and noise, and each channel (red, green, and blue, or RGB) contains varying amounts of grain or noise that are usually expressed in terms of size and amplitude. The red and green channels typically have similar grain or noise characteristics, while the blue channel contains the most grain and noise. That's why pulling a key, or extracting something shot on blue screen, can be problematic.

Most image editing and compositing applications have an automated grain-analysis tool (such as Shake's FilmGrain node). These tools analyze a background plate and then re-create the grain pattern so that it can be applied to a foreground element.

But even if you have such a tool at your disposal, you'll still need to evaluate the effectiveness of the analysis to ensure that everything went according to plan. So it's useful to know how to grain match by hand.

The following manual procedure is useful for making sure your synthetic grain is the best possible match for the original.

Manual Grain Matching

Original grainy background plate

The first step is to create a duplicate copy of the original background plate. Then you need to remove the grain from that duplicate. This is easier than you might think.

By applying a blur, you cause neighboring pixels to be averaged together, removing the variation that is due to the grain. Your image becomes too soft to use, but that's OK for the purposes of this exercise.

Background plate with blur applied

Next, apply a grain-simulation filter to the blurred image, and then compare the two images. If your compositing application doesn't support split comparisons in the viewer, create a split screen composite to achieve the same result.

Blurred background plate in split-screen compare with original plate, ready for grain simulation filter to be applied.

TIP Try to compare homogeneous regions of the image so that you don't get confused by the fine details in the actual photography.

Set the viewer to preview the red, green, and blue channels of the compared images in turn. For each channel, adjust the size and intensity of the grain in your grain filter until the original image and the regrained image match.

Comparing and matching the blue channels of the original and the regrained image

Once all three channels are matched, your grain simulation is correctly calibrated to the background plate.

The final step is to copy and paste the grain-analysis filter into whatever foreground element you are adding that needs grain.

TIP ▶ Be sure to apply grain to foreground elements in an unpremultiplied state to avoid adding grain to the background plate.

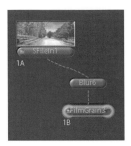

Grain Removal

DEFINITION ▶ The digital removal of film grain from an image. *Related terms:* ADDMix; blurring blue; crawl warping; degraining; frame blending; grain reduction; median filter

SEE ALSO ▶ grain matching; grain removal via warp

Grain creates warm fuzzies for many film lovers, much in the way the analog crackle of a vinyl LP record is treasured by nostalgic audiophiles. For the poor compositor, it's another story.

Grain is a weed that keeps our gardens from passing the homeowners' association inspection. It's the one little cloud that spoils our picnic. It's the dust that sticks to our toast when it falls facedown in the kitchen.

Grain confuses trackers, makes keyed edges crawl and chatter, and thwarts high-contrast color correction. It's easy enough to add grain; removing it is the trick.

Let's get this out of the way first: The best way to remove grain is to buy a plug-in or stand-alone application for the job, even if you're really cheap. At the time of this writing, software such as PictureCode's Noise Ninja (www.picturecode.com) typically sold for $50 to $100 and performed amazing grain reduction at 16 bits per channel—adequate for most visual effects work.

In addition to stand-alone applications, several techniques can help you remove grain in specific circumstances. We've listed the most common here: a median filter, frame blending, edge detection and isolation, and warping.

TIP Grain is most prominent in the blue channel of images. It's sometimes useful to focus on removing grain from the blue channel (using the various methods described below) and leave the other channels unaffected. This can sometimes alleviate the grain problems without significantly damaging image detail.

Median Filter

No, it doesn't do a great job, but a median filter does something. In many cases, the fastest solution is to just slap on a median filter and see if it pulls down the grain enough for you to breathe easier.

Before median filter

After median filter

Before median filter

After median filter

Notice how much softer the image appears after the median filter has been applied. As is usually the case, some kind of sharpening will need to be performed once the image has been degrained.

Frame Blending

Due to its very nature, grain is completely different from frame to frame. If certain elements in your shot are static, you can blend the frames together, effectively averaging out the grain and eliminating it.

A locked-down shot before and after five frames have been blended together to remove grain.

Beware of unanticipated movement when using this technique. You may first need to stabilize the plate to remove motion artifacts like gate weave, and you need to watch out for subtle movements like swaying tree branches. Such subtle movements will produce a time blur effect that may be too surreal for your subject matter.

This technique is particularly effective as a partial solution to a grainy blue or green screen. Apply it to portions of the plate that are static, then treat the moving parts of the scene separately (yes, that might mean rotoscoping).

In Shake, frame blending can be performed in the FileIn, where you can specify exactly how many frames you want blended to produce the final result.

Edge Detection and Isolation

Another technique that can occasionally save the day (although not in keying situations) is to generate an edge matte using an edge detection algorithm. Then blur the footage to remove the grain, and replace the edge detail from the original image over the top.

This is more a stylistic solution than anything else. See skin repair, digital foundation for more details on edge mattes.

Warping

For more information on warping, see grain removal via warp.

Grain Removal via Warp

DEFINITION ▶ The use of a warper to smear film grain to reduce buzzing at key edges.

SEE ALSO ▶ grain removal

Trying to key layered hair with grainy footage is about as fun as cleaning an old mouse ball with your fingernails. (How come I never get to work on those 1984-like sci-fi shows where everyone's bald?) The problem is that the grain buzzes like crazy over the hair after you pull the key. Once you've exhausted your favorite noise-removal software, try this last resort: cheat.

Using a warper, you can gently "smush" in the edges of the hair. Do it too much and things will look weird. Do it just a touch and you'll have smushed the grain, killing the buzz. The hair should still look natural, albeit a little less frizzy (which may make the on-set stylist happy).

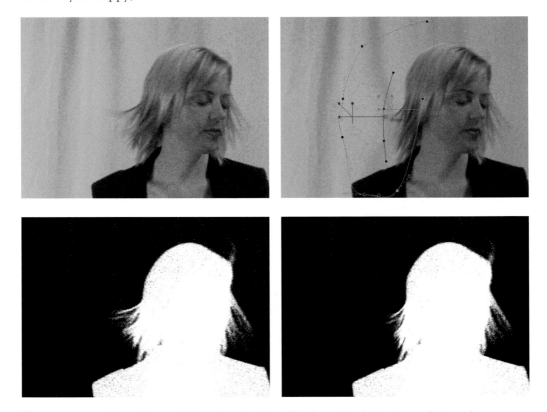

The warp smears the grain enough to reduce buzzing at the key edge, but not enough to produce an unnatural look to the hair.

If you're careful about setting the boundaries on your warp, the result will often be completely unnoticeable. Then you'll have to decide if you should tell the director about your virtual hairstyling, depending on whether you've smoothed away a bit of annoying flyaway frizz or the signature look of the mountain-roaming goat witch.

Gray Ball

DEFINITION ▶ A matte-finish gray sphere used to make lighting comparisons between the actual light conditions on a set and the computer-generated 3D lighting conditions.

When 3D objects or characters will be blended into live action footage, it's critically important to obtain accurate lighting information. Typically, two spheres are photographed on the set: a gray ball and a mirrored ball.

In postproduction, a digital ball is placed beside the photograph of the gray ball to compare the digital 3D lighting with the real lighting on the set; this comparison is most easily made with a perfectly spherical neutral ball. The mirrored ball is useful for extracting environmental reflections and lighting information from the scene. *Related terms:* gray sphere; set survey

SEE ALSO ▶ light probe

Green Screen

DEFINITION ▶ A solid green background placed behind a subject and photographed so that later the subject can be extracted and composited into another image.

SEE ALSO ▶ blue screen; Keying Fundamentals chapter

Grunge Pass

DEFINITION ▶ A special 3D pass used to simulate the deleterious effects of dirt and smudges on surface properties.

Cameo

Slicing Time—
Tim Macmillan

Perhaps the freshest innovation to play across entertainment screens in the last 15 years is *frozen time*, an effect created and named by Tim Macmillan of Time-Slice Films (see Contributors, page v). The effect came to widespread attention in the 1999 science fiction film *The Matrix*. Viewers marveled as bullets sliced through the air all around Keanu Reeves while the camera revolved around his frozen image.

When the effect debuted to BBC television audiences in 1993, Tim had already been working for more than ten years developing cameras that seemed to freeze time. He first discovered the idea of the frozen-time effect as a painting student at the Bath Academy of Art in England. He was fascinated with the cubist art movement, which led to his attempts at capturing the relationship between time and space. He wanted to combine the cubist philosophy with modern technology. He realized that if he exposed a single long strip of film using multiple lenses, all shooting at the same time, he'd capture a moment in time from many different angles, much the way cubist painters attempted to depict multiple simultaneous views of a subject.

For his first attempts, Tim used 16 mm film and built a long housing to hold the film. Each frame of film had its own aperture. The camera mechanism was built in a straight path and had relatively slow shutters that would simultaneously expose every frame of film. Tim hadn't anticipated how extraordinary the images would be. In fact, they were very powerful, almost eerie.

Because of the slow shutter speed, the initial images of moving subjects were blurry. So, Tim moved his setup onto a dark stage and illuminated his subjects with strobe lights. The high speed of the strobes greatly sharpened the image quality.

Tim's next innovation was to build a semicircular camera rig that could expose film frames positioned around subjects. These early rigs used pinhole openings and exposed 300–360 frames of film per shot.

After many years and many more frozen-time efforts, he refined his cameras. Zeiss lenses from compact cameras replaced the pinhole openings. With the addition of the larger and better-quality glass lenses, the length of the film was decreased to 72–120 frames. Tim found that if the camera was too long, frames at each end of the camera would capture the other end of the camera. Eventually, Tim arrived at an optimum configuration built on a 3-meter radius that used 120 frames of 35 mm film in the VistaVision format and had an overall length of 6 meters. Image-stabilization software was the final element that helped to make the images more usable.

In 1993, the TV show *Tomorrow's World* profiled the time slice effect and kick-started an interest in the technique. A BBC natural history program quickly commissioned Tim to use frozen time to study crickets, beetles, and other insects.

The commercial production world also embraced the technique. While some advertisers loved the novel effect, others were not so sure how they could sell their products with such unusual images. Nonetheless, within five years of seeing competitors and colleagues integrate stunning frozen-time images in their ads, the doubters had jumped on the bandwagon.

From commercials, frozen time moved on to feature films, most visibly in the Wachowski brother's *Matrix* trilogy (Warner Bros.). The visual effects personnel on that film used hundreds of Nikon cameras on a curved rigging to duplicate the look of Tim's frozen time. The feature film world definitely took notice, and the film received a 1999 Oscar for visual effects.

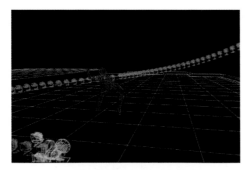

With the advance of digital technology, Tim's frozen-time process has shifted from sprocket-and-film technology to a software-based effect. He now uses off-the-shelf digital still cameras to capture his frozen-time images. With the refinement of frame interpolation, he needs only 12 cameras to create the same views his early 120-lens cameras used to make.

From art to technology and back, Tim Macmillan's frozen-time effect and his company, Time-Slice Films, have gone full circle. Tim invented frozen time as an artist studying the cubist movement, which in turn found inspiration in Eadweard Muybridge's early photographic work using multiple exposures of a galloping horse. While Muybridge explored motion within time, Tim focused on motion beyond time and found himself immersed in intensive technological study. These days, Macmillan's main interest in frozen time is its artistic value, and the ways he can use the technique to advance his art.

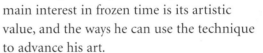

HDR Shop

DEFINITION ▶ A software program that allows users to make and manipulate complex HDR images.

Created at the University of Southern California Institute for Creative Technologies under the leadership of Paul Debevec, HDR Shop was the first publicly available HDRI tool. It is still widely used in the industry because it is excellent at providing accurate HDR control. At time of writing, HDR Shop came in two versions: Version 1 is free to download for personal use, and version 2 requires a commercial license. It can be downloaded from www.hdrshop.com.

SEE ALSO ▶ float space; HDRI; light probe

HDRI (High Dynamic-Range Imaging)

DEFINITION ▶ A file or image that contains a much greater exposure range than a normal digital image or even a 35 mm film image. These images provide valuable data for many visual effects tasks, including realistic renders of 3D images. *Related term:* HDR

SEE ALSO ▶ ambient occlusion passes; float space; HDR Shop; light probe; OpenEXR; radiosity, faux

A typical digitized computer image is stored in a linear 8 bits per channel (bpc) format. That is, for each of the red, green, and blue channels that define an image, there are 8 bits of data available to represent the intensity of a pixel. Eight bits provide 256 discrete steps of brightness. While this is enough color data to provide a visually pleasing reproduction of images on a computer screen, it is *not* enough to accurately depict the dynamic range of real lighting. In a typical outdoor film shoot, the brightest parts of the scene may be several thousand times brighter than the darkest parts.

High dynamic-range imaging solves this problem by storing extreme ranges of data in float space, which provides the data space required to store wide variations in intensity. HDR files are commonly created by combining multiple locked-off shots at a range of exposures and are often used to generate photorealistic 3D lighting. File formats for HDR images vary, but the most common format is OpenEXR.

In the image below, a lightbulb has been photographed at full illumination. The top row represents an HDR image, and the bottom row represents a standard 8-bit version of the image. As the images are darkened using a color corrector, the 8-bit image simply flattens in contrast. In the case of the HDR image, the reduction in brightness reveals more of the lightbulb's internal structure, until the filament itself is clearly visible.

A float-based HDR image that is gradually reduced in brightness using a color corrector eventually reveals the fine details of the bulb's internals.

An 8-bit image gradually reduced in brightness flattens in contrast and eventually goes completely dark.

The filament becomes visible because in the HDR version of the image, pixels are stored with values significantly brighter than the surrounding pixels. Since all of the pixels in the area of the bulb appear extremely bright, this isn't obvious in the initial image. (The computer monitor is unable to display, and the human perceptual system is similarly unable to perceive, the full dynamic range of the brightest portions of the image.) When most pixels are darkened by the color correction, however, the extreme values in the area of the filament leave those pixels clearly illuminated, while the surrounding pixels fade to black.

HDR images are useful for generating light probes, and are also useful for background elements and rendered 3D content.

Experimenting with HDR Images

NOTE ▶ The following demonstration requires that your Mac be running Mac OS X v10.4 or later.

1   To see an example of the dynamic range built into an HDR image, open **CycVFX/ ProjectFiles/Color/HDR/LightBulb.exr** into Preview. (This should automatically occur when you double-click the file.)

2   In Preview, choose Tools > Image Correction.

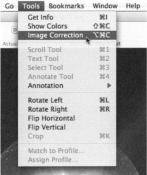

3   Adjust the Exposure up and down, and view the results.

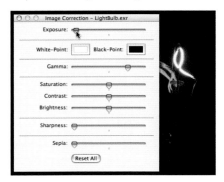

High-Key Images

DEFINITION ▶ Images that are made up of mostly light values.

Histogram

DEFINITION ▶ A window or graph in a software program that displays the relative strength of all luminance values in a video frame, from black to super white. It is useful for comparing two clips in order to match their brightness values more closely.

Holdout Matte

DEFINITION ▶ A matte that is used to prevent the foreground element from being keyed out. *Related terms:* edge ring matte; inner matte; inside matte

SEE ALSO ▶ edge matte/core matte; garbage matte

In today's computer-saturated environment, the holdout matte is sometimes confused with a garbage matte. Both have their origins in the days of optical printing when life was hard and people walked uphill both ways.

Seriously, the holdout matte used to be created via a painstaking process in which each film frame was projected onto a transparent cell and an artist rotoscoped, or traced around, the part of the foreground image that blocked the background so that it could be "held out."

The technique literally involved pouring black paint into the stenciled area. To make a long story longer, the resulting black-and-white articulated matte controlled which parts of the image were exposed on another piece of film and which parts were not. In basic terms, a holdout matte is latent-image photography or double exposures on a sequence of frames.

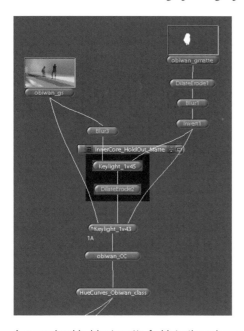

A procedural holdout matte fed into the primary key

It's very common to pull a solid key, only to end up with holes in the center of the matte. This is often caused by onscreen talent wearing blue clothing on a blue screen, or by excessive spill resulting from talent standing too close to the backing screen.

The solution is to create a custom matte that covers just those holes, and use it to "hold out" those portions of the matte. Be careful not to let your custom matte cover the precious soft edge created by the keyer. That is, make sure you color your holdout matte "within the lines" of your main, keyed matte. The holdout matte will, of course, need to be animated over time as the keyed subject moves.

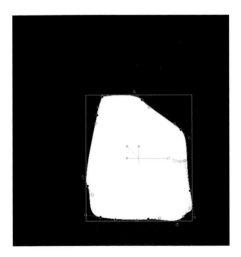

Combining the two mattes produces the desired result.

 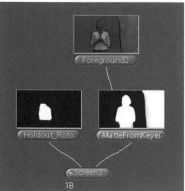

You may sometimes need to apply a slight blur to the holdout matte to blend it smoothly with the original matte.

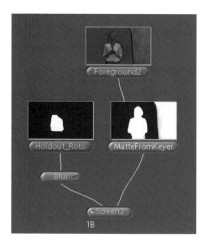

This process is essentially the same as creating an edge matte/core matte, though in this case the core matte is manually generated using rotoscoping, rather than using the keyer to generate both mattes.

Hot Spots, Removing

DEFINITION ▶ The removal of unwanted highlights from footage, these highlights often being the result of lighting rig reflections. *Related term:* glare removal

SEE ALSO ▶ clean plates, generating

Some of the most important visual effects work goes completely unnoticed as visual effects. Compositors may, for example, be called on to fix unintended artifacts that occur during a shoot. One common issue is the presence of *hot spots*.

Hot spots are caused by production lights reflecting off scene elements. Since stage lighting is intended to simulate real-world illumination, it should influence the scene without giving away its presence.

TIP ▶ When you aren't sure how much time it will take to fix a hot spot, take your best conservative estimate and double it. The process of removing a hot spot can be as involved as the effects in a summer action blockbuster. Budget accordingly.

Performing the Primary Replacement

The first step toward removing a hot spot is to remove any movement in the problem area. Whenever possible, use a four-point corner pin stabilization to get the best lock. When necessary, fall back to locking position, scale, and rotation.

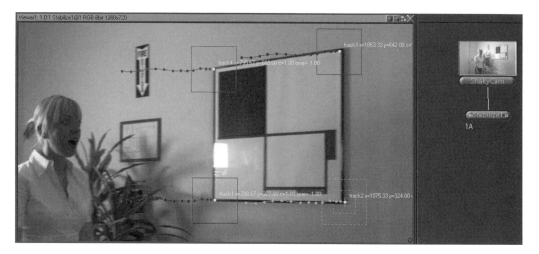

1   In this shot, you'll use the corners of the painting to perform a stabilization.

SHAKE ▼

Open **APTS_CycVFX/ProjectFiles/Tracking/HotNShaky/HotSpotStart.shk**. Add a Transform > Stabilize (trackType = 4 pt, subPixelResolution = 1/256) to ShakyCam. Position the tracking markers over the corners of the hanging picture. Track the shot. Activate applyTransform in Stabilize1.

NOTE ►   For simplicity, only the first 14 frames are included in this shot. Obviously, the woman in the frame is about to cross in front of the picture, which would force you to perform offset tracking if you were working with the complete shot.

Once the shot is stabilized, you'll need to look for a replacement source. In the figure below, the hot spot appears in the blank square at the lower left of a painting. Just looking at the image, you can see that this region is the same color as the upper right region of the painting. So, you can borrow a portion of the upper right area of the painting and use it to replace the hot spot in the lower left area.

2   To replace the hot spot with the borrowed region, you first need to make a matte of the region to be replaced.

SHAKE ▼

Control-Shift-click Image > RotoShape. Looking at ShakyCam in the Viewer, create a shape that covers the square affected by the hot spot.

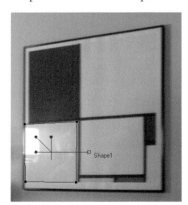

NOTE ▶ The hot spot also covers the black edge of the picture. You won't be able to harvest it from your initial replacement area, so you'll grab it from somewhere else.

3   To perform the replacement, composite the borrowed area over the problem area.

Select Stabilize1 and add a Transform > Move2D node. Control-Shift-click a Layer > KeyMix to add it, then connect Stabilize1 to the first (background) input. Connect Move2D1 to the second (foreground) input, and connect RotoShape1 to the third (key) input. Look at KeyMix1 while accessing the parameters of Move2D1, then pan the Move2D node down and to the left until the problem area is replaced by a uniform patch of the upper right square.

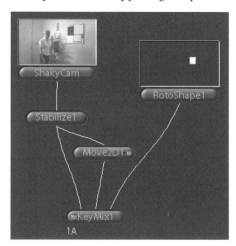

4   Looking at the new composite, you can see that the shading of the borrowed square is too dark for its new surroundings. You now need to color correct it so that it blends more naturally with the background. You can do this by isolating the red, green, and blue channels, and separately color correcting each channel.

Red channel before color correction

Red channel after color correction

Green channel before color correction

Green channel after color correction

Blue channel before color correction

Blue channel after color correction

SHAKE ▼

Add a Color > Mult node after Move2D1. Mouse over the Viewer and press the R key to look only at the red buffer. Looking at KeyMix1, adjust the red channel of Mult1 until the new square blends with its background. Repeat the adjustment for green (the G key) and blue (the B key). With your pointer over the Viewer, press the C key to return to the color channels.

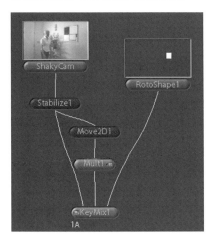

5   The last step in the process is to replace the black border of the picture frame. You can use a section of the border just above the hot spot. The process is exactly the same as the one you used for the square, but this time you'll use a shape that matches the dimensions of the black border affected by the hot spot.

SHAKE ▼

Control-Shift-click Image > RotoShape to add a node. Looking at KeyMix1, create a shape that matches the contour of the black border affected by the hot spot. Create a soft edge on the shape for the top and bottom edges.

Add a Layer > KeyMix node to KeyMix1. Select KeyMix1 and Shift-click a Transform > Move2D to branch a node. Connect Move2D2 to the second (foreground) input of KeyMix2, and RotoShape2 to the third (key) input.

Rotate, pan, and scale as necessary to correctly align the replacement edge with the original edge.

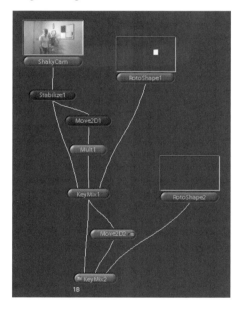

6   For a little cleanup, you'll add a slight blur to the mattes to help smush them in with the background.

SHAKE ▼

Add a Filter > Blur node to RotoShape1. Add
a Filter > Blur node to RotoShape2. Set the
blurs as necessary to blend your shapes into
their backgrounds (probably a value of 2 to
10 pixels).

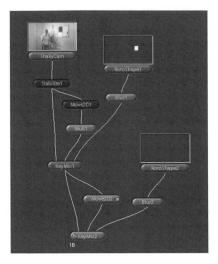

Destabilizing

S

You now have a nicely removed hot spot. The only problem is, your footage is locked
down. You might be tempted to copy and paste the original stabilization to the end of
your composite and set it to matchmove, but that would be bad. The result would be a
double-whammy of subpixel softening at the initial stabilization, and then again at the
matchmove. This should be avoided at all costs.

The superior solution is to remove the stabilization from the primary background element and apply it to the introduced elements as a matchmove. That way the only trans-
formed things are the replacement bits. You can hope that they won't become too soft to
be noticeable. (If they do, a quick sharpening filter might rescue you from disgrace.)

1   To set the movement back to normal, remove the stabilization, then use the same
tracking data to matchmove the two mattes you've used in the project.

SHAKE ▼

Copy Stabilize1, and paste copies after Blur1 and Blur2. Set the inverseTransform
of the two copied Stabilize nodes to "match." Select the original Stabilize1 node and
press the I key to ignore it.

If you try playing back, you'll notice that something is horribly wrong. The black border
shifts over time. That's because you adjusted the transforms based on the stabilized image.

2   To solve the problem, you can sandwich the transforms between two stabilizes: the first set to stabilize, and the second set to match. Thanks to Shake's concatenation of transforms, the three operations will combine to produce a net transform that is appropriate for the shot.

SHAKE ▼

Copy Stabilize1, and paste copies before and after both Move2D1 and Move2D2. Set the applyTransform parameters for the nodes following the Move2D nodes to "match." (The nodes will most likely be called Stabilize5 and Stabilize7, depending on how you pasted them.)

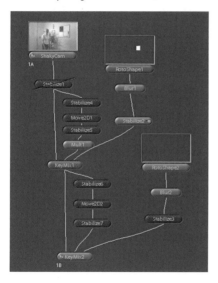

The replacement should now correctly animate over time.

If you step through the shot frame by frame, you may be concerned with slight changes in the black border edges. Be careful not to get too pedantic. At the speed this shot is panning, subtle changes are going to be undetectable when the footage is playing back normally. Don't waste your time and CPU cycles keyframing every subtlety when you and your computer could be off fragging workmates.

Going Further

Most of the grunt work is now completed. If you were really doing this shot, you'd need to offset track the picture and obscure its edges as the girl moves in front of it. Beyond this, there are some other important techniques that should be performed to complete the shot.

First, you may have noticed a reflection in the original picture. You've effectively removed it by adding your replacement square. You could use the exposed side of the girl's face to subtly replace the original reflection.

> **NOTE ▶** Ignore reflections at your own peril. They are one of the strongest signals to a human observer (right up there with shadows) that something ain't right with that there moving picture.

Second, the girl is about to obscure the picture (if the sample footage extends beyond frame 14), which will mess with your tracking efforts and conflict with your patch job. If you were working on the complete shot, you'd need to create a rotoscoped matte of the girl when she intersects with the painting, and subtract that from your two replacement mattes to garbage-matte out that area. (There's no need to replace those areas, since they are of the girl and not the hot spots.)

In this shot, you got lucky. Simple geometry in the picture made it fairly easy to reconstruct. In other situations, you may need to reconstruct the entire painting, which sometimes is actually easier. If possible, check with the director to determine if the original image is still accessible. If so, photograph it (using a polarized filter to remove extraneous reflections) and use the photograph as your replacement image. If the image is not available, try to find an alternative one that could be used as a replacement, or try to locate other shots in the film containing the same image in good view.

For desperate situations, third-party plug-ins like Furnace, from the Foundry (www.thefoundry.co.uk), can clean-plate backgrounds and help to re-create pattern detail from surrounding pixels.

Interlaced Video

DEFINITION ▶ The most common standard-definition video-scanning method used for footage that is intended for display on a television. The method first scans the odd picture lines (field 1), then scans the even picture lines (field 2), and merges the two fields into one single frame of video. Alternatively, some methods scan even lines first, then odd (NTSC DV, for example).

SEE ALSO ▶ 3:2 pull-down removal; deinterlacing

Inverse Core Garbage Matting

DEFINITION ▶ The process of inverting a matte, then eroding it away from the edge of the keyed subject to produce a garbage matte. Essentially the reverse of a core matte.

SEE ALSO ▶ edge matte/core matte; garbage matte

JPEG HDR

DEFINITION ▶ A file format for high dynamic-range imaging (HDRI). The format is unique in that it looks like a normal JPEG file to Web browsers, but offers users of applications like Anyhere Software's Photosphere the ability to adjust exposures using the HDR lighting information contained within the file.

SEE ALSO ▶ HDRI; photosphere

Key

DEFINITION ▶ A matte that has been procedurally generated by a computer. The computer analyzes the image, separates an image element from its background based on specified criteria such as color or luminance, and creates a grayscale matte image of the element. Commonly, a green screen or blue screen background is used when shooting images that will be keyed.

SEE ALSO ▶ keying; Keying Fundamentals chapter

Keyframe

DEFINITION ▶ The point on the Timeline (or on a frame of video) where a specific parameter value is set for a function such as a filter or motion effect.

Keyframes transition from one to another over time, so there must be at least two keyframes representing two different values to see a change in the clip. Some software, particularly animation software, interpolates between keyframes to create the in-between frames from one keyframe to the next.

Keying

DEFINITION ▶ The process of creating a matte (or key) to eliminate a specific background area in order to composite foreground elements against a different background.

SEE ALSO ▶ blue screen; chroma keying; depth keying; edge matte/core matte; Keying Fundamentals chapter; keying generic elements; luma edge keying; luma keying; mask; matte; sky keying

Keying Generic Elements

DEFINITION ▶ Keying techniques for adding generic atmospheric elements—such as dust, clouds, mist, fog, or smoke—into a composite. Typically performed using a knock-out method, or ADDMix. *Related terms:* clouds; contrast match; contrast operator; fog; smoke; vapor

SEE ALSO ▶ black levels, checking/gamma slamming; Keying Fundamentals chapter

One challenge that visual effects artists face almost daily is the realistic integration of 3D computer-generated imagery (CGI) and live action background plates. The addition of generic atmospheric elements such as dust, smoke, fog, and mist is one of the most effective ways to make a composite look more integrated and real.

Computer-generated environment with no atmospheric haze

Computer-generated environment with generic haze added using a depth matte

If you are lucky, an effects animator will create a generic element that perfectly follows the movement of the 3D object causing the smoke, fog, or mist. Unfortunately, your odds are better in Vegas. Most of the time, elements such as dust, smoke, fog, and mist are created on a sound stage. If the budget allows, such elements might be shot specifically for each CG shot.

More likely than not, it was decided in the preproduction stage that using stock elements in the shot would be more cost-effective. It falls to the visual effects artist to locate usable elements in a library of generic elements and then animate and integrate them into each shot. This process can be very challenging, depending on the contents of the production's library and on the level of interaction that is supposed to occur between the live-action and CGI elements.

Knowing the best keying technique to integrate the generic element can mean the difference between a good comp and a bad one. If a great composite looks 98 percent real, then the holy grail is finding the generic element that perfectly bridges the gap between 3D CGI and live action and provides that last 2 percent to really sell the shot.

Generic elements are often shot against a dark surface like black velvet or Duvateen. This allows for easier extraction and integration, especially when using layering methods such as Add and Screen (see the Keying Fundamentals chapter).

Computer-generated haze added with practical generic smoke (brightened to show detail)

Using Color for the Key

One of the advantages of shooting generic elements against a black background is that you get a nice luminance matte for free.

1   Reorder (shuffle) the red, green, or blue color channel into the alpha channel and— *voila!*—instant matte.

SHAKE ▼

Open **APTS_CycVFX/ProjectFiles/Keying/Keying_Generic_Elements/Reorder. shk**. Notice that we have applied a Reorder node (channels = rgbr) to dustdevil.

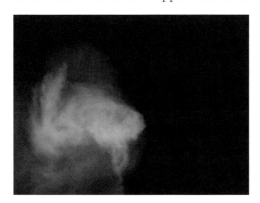 

2   Moving the red channel into the alpha channel (rgbr) creates a basic key or matte for the generic dust element. A contrast adjustment to make the blacks blacker and the whites whiter can be made before the Reorder node.

SHAKE ▼

Use a ContrastLum node (center = 1.5, softClip = 0.2). Adjust the value parameter to 1.5 or until the black area becomes zero (0) black.

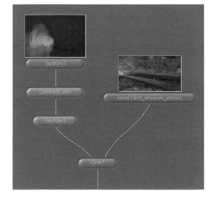

In this exercise, you are basically color correcting the RGB channels before reordering one of the channels into the alpha channel. (In this example, the red channel has the most contrast.)

> **TIP** Be very gentle when manipulating detailed, soft images. A little adjustment goes a long way in retaining intricate detail. This also applies to things like hair and clothes.

3   The image can be placed over the background at this point. However, you should note that an Over node expects a premultiplied image. Multiplying the RGB channels by the image's new alpha channel will give you a premultiplied image that will behave realistically. In the images below, the composite without premultiplication has more wispy detail that you may or may not want to retain, depending on what your overall objective is and how the element is affecting the composite.

SHAKE ▼

Use an Over node (preMultiply = 1). Toggle on and off the preMultiply parameter.

Without premultiplication

With premultiplication

Using the Generic Element as a Matte

S

You've examined the process of harvesting different channels to create an alpha channel matte. Premultiplying the RBG by the alpha matte gives you an image that has density. In other words, when you place a premultiplied generic element over the background, parts of the background are occluded and become difficult to see through the fog. This phenomenon is what we see in nature, though it has been exaggerated in the example images. Premultiplying can make nice wispy detail disappear. Loss of detail can be prevented if you use only the generic element for its alpha channel (matte) and fill in the color information with a color card (see below).

SHAKE ▼

Open **APTS_CycVFX/ProjectFiles/Keying/KeyingVapors/Premult.shk**. Double-click each node to see how it is affecting the image. Drag the noodle from the bottom of the Color_Card node into the top of the SwitchMatte_premult node to compare the different results of the two techniques.

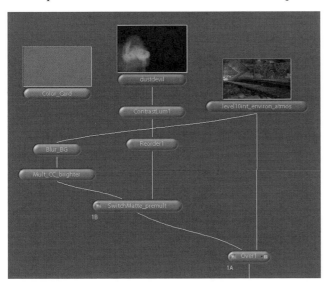

For even better results, use a huge blur on the background so that it looks like a big fuzzy blob. With this technique, you get the best of both worlds: a highly detailed matte combined with the light and dark areas of the blurred background. Techniques like this allow your generic elements to seamlessly integrate into the comp for free!

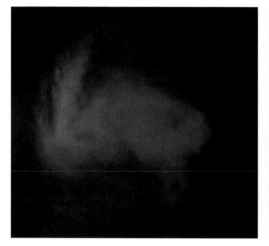

A highly blurred background premultiplied (joined) with a reordered matte

The premultiplied generic element placed over the background

Knot

DEFINITION ▶ A point on an animation curve or shape.

Kodak Cineon

DEFINITION ▶ A 10-bit logarithmic file format that uses an efficient color-compression scheme based on the idea that the human eye is more sensitive to shadows and midtones than to highlights.

There Goes the Neighborhood —Marshall Krasser

THE WORLD IS RIPPED APART as Tom Cruise's character escapes with his family in a stolen van. Shot RH010 is one of the highlights of Steven Spielberg's *War of the Worlds*, and it was created by an Industrial Light & Magic team led by compositing supervisor Marshall Krasser (see Contributors, page v).

Originally, the shot was not in the film; it was conceived by director Spielberg as a teaser shot for a Super Bowl ad. But after a month of intensive work, the teaser shot was so exciting that Spielberg decided to include it in the movie. To enhance the shot to an epic scale, Marshall and his team added several more vehicles to the road, as well as additional dust and smoke elements. The shot went on to win the Visual Effects Society (VES) award for best visual effects shot of the year.

The shot had to convey the unrelenting destruction engulfing the fleeing family. The goal was to wrap the audience into the shot, making viewers feel as if they were with the characters, holding their breath, praying for escape.

But the plate was shot with no destruction or interactive events. Everything that was destroyed had to be added. Portraying this mayhem became so complex, and the completion time so limited, that Marshall divided the work between traditional compositors and compositors using ILM's Sabre system. Two traditional compositors handled the first part of the 30-second shot, and three Sabre artists tackled the latter part of the shot.

In the end, nearly 350 layers were combined to match the gritty plate that was shot in New Jersey. These layers included CGI elements, miniatures built in the model shop, and 3D elements created in Sabre. Furthermore, the original plate was shot from a moving car and required a complicated matchmove.

Once the matchmove was completed, the broad elements of the shot could be blocked in. A collapsing CGI bridge was added in the distance. Next, the pylons that hold up the exploding roadway were added. The pylons were built in the model shop and shot onstage. Supervisor Dennis Muren requested that the roadway be created as a CGI element so that he could accurately choreograph the "peeling apart" of the roadbed as it rips away from the pylons. CGI vehicles were added on top of the roadway.

Next, the hero's van turns a corner onto a narrow street, and two houses are destroyed as a semitrailer truck crashes into them. The houses existed in the plate, and exact duplicates were built in miniature. A miniature truck was built and crashed into the model homes in front of a blue screen.

Finally, death rays were added that blaze down from above, along with exploding debris and fireballs that blast into the frame as the van narrowly escapes.

The team laid out the broad events of the shot and then went to work finessing the elements into the plate. Marshall stressed the importance of replicating what happens in the real world. In the plate, the day was hazy and cold, yet the sky was bright white. The initial observation on such a day is that distant objects are softer than closer objects. But a simple element blur would not produce an adequate result.

In reality, when a darker object moves against a brighter sky, the light "wraps" around the edges of the darker object because light particles scatter more where areas of brightness and darkness meet. Plus, as the camera moves away from objects during the shot, this *depth hazing* changes.

To re-create an accurate sense of depth hazing in the composite, a lot of postprocessing was applied to each element that went into the shot. As an example, a single section of the buckling roadbed required several different procedures using plug-ins to properly integrate it into the shot.

First, a plate flash was added to the element. Then, a percentage of that flash was added back over the edges of the element. An edge blend helped soften just the edges of that element. A dither displace layer further controlled the edges. Finally, a pixel scatter diffused the entire element.

Once the roadway pieces were in place, additional smoke and dust elements were requested for dramatic effect. For these new dust elements, compositors hand-fit the roadbed elements that were engulfed in the dust clouds to make them seem more organically integrated into the shot.

As the color and density of elements were integrated into the plate, an army of roto-scope artists worked frame by frame to create spline files, producing a virtual matte that positioned distant objects behind foreground objects. Numerous telephone lines, stoplights, houses, cars, and people were rotoscoped to combine the hundreds of elements within this shot.

In the second part of the shot, the van heads up a sidestreet. Early on, the choice was made to use Sabre systems to composite the numerous elements in this part of the shot. Sabre artists, led by Chad Taylor, blended in numerous alien laser beams, destroyed houses, explosions, flames, and assorted debris elements.

Sabre can take in the matchmove, and elements can then be moved very quickly in 3D space. Marshall points out that in Sabre you can paint right on the composite, and this second part of the shot needed a lot of paint work.

As Marshall recalls, five compositors completed this award-winning, 350-layer shot in just four weeks with a great team effort and brute-force compositing.

Lens Diffusion Simulation

SEE ► camera diffusion simulation

Lens Flare

DEFINITION ► A common artifact created by the camera lens during shooting. When the camera is pointed directly at a light source, the lens visibly refracts the light and the film is overexposed, resulting in shafts or streaks of light, or a telltale halo effect. Depending on the desired effect, lens flares may be removed or added during compositing to create verisimilitude in CG or composited elements.

Lens flares are products of camera optics and therefore are always composited *after* everything else has been added to the scene.

SEE ALSO ► camera diffusion simulation

Lens Warping

DEFINITION ► Spherically warping an image to introduce or remove lens distortion artifacts. *Related terms:* lens distortion; pincushion effects

SEE ALSO ► camera diffusion simulation

Camera lenses are round. Movie and TV screens are square. Despite Herculean efforts on the part of optical engineers, images acquired with a camera lens inevitably end up with some kind of spherical distortion.

This spherical distortion concerns compositors in two fundamental ways. First, the distortion needs to be removed for many compositing processes. For example, perspective tracks will be confused by the spherical distortion, since the relative distance between the four corner points of the track will also be distorted.

Second, distortion needs to be introduced into elements being added to a live action shot. Since most 3D applications render images *without* any distortion, some spherical distortion needs to be added to CGI elements if they're going to convincingly integrate into the background plate.

Analyzing Distortion

It is possible to fix lens distortion using a basic spherical displacement filter, but why use a hammer when you have a compressor and a fully loaded nail gun? Shake includes a LensWarp node in the Warp tab that is specifically designed to analyze and then remove *or introduce* lens distortion. After Effects includes the Optics Compensation effect, which also introduces and removes lens distortion, but lacks the automated analysis that Shake offers.

SHAKE ▼

Apply a LensWarp node, then draw spline lines along feature lines in the image that you know *should* be straight. Make sure each line has at least three points: The node needs an angle in each line to calculate the distortion. Since the most extreme distortion occurs at the outer edges of images, make sure you have as many spline lines as possible at the periphery. Try to create a good balance of horizontal and vertical splines.

Click the Analyze button when you're done.

What do you do if there are no straight lines in your image? Fall back on making basic adjustments to the scaling parameters of your warping filter. And next time, see if the director of photography can shoot a leader shot of a grid sheet.

> **TIP** When manually adjusting a lens-warping filter, don't always assume that the center of the distortion is the center of the image you're working on. You'll often find that the image has been cropped in some way during acquisition to remove unwanted regions (like the sound strip area on traditional film). In such cases, you'll need to adjust the center position to suit.

Removing and Introducing Lens Distortion

After you analyze or manually adjust filter settings, simply set the lens-warping filter of your choice to remove the distortion. If you're not performing any kind of tracking on the shot, you'll probably just want to introduce the distortion to other elements being added to the shot. Most filters (including Shake's LensWarp and After Effects' Optics Compensation) have a simple toggle for reversing the effect so that the distortion is added, not removed.

When adding distortion to an element, make sure that the element has been framed to match the background first. That is, if the background is 1920 x 1080 pixels, be sure that the foreground element has been positioned correctly and is framed to 1920 x 1080 before applying the lens distortion.

LIDAR

DEFINITION ▶ LIDAR (Light Detection and Ranging, or Laser Imaging Detection and Ranging) is a technology that determines distance to an object or surface using laser pulses. As with the similar radar technology, which uses radio waves instead of light, the distance to an object is determined by measuring the time delay between transmission of a pulse and the detection of the reflected signal.

While it has applications in geology, seismology, and other sciences, LIDAR is used in the film industry to obtain accurate measurements of set dimensions. Accurate set dimensions are particularly important in 3D modeling, building scale models, and creating and lighting CG elements.

Light Probe

DEFINITION ▶ A mirrored ball used to sample on-set light conditions and extract environmental reflections and lighting information from a scene. *Related terms:* mirrored sphere; set survey

SEE ALSO ▶ gray ball; HDRI; HDR Shop; light probe, lighting 3D scenes with; light stage

Photographers sample light in a particular location by photographing a mirrored ball at varying exposures and then combining the result into a single HDRI file. Compositors use this file to compare the environmental reflections and radiosity (or *bounce lighting*) in a digital 3D scene with the real lighting on the set.

Any mirrored ball can be used as a light probe. Garden supply stores sell "contemplation" spheres that work well when large mirrored balls are needed. For desktop work, stainless steel juggling balls from Dubé (www.dube.com) are popular, as are untinted mirrored Christmas tree decorations.

Programs such as HDR Shop can combine HDR images to produce a more accurate image that doesn't include the photographer's reflection. Adobe Photoshop CS2's cloning brush also provides the ability to paint out the photographer's reflection.

Light Probe, Lighting 3D Scenes With

DEFINITION ▶ Using a photographed image of a mirrored sphere taken on the set of a live action shoot to create an environmental reflection map or to generate a radiosity map for lighting 3D objects. *Related terms:* 3D lighting techniques; global illumination; radiosity; mirrored sphere

SEE ALSO ▶ HDRI; light probe; matchmoving in perspective; multipass, basic passes; reflections, faux

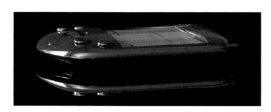

An image rendered using a light probe image

The rendered image integrated into the live action scene in which the light probe was recorded.

Light probe images are a powerful way to match the illumination of a live action set when rendering CG elements. Firstly, they provide the ideal reflection map, since they genuinely depict the scene elements that should appear in a CG item's reflection. Secondly—and perhaps more importantly—they record the position, color, and intensity of light sources in the original live action scene, allowing 3D rendering applications to synthetically re-create the same lighting.

NOTE ▶ Be careful when working with heavily animated live action scenes. The light probe is usually a still image and will therefore fail to account for motion in the reflected scene. In such cases, custom reflection passes should be created from visible elements of the live action footage. (See **reflections, faux** for ideas on how to attempt this.)

When shooting a light probe image for 3D lighting, try to take the image from the same direction as the camera shooting the main scene. Also be very careful to shoot with the same lighting conditions as in the original. Make sure that all studio lights are the same intensity, and if shooting with natural lighting sources (sky and sunlight), shoot at the same time of day as in the main shoot. If the shoot continues throughout the day on a naturally lit set, multiple light probe images may need to be taken.

Also be sure that set conditions remain the same. If a crew member was standing in front of a light during the main shoot, she should also obstruct that lighting source in the same fashion for the light probe shot.

NOTE ▶ While it's useful to remove the camera and operator from the light probe image for creating environmental reflection maps, doing so may actually change the lighting if the image is intended for **radiosity** rendering. This is because the original live action scene would not have received any light blocked by the camera operator and his rig.

If the camera moves to follow the action during a scene, it is ideal to generate several light probe images, representing the point of focus of the camera at different moments in the scene. These images can then be blended over time in the 3D rendering application to help keep the light probe image current as the camera animates.

The Poor Man's Light Probe

Creating HDR light probe images requires the use of a camera with manual focus, exposure, and aperture settings. If a manual camera is unavailable, two other solutions are possible.

Using Non-HDR Light Probe Images

While HDR light probe images produce exceptional sources for radiosity lighting in 3D, there's no reason why a standard, low dynamic range image can't be used. In such situations, take a single photograph of a mirrored sphere, being careful to capture as much dynamic range in the image as possible. In scenes with extreme contrast, you can slightly underexpose the image if necessary, in order to retain as much detail as possible in the brighter light sources.

Using an Automated Point-and-Shoot Camera

You can attempt to generate HDR light probe images even if your camera does not support manual settings by varying the exposure of the scene using other methods. These methods can include applying a neutral density filter to the camera, or changing the ISO speed of the camera.

> **NOTE ▶** On low-end digital cameras, high ISO numbers typically produce extremely noisy images, but the resulting image may still be useful for radiosity lighting purposes.

Focus may be a problem with this approach. A point-and-shoot camera often sets automatic focus for every shot. If this is the case with your camera, you may need to stabilize the images after acquiring them, just in case the focus has changed slightly. A high quality corner pin stabilization should suffice. Just treat the series of different exposures as an image sequence and run them through the stabilizer. (See tracking.)

Another complication with this method is assembling the images in the HDR utility. Since the images were not taken with specific different exposures, a certain amount of guesswork will be required to determine how many f-stops the images are. The EXIF information may help in some situations, but if external ND filters were used, that information will be inaccurate.

> **TIP ▶** HDR Shop is good at guessing f-stop values. Choose "assemble HDR from image sequence," import your images (ignoring error messages that may appear), click the Calculate button and then the Generate button, and hey presto—a slightly kludged but usable HDR. You can specify incremental f-stop settings as well if you want better results.

Orienting the Light Probe Image

Once a light probe image has been acquired, it's important to ensure that it matches the orientation of the scene. Make sure you have set up a scene with camera and orientation that matches the original, live-action set.

1 Apply the light probe image to the scene.

Most modern 3D applications include a plug-in or utility for adding the light probe image to the scene. If such a utility is unavailable, you can attempt to create one manually. Generate an extremely large sphere object with surface normals facing inward, then front-projection-map the probe image onto its surface. This will generally produce poorer results than using a dedicated plug-in.

TIP The name of the process used to generate lighting from HDR images can vary. Look in your applications manual under the terms *HDR, HDRI, radiosity, final gather,* or *global illumination* to identify the appropriate method.

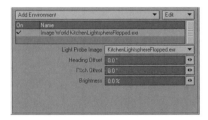

2 Apply the live action plate as a background image for the scene.

3 Create a sphere object in the 3D application that perfectly matches the original radius of the mirrored sphere you used to generate the light probe image. (This assumes you used real measurement—centimeters, inches, and so on—when building the 3D scene.) Give this object a 100 percent reflective surface, with no diffuse or luminous (self-illuminating) properties, and position it in the same location as the original mirrored sphere used to generate the HDR light probe.

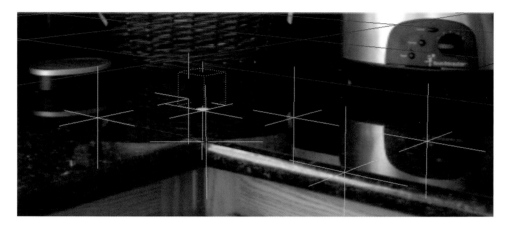

4 Render the scene, making sure that the sphere is set up to receive the reflection from the light probe. Then compare the render to the original light probe image. Most likely, you'll find that the reflection in the rendered sphere does not match the orientation of the original.

5   Using the settings provided in the light probe plug-in, rotate the light probe image until the rendered sphere matches the reflection of the original image.

 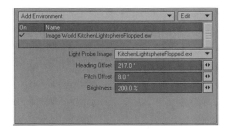

6   Remove the sphere from the shot and replace it with the actual object intended for render.

Rendering the Radiosity Passes

To effectively composite a 3D image into a background using the light probe, two main passes are always required: the main beauty pass and a shadow pass. If the CG object will reflect onto other surfaces in the live action plate, an additional reflection pass will be required.

NOTE ► For simplicity, this exercise was created with a basic beauty pass and a shadow pass. However, for more adaptive control, it's recommended that objects also be broken into the standard diffuse, specular, and reflection passes (see **multipass, basic passes**).

1   To create a radiosity beauty pass, import and position the object to be rendered in the correct location in the scene. Ideally, this will be the same location as the mirrored sphere on the original set.

2   Any object in the live action scene that will receive a shadow or reflection from the introduced 3D object will need to be modeled. To do so, create basic geometry that matches the shadowed or reflective surfaces. If the surfaces are irregular, this should be included in the geometry.

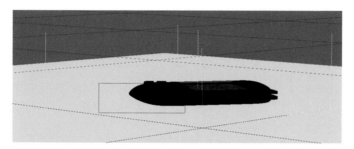

3   First, render the beauty pass with reflections. Give reflective surface properties to any portions of your stand-in geometry that will receive reflections from the 3D object. There's no need to add diffusion to reflections unless the scene is an extreme close-up, since this can be generated during the composite using a blur. Do not render shadows at this point. You'll do that later. Also render an alpha (matte) version of the scene including only the main 3D object, and not the additional surface geometry. This will allow you to perform separate operations on these elements using the generated alpha during the composite.

4 Now render a shadow pass. This is done by setting the main object so that it's unseen by the camera, but it's still visible to the renderer for calculating shadows. Set your "stand-in" geometry to a diffuse white and render.

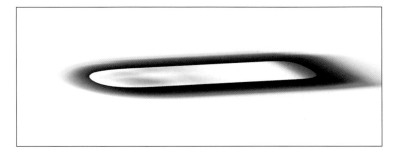

With these elements rendered, you're ready to perform the composite.

Composite the Rendered Elements

Although the final goal here is to composite the rendered object (a PDA) over the live action background plate, you'll begin by working only with the background, adding the reflections, then moving on to the shadows.

1 A matte is required to correctly composite the PDA's reflection over the background. Since the reflection was generated in the 3D application using a ground "stand-in" plane, there is no matte matching this reflection (since there was no "reflection-shaped" geometry from which to create the matte). In this exercise, you can use a luma key and some quick rotoscoping to generate the provided matte, ReflectionMatte.

> **TIP** With very dark backgrounds, you may get away with adding or screening the reflections, which don't require a matte. Another option is to pull a partial luma key and use it to knock out the portions of the background that would otherwise be blown out by the add or screen operations.

SHAKE ▼

Open **APTS_CycVFX/ProjectFiles/CG/HDR/LightProbe.shk**. Add a Layer >
KeyMix node to the Kitchen node, insert PDA into the second input node, and insert
ReflectionMatte into the third input node.

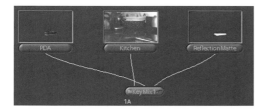

The reflection is much too strong, but you'll adjust that when the composite is fully
assembled.

2   Next, add a little diffusion to the reflection to account for irregularities in the surface
of the marble counter.

SHAKE ▼

Add a Filter > Blur to PDA (pixels = 5,5), copy the new Blur node, then paste a linked
version and insert it between ReflectionMatte and KeyMix1.

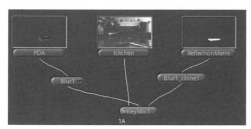

3 Now add the shadow pass. Since the shadow pass was rendered as a positive, you need to invert it to use it as a matte.

SHAKE ▼

Add a Color > Invert node to PDA_Shadow.

4 With shadow passes rendered in float, it's essential to make sure there are no negative values in the image. Negative values will actually cause the background image to lighten in some areas, not something shadows are supposed to do.

SHAKE ▼

At the base of the Viewer, from the Viewer scripts pop-up menu, choose the float viewer script.

The float viewer script indicates whether pixels in a float image fall within the normal linear range of 0–1 (displayed as gray), are greater than 1 (displayed as white), or are less than 0 (displayed as black).

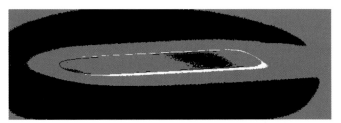

5 It's clearly visible in the Viewer that many of the pixels in your shadow matte do contain subzero values (that is, they appear black in the viewer). These pixels will cause the background to unintentionally brighten, so you'll clamp these values to eliminate pixel values beyond the normal 0–1 range.

SHAKE ▼

Add a Color > Clamp to Invert1, noting the change in the viewer. Click the Viewer script button once to deactivate the float viewer script.

With the clamp applied, the viewer turned pure gray, indicating that all the non-normal pixel values have been clamped to 0 or 1.

6   It's now time to apply the shadow matte.

SHAKE ▼

Add a Layer > ISub node to KeyMix1, and then connect Clamp1 to the second input.

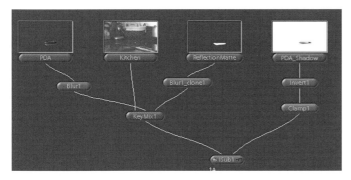

The resulting shadow is inappropriately dark. As with the reflection intensity, you'll fix this when the rest of the composite has been assembled.

7   The final assembly step is to composite the PDA over the treated background. In
the process, you'll premultiply the PDA against its matte to remove the unneeded
reflection.

SHAKE ▼

Branch (Shift-click) a Color > MMult off PDA. Add a Layer > Over node to MMult1,
and connect ISub1 to the second input of the Over.

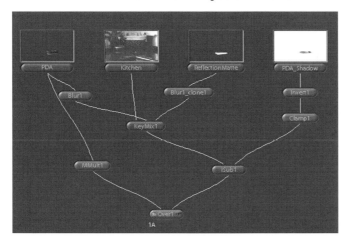

The scene is assembled, but it now requires finessing to create a convincing integration.
The first step is to modify the levels of the reflection and the shadow.

8 Looking at the gray base of the espresso machine on the left, it's clear that the reflected gray plastic is significantly dimmer than the original. You can use this to gauge how much to reduce the PDA's reflection.

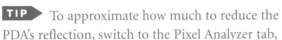 To approximate how much to reduce the PDA's reflection, switch to the Pixel Analyzer tab, set the sample mode to Average, and scrub over only the highlight on the gray plastic. Note the luminance value listed in the L box. It should be around 0.9. Repeat the process for the identical area of the reflected image. It should yield a luminance value of around 0.5. Divide the reflection's value by the original value, multiply by 100, and you should have an approximate value for the percentage of reduction.

SHAKE ▼

In the parameters for KeyMix1, set the percent to *56*.

9 Reduce the shadow to a much more moderate level, visually comparing it with other portions of the scene. It's hard to see from the other elements in the shot, but the shadows are fairly muted. You'll perform a fairly dramatic reduction.

SHAKE ▼

In the parameters for ISub1, set the percent to *3*.

10 To complete the shot, the CG needs to be treated to match the photographic processes inherent in the live-action background. To do that, you should apply a camera diffusion simulation, and add film grain.

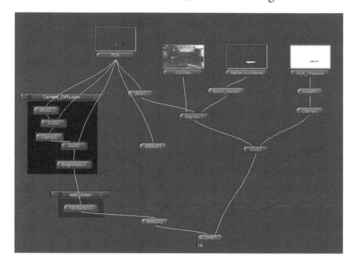

Light Wrap

SEE ▶ background wrap

Lightsaber, Creating

DEFINITION ▶ Techniques for generating light sword effects.

SEE ALSO ▶ edge matte/core matte; rotoscoping

Original Obi-Wan green screen with rotoscoped spline

Obi-Wan with lightsaber, combined core, and glow mattes with color correction

Of the many things brought to us by the creative mind of George Lucas, few are more memorable than the lightsaber.

Before computer graphics found their way into film, lightsabers were made by projecting each frame of the film onto an animation cel (a clear piece of plastic). Then, the artist would hand-trace the broomstick stand-in of each lightsaber and fill it with the appropriate color. This process was repeated frame by frame, 24 frames per second. Once completed, these cels with colored sticks were placed over a black background and projected onto another piece of film through a lens diffuser to add the characteristic lightsaber glow. The lightsaber element was then double-exposed onto the actual movie footage, covering the broomstick props and creating the lightsaber effect we all know and love.

Today, plug-ins using proprietary compositing software create the look and feel of the lightsaber. Nevertheless, computer-generated splines (shapes) must still be hand-drawn using rotoscoping tools, frame by frame. Fortunately, creating the look of the lightsaber is no longer a photochemical process and can be achieved with a combination of rotoscoped mattes, blurs, and color correction.

TIP ▶ "The look of the sabers varies a lot from shot to shot, and even from frame to frame within each shot. This is good; it makes the sabers look more dangerous, more alive, less CG." —Mike Conte, Compositing Supervisor, ILM

The birth of a lightsaber, a rotoscoped spline made up of eight control vertices, or points

The lightsaber has a humble beginning as two simple mattes.

Saber Spare Parts

Before you embark on creating one of the coolest visual effects in film history, you need to understand a few saber ground rules.

First and foremost, a lightsaber is made up of two mattes: a core matte and a pom matte. These mattes are blurred and made into glow mattes.

The core matte is about the width of the hilt and three times the length of the prop hilt used by the actors. It is rounded at the base and tapers slightly along its length. The tip of the saber is not pointed like a pencil or rounded like a Popsicle stick but shaped somewhere in between.

Actors wielding a lightsaber usually use a prop hilt with a thin plastic tube representing the blade. The plastic tube helps identify the size and shape of the blade in 3D space. Although the plastic tube sometimes bends during swinging and sparing, the core matte should always be straight.

The pom matte is an egg-shaped matte that sits at the base of the hilt and is used to widen and hide the connection point between the core matte (blade) and the hilt of the prop saber.

> **TIP** "There is an eight-point system for creating a lightsaber matte. All the mattes in these films (Star Wars Episodes I, II, III) hold to this eight-point system. There are three points for the base of the blade: hard right angles on the outer two, with the inner point used for providing the appearance of volume. Five points are used for the tip: the first pair for setting the beginning of the tip's tapering off, and also to suggest the slight inward draw that the blade makes from its width at the base. The next pair is used to give the tip a rounded appearance, and the final point is the literal tip of the saber."   —Alan Travis, Lightsaber Supervisor, ILM

The Dark Side

Now that you grasp the basics, you can get in touch with your midi-chlorians and create a lightsaber!

> **TIP** **APTS_CycVFX/ProjectFiles/Keying/Lightsabres/LightSabre_finish2.shk** is a 'finished' version of the script that is available for reference and reverse engineering.

1   Start by opening the lightsaber script.

SHAKE ▼

Open **APTS_CycVFX/ProjectFiles/Keying/Lightsabres/LightSabre_start2.shk**. Make sure the current frame on the Time Bar at the bottom is at frame 20. Select the Image tab and add a RotoShape node. Select the left side of the obiwan_greenscreen_1k node to place the footage in the Viewer.

Select the right side of the RotoShape1 node. This should add the RotoShape1 controls to the Viewer.

Now you can make the core and pom mattes while viewing the footage.

Click and add three points (control vertices) at the base of the hilt. Continue down the length of the plastic. Add another point near Obi-Wan's hand. Add three more points at the tip of the blade, remembering to add extra length. Add another point near Obi-Wan's hand and then click on the initial point to close the shape (see image below).

 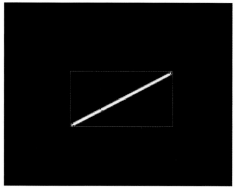

At this stage, it is vitally important that you are creating the RotoShape1 while viewing the **Obiwan_greenscreen_1k** footage. You are basically *rotoscoping,* or tracing, the plastic tube of the lightsaber prop using the eight-point system described by Alan Travis.

Once you have placed eight points and have a closed shape, be sure the points are straight. Obi-Wan might feel like less of a Jedi if you give him a crooked or bent lightsaber!

2   Now you need to add a pom matte. This is the egg-shaped matte that helps blend and connect the main core matte to the prop hilt.

SHAKE ▼

Select the Image tab and add a second RotoShape node. Once again, select the left side of the Obiwan_greenscreen_1k node to bring the footage into the Viewer. Now select the right side of the RotoShape 2 node, so you can view the footage while making the core and pom mattes.

Click and add three points (control vertices) at the base of the hilt. Add three more points a little farther down the length of the blade. Click on the initial point to close the shape (see images below).

The bean-shaped pom matte used to bridge any gap between the main core matte and the prop hilt

The bean-shaped pom matte in all its glory

As before, it is vitally important at this stage that you are creating the RotoShape2 node while viewing the **Obiwan_greenscreen_1k** footage.

Now you have two RotoShape nodes that trace the lightsaber prop for frame 20. The fun part is going to each frame and changing the shape of both the core and pom RotoShapes to match the new shape and location of the prop saber. This is usually done to every frame.

Examining the footage, one notices the lack of extreme movement in Obi-Wan's lightsaber. To speed things up, you can set the Increment value on the Timeline to 2 so that you have to set only half the keyframes for the core and pom RotoShapes. Note that the entire shot of all the elements has been included for your rotoscoping pleasure!

> **TIP** ▶ Whatever you do, make sure keyframing is turned on. There is nothing worse than to animate a RotoShape and then to discover that the only keyframe set is the last one.

3   Continue with the keyframing process.

SHAKE ▼

Select the right side of the RotoShape1 node (your core matte) to place the onscreen controls in the Viewer. Select the Key icon so that it becomes green, if it is not already green. This means keyframing is turned on. When you move to a different frame and change the shape of the core matte, Shake will automatically create a new keyframe at that frame. The RotoShape will now animate from frame to frame.

Go to the bottom of the Shake interface and change the Inc (increment) from 1 to 2. Press the right arrow key to advance from frame 20 to frame 22. The **obiwan_greenscreen_1k** footage should change. If it does not, select the left side of the node to place it in the Viewer. A small triangle should be visible in the Timeline showing the keyframe at frame 20. (Make sure the Update button in the upper right corner of the interface is set to Always, so your footage will update as you move to different frames in the Timeline.)

Press the + (plus) key to zoom in to the core matte so that you can more easily see what you are doing. Place the onscreen controls into the Viewer, if they are not already there, by selecting the right side of the RotoShape1 node. In the Viewer, drag a selection around the points (control vertices) that make up the saber core matte. Once they're selected, very carefully click the point closest to the prop hilt and drag the entire shape to the prop hilt's new location. Adjust the individual points, if necessary.

Advance two frames by pressing the right arrow key, and repeat the previous process until every other frame has its own keyframe indicator.

Remember that you should go back to frame 20 and use the left arrow key to move back in time, and move the core shape and set keyframes for those frames as well.

The Shake user interface. The Inc value (increment, in the lower right corner) is set to 2, indicating that you are on frame 22, and have selected and moved the core spline to match the new location of the saber prop hilt.

Repeat this entire process for the pom matte so that both RotoShapes animate and follow the lightsaber prop hilt and plastic tube (frames 1–19).

NOTE ▶ Obi-Wan lightsaber core and glow elements have been provided for reference. They can be found in both the "start" and "finish" project files: **APTS_CycVFX/ ProjectFiles/Keying/Lightsabres/LightSabre_finish2.shk**.

Use the Force

You have gone through the arduous task of creating and animating both the core and pom parts of Obi-Wan's lightsaber. Now you need to add the characteristics that make up the lightsaber's look.

As is the case throughout this book, you are going to reuse a matte to create new elements. Here, you are going to combine the core and pom mattes, and use them to make the saber glow.

> **TIP** ▶ "There are four layers to the saber—an inner and outer white core (actually it's slightly yellow) and an inner and outer colored glow. Each layer is created by blurring the 'core' matte progressively more." —Mike Conte, Compositing Supervisor, ILM

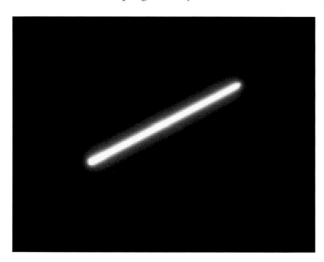

What your lightsaber element should look like at the end of this section

1   The first thing you need to do is combine the core and pom mattes.

SHAKE ▼

Select the RotoShape1 node (core). Go to the Layer tab and add a Screen. Under the RotoShape2 node (pom), drag the noodle into the BG of the Screen1 node.

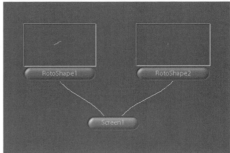

The combined core and pom mattes

The Shake tree of the combined mattes

As Mike Conte said, a lightsaber is made up of four separate mattes that are each color corrected and blurred separately. These are combined to make the final saber look.

2   You can start with the inner core.

The lightsaber is not fully white but slightly yellow. We need to add a Mult node and color correct the combined core. This will be the "inner core" element.

SHAKE ▼

Select the Screen1 node. In the Color tab, add a Mult node. Double-click that node to place the controls for the Mult1 node into the Parameters1 window. Change the Blue parameter to .7 (Color = (R) 1 (G) 1 (B) .7).

The combined core and pom mattes color corrected using a Mult. This is your inner core element.

3 Next you'll need to make a slightly blurred "outer core" element. We will be using the same "base" matte for all our elements.

SHAKE ▼

Select the Screen1 node. In the Filter tab, Shift-click the Blur to add it on its own branch. Double-click Blur to place the controls for the Blur3 node into the Parameters1 window. Change the xPixels Blur value to 11.

Now, in the Color tab, add a Brightness node below the Blur3 node. Change the Brightness value to 1.6.

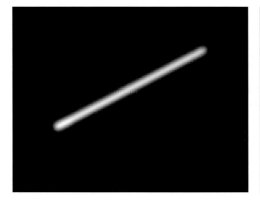

The slightly blurred outer core element

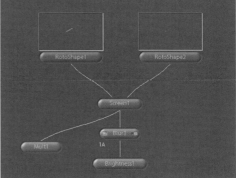

The Shake tree of the slightly blurred, brightened outer core element

4 To finish off your main core matte, now turned into an element, you need to combine the inner and outer core elements. An elegant way to do this is to use a Screen to combine them.

SHAKE ▼

Select the Mult1 node (inner core). In the Layer tab, add a Screen. Under the Brightness1 node (outer core), drag the noodle into the BG of the Screen3 node.

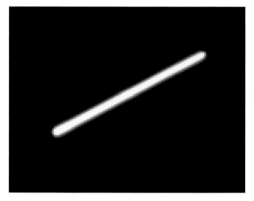

The combined inner and outer core elements

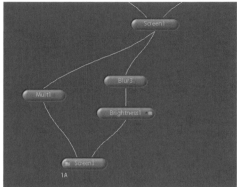

The Shake tree of the combined inner and outer core elements

5   Similar to the way you made the combined core element, you now need to make an inner glow element. Later, this will be combined with an outer glow element.

SHAKE ▼

Select the Screen1 node. In the Color tab, Shift-click the Mult node to add it on its own branch. Double-click the Mult2 node to place the controls into the Parameters1 window. Change the color value of the Red to *0*, the Green to *.2*, and the Blue to *3*.

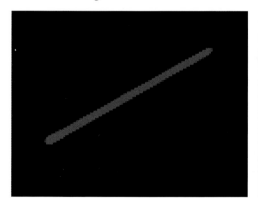

The color-corrected inner glow element

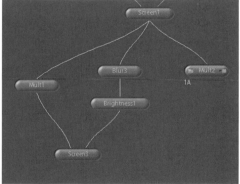

The Shake tree of the color-corrected inner glow element

6   You have the beginnings of an inner glow element. You need to blur it out, brighten it, and take out a bit of saturation. This will boost the inner glow element, yet prevent the blue from getting too crunchy.

SHAKE ▼

Select the Mult2 node. In the Filter tab, add a Blur. Double-click it to place the controls for the Blur5 node into the Parameters1 window. Change the xPixels Blur value to 21.

Now, add a Brightness node below the Blur5 node. In the Brightness2 node, change the value to 2. Finally, also in the Color tab, add a Saturation1 note and reduce the saturation to .9.

The slightly blurred and brightened inner glow element

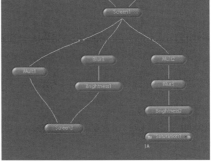

The Shake tree of the slightly blurred and brightened inner glow element

7   Now use a Screen to add the inner glow element to the combined core element that you made earlier.

SHAKE ▼

Select the Screen3 node (combined core). In the Layer tab, add a Screen. Under the Saturation1 node (inner glow), drag the noodle into the BG of the Screen4 node.

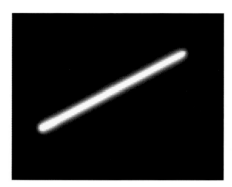

The combined core element with the inner glow element

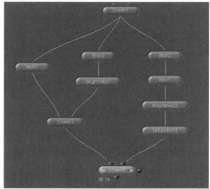

The Shake tree of the combined core element with the inner glow element

8   What would an inner glow be without an outer glow element? As before, you need to blur it and brighten it even more. This will be the last lightsaber element that provides a nice big blue glow.

SHAKE ▼

Select the Mult2 node. In the Filter tab, press Shift and add a Blur node. Double-click it to place the controls for the Blur6 node into the Parameters1 window. Change the xPixels Blur value to 41.

Now, add a Brightness node below the Blur6 node. In the Brightness4 node, change the value to 3.

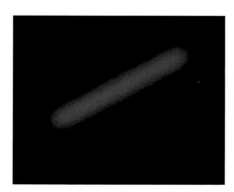

The outer glow element with more blur and brightness

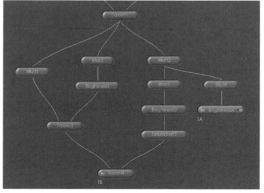

The Shake tree of the outer glow element with more blur and brightness

9   Finally, add the big outer glow element to the rest of the combined elements. This will give you the lightsaber look we all know and love.

SHAKE ▼

Select the Screen4 node (combined core and inner glow). In the Layer tab, add a Screen. Under the Brightness4 node (outer glow), drag the noodle into the BG of the newly added Screen5 node.

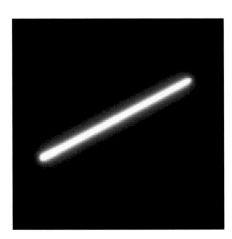

The combined inner and outer core elements with the inner and outer glow elements

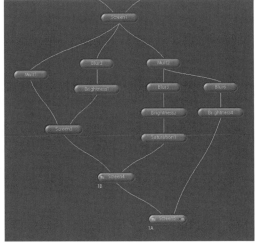

The Shake tree of the combined inner and outer core elements with the inner and outer glow elements

10   At this point you can add this final lightsaber element to the main composite. Typically, the lightsaber is placed over the background using an Add or a Screen.

SHAKE ▼

Now you need to add your lightsaber and glow elements over Obi-Wan and the background. Drag the output of the Screen5 node into the Screen2 node of the composite of Obi-Wan over the Background_Precomp_Group.

TIP ▶ When creating lightsabers, it is sometimes possible to skip frames and still end up with a nice-looking lightsaber in less time. Using an increment of 2 means that the spline is animated with fewer keyframes in half the time. It is easy to go back and tighten up the animation of the RotoShapes by adding keyframes to those frames that were skipped.

Depending on the shot, it might also be possible to track the lightsaber prop and apply the tracking data to move the RotoShapes. This procedural method then requires small adjustments instead of large changes to the rotospline shapes and locations. Plus, it might save time.

Saber Flicker

Although one of the elements that make a lightsaber feel dangerous and live is its slight undulations in size, that level of detail is beyond the scope of the current exercise.

However, note that the separate outer core and inner glow elements flicker randomly. Neither element should ever get too bright or too dark. If you're brave enough to venture on, be warned that the rest of this exercise is fairly advanced.

1   When adding flicker, think subtlety.

SHAKE ▼

Select the Brightness1 node of the outer core. Add a new Brightness node and enter the following Brightness Value parameters for your new Brightness5 node: noise(time/2)/3+.9

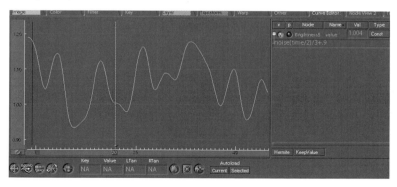

An example flicker curve for the outer core element

Select the Brightness2 node of the inner glow. Add a new Brightness node and enter the following Brightness Value parameters for your new Brightness6 node:

noise(time/3)/1.5+.7

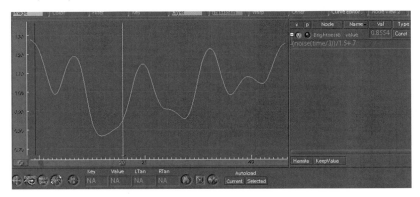

An example flicker curve for the inner glow element

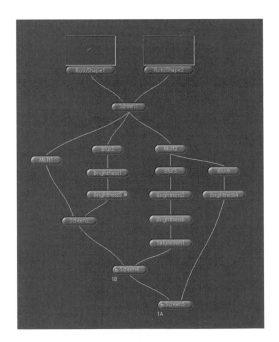

TIP ▶ "For Episode III, [we] wanted Grievous to have 3D-modeled sabers, which lightened the lightsaber group's workload. We were not looking forward to hand-animating Grievous's helicopter-blade swordfighting technique. Although some shots ended up being helped by 2D, most of the Grievous shots are 3D-modeled sabers and I think they fit in seamlessly with the others in the prequels."

—Alan Travis, Lightsaber Supervisor, ILM

Saber Extras

Just when you thought it was safe to go back to Tatooine…

▶ When a saber is turned on, the core must be animated to grow from the prop hilt to the final shape in five frames (a sequence that is reversed when turning it off).

▶ If a Jedi drops his lightsaber, it should stay on for three frames before starting the five-frame turn-off animation.

▶ When a saber turns on or off, a small "ignition flash" occurs that consists mostly of a horizontal bar. The ignition flash is the same color as the saber.

▶ When a saber is swung through the air, it is always opaque and never motion blurred. The core matte is drawn in a wedge shape to match the motion blur of the prop plastic pole.

▶ When a saber contacts something, there is a large reddish-yellow flash. The flash is always reddish yellow, no matter what color the saber is, or what is hit. The size, brightness, and color of the flash varies frame by frame for a more organic look.

▶ When a saber hits something metal, it throws off sparks in the direction of travel, along with some smoke.

▶ When one saber hits another saber, there is a big flash. Don't be afraid to blow out the entire frame.

▶ Most saber hits are two frames long (small-big or big-small flash); larger hits are three frames (small-big-small).

▶ A nice touch is to add fake interactive light from the saber by taking a luminance matte of any object close to the saber (usually cheek highlights) and changing the color to match the saber.

▶ Don't forget to add reflections of the saber in any surface that would naturally warrant it, like shiny floors.

Saber Lore

Even "in a galaxy far, far away," certain rules must be adhered to. George Lucas knew this all too well when creating the *Star Wars* universe. A lightsaber has to obey the rules of a lightsaber, not just to appease the curious fan, but also to establish a believable consistency (and to avoid driving the effects artists crazy). Here are some of those rules, and a few insider stories:

▶ Blue is the hardest color to make. It's either too transparent, or the glow is too saturated and crunchy. The most frequently seen saber is Obi-Wan's, which is blue.

▶ Good guys have blue or green sabers. Bad guys have red sabers. The one exception is Mace Windu, who has a purple saber. I was told Samuel L. Jackson specifically asked Lucas for a purple saber.

▶ In *Episode I*, lightsabers don't cast any light onto surrounding objects. In *Episode II*, a few shots do include interactive light, particularly when Anakin is fighting Dooku. In *Episode III*, there is a lot of interactive light. This reflects how much better we got at doing saber glow, rather than a change in the *Star Wars* universe.

▶ When *Episode I* came out, *Vanity Fair* ran a photo of Darth Maul and Qui-Gon fighting in the desert. On the sand was a distinct shadow from the sticks the actors were holding, which someone forgot to paint out. As a result, we got a letter from a 12-year-old that prompted a daylong discussion on the company message boards about whether lightsabers could cast shadows. The short answer is, yes, they can—just look at that one there. The longer answer is, yes, they can—in the proper circumstances—the same way a fluorescent lightbulb can cast a shadow if you point a brighter light source at it.

▶ We always wanted to add baconlike smoke and sizzle when the sabers touch people, as when Qui-Gon gets stabbed at the end of *Episode I* or Anakin rampages in *Episode III*; but Lucas thought it was too gruesome. On *Episode III*, we did add a burning steel-wool look along cut edges; but for the most part, any smoke and sizzle you see is limited to inanimate objects such as droids.

TIP ▶ "In the end, while it may sound like there were a lot of hard and fast rules about how these things should look, most of the time we would just try something and, if it looked cool, we went for it. There was more than one occasion where I added little spins of the saber where the actor had simply held it still because it looked great and you couldn't tell that he hadn't really done it. 'Make it look cool' was our mantra, and we went for it on every shot."

—Alan Travis, Lightsaber Supervisor, ILM

The composite with your home-brewed lightsabers

For more on the rendering and compositing of this shot, see Brian Connor's "Anatomy of a Lightsaber Duel," on page 155.

Light Stage

DEFINITION ▶ A device that re-creates HDRI-derived lighting effects.

SEE ALSO ▶ HDRI; HDR Shop; light probe

Developed by a team led by Paul Debevec at the University of Southern California Institute for Creative Technologies (ICS), Light Stage uses a light probe recorded on location and a sphere of computer-controlled LEDs to re-create the exact match of the lighting derived from any HDRI onto, say, the face of a live actor.

The ICS team's 2005 SIGGRAPH paper demonstrated how a Light Stage can be used to capture an actor's performance at 4000 fps with a range of lighting permutations that allow the recorded performance to be played back with *any* lighting scheme. This technique has the potential to dramatically alter visual effects practices, but it is still in the prototype stage. (More information is available at http://projects.ict.usc.edu/graphics/research/LS5/index-s2005.html.)

Low-Key Images

DEFINITION ▶ Images that are made up mostly of dark values.

Luma

DEFINITION ▶ Short for *luminance*. A value describing the brightness information of the video signal without color (chroma). Equivalent to a color television broadcast viewed on a black-and-white television set.

SEE ALSO ▶ luminance, weighted; YIQ; YUV

Luma Edge Keying

DEFINITION ▶ Using a luma key to produce a full-detail edge matte, then using the color difference keyer to extract a core matte. *Related terms:* DV keying; luma edge matte; 4:x:x

SEE ALSO ▶ chroma blur; difference matte; edge matte/core matte; luma keying

Edge detail is of paramount importance when pulling a key. Unfortunately, many of the compression schemes used to store media digitally subsample the chrominance, producing jagged edges during the keying process. Leveraging the edge matte/core matte technique to combine a luma key with a color-difference key, you can create a solution that occasionally performs better than applying a chroma blur.

Here's how it works: Use a luma key to extract a matte for edge detail, and then use a color-based keying method (such as color-difference keying) for the center of the matted object. In this setup, the luma key is obviously the edge matte, and the color-difference key is the core matte. You'll most likely also need to use a reverse of the core matte to garbage-matte the outside of the luminance key.

This technique has pros and cons. On the plus side, a luma key will produce higher-resolution edge detail than a key based on the subsampled chroma components. (That makes sense, since the luminance component of an image is always sampled at full resolution.) The fundamental problem is that if the footage has been sharpened, it will not produce a soft-edged matte when luma keyed. You can turn off sharpening in the camera or acquisition system, but unfortunately, many prosumer-type cameras automatically apply sharpening and provide no menu function for deactivating it.

If you use this method, follow the "blonds on blue" principle: If you're shooting light hair or light-colored objects, shoot against a blue screen and slightly overlight the foreground subject to enhance the contrast between foreground and background in order to produce a better key. The reverse is also true: Dark hair or dark objects should be shot against the higher luminance of a green screen and slightly underlit to produce a nice contrast for the luma keyer.

Luma edge keying is a very useful tool for partial matte edge repair, so don't forget it's available when you're struggling to fix a small portion of a stubborn edge. However, the problems this technique creates may not be worth the effort, so be sure to test it with your equipment before using it.

Luma Keying

DEFINITION ▶ Extracting a key based on luminance information in an image. *Related terms:* keying brightness; luminance keying

SEE ALSO ▶ chroma keying; keying generic elements; luma edge keying

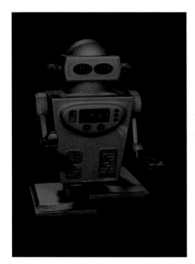 

Keying based on the luminance (brightness) information in an image is an essential part of the compositor's tool kit. It allows you to harvest specular highlights, replace skies, and extract shadows. Luma keyers are also among the simplest filters to operate.

Most luma key filters have one control for a low threshold and another for a high threshold. First, adjust the low threshold until you've isolated the pixels in which you're interested.

TIP ▶ In Shake, you'll need to be watching the alpha channel of your image to see the result, unless you check the matteMult LED.

Then, reduce the high threshold until you have a solid white matte that suits your purposes.

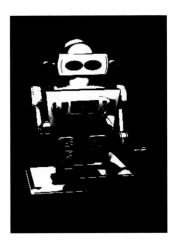

At this point, you may find that the edges of the matte are unpleasantly aliased. With any luck, your luma key filter will have smoothing adjustments for both the high and low thresholds. These smoothing parameters can add a graceful falloff curve to each of the thresholds, instead of the harsh clipping evident in the aliasing mentioned above. They will "loosen" the key—adding some pixels beyond the range you've selected—but they'll reduce the unpleasant aliasing at the extremities of your matte.

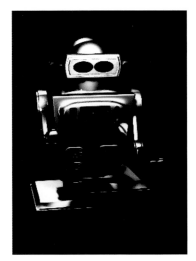

Sample adjustments used to produce the luma key shown above.

Luminance

SEE ▶ luma; luminance, weighted

Luminance, Weighted

DEFINITION ▶ A technique used to create a contrast-accurate black-and-white version of a color image. *Related terms:* broadcast luma; YIQ; YUV

When attempting to create a visually accurate black-and-white version of a color image, designers are often tempted to simply take one-third of the red information, one-third of the green, and one-third of the blue and add them together to create the new image. That is what is referred to as a *nonweighted luminance* and will actually cause a skew in the perception of contrast of the image.

For a black-and-white version of an image to maintain the appropriate sense of contrast between elements in the scene, a weighted luminance must be used.

Put in very simple terms, the human perceptual system is most sensitive to variations in the contrast of green light. It is much less sensitive to contrast changes in red light, and even less sensitive to contrast changes in blue light. Our overall perception of a scene's contrast is therefore *weighted*; roughly 59 percent comes from green light levels, 30 percent from red light levels, and 11 percent from blue light levels. Experts will argue over the exact percentages, but a black-and-white television signal is based on the values quoted above. More precisely, the full luminance TV signal is the result of combining 0.299 of the red signal, 0.587 of the green signal, and 0.114 of the blue signal.

When color television appeared on the scene, the original black-and-white signal was left untouched, but two subcarrier signals containing the extra color information were added. A black-and-white television ignores this information; a color television uses the subcarrier luminance information to extract the original red, green, and blue signals.

To create a weighted luminance version of an image:

In Shake, apply Color > Monochrome or Color > Saturation.

In After Effects, choose Effect > Adjust > Hue/Saturation.

In Motion, choose Add Filter > Color Correction > Desaturate.

The Art of Matte Painting— Yanick Dusseault

AT THE END of *Star Wars: Episode III—Revenge of the Sith*, the body of Padmé was returned to her native planet, Naboo, for burial. The wide shot of Naboo and the city of Theed on the distant bluff was a matte painting by Yanick Dusseault (see Contributors, page iv).

At this point in the movie the tone was somber, and a sense of final resolution prevailed. Though the shot of Naboo had been fairly well blocked out in previsualization, and a sketched storyboard existed, the feeling of the shot was open to interpretation. The painting could have been done in one of many different styles (in fact, George Lucas first envisioned the scene at night).

But over time, the storyboard simply stated, "magic hour." To capture this moment of passing, Yanick decided *not* to use the clichéd image of the sun just setting over the horizon. To redirect and unbalance audience expectations, he selected a moment that was just before, or just after, that more traditional visual moment.

This shot, like every **matte painting**, was about more than the basic shapes of the composition. It was about tone and feeling, the emotional resonance that color and texture and light create. In this case, Yanick wanted Naboo to feel rich and comfortably soft, with a soothing light and a touch of the ethereal. To that end, he avoided the active oranges of sunset and went with a palette of soft green, embracing colors.

Being a fan of wide, beautiful vistas, Yanick loved the original representations of Theed and Naboo that had appeared in the previous two films. Those early works became the basis of his inspiration for the matte painting of Naboo in *Episode III*.

Yanick said that the sky defines the feeling an audience gets from a matte painting, and that's where he starts to craft his images. "In the sky we find the color palette, the lighting, and the mood of a pictorial image," he stated.

So Yanick began to look for the proper sky. Just before starting work on the shot, he was traveling north on Interstate 5 from Los Angeles to San Francisco. As he drove down a steep grade, he found an inspirational sky. He grabbed his digital camera and began snapping away at 70 mph. The vista was perfect, down to the rolling hills in the distance. Ultimately, these 70 mph stills became most of his foreground sky. They embodied the somber feeling he wanted his painting of Naboo to evoke from the audience. Further down the road he photographed more distant clouds, and these became the distant clouds at the horizon of the painting.

"Once the feel and mood of the sky is in place, the lighting of every other part of the painting falls into place," said Yanick. In the shot, the sun was low, with the light just peeking under the overhead clouds, causing the spires of the palace to throw long shadows across the entire valley below. The landing strip where the spacecraft settles down was cast in the larger soft shadow of the entire cliff above it. The mood was soft and beautiful and welcoming. Once the mood for the painting was defined, the execution of the painting became fairly straightforward.

The bulk of modern matte painting is a form of collage that might be composed of two-thirds digital image pictures and one-third painting. Since the camera pushes in during the shot, Yanick started his painting at the end of the move when the camera is closest to the terrain. Then he backed the camera out, filling in areas as necessary.

His 2D pictures were projected onto the 3D geometry of the terrain. To do his 3D work, and being familiar with Softimage, Yanick used that software program rather than the newer XSI package. All of the manmade objects, such as buildings and runways, were built in 3D, along with the cliffs and rock faces. The push-in camera move on the city of Theed came from the previsualization element. The spaceship was CGI, and the waterfalls, including luminance mattes, were extracted from preexisting footage. The God rays in the sky were composed of multiple 3D cards from 2D images. Each God ray card was offset from the next, so when the camera moved, it created the illusion of three-dimensional space.

For this painting, Yanick estimated that 70 percent of the matte painting came from still images and 30 percent was hand painted in Adobe Photoshop. Though a large

percentage of the piece consists of still images, the hand painting ultimately blends, reshapes, and defines the work. The hand painting is the *art* of the process, the veil through which the audience sees the shot and, more important, feels the mood.

In summing up this matte painting of Naboo and all his work in general, Yanick

said, "I try to get as much drama as I can on the screen as quick as I can. Then it becomes simple 3D tricks with pictures, textures, and paintings."

Macros

DEFINITION ▶ The combination of multiple functions into a single new function. In Shake, macros let you control what parameters are exposed and hide parameters that don't need to be changed.

SEE ALSO ▶ Sample Shake macros on accompanying DVD

Mask

DEFINITION ▶ An application of a matte, usually used to limit or constrain an effect. More broadly, an image, clip, or shape used to define areas of transparency in another clip. Compositors, for example, commonly mask specific areas to be color corrected while leaving the rest of the image untouched.

In the process of masking, a matte is used to determine where a certain effect will be applied and where the source image will remain unaffected. The mask acts like an external alpha channel.

SEE ALSO ▶ alpha channel; depth keying; difference matte; Keying Fundamentals chapter; matte

Master Shot

DEFINITION ▶ A single, long shot of dramatic action into which shorter cuts, such as close-ups and medium shots, are placed in order to fill out the story.

Matchmoving

DEFINITION ▶ A compositing technique that uses tracking data to create identical movement in foreground elements that are being added to a moving background plate. Creates the illusion that the new element is moving with the background.

SEE ALSO ▶ matchmoving in perspective; tracking; Tracking Fundamentals chapter

Matchmoving in Perspective

DEFINITION ▶ The process for matching the movement of a foreground element to movement in a background plate in perspective. The technique usually entails first position and rotation matchmoves, then perspective matchmoves. *Related terms:* corner pin matching; display replacement; sign replacement

SEE ALSO ▶ perspective match; screen replacement; Tracking Fundamentals chapter

Matchmoving in perspective is used for screen and sign replacements (see screen replacement) and is one of the most common tracking tasks performed by a visual effects compositor. To track the perspective of a plane, you technically need to track only three points, but most compositing packages require four points to perform corner pin translations (one tracked point for each corner of a corner-pinned rectangle).

One of the biggest problems with matchmoving perspective occurs when there aren't four points to track. For an accurate track, the four points must be co-planar (sharing the same flat plane in 3D space) and fixed relative to each other (that is, "glued" to that plane). When four such points are unavailable, you move into the territory of *offset tracking*. For more information on offset tracking, see the Tracking Fundamentals chapter.

TIP ▶ Get to know and love offset tracking. It will make the difference between a difficult shot and an impossible one.

When shooting footage for a perspective matchmove, make sure that four corner points are visible *at all times*. If they aren't, try to add tracking markers close to the points that are becoming obscured.

Procedure

The following exercise is typical for a screen replacement. You'll begin by tracking the screen, then applying the tracking data to a foreground element to replace the screen. The same process could be used to replace a sign or any other planar element.

The procedure is laid out here for Shake, but the process in After Effects is the same in principle: Choose Animation > Track Motion from After Effects' main menu, then choose a perspective corner pin track type. Read the After Effects tracking documentation for specifics on how to operate the tracking system.

1   Position the tracking markers. Be sure to keep the order of the points counterclockwise from track point 1 to track point 4 (if you don't want your track ending up like a Möbius strip).

In the current track, the right edge of the laptop screen is obscured at frame 1, so you'll begin at frame 150 and track backward.

SHAKE ▼

Open **APTS_CycVFX/ProjectFiles/Tracking/Perspective/ Start.shk**. Locate frame 150. Attach a Transform > Stabilize (subPixelResolution = 1/256) to the Main node. Set the trackType to 4 pt. Align the four onscreen tracking controls to the four corners of the laptop.

2   It's now time to track. Since you've already seen that the right side of the laptop is off-screen at frame 1, you know that the track will fail at some point. Be prepared to stop the track (by pressing the Esc key) as soon as things go awry.

SHAKE ▼

In the Viewer shelf controls, click the Track Backward button .

Press the Esc key to stop the track when the tracking points to the right of the laptop screen are no longer aligned with the corners of the screen.

If you left your pattern and search regions at their defaults, you probably found that the track turned bad around about frame 63. It's time to take evasive action.

3   The most important step in a good offset track is to back up to the last good frame—the last time the track point was correctly aligned with its target. Back up to a point after that, and you're in trouble. You'll end up with a kink in your tracking data.

SHAKE ▼

Use the right arrow key to step backward to the point at which the tracked points are clearly traveling in concert with the corners being tracked. If in doubt, back up an extra frame. It's better to overlap the track sessions than to leave errant tracking data in your Timeline.

4   You can now enter offset tracking mode and identify appropriate alternative targets. It's essential that the replacement points be as close to the originals as possible to reduce distortion of the final corner pin. To create a good track, it's also important that the new tracking target have high contrast, so this will dictate just how close you can get to the original target.

SHAKE ▼

In the Viewer shelf, click the Offset Track button 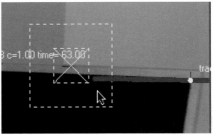.

Move the pattern regions of the two rightmost tracking markers to new tracking features that will be present onscreen at frame 1. Click the Track Backward button to resume the track.

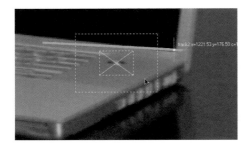

You should now be able to track all the way to frame 1.

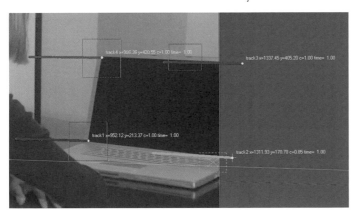

5   Although you'll be performing a matchmove operation, the easiest way to test the accuracy of tracking data is to perform a stabilization. You can do this using the fingernail test: While the stabilized footage is playing back, position a finger over each corner (or the mouse pointer—fewer marks on the display that way). You'll quickly be able to identify any drift that's occurring. If there's drift, then you have a bad track. The remedy for a bad track is (A) to track again, or (B) to apply a corner pin after the stabilization and keyframe it manually to realign the corners anytime they stray. Option B is messy, so at least give option A some serious effort before giving up.

Step-by-Step

In the current shot, you'll need to set the reference frame to 150 instead of the default, frame 1. The reference frame determines the initial perspective to which all other frames are forced to conform; that is, all other frames are corner-pinned in such a way that their tracked corners match the reference frame. If you leave the default at frame 1, the laptop will be stabilized partially offscreen (as it appears at frame 1). By setting the reference frame to 150, you'll see the entire laptop in all frames (although it obviously will be cropped at the earlier frames in which the camera didn't capture the full laptop display).

Remember to ignore the bizarre shaking of the rest of the image. You simply want to ensure that the laptop screen remains stabilized to a fixed perspective.

TIP ▶ In Shake, if you've got a decent track but want to try for a better one, copy and paste the original tracking node (in this case, a Stabilize node). That way, if you screw things up, you can always throw away the copy and go back to the untouched original.

SHAKE ▼

In the parameters for Stabilize1, set the refFrame to 150 and activate applyTransform. Launch a flipbook and perform the fingernail test.

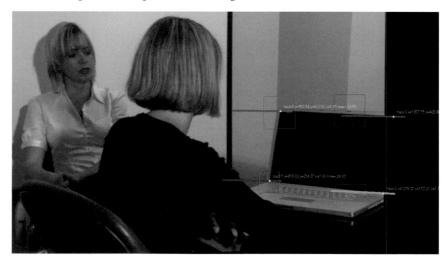

6   Now set up the replacement graphic. Begin by corner-pinning the graphic to the screen.

SHAKE ▼

Move to frame 150. Add a Color > SetAlpha to Screenshot. (The SetAlpha creates an alpha channel so you can use an Over node to composite the image.) Add a Transform > CornerPin to SetAlpha1. While still accessing the parameters for CornerPin1, load Main into the Viewer. Move the corners of the corner pin's onscreen controls to align with the corners of the laptop screen. You may need to zoom out of the Viewer to initially access the corners of the onscreen controls.

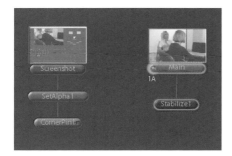

7   The final step before the composite is to apply the tracking data to the foreground screen shot. The tracking data is currently attached to the background clip, Main, acting as a stabilization. You need to move it and change its role.

Step-by-Step

SHAKE ▼

From Main, extract Stabilize1 and attach it to the output of CornerPin1. In the parameters for Stabilize1, set the inverseTransform to match.

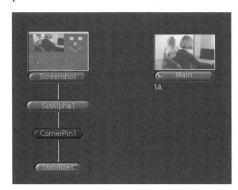

The CornerPin1 node establishes an initial matching perspective for Screenshot, and the Stabilize1 node makes sure that Screenshot always keeps up with perspective changes occurring to the laptop in Main.

8   Now, of course, you composite.

SHAKE ▼

Add a Layer > Over to Stabilize1. Connect Main to the second (background) input of Over1.

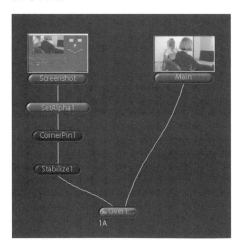

And there's your perspective match.

Going Further

Matching the perspective is just the beginning of this procedure. With the graphic matched to the laptop, you must add the effects necessary to make the composite convincing. These effects include camera diffusion simulation, grain matching, adding specular screen glare, and bedding the edges of the graphic. (See also screen replacement.)

Matte

DEFINITION ▶ An image that controls the opacity of another image.

SEE ALSO ▶ alpha channel; clamping mattes; difference matte; edge matte; edge matte/core matte; garbage matte; holdout matte; inverse core garbage matting; Keying Fundamentals chapter; mask; mattes, combining; mattes, shrinking and expanding

Matte Painting

DEFINITION ▶ An image used as a way to fill in detail in a shot without building those elements on a practical set. Often used for set extension, where the foreground areas are built as a practical set, then distant mountains and buildings are added via the painting. Foreground objects are also occasionally included on the matte painting. Originally hand painted, matte paintings are now frequently a combination of hand painting, 3D rendering, and cloning of real-world photography. For more on matte painting, see Yannick Dusseault's "The Art of Matte Painting," on page 339. *Related term:* set extension

Mattes, Combining

DEFINITION ▶ Techniques to combine two or more mattes into a single new matte, using various blend modes such as Add, Screen, and Difference blending. *Related terms:* adding mattes; maxing mattes; merging mattes; screening mattes

Creating a good matte often requires combining smaller ones. Several methods are in common use.

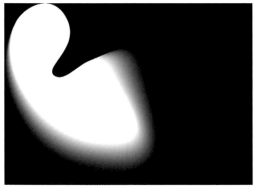

Sample matte 1   Sample matte 2

Adding Mattes

Using an IAdd in Shake or the Add blending mode (also known as the *transfer mode*) in After Effects and Motion will simply sum the pixels of two mattes. The result will be a combined matte, but soft edge detail may be clipped. This is generally not the best technique for combining mattes, although it can be used on the rare occasion that a matte requires float data.

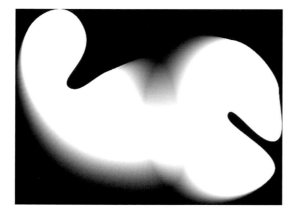

Screening Mattes

Screening mattes (using Screen in Shake or the Screen blend mode in After Effects and Motion) is one of the best methods for combining mattes, as it gracefully builds up bright areas without any harsh clipping. First, make sure the input mattes are clamped to remove float values, because the screen operator's math will not work correctly in float. (See clamping mattes.)

Maxing Mattes

A Max operation is a great way to combine mattes without affecting soft edge detail. Rather than building up soft edge areas as a Screen operation does, the soft edge resulting from a Max operation is only as bright as the brightest of the original image pixels.

Subtracting Mattes

Subtracting one matte from another (using an ISub in Shake, or the Difference blending mode in After Effects and Motion) effectively cuts a hole in one matte using another matte. Again, make sure you've clamped any float values before performing this operation. Negative values in your blacks will add to the matte, which you almost certainly do not want to happen.

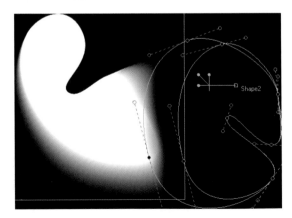

Mattes, Shrinking and Expanding

DEFINITION ▶ Resizing mattes to accommodate problems such as 4:2:2 artifacts, excess spill, and gray pixels. Includes *choking* (the process of removing unwanted pixels at the edge of a matte). *Related terms:* choking mattes; dilate/erode mattes; resizing mattes

SEE ALSO ▶ chroma blur; difference matte; edge matte/core matte

A typical DV key with edge artifacts

The same DV key with a choked (shrunk) matte. (OK, and a little chroma blur to clean up.)

In a perfect world, you'd take a matte, use it to composite your foreground over your background, and end up with a flawless final shot. This is not a perfect world. (For more information, see taxes, death and.) Mattes frequently need to be expanded or shrunk to best fit the final composite.

Many issues require mattes to be choked (shrunk). These include unwanted fringe pixels resulting from sharpening in blue and green screens, chrominance subsampling artifacts (keying from 4:2:2, 4:1:1, and so on), and edge matte/core matte.

Poor keying techniques, or being forced to compensate for extreme grain and other noise, may generate a matte that is too tight for the subject being composited. Using the matte would result in the edges of the foreground object being cropped out. The solution is to expand the matte. Note that this may also introduce unwanted background, so it's worthwhile to try generating a more accurate key before resorting to matte expansion.

When expanding and choking mattes, it's highly desirable to perform subpixel increments and decrements. That is, changes to the matte should occur in fractions of pixels, rather than in discrete steps.

Using Blur to Modify the Matte

A simple approach to resizing the edge of a matte is to blur and contrast. In this approach, the matte is blurred slightly to create a wider soft edge than in the original.

SHAKE ▼

Open **APTS_CycVFX/ProjectFiles/Keying/Choke/GingyStart.shk**. Apply a Blur node (xPixels = 5) to Gingy.

MOTION ▼

Open **APTS_CycVFX/ProjectFiles/Keying/Choke/GingyStart.motn**. Add a Filter > Gaussian Blur (Amount = 1) to Gingy.

AFTER EFFECTS ▼

Open **APTS_CycVFX/ProjectFiles/Keying/Choke/GingyStart.aep**. Add a Blur & Sharpen > Gaussian Blur filter (Blurriness = 1.0) to Gingy.png.

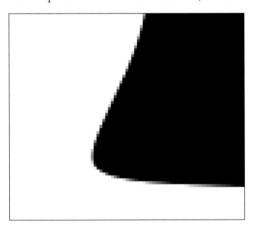 

This creates some play in the edge. A contrast adjustment is then used to pull the midtone grays closer to black, tightening the edge and shrinking it in the process.

SHAKE ▼

Use a ContrastLum (center = 1, softClip = 0.3). Adjust the value parameter until the edge tightens to match the original edge width. You can then adjust the center parameter up to vary the amount of expansion.

MOTION ▼

Use the Levels filter and push the black point closer to the white point, consequently crushing the grays to black. Move up until the edge tightens to match the original edge width.

AFTER EFFECTS ▼

Use the Levels filter and push the black point closer to the white point, consequently crushing the grays to black. Move up until the edge tightens to match the original edge width.

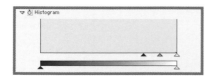

The original edge

The edge after blur and contrast adjustments

This technique works well for modest edge reductions with well-defined edges. It does *not* work so well with edges that possess a high degree of edge softness before the operation.

Here the same settings as used with the previous figures successfully trim the hard edges, but they produce an unwanted haircut at the same time.

Expanding the Matte Using Blur and Contrast

To expand the matte, simply perform the contrast adjustment in the reverse direction, pushing the mid-grays toward white.

SHAKE ▼

Set the ContrastLum's center. Adjust the value parameter until the edge tightens to match the original edge width. You can then adjust the center parameter down to vary the amount of expansion.

MOTION ▼

Use the Levels filter and push the black point closer to the white point, consequently crushing the grays to black.

AFTER EFFECTS ▼

Use the Levels filter and push the black point closer to the white point, consequently crushing the grays to black.

Again, the technique works well for subtle adjustments but has dramatic effects on initially soft edges.

Using DilateErode to Modify the Matte

A more accurate way to expand and shrink mattes is to use a DilateErode node in Shake. This analyzes pixels, and expands or reduces the matte based on the pixels specified.

> **TIP** To speed up the DilateErode, set the Channels field to include only the channels you need to modify. For example, if you're only shrinking the alpha channel, set Channels to "a."

A major limitation of DilateErode is that it chokes and expands in discrete, single-pixel increments. That is, it is *not* a subpixel operator. I know what the Shake docs say: turn on the "soften" option. Unfortunately it doesn't do what you'd expect. (Please feel free to try.)

The solution is to blend between two instances of DilateErode nodes set a single pixel apart to create in-between edges. This won't animate well, so if you need to animate the erosion, use the blur/contrast method instead. See the macro SubDilateErode (**APTS_CycVFX/Macros/SubDilateErode.h** and **SubDilateErodeUI.h**) for an example.

DilateErode successfully trims Gingy's edges without causing any significant damage to his stylish coiffure.

Motion Tracking

DEFINITION ▶ A technique that involves selecting a particular region of an image and analyzing its motion over time.

SEE ALSO ▶ Tracking Fundamentals chapter

Motion Vector Pass

DEFINITION ► A method of using mattes rendered from a 3D application to encode the horizontal and vertical velocity of pixels in an image. Motion vectors can also be derived for live action footage using optical flow algorithms. *Related terms:* vector pass; velocity pass

Motion vector passes typically use the red channel to encode the horizontal speed of a pixel from one frame to the next; they encode the vertical speed of a pixel in the green channel.

A motion vector in its raw form doesn't seem to have much going on:

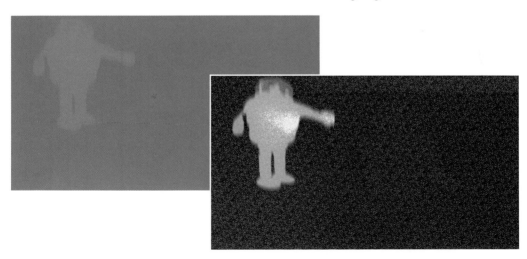

After a compression color correction is applied, however, the pixel motion becomes much more obvious.

Motion vectors are typically fed into other filters to produce special effects. They can be fed into warp and displacement filters to create "time ripples" or used on particles to have them change color with kinetic energy, among other surreal techniques. However, they are most commonly used to create a smooth motion blur during the compositing stage.

Motion blur is extremely render intensive in 3D applications, and it usually produces distinct steps rather than a smooth blur in the resulting image. To achieve the smoothness of a real motion blur, render times must increase dramatically.

Motion vectors can be used to create a smooth motion blur in the postrendering stage. The trick is, you do not render the image from your 3D application with no blur. Rather, you should apply motion blur with a minimal number of render passes, then use the compositing application to smooth the passes into the final blur.

Rendering with no blur produces all kinds of complications at object borders and around transparencies. It's much wiser to work with some initial blur, albeit unpleasantly stepped.

Applying the Motion Vector Pass
Motion blur can be created using generic filters, but these methods usually fall prey to the same kinds of stepping artifacts found in 3D motion-blurred renders. For this particular case, you really need to call in an expert.

A good expert plug-in for the job is RE:Vision Effects' ReelSmart Motion Blur (www. revisionfx.com). ReelSmart uses the motion vector pass to apply a smooth blurring to the supplied image. The RE:Vision site even contains white papers on setting up motion vector passes in your 3D renderer of choice.

Multipass Compositing

DEFINITION ▶ Compositing using multiple render passes (*multipass rendering*), rather than a single render pass.

The advantage of using multiple passes is that it gives you more flexibility to isolate, manipulate, and adjust the lighting of disparate elements in a composited scene.

Typically, multipass rendering breaks up renders into four separate passes—the diffuse, specular, reflection, and shadow passes.

SEE ALSO ▶ multipass, basic passes; multipass, per light

Multipass, Basic Passes

DEFINITION ▶ Techniques for rendering and compositing the four basic render passes—diffuse, specular, reflection, and shadow—that are commonly used in multipass compositing.

SEE ALSO ▶ multipass, per light

Diffuse pass   Specular pass   Reflection pass   Shadow pass

A multipass rendering can be diced in many ways, but four passes are of primary importance: diffuse, specular, reflection, and shadow. After those four passes, you can create additional passes as necessary.

NOTE ▶ It's a good idea to become acquainted with a multipass rendering plug-in or utility for your 3D software. Free utilities are available in most 3D animation communities, and there are several more robust commercial products. Many of these products enable you to break scenes into multiple passes with a few mouse clicks, and once some time is spent creating the initial passes, future scenes can be rendered with a minimum of hassle.

In the real world, there's no true distinction between diffuse light, specular light, and reflective light bouncing off an object toward an observer. It's all the same light. Depending on the surface properties of an object, however, some light will scatter, some will gather, and some will reflect perfectly (more on this in the following sections). For simplicity, most 3D rendering engines treat these as distinct actions. That is, the diffuse, specular, and reflective light bounces are calculated independently. This is perfect for multipass compositing, since isolating each computation allows you to adjust the mixture of the components, altering the perceived surface qualities of a given object in the scene.

Diffuse Pass

The diffuse pass represents the basic shading and color information of a scene. *Diffuse* refers to the light scattered by an object's surface when it bounces off that object. Scattered light produces no visible reflection. A good example of a completely diffuse surface is felt; the uneven texture of the felt causes light to scatter off the surface in random directions rather than bounce in a concentrated, straight line.

Rendering a Diffuse Pass

The method used to render a diffuse pass will depend on the software used. Most 3D renderers will allow you to turn the diffuse and specular components on and off for each light. To create a diffuse pass, turn off the specular component of each light to be rendered, and make sure no scene reflections will be rendered. (That is usually simply a matter of turning off ray tracing, but you must make sure no environment reflection maps are being used.)

When creating a diffuse pass, it's important to understand the distinction between *self shadows* and *cast shadows*. Self shadowing results when an object casts shadows back onto itself. It's certainly possible in most 3D applications to render this out in a separate pass, but for most multipass composites it's easier to

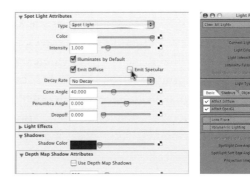

Sample parameters from Maya (left) and LightWave (right).

simply incorporate these shadows into the diffuse pass. This will automatically occur with the diffuse setup just described.

> **NOTE** ▶ Some software packages have a single-button option for each type of pass. While these can be dramatic time-savers, make sure the output is as intended—the default settings often yield unsatisfactory results, especially when combined with ray-traced reflections and refractions.

Specular Pass

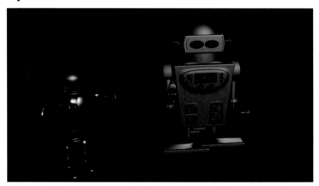

Specular, or semireflective, surfaces "gather" light at specific locations, referred to as *specular highlights*. The size and intensity of these highlights vary from surface to surface. Specular surfaces include metallics, glass, plastic, and glossy paint.

Rendering a Specular Pass

Rendering a specular pass is essentially the opposite of rendering a diffuse pass. Simply turn off the diffuse contribution of each lighting source and leave on the specular contri-

bution. Depending on the shaders (textures) used for your models, you may need to turn ray tracing on for some specular effects, but make sure the ray tracing of reflections is *not* turned on. You may wish to render caustic effects with this pass if your scene calls for them.

Reflection Pass

The reflection pass should contain direct reflections from a 3D surface. Whereas the specular properties of a surface gather light to a point, the reflective properties cause light to be reflected in a predictable pattern based on the surface normal of the object. In plain English, these are the mirrorlike reflections.

A typical 3D scene has two kinds of reflections: ray traced and environment mapped. Ray-traced reflections are reflections of the 3D objects in the scene. Environment-mapped reflections (sometimes simply called *reflection maps*) are produced by projecting an image wrapped around a sphere—located at an infinite distance from the objects in the scene— onto the reflective objects in the scene.

These reflection types can be rendered as separate passes, but for convenience and simplicity they are usually rendered together.

Rendering a Reflection Pass

Reflection passes can sometimes be difficult to achieve. In many cases, it's simply a matter of turning off diffuse and specular shading (and ambient lighting if it's on). In some applications, however, reflections may not be rendered if no diffuse lighting is active.

The biggest problem with reflection passes is that they require each object in the scene to be visible to other objects in the scene. Some rendering software packages have difficulties in seeing reflected objects when the diffuse lighting is disabled.

Many 3D rendering engines make the reflection buffer available for export. Use this feature whenever possible, as it will produce the most accurate results. It also requires no additional rendering; if a **beauty pass** is being produced, the reflection buffer can be exported at the same time. Be careful not to confuse the reflection buffer with a reflection *matte*, which will be a grayscale image indicating the reflectivity of objects in the scene and *not* a color image of the reflections.

If all else fails, the following steps will produce an accurate reflection: First, render the diffuse and specular passes. Then, render a beauty pass without the cast shadows (a beauty pass is the full, complete rendering of the scene, not broken into passes). In other words, render the scene as you normally would, but turn off shadows for the scene lights. Then, in the compositor, subtract the diffuse and specular images (see figure below). What remains will be the reflection pass. If all of the components were rendered in float (see **float space** for more information), there should be sufficient color resolution to preserve the data and produce an accurate isolated reflection pass.

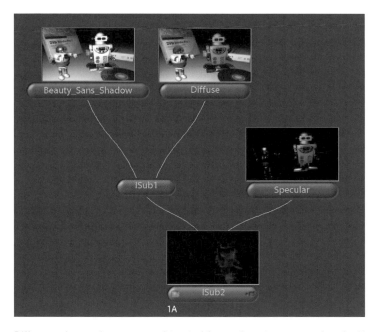

Diffuse and specular passes subtracted from a beauty pass rendered without cast shadows

Shadow Pass

A shadow pass indicates the areas where shadows fall over objects in the scene. For live action integration, create a "dummy" ground plane that matches the topography of the live action surface upon which the 3D object is intended to rest. Note that the shadowed areas appear in white—the wrong color for shadows themselves, but useful as a matte for performing color corrections.

Rendering a Shadow Pass

There are several ways to produce a shadow pass. When possible, use a shadow buffer export to save time, but try to avoid including self shadowing—that should be included in the diffuse pass unless it absolutely must be rendered separately (and if self shadowing must be rendered separately, it should be rendered as a distinct pass to the cast shadows).

If a shadow buffer is unavailable, shadow passes can be produced in the following manner: First, give all the objects in the scene a generic white diffuse surface (although transparencies should still be taken into account). Then, set all the lights in the scene to pure black. Finally, set the shadows of the lights to pure white. This produces a shadow pass in line with that produced by a standard shadow buffer pass.

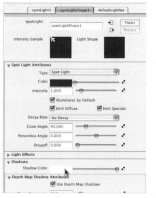

Compositing the Passes

Once the four basic passes have been rendered, it's time to composite them into a single image.

1 Combine the diffuse and specular passes using a simple addition of pixel values.

> **TIP** ▶ While simple addition is being used to combine the specular pass with the diffuse pass, a screen operation may produce a more pleasing result in certain circumstances. Be aware, however, that when working in float space, screening images with pixels outside the normal color range can produce undesirable results.

SHAKE ▼

Open **APTS_CycVFX/ProjectFiles/CG/Multipass/BasicMultipass_Start.shk**. Add a Layer > IAdd node after Key_Diffuse, and connect Key_Specular to the second input.

AFTER EFFECTS ▼

Open **APTS_CycVFX/ProjectFiles/CG/Multipass/BasicMultipass_Start.aep**. Drag Key_Specular from the Project panel to the Timeline panel, positioning it above Key_Diffuse. In the Mode pop-up menu, choose Add.

MOTION ▼

Open **APTS_CycVFX/ProjectFiles/CG/Multipass/BasicMultipass_Start. motn**. Navigate in the File Browser to APTS_CycVFX/ProjectFiles/CG/Multipass/ EightBit. Drag Key_Specular from the File Browser to the Project pane, positioning it above Key_Diffuse. In the Blend Mode pop-up menu, choose Add.

2   Once the diffuse and specular passes are combined, use the same method to add the reflection pass.

SHAKE ▼

Add a Layer > IAdd node after Key_Specular, and connect Key_Reflection to the second input.

AFTER EFFECTS ▼

Drag Key_Reflection from the Project panel to the Timeline panel, positioning it above Key_ Specular. In the Mode pop-up menu, choose Add.

MOTION ▼

Drag Key_Reflection from the File Browser to the Project pane, positioning it above Key_Specular. In the Blend Mode pop-up menu, choose Add.

3   Use subtraction to combine the shadow pass. (There are two primary methods for combining the shadow pass: subtraction and multiplication. Since shadows in the shadow pass appear white, the addition operation used to combine the diffuse, specular, and reflection passes would cause the image to *brighten* in the shadowed regions.)

NOTE ► In the absence of a subtract mode in After Effects, use Multiply with an inverted version of the shadow matte.

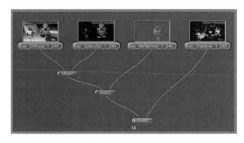

SHAKE ▼

Add a Layer > ISub node after Key_Reflection, and connect Key_Shadow to the second input.

AFTER EFFECTS ▼

Drag Key_Shadow from the Project panel to the Timeline panel, positioning it above Key_ Reflection. Choose Effect > Channel > Invert, then in the Mode pop-up menu choose Multiply.

MOTION ▼

Drag Key_Shadow from the File Browser to the Project pane, positioning it above Key_ Reflection. From the Blend Mode pop-up menu, choose Subtract.

NOTE ▶ Be careful when combining shadow passes generated in float—there may be subzero values hiding in the black regions of the matte. In such cases, only pixels with a value less than 0 should be clamped to 0; pixels with values greater than 1 should keep their values, since these provide greater detail when the shadow intensity is adjusted (see **clamping, subzero**).

In After Effects 7.0, the Invert filter only works in linear space, so it automatically clamped the shadow pass by forcing it to linear space. While this is helpful here, it's not always a good thing (you want your float data preserved wherever possible). After Effects warns you if a filter is clamping your image to linear space by displaying a yellow triangle with an exclamation mark next to the filter name.

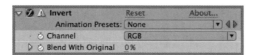

4   Now that the final composite is assembled, you can adjust levels by changing how much of the specular, reflection, and shadow passes are added to the diffuse pass. To adjust the overall level, you can make a global brightness adjustment to all the passes at once.

SHAKE ▼

Adjust the percent slider in the parameters of IAdd1, IAdd2, and ISub1 to modify the levels of the specular, reflection, and shadow passes, respectively. To adjust the overall intensity of the image, add a Color > Brightness node directly after ISub1.

AFTER EFFECTS ▼

Select the Shadow, Reflection, and Specular layers, then press the T key to access the opacity settings of these layers. Adjust as desired. To adjust the overall intensity of the image, precompose the layers, then adjust the opacity of the new nested comp.

MOTION ▼

Click the arrow in the upper right corner of the Project pane and choose Opacity from the pop-up menu. Opacity sliders will be added for each pass and can be adjusted as desired. To adjust the overall intensity of the image, adjust the opacity of the master layer.

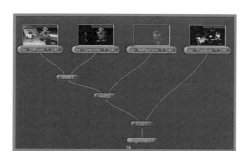

Multipass, per Light

DEFINITION ▶ A rendering technique in which multiple renders are made of each light or group of lights in a scene.

Per light multipass enables the extreme relighting of scenes without the need to re-render them. In many ways, it's the equivalent of an interactive preview renderer (IPR) in a 3D application, but with complete anti-aliasing and surface detail.

SEE ALSO ▶ multipass, basic passes

The same scene relit during compositing. No re-rendering was required to produce the various results.

Surface properties of the two robots are altered without re-rendering the scene.

To perform a per light multipass composite, you'll first break down the scene into lighting groups, then render each group as a separate set of basic passes (see multipass, basic passes).

Grouping Passes

In a classic three-light staging—with a key light, a fill light, and a rim light (also known as a backlight)—the setup is simple: Each of the three lights is rendered into the four basic passes. In more complex scenes, however, there may be dozens or even hundreds of lights. In such situations, it's impractical and inefficient to create a group of rendering passes for each light. Instead, several lights can be grouped together for a single set of passes.

TIP If your rim light is extremely subtle, you might get away with only rendering a diffuse and specular pass. In situations with minor rim light, the reflections are usually taken care of by other light sources, and the shadows actually detract from the scene rather than enhancing it.

Consider a situation in which a CGI character is to be composited over a lawn on a sunny day. To simulate the bounce lighting of the grass on the underside of the character, five or six green lights may have been pointed upward from ground level. Since all of these lights are creating the same effect, it would make sense to consider them as a single light source and render a single set of passes for them.

Be careful when grouping lights into passes: make sure you have no need to vary the intensity of the individual lights inside the group. Once the group is rendered, the intensity of the lights inside the group relative to each other can't be modified.

TIP If you really need to make changes to the intensity of a light that was rendered as part of a group of lights, you can go back and re-render a pass with just that light. You can then add that light to the final composite for individual control of that single lighting source. If it was rendered in **float,** you'll even be able to subtract the new light's passes from the original comp, thereby reducing the intensity of the light relative to the rest of the group.

Neutralizing Lights Before Rendering

While scene lighting is often developed and adjusted within the 3D application itself, it makes sense to neutralize this lighting if the scene is going to be composited using a multipass setup in a compositing package. To do this, simply set the color of the lights back to pure white. If the lights within a group vary in color, though, it's wiser to make an exception and leave them set at their distinct colors; once they're rendered, it will be impossible to assign separate colors to the lights inside the group, since the compositing application will only be able to color correct the group as a whole.

The three light sources of this scene have been neutralized in preparation for their manipulation during compositing.

When neutralizing the color of the lights, it's important to take note of the original colors; these colors can be reintroduced using color correction in the compositing stage.

Combining Passes

Once passes have been generated for each of the lights (or groups of lights), they are simply added together to produce the final composite. The relative intensities of the groups can then be adjusted to relight the scene. If the color of the lights has been neutralized, it can also be easily modified as desired.

Changing Object Properties

The original image

Left robot with modified diffuse color

Right robot with reduced specularity and modified diffuse color

One of the most important features of multipass compositing is the ease with which you can modify the surface properties of individual objects. You can easily single out objects and adjust their color, reflectivity, and specularity as desired. Doing so requires adding matte passes for each object, a relatively simple task for most modern 3D applications.

An example of a matte pass.

Production Considerations

When deciding whether to render a scene using per light multipass, it's important to ask the following questions:

▶ Is the rendered 3D content going to be incorporated into a live action background? If this is the case, it may be better to render each object as a group of separate passes. This way, rotoscoped live action elements can be composited *in between* the 3D objects.

▶ Is there going to be much depth-of-field simulation? If so, portions of the scene at different depths should be rendered as discrete elements to allow for more realistic defocus blurring. (Alternatively, background hole filling can be attempted instead.)

▶ Are there overlapping transparent surfaces through which a live action background should be visible or refracted? In such cases it's usually better to render objects separately.

Even in situations where objects must be rendered separately, it is still possible to employ per light multipass. However, since it will be performed for each object, the scene's complexity will increase exponentially, so this use is justified only when exacting control of scene elements is required.

Procedure: Relighting a Multipass Scene   <kbd>S</kbd> <kbd>AE</kbd>

Once each group of lighting passes has been assembled and the resulting comps added together, color-correction operations can be performed to modify the scene lighting.

1   Begin by setting up the scene with a blue key light and complementary colors for the rim and fill lights.

NOTE ▶ The Shake version of this tutorial requires that the Multipass macro (included on the included DVD) is installed on your system.

SHAKE ▼

Open **APTS_CycVFX/ProjectFiles/CG/Multipass/PerLightMultipass_Start. shk**. Set the following values: Key_MPass (Light Color = 0.14, 0.14, 0.7, masterLevel = 1), Fill_MPass (Light Color = 0.5, 0.26, 0.15, masterLevel = 0.7), Rim_MPass (Light Color = 0.19, 0.5, 0.16, masterLevel = 0.4).

AFTER EFFECTS ▼

Open **APTS_CycVFX/ProjectFiles/CG/Multipass/PerLightMultipass_Start. aep**. Set the opacity for Rim_Comp, Fill_Comp, and Key_Comp to *40%, 70%,* and *100%*, respectively. In the Levels Effect Controls pane for Rim_Comp, set Red Output White to *0.19*, Green Output White to *0.5*, and Blue Output White to *0.16*. In the Levels Effect Controls pane for Fill_Comp, set Red Output White to *0.5*, Green Output White to *0.26*, and Blue Output White to *0.15*. In the Levels Effect Controls pane for Key_Comp, set Red Output White to *0.14*, Green Output White to *0.14*, and Blue Output White to *0.7*.

NOTE ▶ Adjusting the Output White isn't exactly the easiest way to modify color in After Effects, but at least the Levels filter doesn't clamp the images down to linear space. At time of writing, most of the more convenient color correctors in After Effects 7 only operated in linear space. See the note in the "Compositing the Passes" section of the technique **multipass, basic passes** for more information on After Effects' handling of float by its filters.

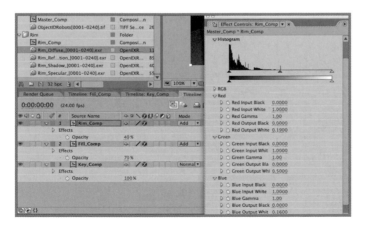

2   The light levels are adjusted, but notice that multiple shadows are visible for each light. In the real world, multiple shadows are the bane of the photographer. In the digital world, we can easily select which lights will contribute shadows and which won't.

SHAKE ▼

Open Light Properties in Fill_MPass, and set the shadowLevel to *0.15*. Set the shad-owLevel for Rim_MPass to *0.2*.

AFTER EFFECTS ▼

In the Fill_Comp, set the Opacity of Fill_Shadow to *15%*. In Rim_Comp, set the Opacity of Rim_Shadow to *20%*.

The shadows are now comfortably modified. If the scene requires relighting, it's simply a matter of adjusting the levels and color corrections to create a new look. Feel free to experiment.

Procedure: Modifying Object Properties

So far you've been able to change the lighting of a scene without re-rendering. But what if some of the properties of an object's surface change? In such cases the use of a matte pass can enable dramatic modifications to the surfaces of objects, again without re-rendering.

NOTE ▶ It must be mentioned that while multipass techniques allow the modification of light intensities and color without re-rendering, a change in the positions of lights will necessarily require a fresh render. A work-around for this is to use **surface normal lighting**.

A matte can be used to isolate the color correction of a given pass (diffuse, specular, reflection, or shadow) to a specific area of the image. In the following exercise, you'll modify the color of the left robot. A matte in exactly the same shape as the robot will mask the color correction so that only the robot is modified, not the entire scene. Different properties can be adjusted by color correcting different passes. To reduce the specularity of an object's surface, for example, the specular pass could be darkened in that area of the scene.

It's important that the identical color correction is performed on all light groups to achieve a true surface change. The effect is illustrated here in Shake for simplicity. In After Effects, duplicate copies of each layer would be required, making the implementation possible but somewhat cumbersome.

1   Apply a color correction to the diffuse channels of the image, since this is the channel in which basic surface-color information lives.

SHAKE ▼

Add a Color > Mult node to the Key_Diffuse. Copy this Mult node and paste a linked version (Command-Shift-V) into a vacant area of the node view. Connect the linked version directly after Fill_Diffuse. Paste a second linked version and connect it directly after Rim_Diffuse.

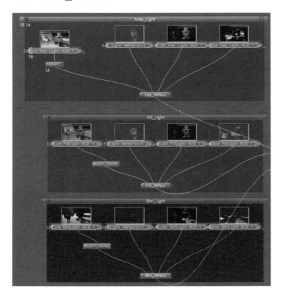

2 Before applying the color correction, you need to mask off the area on the small robot where the color correction will be applied.

SHAKE ▼

Add a Color > Reorder node (channels = "rgbr") after ObjectIDRobots. Connect Reorder1 to the side mask input of the three Mult nodes added in the previous step.

3 Modify the color. You'll need to adjust the color only in the first Mult, since the others are linked.

SHAKE ▼

Set Mult1's RGB values to *0.6, 0.6,* and *1.3.* The robot is now tinted blue.

MultiPlane Compositing

DEFINITION ▶ The process of compositing 2D layers in a 3D space. A virtual camera, similar to those found in 3D animation packages, controls the view of the output image. This camera can be animated by keyframing parameters or by importing 3D camera and tracking data from third-party programs.

Nest

DEFINITION ▶ To place a layer into another layer so that it effectively acts as a single object in the new layer.

Neutralizing Black and White Points

DEFINITION ▶ The process of removing color bias from black and white points in preparation for a key. Also useful for correcting day scenes shot with tungsten film and the reverse. *Related term:* stock fixing

If you've worked exclusively in the video world, you're probably familiar with white-balancing problems. It's also an issue for film since there are different film stocks for shooting in daylight, at night, or inside using tungsten lighting. From time to time, some-one loads the camera with the wrong kind of film for the shoot going on, throwing off the color of the entire shot. The solution? Neutralize.

One of the most important parts of keying is successfully integrating the keyed fore-ground element into the color space of its new background. You can get things off to a good start by neutralizing the black and white points of the shot before pulling the key.

Whether you're encountering this problem in film or video, the following technique should help clear up the shot.

TIP ▶ This technique is very easy, but clients will often come to you terrified that they'll need to reshoot and will perceive your fix as a miracle. Charge accordingly.

Expand the Shot

The first step is to perform an expand operation. In After Effects and Motion, you can use the Levels operator to perform the task, but you'll need to adjust the R, G, and B levels separately.

Then add a slice tool. In Shake, make sure you have the UberSlice macro installed (included with this book's DVD) and add one (an UberSlice node, for example) from the Other tab. In the Viewer, position the two crosshairs to create a line through a white area of the shot (or at least something that should be white). Try to slice a section that's away from the blue screen or green screen border to avoid biasing your results with excessive spill.

NOTE ▶ This technique works only if there are true whites and blacks (or at least light and dark grays) in the shot. If there aren't, you're back to best-guessing. Remember to shoot a reference card next time.

In the figure above, notice that the three colors are separated. In true white (or gray) the three colors would overlap. The solution here is to adjust the blue and green of the expand's high color to match the red level. Always try to move the lowest two colors up to meet the highest, unless the distances are extreme; in such situations you risk developing banding in the shot. Looking at the UberSlice node, you can adjust the levels of the high color until the three graph curves align.

Now that the white is neutralized, move the UberSlice crosshairs to slice through a black region in the image, preferably the darkest.

> **TIP** ▶ A common mistake when sampling black points is to sample the darkest pixel in the image. This may actually be a pixel in the matte box of a masked image, or a pure black border introduced during some intermediate standards conversion. Instead, make sure your selected black point is part of the actual shot that will be seen by the audience.

This time, adjust the colors down to meet the lowest of the three curves. Make the adjustments to the expand's low color.

TIP If the black level is close to pure 0 (as it is in the figure above), be careful not to clip your other channels as you adjust them down.

With that done, remove the UberSlice and you should have a much more natural-looking tint to your shot.

Nonsquare Pixel

DEFINITION ► A pixel whose height is different from its width. An NTSC pixel is taller than it is wide, and a PAL pixel is wider than it is tall.

SEE ALSO ► aspect ratio; pixel aspect ratio

NTSC

DEFINITION ► Stands for *National Television Standards Committee*, which developed the color transmission system used in the United States. The standard of color TV broadcasting used mainly in North America, Mexico, and Japan, consisting of 525 lines per frame, 29.97 frames per second, and 720 × 486 pixels per frame (720 × 480 for DV). Compare with PAL.

NTSC Legal

DEFINITION ► The range of color that can be broadcast free of distortion according to the NTSC standards, with maximum allowable video at 100 IRE units and black at 7.5 IRE units.

Offset Tracking

DEFINITION ▶ A tracking process that is used when the tracking reference pattern becomes obscured. With offset tracking, the track point follows the same path, but a new search region and reference pattern are used to acquire the tracking data.

SEE ALSO ▶ screen replacement; Tracking Fundamentals chapter

Opacity

DEFINITION ▶ The degree to which an image is transparent, allowing images behind it to show through. An opacity of 0 percent means an object is invisible; an opacity of 100 percent means the object is completely opaque.

OpenEXR

DEFINITION ▶ A data-storage file format invented by Industrial Light & Magic. OpenEXR is known as a *half float* format, meaning that it represents images using floating-point information, but also makes allowances to reduce file size.

OpenEXR is a popular format for HDRI images, and it is also used to hold other floating-point information in multipass rendering pipelines.

SEE ALSO ▶ float space; HDRI; radiance

Cameo

The Sands of *Jarhead*— Martin Rosenberg

IN SAM MENDES'S FILM *Jarhead*, Corporal Swofford (Jake Gyllenhaal) has a nightmare in which he enters a latrine and sees his girlfriend's face in a mirror. He's so distressed that he vomits rivers of sand, filling an entire sink.

To reinforce the nightmarish mood, the effect needed to look surreal, with sand shooting out of the actor's mouth in a constant stream, like water from a fire hose—a challenge for an effects team at Industrial Light & Magic (see Contributors: Martin Rosenberg, page v).

Finding sand in northern California that was the right size and color to pass for desert sand was difficult in itself, without adding the burden of finding smaller material that could pass for sand in a miniature. So we chose to shoot this element as a full-size event.

> **NOTE** ▶ Many fine powders like fuller's earth or microballoons will pass as miniature ground cover if they don't move; but when powders like fuller's earth fall, they tend to float, and microballoons don't have the edge finesse of falling sand.

The plate has a close-up of Swofford as he sees his girlfriend's image in the mirror. Just as he throws up, the camera tilts down to the sink as it fills with sand. The timing of the sand coming out of his mouth and the start of the camera tilt onstage would have to be perfect, or another take would be required. One possible solution for this would be to build a motion-control rig that controlled the sand-delivery system and the effects camera.

Rather than burning take after take for the sake of this timing alone or investing in an expensive motion-control rig, another option was available. Industrial Light & Magic uses the VistaVision format. The VistaVision frame is approximately twice the size of a normal motion picture frame. The choice was made to use a VistaVision camera that was rolled 90 degrees on its side and, in postproduction, to perform a pan-and-scan down the larger VistaVision negative to match the original camera move.

> **NOTE** ▶ VistaVision's vertical measurement is approximately the same as a standard motion picture camera's horizontal measurement.

Therefore, on the day of the shoot, we only had to concentrate on sand action and lighting. We purchased a sink similar to the one used on set and painted it blue. We put this in front of a blue screen and lined it up exactly with the plate. We built a sand-delivery device out of 2-inch PVC, cut to a length that could hold enough sand to fill the sink, and then fitted a spill-proof trap door to the delivery end. The device was attached to a pipe rig that could be moved by hand to give the sand the articulation it needed to match Swofford's head motion.

We positioned the device above the blue sink the same distance above the sink as the actor's head, matched the complex broken gridwork lighting on the sink, and also lit the path of the sand. With this setup, the only performance variations would be the volume and speed of the sand. We dumped ten different-sized streams with different motion added at the moment of release to give the director a choice of footage.

The actor's mouth was rotoscoped, and our live element was tracked to fit the mouth. The live action camera tilt was matchmoved, and we used the move data to scan down the larger VistaVision negative in order to lock our element to the plate. Using the larger-format negative on its side, and a postproduction 2D move across the sand element, we turned this shoot into a task that involved a few hours instead of a full day of shooting and rig building.

Another *Jarhead* shot presented us with a completely different set of choices. We had to shoot an airport in Iraq being leveled by American bombers. Choosing to do a miniature shoot was easy in this case; the dilemma was that time and budget restrictions made a composite shot undesirable.

Our supervisor, Pablo Helman, knew that a lot of fine, wispy gray smoke against a blue screen would create a time-consuming compositing job. Though the shot was finally used only as a reflection in a pane of glass, at the time we had to make sure the shot worked on the large screen.

Pablo decided to shoot it against a real sky. That sounded good, but if we plopped the miniature on the ground behind ILM, our best view would include plenty of northern California in the background. After a search, we realized there wasn't anywhere in the Bay Area that could give us an unobstructed view of the sky and remain a practical place to shoot.

Returning our focus to the backyard at ILM, a quick calculation told me we needed to shoot at 3:30 p.m. to match the lighting in the surrounding footage. The best shooting position for that time of day was under some high-tension lines that included views of a Cyclone fence, the Richmond–San Rafael Bridge, and the East Bay hills. So the challenge was how to eliminate these obstacles.

The 8-foot-tall Cyclone fence was fairly easy to eliminate. I knew we could easily and inexpensively rent some metal truck containers and raise up our set 10 feet. Deeper in the backlot, I found a couple of discarded, barely acceptable, sunworn 20-by-40-foot platforms made out of plywood and Trus Joist. This wood base gave us something we could anchor the set to and then paint with the proper color.

Our set was raised just over 11 feet, enough to get our view above the Cyclone fence. The 300-foot-high Richmond–San Rafael Bridge, about two miles away, and the 900-foot East Bay hills, another five miles away, weren't so easy to overlook. When we used the appropriate lens at the properly scaled distance and height, the 11-foot rise didn't come close to eliminating the higher obstacles in the distance.

While standing on a ladder by the camera, I began to ponder a slight rotation of the set. Normally, the last thing you want to do is mess with Mother Nature and gravity; but after doing some math, it turned out that a 3- to 4-degree rotation would just barely hide the bridge and distant hills. If we precisely positioned the set at the needed pitch, we could keep the overhead high-tension lines out of the shot and avoid the higher obstacles.

Gravity was the only real issue. I reasoned that the debris thrown forward would appear to fall slightly more at us than in the original setup, and the smoke drifting backward would appear to be hitting a slight downdraft. Both were completely acceptable events. We ended up building a one-sixth scale miniature that was 80 feet wide and stood about 12 feet high at the control tower. The camera and the set world were tilted up 3.5 degrees in the back, providing a clear blue "Iraqi" sky. Two cameras shot the one-take-only pyro event at 72 fps, just slightly over the proper scale film rate. Nothing that fell to the ground or drifted in the air could be identified as a shot breaker, and considerable time was saved by avoiding a difficult composite shot.

PAL

DEFINITION ▶ Stands for *Phase Alternating Line*. The European color TV broadcasting standard, consisting of 625 lines per frame, running at 25 frames per second and 720 × 576 pixels per frame. Compare with **NTSC**.

Pan

DEFINITION ▶ To move a camera left or right without changing its position. The term has been adapted in computer graphics to refer to the movement of individual video elements.

SEE ALSO ▶ dolly

Penumbra of Shadows, Varying

SEE ▶ shadows, faux

Perspective Match

DEFINITION ▶ Distorting one image to match the perspective of another image. *Related term:* perspective simulation

SEE ALSO ▶ matchmoving in perspective

One of the great tragedies of modern postproduction is ignorance of perspective. The ease with which compositors can combine elements leads many film and video crews to shoot the components of a final composite at conflicting perspectives. However, perspective is something that cannot fully be replicated in postproduction, since different vantage points provide unique information about a 3D object that is simply unavailable to the compositor. Until omniscient 3D set-scanning devices are commonplace (they're currently only available inside Area 51 and on Neverland Ranch), the only way to produce truly correct perspective is in the camera.

Get It Right on the Set

Whenever possible, shoot perspectives correctly. If the background plate of a beach is shot with the camera at shoulder level, shoot the green screen talent at shoulder level, too. If the ground the talent will be composited onto is 20 feet from the camera, shoot the green screen talent 20 feet from the camera.

If there are live action characters in a fantasy CGI environment and they are supposed to be 300 feet from the virtual camera, shoot them outdoors 300 feet from camera, and use rotoscoping to extract them if a blue screen or green screen background at that scale is cost prohibitive.

Fixing in Postproduction

Although it's impossible to re-create a different camera perspective in two dimensions, you can fudge elements to improve the dimensional look. Corner-pinning is the easiest way to approximate the look.

Big Head, Small Boots

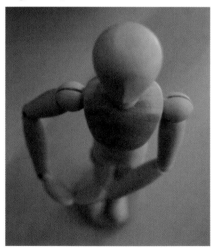

If you have an initial image that was filmed from a perspective *lower* than the perspective of the image you're matching it to, you'll need to stretch the top of your initial image to compensate (or, conversely, shrink the bottom). The higher the camera, the larger the top of an image will appear. Think of cartoons in which roofs of buildings begin as large squares and scale away to nothing at the street level.

Subtlety is key here: An exaggerated stretch will just look weird. It's better to leave a slight mismatch in perspective than to overdistort the effect.

Big Boots, Small Head

If you have an initial image that was filmed from a perspective *higher* than the perspective of the image you're matching it to, you'll need to stretch the bottom of your image to compensate (or, conversely, shrink the top). The lower the camera, the larger the bottom of the image will appear. Think of mouse P.O.V. cartoons in which people appear as enormous feet with tiny heads.

Adding Perspective Simulation to Postproduction Moves

It's very common to create postproduction camera moves by scaling a shot, then moving it left to right or top to bottom over the course of the shot. Directors hate locked-down shots (because, well, they're boring), and this is a reasonable compromise if the shot was locked down on the set for clean plate reasons.

A true live-action camera move produces a perspective distortion as the camera tilts through its motion on the tripod head. You can simulate this distortion by animating a corner pin through the move that you're adding in postproduction.

Photogenics

DEFINITION ▸ A robust software program used for editing, painting, and manipulating high dynamic range images. Manufactured by Idruna Software (www.idruna.com), Photogenics runs on Windows and Linux operating systems.

SEE ALSO ▸ HDRI; light probe; Photosphere

Photosphere

DEFINITION ▶ A shareware program, created by Greg Ward's Anyhere Software (www.anyhere.com), that builds and manages high dynamic range images and digital imagery. The program offers exceptional alignment and calibration tools that are not found in other programs. Photosphere runs under Mac OS X.

SEE ALSO ▶ HDRI; light probe; Photogenics

Pixel

DEFINITION ▶ Short for *picture element*. The smallest element of a digital image. One dot in a video or still image.

Pixel Aspect Ratio

DEFINITION ▶ The width-to-height ratio for the pixels that compose an image. Pixels on computer screens and in high-definition video signals are square (1:1 ratio). Pixels in standard-definition video signals are nonsquare.

SEE ALSO ▶ aspect ratio

Plate

DEFINITION ▶ A piece of original photography that is intended to be used as an element in a composite. A still frame of film footage.

Point Cloud

DEFINITION ▶ A series of tracked points that echo or follow along with features in an image.

Post

DEFINITION ▶ Short for *postproduction*. *Production* refers to all the work done during the film or video shoot. *Postproduction* refers to everything that's done to the footage after the shoot.

Premultiplication

DEFINITION ▶ The process of multiplying the RGB channels in an image by that image's alpha channel.

Primatte

DEFINITION ▶ A proprietary plug-in from Red Giant Software that is used for keying blue screen and green screen shots. Uses a three-dimensional mathematical model to perform its operations.

Process Tree

DEFINITION ▶ In Shake, a treelike structure comprising interconnected images and processes (*nodes*) such as color corrections, layering commands, and keying functions.

Production

SEE ▶ post

Proxy

DEFINITION ▶ A lower-resolution copy that you substitute for a high-resolution image. A *proxy ratio* determines the size relationship of the proxy to the original file.

Radiance

DEFINITION ▶ Ray tracing software used in architecture and lighting simulations.

SEE ALSO ▶ HDRI; OpenEXR

In physics, radiance is the light (or energy) falling on a point or surface. In the world of visual effects, Radiance is the name of a ray tracing software package written largely by Greg Ward of Anyhere Software and used in architecture and lighting simulations. Prior to the development of OpenEXR, Radiance was also one of the most common file formats for HDRI.

Radiosity

DEFINITION ▶ The interactive bounce lighting that produces the subtle shading detail of the physical world.

SEE ALSO ▶ radiosity, faux

Radiosity, Faux

DEFINITION ▶ The simulation of bounce lighting through color correction. *Related terms:* bounce lighting simulation, radiosity simulation, interactive lighting

SEE ALSO ▶ 3D Fundamentals chapter; HDRI; light probe, lighting 3D scenes with

Before faux radiosity

After faux radiosity

Light bounces off walls, floors, kitchen tables, fluffy white kitties, even ugly brown '70s sofas. Each time light reflects off an object, the reflected light combines the light's original color with the color of the object. So, light bouncing off that brown sofa should appear brown. The 3D rendering simulation of this bounce-lighting effect is often referred to as *radiosity*.

If you composite a foreign element—like a fluffy white kitty—into a scene, it's important to create the illusion that the object is receiving bounce lighting from its surroundings. If the fluffy white kitty is sitting on the sofa, its fur will have a tinge of brown as a result of the radiosity lighting (either that, or someone failed to change the kitty litter for the second week in a row).

You can simulate radiosity very simply by sampling the color tint from a large uniform surface, such as a wall. Just sample the color of the surface, and then colorize the foreground with that sample. In Shake, a Mult node will usually suffice for this simulation. In After Effects, use the Tint and Colorize filters, respectively. In Motion, use the Tint and Colorize filters, respectively.

As you can see in the preceding image, the result may appear a little wrong. Chances are, the tint will be far too extreme. The solution is to reduce the saturation of the sampled color until the effect becomes subtle. In Shake, reduce the saturation by holding down the S key while clicking the sample swatch and dragging to the left. In After Effects, adjust the saturation level in the color wheel for the appropriate swatch. In Motion, adjust the saturation level in the Color Picker for the appropriate swatch.

Ramping

DEFINITION ▶ Employing variable speed effects to vary a clip's speed throughout playback. Traditionally achieved by varying the crank speed of the camera during filming. Now often performed in postproduction using optical flow algorithms. *Related terms:* optical flow; retiming; time remapping; variable crank; variable speed effects

SEE ALSO ▶ blink repair; time remapping

Ramping using frame blending

Ramping using optical flow

Ramping is one of the most overused effects in modern video editing. It's become so ubiquitous that its presence is almost subliminal to the average viewer. Even if you didn't recognize it, you've seen ramping a thousand times: an overpriced sedan comes racing into a turn at the speed of light, then instantly slows to super-slow motion with puddle spray gracefully floating toward the camera. And then, as in an ephemeral dream, it darts away, leaving us with a lingering mental image of where our children's college fund is about to be spent.

Regardless of its overuse, ramping is a valuable tool. And the job of ramping often falls to the compositor because most stock edit bays lack the sophisticated algorithms required for good retiming.

Both Shake 4.1 and After Effects 7.0 ship with optical flow retiming systems. Optical flow algorithms estimate where pixels are moving from one frame to the next, enabling them to synthesize in-between frames as necessary. This process is worlds apart from the frame blending of yesteryear, when new in-between frames were simply the product of cross-dissolving two adjacent frames.

In Shake, use the Remap retiming mode in the FileIn parameters of a given footage node. In After Effects, use the Timewarp filter.

Workflow

Optical flow algorithms are extremely render intensive. When adjusting and previewing a ramping effect, temporarily set the interpolation method to display only the original frames. This will result in very rough, stuttering animation, but it should give you a decent sense of how the ramping will look and feel—and without continually subjecting you to the crazy render times of optical flow.

In Shake, retimeMode should be set to Nearest (Blend being the equivalent of traditional frame blending).

In After Effects, the method option should be set to Whole Frames for previewing. (Frame Mix will provide a traditional frame blend preview.)

When you're happy with the results, set the retiming method back to Pixel Motion (After Effects) or Adaptive (Shake) for the final, full-quality render.

Problems with Optical Flow Retiming

Optical flow algorithms are not perfect, and elements such as random particles can create situations that are essentially impossible for the algorithms to solve. In difficult situations, you may find that Shake provides the most flexibility for adjusting the retiming effect. After Effects' retiming is based on Kronos, The Foundry's (www.thefoundry.co.uk) industry-tested optical flow engine. Unfortunately, with this cut-down version of Kronos, After Effects lacks fine-tuning options when things go awry.

For extremely difficult cases, try creating a split screen composite of the optical flow retimed footage and the same footage retimed using frame blending (see split screen composites).

Real Time

DEFINITION ▶ Refers to the ability to play back video content during preview at exactly the same frame rate as that of the final intended output. Can also refer to the ability to update parameters and instantly see the results of the change without requiring rendering first, as in *real-time effects*.

Reflection Pass

SEE ▶ 3D Fundamentals chapter; multipass, basic passes

Reflections, Faux

DEFINITION ▶ The simulation of surface reflections when compositing an object into a reflective scene. *Related terms:* reflection match; surface reflections

SEE ALSO ▶ Fresnel shading pass; light probe, lighting 3D scenes with; surface normal lighting

The simulated reflection below the feet of the robot (right) is subtle, but enough to add an important cue to the integration of this CG element into a live action background.

Like shadows, reflections are among the great giveaways to the integrity of a shot. If reflections are missing, the human observer quickly detects that something is awry. He may not be able to identify what's wrong with the shot, but somewhere in his cerebral cortex a check box is not checked, and the perceptual alarm box is triggered. (OK, so I have no idea if it's in the cerebral cortex—please, no nasty neurological letters of errata to the publisher.)

However, humans can be quite forgiving about the quality of the reflections. As a result, the process for generating reflections is often quite simple.

Deriving the Reflection

The first step in creating a reflection is to find a reflection source. This can be extremely trivial or extremely complex; there's rarely any middle ground. In the case of an object whose base is parallel to the camera, a simple flip of the camera will produce a reflection.

A true reflection (left) compared with a faux reflection (right) created by flipping the original object. Notice that while the faux reflection is similar, it lacks the perspective of the true reflection.

If the object *isn't* flush to the camera, then you're not so lucky.

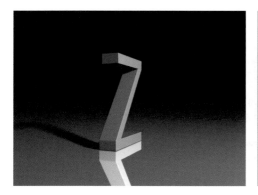 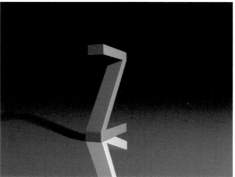

The true reflection of a skewed object (left), and a simulation attempted by flipping the original object (right).

In this situation, you can try warping the reflection into the appropriate shape. After that, your next step is to try to shoot the object from the angle of the reflection, which unfortunately won't work so well if the object is animated and the movement unreproducible. The last resort is a trip to your favorite 3D application for some serious camera mapping.

Creating the Reflection

Once you've obtained a reflection source, you need to composite it into the scene. In this example, you can take the easy road and assume you have an object flush with its ground plane and fairly parallel to the camera. Flipping the object will generate the reflection source.

> **NOTE** ▸ To work through the following examples, use the **ReflectionStart** project file on the disc in APTS_CycVFX/ProjectFiles/CG/BotBoy.

> **NOTE** ▸ Rotating the object 180 degrees is *not* the same as flipping. When the object is flipped, it is also reversed horizontally. Letters appear to read backward just as in a real-world mirror.

Composite the reflection source over the background plate.

Next, composite the object over the top of the reflection and background.

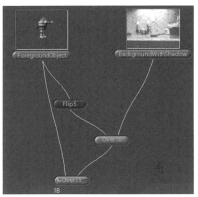

Now the reflection should be moved into its appropriate position. Make sure the reflection completely overlaps the base of the object. It's better to tuck the reflection in too far than to leave a noticeable gap.

Here on earth, there's no such thing as a perfect reflector. All objects have some degree of diffusion, due to the roughness of their surface. The result is that reflected light is scattered somewhat before it reaches the observer. A good old-fashioned blur will simulate the diffusion.

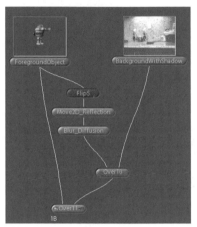

Having mimicked the diffusion with a blur, it's time to dial back the intensity of the reflection, making it more transparent.

> **NOTE** ▸ Don't be afraid to significantly reduce the strength of the reflection. It's better to keep it subtle than to draw attention to it. After all, it *is* a fake—the last thing you want is increased audience scrutiny.

The final step is to mask off nonreflective areas. This can be as simple as creating a mask to clip the edge of the reflective plane, as in the current example. In other cases, you may need to create a custom reflection map—a matte identifying which areas will reflect and which will not. For example, a wet floor might have puddles that produce a strong reflection, along with dry portions that produce a very small and extremely diffuse reflection.

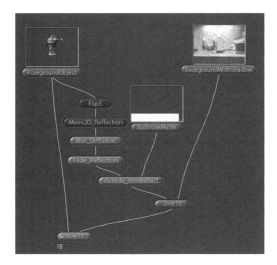

The resulting reflection may appear extremely subtle, but it's important. It will most likely also appear much more pronounced when you view your shot as an animated sequence.

Render

DEFINITION ▶ The process by which the computer calculates the final frames for a project, applying all specified transitions, filters, and other effects. Also, to convert 3D scene geometry, lights, and shading information into a fully formed 3D image.

SEE ALSO ▶ 3D Fundamentals chapter

Render File

DEFINITION ▶ The file produced by rendering a clip to disk. Commonly referred to as a *render*.

Roto

SEE ▶ rotoscoping

Rotoscoping

DEFINITION ▶ A frame-by-frame hand-painting technique to create images over time. Also, the process of generating a matte by manual articulation (commonly referred to as *rotosplines*). That is, instead of the computer determining which pixels should be transparent and which opaque, the user manually specifies—by use of points, curves, or paint—the opacity of the pixels in an image.

For an example of a rotoscoping technique, see J Bills's "Bringing Frank Sinatra 'Back to Life,'" on page 453.

NOTE ▶ The original *rotoscope* was a device that enabled animators to trace live action movement, frame by frame, for use in animated cartoons. Invented by Max Fleischer in 1914.

Rushes

DEFINITION ▶ A British and European term for dailies.

Cameo

Harry Potter's 2D Wizardry—Tim Alexander

RESOURCE MANAGEMENT IS a part of every effects supervisor's job. No show seems to have enough time or money to produce the effects at their ideal level. As a result, good initial decisions regarding the methods and techniques to be used are essential to the overall success of a show.

The key to any successful show is to determine the minimum requirements necessary to achieve the desired results. As always, when effects supervisor Tim Alexander (see Contributors, page iv) began working on *Harry Potter and the Goblet of Fire* (Warner Bros.) for Industrial Light & Magic, he had to make many choices related to time and technique.

On one series of shots, Tim discovered a low-tech approach that worked beautifully and saved time and money for other, more challenging effects.

The shots in question occurred during an early scene in the film in which Harry and three other contestants compete to capture a dragon egg outside the mist-shrouded Hogwarts castle. While using Apple's Motion, Tim became familiar with its particle system. Following a few quick tests, he realized that Motion's 2D, sprite-based particle system was more than adequate to create the look he needed for the mist and fog elements of this dragon sequence.

Although Motion is a strictly 2D program, creative use of it can add a sense of depth and movement to elements such as fog and mist. During the Triwizard Tournament competition at Hogwarts, the client wanted fog and mist added to every shot to enhance the mood. A simple foreground element blowing across the frame wouldn't be sufficiently convincing. Every shot needed fog or mist blowing toward or away from the camera.

Using Motion's particle system, small images were mapped onto each sprite-based particle—in this case, pictures of clouds. In Motion, each sprite is quick to generate and can have a programmable velocity, direction, rotation, and life span. By manipulating these parameters, you can combine sprites to create many different looks.

In the case of mist blowing at the lens, the life of a particle determined the opacity of the mist. When a sprite was born, it had zero opacity. It faded up to have a denser look, and then faded away, revealing other growing sprites. This movement gave the sprites life.

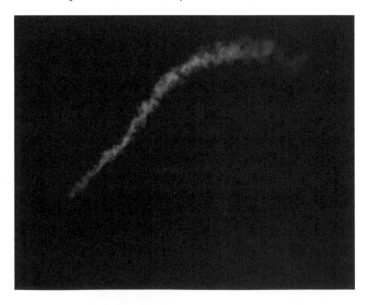

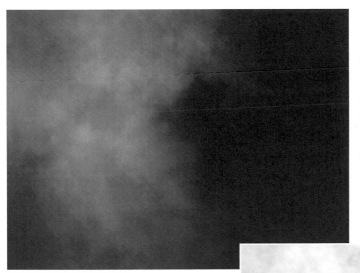

Next, scaling was used to enlarge each sprite through time to make it appear to be approaching the camera. To impart more character to the mist, rotation was used to create the look of swirling, wind-blown mist. The more complex the programming of each sprite, the more random and real the fog and mist looked.

Once individual sprites were programmed, several layers of sprites were piled on top of each other. Together they formed a contiguous whole that made up a dimensional mist and fog.

If the fog and mist elements had needed to interact with some other element in the frame—such as a broom-riding character who roils the atmosphere in his wake— Alexander probably would have needed to shoot practical elements on a stage or create 3D-generated objects. In these shots, however, no interaction was required. So, the skillful use of 2D elements in Motion was more than adequate to the task, and the more complex and costly 3D solutions were saved for shots in which they were really required.

Saturation

DEFINITION ▶ The intensity of a color. Saturation is represented on a color wheel as a point along a radius from the center of the wheel to the outer rim. As saturation is decreased, the color moves toward gray.

SEE ALSO ▶ color matching

Screen Blur Composite

DEFINITION ▶ Adding a soft glow by compositing a blur over the original shot. *Related terms:* glow; instant sex

The technique of screen blur composite gained considerable momentum in the 1990s when it was thrust into the mainstream by motion-graphics-gurus and super-compositing-author-duo Trish and Chris Meyer. They appropriately dubbed the effect "instant sex." Perhaps the tag is derived from DPs who were shooting romantic comedies and had an affinity for applying diffusion filters to the lens (as in *Jerry Maguire*), or possibly it's a shout out to the cheap pantyhose-diffused shots that were commonly used in the '70s adult-film industry (or so I'm told).

If you watch carefully for it, you'll notice that screen blur is the go-to effect for many hazy dream sequences. This is also a hot effect in mainstream sports circles, as the NBA adopted it for in-game highlight reels to add a hyperrealism to the most recent barrage of slam dunks.

Even after ten-plus years of heavy usage, screen blur remains a compelling, valid treatment.

In Shake, the source footage (FileIn) is duplicated and layered over itself with a screen operation. The screened input is then blurred and dialed back with a Fade node as necessary, to make the effect as bold or subtle as the scene dictates. As icing on the cake, you can add an Expand node following the FileIn that is being screened to feed an image with more contrast to the screen operation.

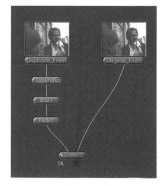

Before

After (with bold, dreamlike settings)

After (with a more subtle diffusion, also common)

For the bold example above, a Blur of 35 was used, and the white point on the Expand node was dipped slightly to .95. Finally, the Fade value was set to .75.

> **TIP** While the bold look may be tempting, it's been used frequently in the last few years to dress up footage shot on video instead of film. As a consequence it can actually appear to be on the "amateur" side—think twice before using it for shots on your reel.

The effect works best on well-lit scenes, as the screen operation depends on a fair amount of brightness. It definitely adds an element of atmospheric weight to the scene. Screen-blurring a shot also is commonly used to smooth out harsh edges or hide jagged edges that result from upscaling an element, as it has a knack for naturally finding contrast in an image and fuzzing it.

In the past, most artists' toolboxes contained a subtle screen blur for giving video the always-in-demand "film look," but recently many compositors have replaced the effect with faster low-level diffusion rendering methods using plug-ins better suited to the task. However, you might want to note that if those expensive plug-ins aren't available on a job, reviving a good old subtle screen blur might do.

Screen Color Selection

DEFINITION ▶ The process of choosing a backing screen color when shooting footage to be extracted in postproduction using a keyer. *Related terms:* backing screen color; key color selection

SEE ALSO ▶ blue screen; Keying Fundamentals chapter; sky keying

Due to the nature of the most common keying method—the color difference key—the only appropriate backing screen colors for the standard keying process are additive color primaries: red, green, and blue.

The actual hue of the backing screen should be as close to the selected primary as possible. For example, in the case of a green screen, the pigment used for the background should diffusely reflect as much green light as possible, while absorbing as much red and blue light as possible.

While red backgrounds are occasionally used for miniature work, the predominantly red hue of skin tone makes their use uncommon. This leaves a decision for background color between chroma-key green and chroma-key blue. When deciding between using a blue or green screen, the following issues are important to consider.

Subject Color

If the color of the camera subject includes a large amount of blue, a green screen would be the most appropriate choice. Likewise, if there is a great deal of green in the foreground, chroma-key blue would be the best choice. Keep in mind that something like a blue logo on a T-shirt may not be a major concern, since a holdout matte can be created easily to compensate for any false transparency generated in the matte.

Clothing items like blue jeans also may not cause significant problems with the keying process, depending on the closeness of their color to the backing screen color. Nonetheless, such clothing can experience a significant color shift during de-spill operations, so the alternate backing color (in the case of blue jeans, a green screen) usually is the preferable choice.

Many issues can be resolved in wardrobe selection. Wherever scene continuity permits, colors should be chosen that differ significantly from the backing color.

Final Composite Background Color

Just as important in choosing a screen color is the general color scheme of the background image into which the keyed object will be composited. If the color scheme of the background plate is predominantly blue (as is quite often the case), a blue screen would be the best choice, since excess spill might pass as radiosity lighting from the background.

The Blond on Blue Principle

Another criterion in the screen color decision is hair color. Fine hair detail is one of the most difficult elements to key convincingly, and choosing the right backing color can significantly improve the chances of retaining clarity in those areas of the key.

The Blond on Blue principle suggests that blond hair keys better when set against a blue screen. Since blond hair has a high luminance value, and blue screens have a relatively low luminance value (at least relative to green screens), the combination of blond and blue results in a more dramatic contrast between foreground and background. This is particularly true for the luma edge keying technique.

Dark hair will benefit from a green screen, since the high luminance of a green screen will present a strong contrast with the relatively low luminance of dark hair.

When using the luma edge keying technique, lighting can be adjusted to make the contrast between foreground and background even more dramatic. In the case of a blonde in front of a blue screen, slightly overlighting the foreground subject can help to accentuate the contrast. When using a green screen, slightly underlighting the foreground may increase the contrast. Obviously, neither technique should be used at the expense of a shot's intended lighting effects.

As with the luma edge matte, it is essential that any sharpening algorithm be turned off at the camera, telecine, or film scanner.

> **NOTE** ▶ Unfortunately, the majority of prosumer DV cameras have sharpening permanently enabled. When shooting with these cameras, the artifacts caused by sharpening can sometimes create more of a problem for the key than the poorly subsampled color space of DV. In such cases, the variation in luminance between the backing screen and the subject should not be emphasized, as this would encourage the sharpening to be more extreme at the borders of the subject, compromising the highly coveted soft edge.

Digital Color Space

Contrary to a common belief, the subsampled color space of digital video is *not* an appropriate determinant when choosing screen color. It is true that a fully sampled luminance channel of digital video is predominantly green, but choosing a green screen will not necessarily generate a more accurate key in subsampled video spaces, since the lower-resolution subcarrier channels are still involved in extracting the key.

Cost

As in every other area of production, cost is a major issue. Soundstages and studio spaces often have been painted blue or green. The cost of painting a space to a different backing color may be prohibitive. In such cases, appropriate lighting and careful wardrobe choice can yield adequate results regardless of the backing color.

In the case of the Reflecmedia keying system, you can instantly alter the screen color by changing the LED ring at the front of the camera lens.

Poor Man's Chroma-Key

There is a strong temptation to use standard blue or green paint for keying instead of the specially formulated chroma-key blue and chroma-key green offered by staging supply companies. After a great deal of experimentation with different paint pigments, you may be able to produce adequate keying results. However, the price of the specially formulated pigments is quite modest and unlikely to create serious damage to even a shoestring production budget.

Another good alternative is the use of Velcro backing in chroma blue or chroma green. This highly diffuse material has the benefit of being portable and reusable, and it is surprisingly affordable.

For the truly thrifty, the blue sky can sometimes be used as an alternative backing screen. See sky keying.

Screen Replacement

DEFINITION ▶ Using tracking and matting techniques to replace flat, polygonal objects—such as TV screens, billboards, and signs—in a composite. *Related terms:* sign replacement; watch replacement; display replacement.

SEE ALSO ▶ grain matching; matchmoving in perspective; spill suppression; Tracking Fundamentals chapter

Screen replacement is among the most common tasks in compositing. In general terms, it can be thought of as *plane* replacement, and it covers the replacement of such items as TV screens, cell phone screens (or mobile phone screens, for everyone outside of North America), watch faces, billboards, and license plates. (That's "plane" as in "flat, polygonal surface," not as in "just missed the last one out of Denver.")

Most replacement shots involve tracking a plane and then applying the replacement image. Tracking a plane is described in matchmoving in perspective. This exercise covers the integration of the replacement screen after the tracking has been done.

NOTE ▶ In addition to the **matchmoving in perspective** entry, review the Tracking Fundamentals chapter for more information on tracking a plane.

Production Considerations

There are several production issues to consider when preparing a screen replacement. The first is the most critical: Make sure the corners of the replacement plane are clearly defined and visible throughout the shot.

A common practice is to insert tracking markers near the corners of the screen or sign. This is useful when there is poor edge definition, but it may be unnecessary if the edge detail is already sharp and defined. Always remember that tracking markers added during production must be removed in postproduction. These markers can also cause issues with highlight harvesting (see below).

The tracking markers in the corners of the screen, while much appreciated, are probably unnecessary here given the high contrast between the black screen and the crisp metallic edges of the screen border.

If the corners of the tracked plane become obscured by a foreground element, make sure a trackable element is available nearby (on the *same* surface as the obscured corner) for offset tracking while the corner is obscured. In such a case, the addition of tracking markers may be desirable.

The type of placeholder image used during the shoot is another production consideration. When replacing a sign or a piece of paper, the color and texture of the placeholder should match the native color and texture of the final replacement item. For example, when placing a blue billboard graphic, the filmed placeholder also should be blue.

For screen replacements, a black background is almost always the most desirable. It allows you to harvest the specular highlights from the screen and "paste" them back over the final composite to enhance the illusion that the replacement image is truly encased in glass. This can be faked in postproduction, but it's surprisingly difficult to simulate the movement of specular highlights on a screen without having detailed knowledge of the light sources and 3D movement.

Procedure

In this exercise, you're dealing with a locked-down image of a laptop computer. The background will be replaced with an out-of-focus image, the screen will be replaced, and a hand will be added in front that is touching the screen. While this shot includes techniques beyond basic screen replacement, it's worth examining them in detail, because many of these techniques are commonly used to solve screen-replacement problems.

Replacing the Background   S

1   Begin by replacing the background. Since the laptop is highly reflective, you can anticipate a lot of spill on the foreground and, therefore, a lot of holes in the matte generated by a keyer. The good news is that the shot is static, so rotoscoping the laptop is a quick and easy solution.

SHAKE ▼

Open **APTS_CycVFX/ProjectFiles/Keying/ScreenReplace/Start.shk**. Attach a Layer > KeyMix to BG. Connect ScreenTouchFG to the second (foreground) input, and connect Powerbook_Outline_RShape to the third (key) input. Or, if you're feel-ing brave, create your own RotoShape of the laptop and substitute it for Notebook_Outline_RShape.

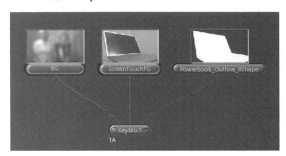

2 You'll immediately notice how green the PowerBook appears. Of the many methods for spill suppression, the most reliable method here will be to limit the green chan-nel to the average of red and green. Since the laptop computer is a metallic (and gray) object, red, green, and blue should be of equal intensity. So, by limiting green to the average, you should get the most neutral spill suppression results.

SHAKE ▼

Add a ColorX node (gExpr = $g>(r+b)/2?(r+b)/2:g$) after ScreenTouchFG. Group the cur-rent nodes for organization's sake, if you desire.

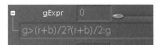

Treating the Replacement Image

1 With the spill neutralized, you can prepare the replacement screen image. The clip, **DropletImage**, doesn't have an alpha channel. You'll need one once you've corner-pinned the clip into the PowerBook screen.

SHAKE ▼

Apply a Color > SetAlpha node to DropletImage.

By default, this creates a pure white (fully opaque) alpha channel.

2   Now you should corner-pin the image.

SHAKE ▼

Add a Transform > CornerPin node after SetAlpha1. Open **KeyMix1** into the Viewer while keeping CornerPin1's parameters active. Position the corners of the CornerPin onscreen controls so that they align with the corners of the laptop's screen.

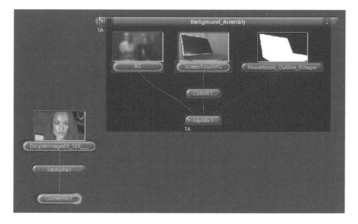

Feel free to overlap the image a little with the edges of the screen; you'll be trimming the image in the next step. In fact, when working with TV-screen replacements, you should always anticipate the portion of the image outside action safe that would naturally be cropped out by a standard set.

3   Next, you need to ensure that the image fits inside the bounds of the laptop's display.

SHAKE ▼

Add a Layer > Inside node to CornerPin1. Connect Screen_RShape to the second input of Inside1. (Or you can create your own RotoShape for the screen boundaries.)

NOTE ▶ The logical method when rotoscoping the display area is to use four points for the four corners of the shape. In practice, you'll need to use more points than that because lens distortion causes the straight geometry of the image to appear bowed. The conventional procedure would be to start by removing lens distortion from the image. However, since this causes subpixel softening, it's often easier, if unconventional, to bend your mattes to accommodate. The lens distortion is not extreme here, so the unconventional solution is preferable.

If you look at the original **ScreenTouchFG** image, you'll notice that the top and left of the screen are shadowed due to the scene lighting. The shadow mainly involves the top of the screen. Also, the left recess is obscured by the camera angle, but you can ignore that situation in this exercise. Of course, if you ignore it on the job, you'll probably get fired.

4   Use an emboss node to simulate the shadow direction.

SHAKE ▼

Select Screen_RShape, and Shift-click Filter > Emboss (gain = 1.0, elevation = 0) to branch an emboss node.

Add a Color > Brightness node (value = 0.4) after Inside1. Feed the Emboss1 into the mask input of Brightness1, and set the mask channel in Brightness1's parameters to R.

The effect is subtle, but the high-intensity illumination of the display would prevent any significantly dark shadows. The value of 0.4 is probably already stronger than what you would normally see, but it helps to "bed in" the graphic.

TIP ▶ The azimuth angle of 135 happened to be the value you needed, but you can adjust this angle for different lighting directions.

5   Finally, you can composite the replacement screen into the shot. Thanks to the alpha channel that you created using the SetAlpha node, you can use an Over operation for the composite.

SHAKE ▼

Add a Layer > Over node directly after Brightness1. Insert KeyMix1 into the second (background) input.

Try ignoring the Brightness1 node to see the effect you previously built with the emboss node.

6   The replacement screen is now integrated, but it stands out from the rest of the shot. Some care should be taken to color-correct the image into the shot.

NOTE ▶ The solution has been simplified in this exercise, but if this were a commercial shot, you'd most likely need to do more localized correction. The good news is that a high-luminance image coming from a computer display doesn't need to be brought completely into the scene lighting because it is a light source in and of itself.

The shot also lacks grain, but you'll get to that at the end of the shot.

SHAKE ▼

Add a Color > Gamma node (rGamma = 0.9) after CornerPin1. Group the nodes as desired.

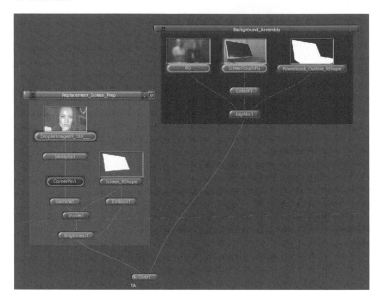

Harvesting Highlights

S

1 Because the laptop was filmed with a dark screen, you can harvest the highlights to overlay on top of the replacement graphic, suggesting that the graphic is encased in glass. In this case, it's a lockdown shot, so the effect isn't particularly impressive. With a traveling shot, the highlights would change with the varying angle of the screen to camera.

SHAKE ▼

Branch a Layer > Inside node off KeyMix1. Insert Screen_RShape into the second input.

TIP If you've grouped KeyMix1with the other background nodes, select Inside2 and press Control-G to separate it from the rest of the group.

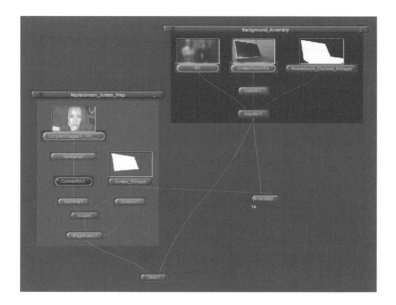

This step ensures that you're dealing only with the part of the image inside the screen area (where you need the highlights).

2   Isolate the highlights with a luma key.

SHAKE ▼

Add a Key > LumaKey node (loVal = 0.05, loSmooth = 0.2, matteMult activated) after Inside2. Add a Color > Brightness node (value = 0.6) after LumaKey1 to reduce the intensity of the highlight a tad.

3   Finally, screen the highlight back over the main display. The Screen operation is commutative, so it doesn't matter which input goes where (unless you're using the mask input).

TIP ▶ If you're working with float images, you'll need to replace the Screen operation with a Layer>IAdd, or risk doing weird things to your non-normalized float data.

SHAKE ▼

Add a Layer > Screen node to Over1. Attach Screen1 to the second input.

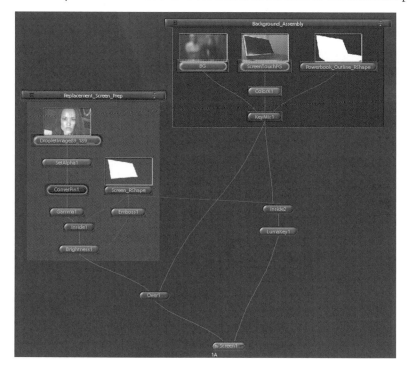

Keying or the Lack Thereof

You're about to add a hand coming in to touch the display. This isn't a keying exercise, so we cheated and provided mattes for the hand and the hand's shadow. Generating those mattes is actually a good exercise to test your keying skills, if you've been working through some of the keying techniques. Here are a few tips if you're trying to key the shot:

▶ Don't try to pull one key for the hand and the hand shadow. (As my mother always says, "When you start being silly, someone always gets hurt.")

▶ Don't panic if you can't pull the hand matte without bringing the shadow along for the ride. At the end of the day, you'll need to rotoscope the shadow matte to separate it from the hand matte. You'll be using them for two different purposes.

▶ Use the inner/outer keying method to get the job done.

▶ Don't be afraid of roto—it's your friend: a nasty, painful friend that hangs around after everyone else has left the party, but a friend nonetheless.

Transforming the Hand Shot

In a perfect world, the elements of a visual effects shot would automatically integrate into the appropriate locations. This is not that sort of world, and as a result, there is invariably a certain amount of "fudging and smudging" necessary to get elements to fit together.

In the current scene, you have two laptop shots using a locked-down camera, one with no green screen cloth (ScreenTouchFG) and one with the cloth (ScreenTouchGS). In theory, the shots should be identical and the laptop should be in exactly the same location in both shots. In reality, an inexperienced grip may have moved the laptop while adding the cloth, and an inexperienced director of photography may have made adjustments to the camera between takes.

These two shots should have identical framing. Unfortunately, they don't. In the right-hand shot, the PowerBook is further to the left of frame.

1 The framing of the laptop is markedly different in each shot. You'll need to compensate for this before continuing with the composite. Obviously, the screen is the most important part of the shot, so you'll make sure it is correctly aligned.

SHAKE ▼

Branch a Transform > CornerPin off ScreenTouchFG. Look at ScreenTouchFG while adjusting the parameters for CornerPin2, and align the edges of the corner pin with the outer edges of the PowerBook display.

2 If you look at the output of CornerPin2, you'll conclude that something has gone horribly wrong. Hang in there; it'll sort itself out in a moment.

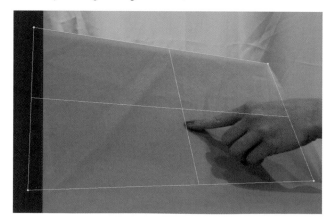

Add a Transform > CornerPin node to ScreenTouchGS. Look at ScreenTouchFG while adjusting the parameters for CornerPin3, and align the edges of the corner pin to the positions where you *estimate* the outer edges of the laptop display might be if the shot framing extended that far.

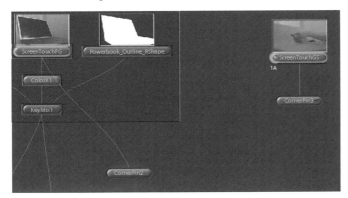

3 Now for the magic trick: Invert the corner pin on the hand clip, and then, from the laptop foreground clip, apply the corner pin to the result. That is, you're removing the original perspective of the hand clip by using the inverted corner pinning, then substituting in the perspective of the laptop clip. The result should match both laptop screens to the same space.

Activate inverseTransform in the parameters of CornerPin3. Extract CornerPin2 from ScreenTouchFG and attach it to the output of CornerPin3.

The resulting image is now aligned to the ScreenTouchFG shot. Are there problems? Yes—the arm has been squished a little. Does it matter? That depends on how important the arm is. If it's the arm of a famous actress, she probably won't appreciate its being misrepresented. In that case, you'll need to use more laborious position, rotation, and (subtle) scaling to align the shots.

Step-by-Step

Adding the Shadow

S

You have a shadow matte–either the one supplied with this tutorial or one created through your own keying and roto efforts. You can use it to darken the final shot.

1 Adjust the matte's position using your perspective fix.

SHAKE ▼

Copy CornerPin3 and CornerPin2, and paste them below ShadowMatte. (Make sure the two CornerPins are still connected.) Connect ShadowMatte to the input of the top pasted CornerPin.

2 The screen is highly luminous, so it would be unrealistic to expect to see significant shadowing. You'll use the matte of the screen area to remove any shadowing that may be present in that portion of ShadowMatte.

SHAKE ▼

Add a Layer > Outside node to CornerPin5 (connected to ShadowMatte). Connect the output of Screen_RShape to the second input of Outside1.

3   Darken the shot with a shadow.

SHAKE ▼

Add a Color > Brightness node (value = 0) after Screen1. Connect Outside1 to the mask input of the Brightness node. Group the shadow nodes, as you desire.

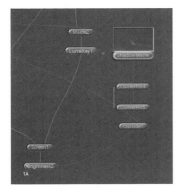

You now have a shadow for the hand.

Adding the Hand

Like the laptop, the hand footage is polluted by green spill.

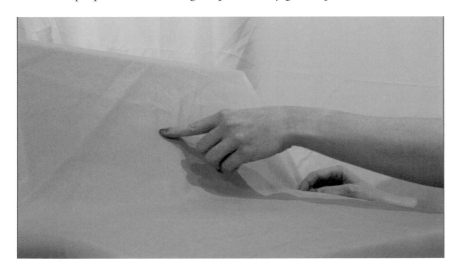

1   Suppress, then add the matte you've created (using the one provided, or using your own keying/roto efforts).

SHAKE ▼

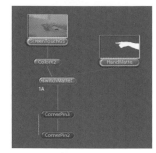

Copy and paste ColorX1, and insert it below ScreenTouchGS. Add a Layer > SwitchMatte node to ColorX2, then connect HandMatte to the second input. Deactivate matteMult in SwitchMatte1's parameters. Make sure the CornerPins are still connected below the SwitchMatte.

TIP ▶   For better spill suppression on the hand, use the following equation in the gExpr channel of the ColorX node: g>(2*b+r)/3?(2*b+r)/3:g

You deactivated matteMult because you'll want to color correct the hand, and you'll want to be a good compositing citizen who obeys the first great law of compositing: "Never color correct a premultiplied image."

2   Perform a quick color correction, and then premultiply.

Add a Color > Gamma node (rGamma = 0.7) after the CornerPins, and then add a Color > MMult node to the Gamma.

3 Finally, slap the hand on top.

Add an Over node after MMult1. Connect the output from Brightness2 to the second input of the Over node. Set the oven to 325 degrees Fahrenheit and group to taste.

And there's your composite.

Adding Some Grain

The composite is assembled, but a few things remain to finish. The first thing is grain. The background clip, **BG**, was defocused as a post process, so it no longer has any grain structure. The screen replacement is a computer-generated element and therefore needs grain added.

1   You can sample grain from the **ScreenTouchFG** clip and use that to add grain to both. Sample the grain yourself (see grain matching), or use the provided Laptop_Filmgrain node.

> **TIP** Sample the grain *after* the spill suppression operation to prevent the grain from being biased toward the green. Also, make sure that grain is applied *after* any transforms (such as your corner-pinning) that might alter the grain structure.

SHAKE ▼

Copy Laptop_Filmgrain, then paste and connect copies after Gamma1 (the gamma connected to DropletImage) and BG.

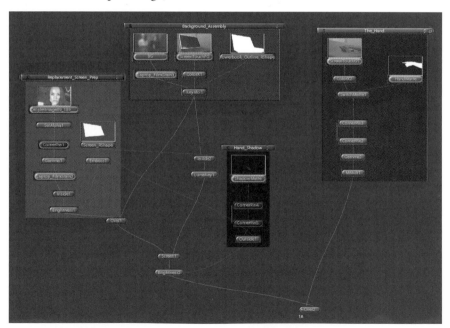

Going Further

As with all shots, there are still plenty more areas to finesse after the fundamentals are completed.

Primarily, the color balance of the elements should be adjusted.

There are also other secondary considerations. One of these is the illumination of the screen itself. You would expect the portion of the hand facing the screen to be illuminated by light coming from the screen. The laptop's keyboard would also receive this illumination.

To create these spill effects, you'll need to make an edge matte of the hand in the area where the spill is applied. (Try using the same trick you previously used with the emboss.) Also, try using an extremely blurred version of the replacement screen as the source for the spill you're adding to the hand.

For the keyboard, try flipping the replacement screen image, blurring and then compositing over the keyboard area. Fade it down significantly—subtlety is essential.

Beyond these considerations, the interactions of the background with the edges of the arm in general should be addressed. Specific areas where the arm is haloed should be color corrected to blend with the background.

> **TIP** ▶ The droplet effect for the replacement screen was created in Motion using the file **APTS_CycVFX/ProjectFiles/Keying/ScreenReplace/Droplet.motn.**

Scrub

> **DEFINITION** ▶ The action of shuttling quickly through an image sequence.

Shadow Displacement Map

> **SEE** ▶ shadows, faux

Shadow Pass

SEE ▶ 3D Fundamentals chapter; Keying Fundamentals chapter; multipass, basic passes

Shadows, Faux

DEFINITION ▶ The process of adding shadows to a scene when the original shadows cast by an object are unavailable or inappropriate. *Related terms*: contact shadow; fake shadow; object as shadow; shadow from matte; shadow density; skewing shadows; variable penumbra shadow

Without faux shadow

With faux shadow

Of all the visual cues a compositor can add to a shot, shadows are probably the most critical. Human beings are acutely aware of the presence of shadows. Shadows anchor objects to their surroundings and are always important, even when they are subtle.

The good news is that human beings don't seem to care so much about the *details* of a shadow, such as its position. For example, many movies filmed outdoors require multiple takes across a single day. When those takes are edited, some of the shots have shadows casting off to the left, others have them casting off to the right. The shadow positions differ depending on the time of day when each take was filmed. For the most part, audiences won't notice this dramatic shifting of shadows. If they do, chances are the movie is *extremely* boring, and not one you'll want to boast about on your personal show reel.

You can leverage this audience inattention to detail to create *faux* shadows.

Faux shadows should be a last resort. Shadows should be harvested from green screen or blue screen content whenever possible, and shadow passes should be rendered for 3D content. If neither a harvested shadow nor a shadow pass is available, it's time to grow your own.

Observing the Background Shadows

The first step in creating a faux shadow is to observe real shadows in the background plate. This step breaks down into several tasks.

Identify the Number of Shadows

Each light source in a scene creates a shadow. Some lighting sources are diffuse and produce negligible effects (like the illumination from a blue sky). Others may be washed out by stronger light sources and produce no visible shadow. The important tasks are to identify distinct, *observable* shadows cast by objects in the background plate, and to note their direction and strength.

If you have any say in the production process, try to record the position, orientation, type, and intensity of lighting on the set. The more information you have, the better.

Additionally, whenever possible, shoot one or more stand-in objects that are about the same size as the objects you're integrating. Separate diffuse and reflective stand-ins are ideal, but don't discount the value of a single stand-in with surface properties similar to those of the objects you're integrating. This will give you the best sense of how shadows should fall in the scene.

A real PDA (left) is used as a reference stand-in for the CG PDA to be integrated (right).

Identify the Strength of Shadows

Is a shadow dark and pronounced, or relatively unnoticeable? Does it remain pronounced across its length or quickly fade to undetectable levels? These are the questions you need to ask about the strength of the scene shadows.

Identify the Edge Sharpness of Shadows

Shadows will have sharp or fuzzy edges, depending on the polarization of photons emitted by a light source. Direct sunlight is an example of a relatively polarized light source. (Light from the sun travels a long distance, so the angle of the arc of radiation reaching the observer is relatively small, creating beams that are not parallel, but close enough for your purposes.)

Once you've determined edge sharpness, employ the variable penumbra shadow technique (described two sections below) to produce a match.

Creating the Shadow

You typically produce a faux shadow from the outline of the object casting the shadow, although in extreme situations you may need to rotoscope a matching shape. Note that the shape of a faux shadow will differ from the shape of a true shadow. When working with the outline of the object, the perspective of the silhouette comes from the observer.

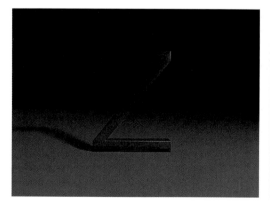 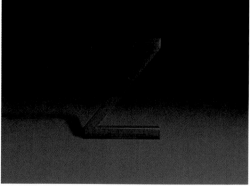

An accurate silhouette (left) compared with the silhouette of a simulated faux shadow (right). Notice the difference in the angle of the shadows' upper right corners. This is because the accurate silhouette is calculated from the light's point of view (see the following image), while the faux shadow is derived from the observer's point of view.

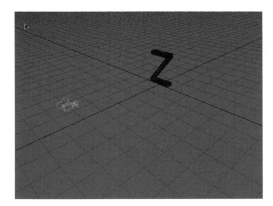

The shadow can usually be derived from the alpha channel of the original object. You create a copy of the alpha channel, transform it, and then use it as a mask for color-correcting the background plate.

There's no need to isolate the alpha channel or copy it to the RGB channels. Instead, make a duplicate copy of the image (or simply branch a Move2D off the original image in Shake), and set your viewer to look at the alpha channel instead of the color channels. (Press the A key while your mouse is over the Viewer in Shake, press Option-4 in After Effects, or press Shift-A in Motion.)

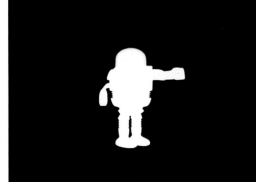

Scaling the Shadow

The first step is to "squash" the shadow into place. Take the copied alpha channel of the original object and position the anchor point (or *pivot* point, depending on your software's terminology) at the point where the shadow connects with the object (usually the base of the object). In Shake, you'll need to apply a Move2D node to obtain transform controls. In After Effects and Motion, transform controls are built into the object by default.

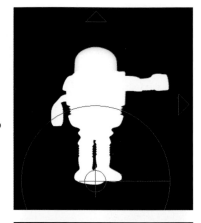

> **NOTE** ▶ To work through the following examples, use the **ShadowStart** project file on the disc in APTS_CycVFX/ProjectFiles/CG/BotBoy.

With the anchor point in place, scale the image vertically until the shadow length is appropriate to the scene. You should be matching the shadow length to the scene based on your earlier observations (see "Observing the Background Shadows," above).

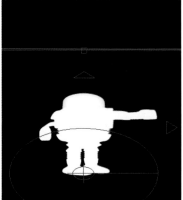

Shearing the Shadow

With the shadow set to the appropriate length, it's time to adjust the angle. Do so using a simple shear (or *skew*, depending on the terminology of your specific software package).

Shear the image horizontally to match the orientation of the light source you're trying to emulate.

> **NOTE** ▶ This section was crying out for a good sheep joke, but the author avoided the temptation on the grounds that it would cause undue hardship to the reader base.

Adding a Contact Shadow

In addition to the obvious shadows in a scene, there's almost always a *contact shadow*. The contact shadow is the dark line you'll see at the front of an object, even if it's sitting flush with the surface it rests on. This shadow is due to the occlusion of light from the under-surface of the object, and it is very important but, alas, oft overlooked.

You can manually articulate a contact shadow by rotoscoping, or you can simply create another copy of the object, blur it slightly, and then shift it down until you're happy with the amount of shadowing. You'll also need to mask off this new shadow, so that you create a shadow only in the small area where the object contacts its resting surface.

TIP ▶ Alternatively, you could try expanding (dilating) the new copy of the object by 1 to 1.5 pixels instead of shifting it down.

When you're done, screen the contact shadow onto your scaled/sheared shadow for a final shadow matte.

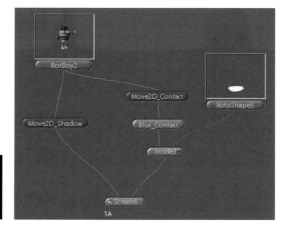

Varying the Penumbra

As mentioned previously, most shadows have a soft *penumbra*, which is the term for the shadow's edge. The simplest way to soften a shadow matte is to blur it. However, in most situations the shadow's blur increases as it moves away from the point of contact with its source object. You can simulate this effect by using an image-based variable blur.

First, create a matte with a soft edge that begins solid at the object's point of contact and then softens as it moves to the outer extremities of the shadow.

> **TIP** ▶ If your software doesn't support a variable soft edge roto tool (like the one from Shake, shown in the image below), you can often get away with using a radial gradient, or with applying a global feather to a hard-edged shape.

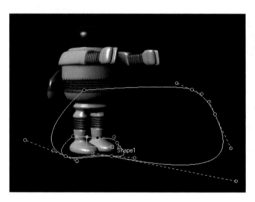
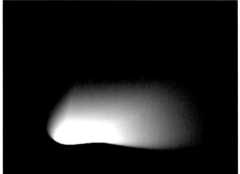

Next, invert the matte. The variable blur will be strongest where the matte is white, and weakest (actually, nonexistent) where the matte is black. If you were to use the matte without inverting, the shadow closest to the point of contact would be blurred the most—exactly the opposite of what you're after.

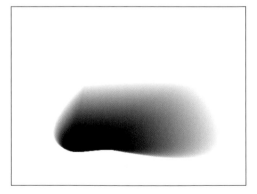

Finally, feed the inverted matte into an image-based blur. In Shake, use an IBlur node; in Motion and After Effects, use a Compound Blur. Adjust the blur to match the background shadows.

TIP ▶ Where necessary, you can adjust the white and black points of the gradient matte you created to modify the minimum and maximum blur settings. Use a Compress node in Shake or the Levels filter in Motion or After Effects. Remember to color correct the alpha channel when doing this, since this is the channel used by the variable blur.

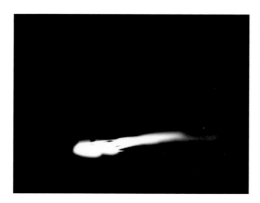 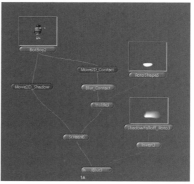

Adding Intensity Falloff

Shadows get fuzzier with distance and lose their intensity. To achieve this, apply a color correction that darkens the alpha channel of your shadow matte, and mask the effect of the color correction with the falloff matte being used to vary the shadow penumbra.

Since this is a nonlinear falloff, you may want to apply a gamma correction to the falloff matte before using it as the mask for the color correction. For extreme adjustments, blur a little after the gamma correction to fix any resultant banding.

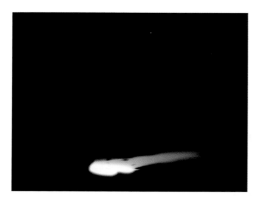 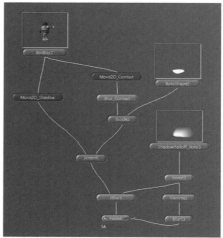

Applying the Shadow

Shadows are the absence of light in portions of a scene that is due to objects' occluding light from those areas. To simulate this, you can darken the background in those locations. Before rushing off to apply a brightness filter, however, it's important to consider an essential physical detail: ambient light.

Adjusting for Ambient Light

Ambient light is general, omnidirectional light and has two primary causes. The first cause is a diffuse lighting source. The most obvious example is blue sky. While sunlight is very directional, blue sky light is a result of sunlight photons' being knocked about by particles in the earth's atmosphere, which causes diffuse blue wavelength light to reach the observer from all directions in which those photons have been scattered.

The second source of ambient light is radiosity. Radiosity is the result of light bouncing off of other objects (such as walls, chairs, and floors) before reaching the observer. Have you ever noticed how opening the door of a dark room just a crack illuminates the entire room, even though the direct light from the doorway encompasses only a thin beam on the opposite wall? That's radiosity at work.

Why is ambient light important when faking a shadow? It's important because when you take away direct light from a portion of a scene (by casting a shadow over it), you don't stop ambient light from reaching it. So, if you create a shadow on a sidewalk on a sunny day by standing in the way of the sun, the sidewalk is still illuminated by blue sky light. That's because the blue sky light is coming from multiple directions and therefore is not obstructed, at least not to the degree that the direct sunlight is.

The upshot? Your shadow is not going to be black, but will, in fact, be tinted *blue*.

The shadow created when the Z occludes a key light in this image is actually blue, due to the blue color of the diffuse ambient light in the scene.

Color Correcting the Background

Except in trivial situations, apply a color corrector to the background that is capable of tinting (or colorizing).

Next, try to identify a neutral, gray, or white portion of the background plate that is close to where the object will be integrated into your shot. In the image below, the wall plate would be the obvious choice. (Of course, you need to be careful not to be led astray by an off-white fitting. Here's yet another case in which on-set survey is critical.)

Sample the color and use it as your tint choice for the shadow. Once you've sampled the color, you still may need to adjust its saturation, but the hue should be correct.

If you're unable to find any true whites or grays in your scene, you'll just have to make a best guess as to the color of the scene's ambient lighting.

Masking the Color Correction

With the color selected, mask off the color correction using the shadow matte that you created earlier.

When using After Effects or Motion, you'll need to nest the previous matte into a single element (a pre-comp in After Effects, a Layer in Motion) and apply a layer image mask. In Shake, just feed the mask into the side input of the color corrector.

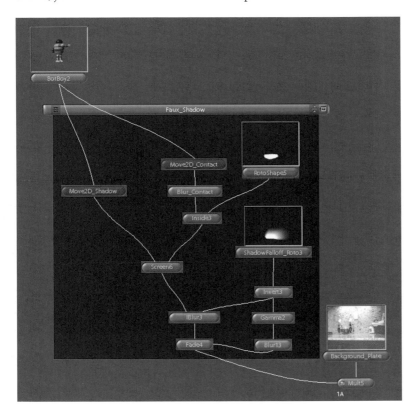

NOTE ▶ In this image, the shadow-creation section was grouped for emphasis.

With the mask in place, darken the background with the color corrector. You can do this by using a brightness slider or by reducing the value of your sampled color (or lightness, or brightness, depending on your specific software terminology).

Adjust the brightness until the shadow intensity is appropriate for the scene. As you work, you may notice a need to adjust some of the shadow matte settings to get a better match of penumbra softness, contact shadow strength, and so on.

Going Further

Once you've set things up, you need to play your entire sequence to see where your shadow work fails . . . and it will. You'll find separating shadows (aka the Peter Pan effect), flickers, shifting blurs, missing shadows, and so on. Adjust and keyframe as necessary, but be prepared to roto the patchier bits.

Displacement over Objects

One additional issue that often crops up is the need to simulate a shadow falling over other objects in the scene. This is where good 3D modeling and shadow pass rendering can really save you some time; but if they're not available, you can try creating a custom-rotoscoped gradient of the object, and then displacing the shadow using the matte.

This works well only for small objects close to the ground plane. Large objects will require custom-rotoscoped mattes.

Shadows, Harvesting

SEE ▶ Keying Fundamentals chapter; shadows, faux

Sharpening

DEFINITION ▶ Increasing edge contrast in an image to create the illusion of crisper focus. *Related terms:* focus enhancement; sharpening simulation

In other sections of this book, the emphasis is on turning *off* sharpening at all stages of the compositing pipeline. Sharpening is a great enemy of compositing. Once it's baked into an image, it's very hard to manipulate. However, it makes images look crisper. Therefore, part of your job is to sharpen images after you're done with the composite.

Matching Sharpness

If you're working with a film that has a mix of visual effects shots and non–visual effects shots, try to get a few frames of a standard shot in order to gauge the sharpness of the untreated scenes. Match your sharpness to those settings.

Applying Sharpness

There are many ways to sharpen, including standard sharpening filters, unsharp masks, and adaptive upsampling filters. Review the specific controls of the sharpening filters you have at hand. The most important point is not to oversharpen. Set the sharpen percentage to a level you think appropriate, and then seriously consider scaling it back. Also, be sure to preview the scene as animated before making a final decision on sharpness settings.

Cameo

Bringing Frank Sinatra "Back to Life"—J Bills

ONE OF THE MOST ambitious rotoscoping jobs the industry had seen in some time was a 2003 Radio City Music Hall production, *Frank Sinatra: His World, His Voice, His Way*. A core group of 12 New York City roto artists (see Contributors: John-Michael "J" Bills, page iv) took on more than 60,000 frames of vintage Sinatra footage with a completion time of six short months. This was a pure roto job of epic proportions with an exceptionally tight deadline.

Frank Sinatra: His World, His Voice, His Way, Radio City Music Hall, 2003

The task was to separate Sinatra from his backgrounds in an incredible 50-year-old performance. VFX-savvy theater vet Des McAnuff's directorial vision was to single out Sinatra and combine this footage with a barrage of other elements, from the kicking legs of the Radio City Rockettes to a gospel choir. All in all, the plan was to completely consume the audience in all things Frank with the help of 17 high-definition video projectors (at the time, the most projectors ever used in a live production), all simultaneously projecting onto screens as high as 60 feet.

One Foot at a Time

The footage was mostly composed of 35 mm reels that Sinatra filmed for his ABC-TV variety show in the mid-1950s. The footage had sat deep inside the Sinatra vault for more than 50 years.

For the most part, the shots were continuous, unedited takes of each song, with simple camera moves. Some of the best moments were long stretches of Sinatra framed from the waist up, centered, intently singing straight into the lens. It was easy to see what excited the production team behind this show. No matter where you were in the crowd, Frank would be singing just to you. Any seat was the best seat in the house! Even the audio was a dream come true for the purposes of the show, as Sinatra had multitracked the recording and his voice had its own track. The perfect setup.

After a few initial tests, the decision was made to use a liquid gate film process during the film transfer. This method runs the film through a liquid that simultaneously cleans it and minimizes dust and scratch artifacts. This was our first line of defense, the first of many automated methods we'd eventually employ to save us as much hard labor as possible. Even so, we still were left with scratches and dust spattering that the liquid gate couldn't address, as well as film tears, sprocket hole damage, grease-pencil marks, hairs, and chemical stains.

A taste of the restoration to come

The Secret Conversion

Another big production issue was how to get these shots distributed to the "dirty dozen"—the 12 hungry artists who would dive in and take on as many frames as we could dish out. But that raised another question: How fast could we dish?

In our case, frames were served from a storage-area network array similar to Apple's XSAN, feeding workstations via a fiber channel connection that was capable of serving about six artists with real-time disk-based 2K playback of source footage. This was a big workflow boost and almost a necessity, given that each shot was typically over 4000 frames!

Raw Cineon scans were converted to versions of the plates that were optimized strictly for the roto phase—something I highly suggest doing on any roto project. This initial **render** was used only to bump contrast and help to "punch out" Sinatra from his background as much as possible. Usually it was done with a simple lookup curve or by manipulating the black-and-white point of the Cineon conversion to give us a clearer edge.

Once we arrived at our golden **alpha channel** for each song, we threw out this roto version of the raw footage and brought back our original plates to be matted off by our final roto'd mattes. The footage was then further manipulated by the colorist and compositors according to the project's design specifications, so no one ever knew of our "roto version" besides the roto crew.

Cutting It Down to Size

When doing this first optimized roto render, we saw a unique chance to really knock our black-and-white image file sizes down. We converted the original 10 bit Cineon log plates to 8 bit grayscale linear, single-channel SGI files. The biggest advantage to doing this conversion was that it scaled down a three-channel image (RGB) and left us with a single-channel image (grayscale, or "BW" in Shake) that was further compressed with SGI's lossless file compression. This was a huge advantage. On disk from the scanner, 2K Cineon scans are 12.2 MB per frame. But our resulting conversions ranged from 1 MB to 3 MB, depending on the content of the frame and how many colors could be grouped.

A raw 10 bit Cineon scan (12.2 MB) versus an optimized grayscale 8 bit SGI (1.2 MB)

Our pipeline benefited in a big way from this optimized render. Preview renders were shorter, we never encountered disk-space problems, transferring files over our network was snappier, and the number of frames we could cache into RAM was exponentially increased.

> **TIP** ▶ This process was possible on the Sinatra project as the footage was strictly in black and white, but on color footage you'll want all three channels to properly see edge detail. You can, however, almost always dump the higher color-depth info in formats like Cineon or **OpenEXR** and work in an 8 bit space for a quick and easy speed boost.

To further reduce file sizes, we noticed that in most shots the framing was such that there were wide expanses of unused "fat," sometime as much as 30 percent of the frame, that we could trim off. We lopped off as much as his movement allowed, and occasionally even animated this crop to track Sinatra as he moved in the frame.

After working with the cropped version of the plates, we would uncrop and restore the footage to full size before rendering the final matte. Working with cropped footage results in a memory footprint that's a fraction of what it would've been. On a couple of songs, we were able to trim as much as 60 percent. When you're dealing with uncut shots and complete songs ranging up to 5000–6000 frames in length, that size reduction can result in a huge gain in interactivity.

The full-aperture scan

The cropped frame

The optional output crop (frame can be moved at compositor's discretion)

The last tightening up we were able to do was of a temporal nature as opposed to spatial. Why roto what you're not going to use? The show was tightly choreographed and edited from day one, which is incredibly important in any roto situation. Ideally, not a frame would be wasted—not to say we didn't provide the *Sinatra* editors with a modest handle of 24 frames in either direction. But when you figure that each shot was usually upwards of four minutes long, 24 frame handles are almost trivial. On a quick-cutting commercial with an edit every second, 8 frame handles might be more typical: just a little headroom in case an editor needs to make a last-minute emergency change, but no more than necessary. As roto is the most time-consuming part of a pipeline, it's important above all else to start with a locked edit.

Roto: The Last Resort

As a rule, the best roto artists reserve roto as a last resort. On *Sinatra*, we tried to coax as much as possible out of the footage procedurally. Even if it was the tiniest little thing, if it saved time, we did it. On one shot we were only able to track a mask to the hat that Sinatra was wearing, and the footage didn't give us anything else. Another shot had Sinatra wearing a jet black suit—jackpot! We were able to luma-key his jacket, pants, shoes, and slicked-back black hair against the light gray background, giving us a clean matte that was 80 percent complete, and turned 12 days of roto into only a couple of days.

A raw frame and resulting luma key; a matte that's about 80 percent usable

The average shot on this project was over 4000 frames long. A lot of roto artists won't see that *total* amount of roto work over an entire feature film assignment. And we were going to do it 15 times over! There had to be a methodology that would get these shots out the door efficiently once we were roto-ing away. After a couple of shots were under our belt, it was clear that the key was collaboration.

We found that we could divide Frank into several pieces. Divide and conquer! Once a lead artist was assigned, that artist would slice up Frank and break him off into a dozen or so discrete parts over the course of a shot.

Cutting a reference frame to use as a guide

The lead artist would cut a reference frame and distribute that to the team as a JPEG or project file with shapes. Then, the assigned pieces would be doled out to each artist on a macro level. They would use this reference frame as a basic guide to see what they needed to cover and where shapes of other artists would likely overlap. Then, each artist would analyze the clip to separate what was moving independently for each shape on a micro level.

To meet our deadlines, we found it most efficient to split into two teams of six artists and pump two songs through our pipelines simultaneously. Given that all of the artists were capable of working at a high level, we usually alternated assignments between a difficult set of shapes, such as snapping fingers, and then dialed back to an easier shape, like a leg. This was important for maintaining some shred of sanity!

As each shape was carried through the shot, a status flipbook was rendered daily to check for any pops or other glitches that we might discover as we worked. Each morning would begin with a quick review of these overnight flipbook renders. If you've never looked at a floating set of ears before, let me say it can sometimes be hard to keep from laughing at the sight of floating body parts, but we did our best.

To give you an idea of how complex a character roto like this can get, I believe our toughest shot had more than 300 shapes along with accompanying stabilizing and cropping. This could have turned into an organizational nightmare if not run tightly.

As you can imagine, running out thousands of frames with motion blur required quite a bit of render time. We were careful to separately render those shapes that we felt might need to be revised from those shapes that we knew were already approved. We then joined the "iffy" renders with the approved ones as a final step in Shake to generate the combined matte. This final render merge was lossless and incredibly quick (as motion blur had already been calculated). This step was important. If revisions were necessary, we only had to re-render specific shapes and not the entire group.

Motion blur became an issue later in the project because we were often compositing Sinatra over black to give the shots the "timeless" and powerful look that the director wanted. Since his original backgrounds were nowhere near black, the usual motion-blur treatment left the much-brighter original backgrounds bleeding through Frank's edges and impulse movements. It was next to impossible to find any method of color correcting the smudges of motion blur to match these new black surroundings. Our solution was to use optical flow data to track Sinatra's pixels as they moved through the frame. This allowed us to generate new motion-blur data and to seamlessly mix in the black background, or any background we wanted.

The roto phase: Before and after

Cleaning It Up

So we completed the marathon roto task. This crew had just roto'd for five months on end, but Frank was still missing something: his background!

Now that the shapes were all in place, it was time to focus on what was inside the mattes. The time had come to tackle the restoration phase of this project.

There was no need to hire a separate crew. As it turns out, the personality and composition of roto artists naturally make them good candidates for animated digital paint work—the kind of grit removal that was necessary to fix 50-year-old film scans.

I think it's safe to assume that most of us 2D types are Adobe Photoshop junkies by nature. We all start somewhere, and for most of us it's simple image manipulation.

Setting up the restoration involved many of the same decisions made during the roto phase. Automation again proved key. The majority of our 60,000 frames had some sort of 50-year-old gunk left on them. Overwhelming! Giving our crew of 12 a much-needed break, a single artist was placed in front of a da Vinci revival system, and a large render farm was able to generate a first pass that was about 80 percent complete. Beyond that, lots of frame-by-frame tweaking was necessary to remove dust and grime and to make this 50-year-old footage look like a brand-new show.

Samples of damaged frames

And what a show it was! Tears were flowing as "New York, New York" closed the show and the gospel choir, the band, the Rockettes, the life-size Rat Pack puppets, and every other cast member came out and took a bow, as a sea of confetti rained down from above. And somewhere in the back, in the shadows of the upper deck, a small row of about a dozen tired-looking artists had to be thinking that the emotional rush of that hour and a half was worth the pain of pushing points and pixels for the previous six months. Worth every second!

Showtime!

CREDITS ▶ Guava NYC
VFX Supervisors—Alex Catchpoole & Manuel Gonzalez
VFX Producer—Mary-Joy Lu
VFX Technical Supervisor—Ari Zohar Klingman
Lead Restoration—Jan Cilliers
VFX Artists—J Bills, Jan Cilliers, Greg Cutler, Michael Eder, Chris Halstead, Noor Kirdar, Ray Lewis, Dan Rubin, Brian Spector, Adam VanDine, Mark Wilhelm, Amber Wilson

Skin Repair (Digital Foundation)

DEFINITION ▶ The digital blurring of an image to even out the skin tone and smooth imperfections in the complexion of onscreen talent. *Related terms:* skin repair; skin retouching; skin tone repair

SEE ALSO ▶ blemish removal; cel shade, live action

Image before digital foundation

Image with extreme digital foundation applied

In the production world, makeup artists go out of their way to smooth the complexions of the talent. Unfortunately, due to age, acne, sunburn, or just plain old vanity, the foundation applied by the makeup artist is sometimes deemed insufficient. In such situations, a digital foundation applied in postproduction can rescue an otherwise embarrassing image. This technique also works well when a surreal perfection is required (such as in music videos).

The idea behind this technique is to blur the image to even out the skin tones. Indiscriminately applying a blur will, of course, wash out the detail in the entire image. A matte must therefore be created to isolate the areas in which the blur is applied. Edge detection is used to isolate the primary features of the image and protect them from being blurred. A final, loose rotoscoped matte protects large areas of the image where blurring is unnecessary.

Production Considerations

Digital foundation is usually classed as a "fix in post" technique and therefore not brought into consideration during production. Nonetheless, if the technique is intended to create an accentuated creative effect, it may be worth increasing the contrast in the facial features during production to help trigger the edge detection used in the process.

Procedure

1   The first step is to apply a blur to the image to determine the appropriate level of softening in the skin tones. Use the files located in **APTS_CycVFX/ProjectFiles/ BlursConv/Digital Foundation**.

    SHAKE ▼

    Open **DigitalFoundationStart.shk**. Apply a Filter > Blur (xPixels = 15) to the DigitalFoundation node.

    AFTER EFFECTS ▼

    Open **DigitalFoundationStart.aep**. Drag a copy of **DigitalFoundation.tif** into the Timeline. Apply an Effect > Blur & Sharpen > Gaussian Blur (Blurriness = 5) to the new layer. Rename the layer *BlurredLayer*.

    MOTION ▼

    Open **DigitalFoundation.motn**. Select the DigitalFoundation object and press Command-D twice to create two duplicates of the object. Rename the DigitalFoundation copy 1 object *MatteObject* and the DigitalFoundation copy object *BlurredObject*. Select BlurredObject and choose Add Filter > Blur > Gaussian Blur (Amount = 2.2). (You can deactivate MatteObject temporarily to confirm the blur. Reactivate when finished.)

    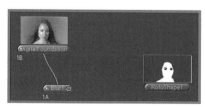

2   Now that the blurred image is prepared, it's time to create the matte that will protect the facial features from being blurred as well. The first step is to apply a median filter. The

median filter will remove small differences in the image (such as grain or video noise) that might falsely trigger the edge detection. If these were allowed to show up in the matte, the very imperfections we're trying to remove would be protected from the blur.

SHAKE ▼

Branch a Filter > Median (defaults) from the DigitalFoundation node.

AFTER EFFECTS ▼

Drag another copy of **DigitalFoundation.tif** into the Timeline above the first copy. Rename the layer *MatteLayer*. Apply an Effect > Noise > Median (Radius = 1) to MatteLayer.

MOTION ▼

Motion has no median filter, so a contrast filter will be used instead to flatten out everything except the major contrasting features of the image. Select MatteObject. Choose Add Filter > Color Correction > Contrast (Contrast = 1.27, Pivot = 0).

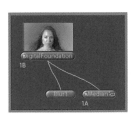

3   Next, edge detection is applied to the image to locate the areas of detail in the skin that need to be preserved.

SHAKE ▼

Add a Filter > EdgeDetect node (strength = 2.9) to Median1.

AFTER EFFECTS ▼

Add an Effect > Stylize > Find Edges (Invert = checked).

MOTION ▼

Choose Add Filter > Stylize > Edges (Intensity = 13).

4   As a result of the edge detection, fine detail throughout the skin area has inappropriately triggered the edge detection algorithm. A threshold filter is therefore added to
isolate only the brightest, and therefore most important, edges. A threshold filter sets
any pixel brightness below a certain value to 0 (black). A crush control can be used
to set all other values to 1 (pure white). (In the case of After Effects and Motion, the
crush is fixed to the "on" position.)

SHAKE ▼

Add a Color > Threshold (R,G, and B = 0.33, crush = 1) to EdgeDetect1.

AFTER EFFECTS ▼

Add an Effect > Stylize > Threshold (Level = 43).

MOTION ▼

Choose Add Filter > Color Correction > Threshold (Threshold = 0.05, Smoothness
= 0). To compensate for some of the detail lost due to the Contrast in step 2, choose
Add Filter > Stylize > MinMax (Mode = Maximum, Radius = 1). This will expand
the masked areas enough to fully cover high-feature areas of the face.

5   A few finishing touches are then applied to the matte. A blur is added to soften the
matte, smoothing the transition between areas where the blurred version of the image
will be applied and where the edges will be protected. After this, the matte is inverted,
so that the feature-protected areas appear dark, and the areas where the blur will be
applied appear white. This is the correct order for the matte: the blur needs to be
composited over the original image in the white areas of the matte.

SHAKE ▼

To the Threshold1 node, add a Filter > Blur node (xPixels = 10) and a Color > Invert node.

AFTER EFFECTS ▼

Add an Effect > Blur & Sharpen > Gaussian Blur (Blurriness = 2.5), then add an Effect > Channel > Invert.

MOTION ▼

Choose Add Filter > Blur > Gaussian Blur (Amount = 2.0). Then choose Add Filter > Color Correction > Invert.

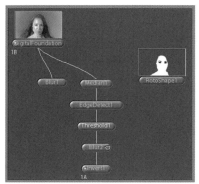

6   At this point, the generated matte could be used to composite the blurred version over the original. You might want such a softening as an exaggerated effect for the entire image. However, in normal situations where only the skin is to be affected, a rotoshape must be generated to protect other areas of the image. The good news is that this rotoshape can be very rough; the edge detection is already doing some significant filtering of border areas. Facial features such as eyes and eyebrows can also be quickly matted out with rotoshapes. These shapes can usually be tracked in place for minimal manual rotoscoping work over time. Once the matte has been created, it can be blurred to smooth transition areas, inverted, and then subtracted from the original matte. (Alternatively, for a more subtle effect, the noninverted version can be multiplied against the original matte.)

TIP ▶ You may find that working specifically with the red channel will produce a nicer skin matte. Often blemishes will be less conspicuous in the red channel.

SHAKE ▼

Select RotoShape1 and add a Filter > Blur node (xPixels = 40) followed by a Color > Invert node. Select Invert1 (at the base of the branch generating the matte) and add a Layer > ISub node. Connect Invert2 (from the RotoShape1 branch) to the second input of ISub1.

AFTER EFFECTS ▼

Select MatteLayer and choose Layer > Pre-compose. Select "Move all attributes into the new composition" and click OK. Double-click MatteLayer Comp 1 in the Project panel to open it. Drag **RotoMask.tif** above MatteLayer in the MatteLayer Comp 1 Timeline. Set the transfer mode for **RotoMask.tif** to Silhouette Luma.

MOTION ▼

Turn off visibility for MatteObject. Drag **RotoMask.tif** into the Layers tab and deactivate its visibility as well. Select BlurredObject and choose Object > Add Image Mask. In the Image Mask Inspector (F4), drag RotoMask from the Layers tab into the image well, set Source Channel = Luminance, and Mask Blend Mode = Subtract.

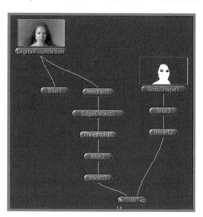

7   Finally, the matte is used to composite the blurred version of the image back over the original to complete the effect. You can adjust the opacity of the blurred version of the image to reveal some of the imperfections beneath for a more subtle effect.

SHAKE ▼

Select DigitalFoundation and shift-click to branch a Layer > KeyMix node (channel = R). Connect Blur1 to the second (foreground) input, and ISub1 to the third (key) input. Adjust Percent in KeyMix1 to reduce the strength of the effect.

AFTER EFFECTS ▼

Select DigitalFoundation Comp 1. In the Timeline, turn off the visibility for MatteLayer Comp 1. Drag another copy of **DigitalFoundation.tif** to the bottom of the Timeline (to serve as the unblurred base image). For BlurredLayer, set the track matte (TrkMat) to Luma Matte "[MatteLayer Comp 1]." Adjust the opacity of BlurredLayer to reduce the strength of the effect.

MOTION ▼

Select BlurredObject again, and add a second image mask by choosing Object > Add Image Mask. In the Image Mask Inspector (F4), drag MatteObject from the Layers tab into the image well, set Source Channel = Luminance, and Mask Blend Mode = Intersect. (Intersect combines this new mask with the original.) Adjust the Opacity of BlurredObject to reduce the strength of the effect.

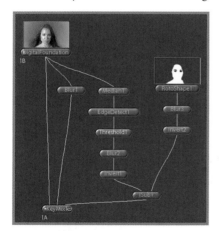

Sky Keying

DEFINITION ▶ Using a blue sky in place of a blue screen or green screen. *Related terms:* outdoor blue screen; sky replacement

SEE ALSO ▶ edge matte

If you just need to get out of the studio for a while, why not use the blue sky as your key background? Blue sky actually makes an ideal choice for keying, and it is sometimes the only choice when the scale of the element to be keyed is beyond the capacity of a soundstage.

Sky keys are most commonly used for scale model photography and, of course, sky-replacement shots.

There are a couple of techniques that will help make a sky key successful (beyond the obvious ones of shooting away from smog-infested cities, and shooting on a clear, sunny day). The first technique is to use a polarizing filter on the camera lens. Polarizing the light before it enters the lens will produce much better contrast in the shot and should tame the brightness of the sky without significantly darkening the all-important foreground elements.

Second, it's crucial that you deactivate sharpening in the camera. The stark border between the sky and the foreground will almost certainly produce strong sharpening artifacts if the camera applies a sharpen filter.

Once the footage is acquired, there's another important factor to consider: spill. The foreground will be affected by the blue spill of the sky light, and that spill will be extremely luminous. If you're replacing the sky with something of a similar intensity, you should have few problems. If you're replacing the sky with a dark, brooding storm, you'll have many more problems.

The dark, brooding storm would produce less spill light, and therefore the foreground should also appear darker. The solution is to apply a color correction to the foreground using an extremely wide edge matte. (See edge matte for details.)

Once the edge matte has been used to attenuate the foreground brightness, the sky should blend much more naturally.

Smoke

SEE ▶ keying generic elements

Smoothing

DEFINITION ▶ The process of using tracking data to remove only the noise in a movement while preserving a smooth motion path for the tracked object. Here, *noise* refers to unwanted movement.

SEE ALSO ▶ Tracking Fundamentals chapter

SMPTE

DEFINITION ▶ Stands for *Society of Motion Picture and Television Engineers*. The organization responsible for establishing various broadcast video standards, such as the SMPTE standard timecode for video playback.

Specular Pass

SEE ▶ 3D Fundamentals chapter; multipass, basic passes

Speed Changes

SEE ▶ ramping

Spill

DEFINITION ▶ The unintentional tinting of areas of the foreground with the background screen color. This results from light reflecting off the background screen and contaminating the foreground, along with backing light diffused into the foreground in the camera optics. Spill must be removed before a shot can be color corrected.

SEE ALSO ▶ spill suppression

Spill Suppression

DEFINITION ▶ Removal of unwanted background light spill from a foreground subject. The spill is usually the color of a blue screen or green screen. *Related terms:* blue spill removal; green spill removal

SEE ALSO ▶ background wrap; compositing outside the keyer; radiosity, faux; screen replacement

Spill from blue screens and green screens is inevitable. Diffusion in the camera's optics will always produce some degree of spill, even if two football fields separate a foreground subject from its background. This spill will tint the subject green or blue (depending on the backing key screen color) and will look very unnatural.

All scenes cast light on objects within that scene (see radiosity, faux), but unless the predominant background color is the same as the key screen, the original spill lighting will be incorrect.

TIP ▶ Are you compositing an actor against a blue sky? Shoot blue screen, not green screen, and then think twice before applying any dramatic spill suppression. The blue spill may be appropriate for the final blue background.

There are many ways to suppress excessive spill, and it's important to have as many methods in your tool kit as possible. Every key screen is a unique little beastie, and a spill suppression method that failed miserably on one key may work like a charm on a different screen.

Applying Spill Suppression

Spill suppression should always be applied to an unpremultiplied image, *never* to an image that is being fed into a keyer to generate the key. If you suppress the color in an image before keying it, you destroy the color contrast that the keyer needs to do its magic.

For more information on spill suppression placement, see compositing outside the keyer.

Problems with Spill Suppression

Spill suppression causes many problems even as it cures one problem.

First, whenever you remove color from an image, you reduce that image's brightness. When removing spill, you'll need to boost the luminance of the affected pixels to compensate for that loss of brightness.

One nice solution to key screen spill is to apply a background wrap to replace the key screen spill lighting with simulated spill lighting from the background.

Another key screen limitation is the destruction of legitimate colored elements. If someone wears blue jeans to a blue screen set, those jeans won't be blue after the spill suppression is done. The solution is to use a holdout matte to protect these legitimate color regions.

Using Filters and Keyer Suppression

Most compositing applications include some form of spill suppression filter. They are usually simple to adjust and *may* work well. Try them first, but expect them to work well in only some situations. As often as not, you'll need to roll your own.

Many keyers also include spill suppression. Since spill suppression is inextricably linked to the process of pulling a key in these keyers, you may compromise the quality of the spill suppression for the sake of the generated matte, or vice versa. A way around this dilemma is to use separate keyers to generate the matte and apply spill suppression (see compositing outside the keyer).

Limiting the Spill Color

A pixel looks blue because that pixel's blue value is higher than its red and green values. If the blue value is the same as either the red or green value, then the pixel can no longer be considered blue. It may appear to be cyan or magenta.

> **NOTE ▶** In some situations, the context of surrounding pixels may create a perception of blue even when the blue value of that pixel is not significantly higher than its red and green values.

The idea, then, is to limit the spill color whenever it exceeds the values of the other two channels.

Take a blue screen as an example. If you limit the blue values of pixels to the green channel, then the blue value will be replaced with the green value whenever the pixel's blue value exceeds the green value. So, if a pixel's blue value is 0.8 and its green value is 0.6, the new blue value after the limiting would be 0.6, and the green value would remain at 0.6.

Whenever the blue value was below the green value, it would remain untouched. A pixel with a blue value of 0.4 and a green value of 0.7 would retain those values after the limiting.

Blue limited to green

In the preceding example, blue was limited to green, but you can just as easily limit blue to the red value. In fact, it's quite common to limit the blue channel to a combination of the other two channels.

To try out various limiting operations, you can use a ColorX node in Shake.

Apply a Color > ColorX node to the image you want to suppress, then change the expression for the key color (to bExpr in the case of a blue screen, for example). The previous example of limiting blue to green would look like this:

The ColorX node syntax may seem daunting, but it's actually quite simple. Whatever appears to the left of the question mark is a question. In this case, the ColorX node asks if the blue pixel value is greater than the green pixel value. The item directly to the right of the question mark gives the result if the answer is yes. The item to the right of the colon gives the result if the answer is no. So in this case, if the blue value *is* greater than the green, the resulting value for bExpr—and therefore the current pixel's blue value—will be the same as the green value. If the blue value *is not* greater than the green value, the resulting value for bExpr will be blue, and the original value of blue will be unchanged.

If you've done any programming, you'll recognize that this is a shorthand form of the "if … then … else" command set common to most programming languages.

There are many ways to limit the key color with ColorX. The examples below are written in terms of blue limiting, but you can limit green just as easily by swapping the b and g values (and by placing the expression in the gExpr parameter).

b>g?g:b—As already mentioned, this expression limits blue to green.

b>r?r:b—This expression limits blue to red.

b>(r+g)/2?(r+g)/2:b—This expression limits blue to the average of red and green. If the image features a wide variety of hues, this will probably produce more balanced results.

b>max(r,g)?max(r,g):b—This expression is an extremely subtle variation. It limits blue to either the red or green value, depending on which is larger. In very mild situations, this may be all the correction that's needed.

b>min(r,g)?min(r,g):b—This expression is the most extreme of the limiting functions. It will suck the blue out of any pixel that ever had a melancholy thought. You should use this only in severe situations (and never in conjunction with prescription antidepressants).

The possibilities are infinite, but if none of the above works, you may be well advised to move on. There are better ways to waste your employer's time and money.

Using Hue Curves

Hue curves, available in Shake's Color tab, are a powerful spill suppression method. They allow you to color correct the pixels in a specific hue range. So when using a blue screen, for example, you can specifically target blue pixels without affecting pixels with hues outside the defined range. You can also use hue curves to reduce the saturation of stubborn spill areas.

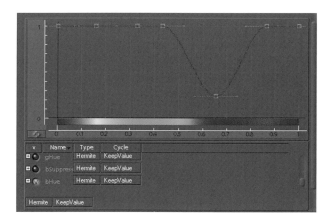

Color Replace

Another way to desaturate specific colors is to use a color-replacement filter. This method is extremely useful for stubborn spill areas that have been unaffected by more general methods. Sample the problem spill area as the source color for the operation. Copy that color and use it as the target color (which will make no difference to the image as yet, because you're setting the filter to shift the pixel colors from an initial value to exactly the same final value). Once the source and target colors are identical, you can reduce the saturation of the target color until you're happy with the result. You can even tint the color as necessary. Remember to adjust hue range and falloff values to encompass exactly the right pixels in your image.

Paint It Out

In extreme cases of spill, you can try to paint away the problem areas. Use a paint tool to create a matte for another operation, such as a desaturating filter.

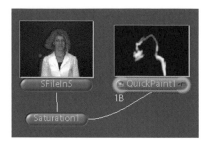

Spill Maps

All of these techniques are useful, but sometimes you want more control over the *amount* of spill being removed. The solution is to create a spill map. A *spill map* is a matte that details where the spill in an image occurs, allowing you to mask off a secondary color correction and adjust the intensity of the suppression.

For example, a spill map of a blue screen limited to the average of red and green (see "Limiting the Spill Color," above) could be generated by the following expression in a ColorX node:

This expression produces a matte on the alpha channel of the image identifying only the areas where blue pixel values exceed the average of red and green values.

This matte can then be fed as a mask to an additive color corrector to remove unwanted spill. (In this case, the additive color corrector will be subtracting, not adding.)

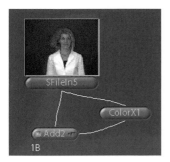

There are many other permutations and combinations of spill suppression techniques, but the techniques described here are good starting points in your efforts to tame spill. Remember, always start with the simple options, and continue until you find a satisfactory result.

One last word of caution: Beware of breaks in scene continuity. If your blue screen or green screen comp is part of a sequence that is intercut with non-VFX shots, make sure that the spill suppression has not significantly changed the coloration of clothing (and skin tones) relative to the standard shots.

Split Screen Composites

> **DEFINITION** ▸ Using a split screen matte to divide the frame. *Related terms:* continuum shot; twin shot

Split screen compositing allows for combining and viewing multiple shots or images simultaneously, such as in "twin" shots or showing both sides of a telephone conversation. Traditionally, the simplest example is dividing the screen into left and right halves, showing action in two separate locations. In the image below (from the music video *Monkey* by New Zealand's The Reveals), a character confronts the dark side of her psyche as she looks into a huge mirror.

Source 1

Source 2

Composite

Although the music video's intended output was TV resolution (PAL, 720 × 576), this shot was framed at a wide-screen aspect ratio (2.35:1). This made it much easier for viewers to digest the side-by-side split screen shots when they were intercut with the full screen (4:3) "regular" material.

An extension of this technique is the twin shot. The same actor delivers a scene twice, once as herself and once as her twin. The actions of each performance are carefully limited to one side of the frame. The two shots are then composited so that the actor's separate performances appear to interact. The camera is typically locked off (or, rarely, motion controlled), and the placement of the line dividing the two scenes is usually buried within a straight-line vector such as a door or window, which can help to mask minor misalignments that can occur between the shots.

In the television series *Friends*, this technique was used extensively in episodes featuring Phoebe and her twin, Ursula—both played by Lisa Kudrow. Other recent examples of split screen compositing may be seen in the films *The Hulk* and *Time Code*. In *The Hulk*, director Ang Lee used split screen compositing to create a comic book–like frame structure during montage sequences, at times showing several onscreen clips arranged in a complex pattern.

In Mike Figgis's *Time Code*, the frame was divided into quadrants, and four shots were shown simultaneously in a unique (and sometimes overlapping) narrative. Audio is always an important consideration when doing a multiscreen composite of multiple locations, and *Time Code* did a brilliant job of ensuring that whichever quadrant had the focus of the action also had its sound mix in the forefront.

Finally, split screens are used by compositors for side-by-side previews of different effect settings or branches of a comp tree, and to present before-and-after renders for clients and supervisors. In fact, Shake's built-in A/B buffer Compare tool is in itself a variation of a split screen comp.

There are production considerations common to most split screen shoots. Typically (but not without exceptions), the shots should tend toward close-ups, as opposed to long shots, because the reduced screen size of each element limits the effectiveness of small details.

It's also best to plan the framing of each shot in advance, rather than depend on cropping when compositing in postproduction. Ask yourself how many sources will be displayed at once, and if the division will be horizontal or vertical. Or, you might be working with a more elaborate split screen design that leaves areas of blank/black space onscreen. Depending on how the frame is going to be split, it may be critical to frame the action in a specific way.

The Shake composite workflow is fairly straightforward for a simple split screen.

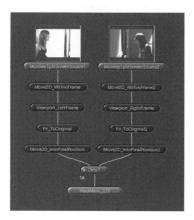

When you bring in the image sources (making sure that auto-alpha is enabled to include any RGB images' alpha information), follow each FileIn node with a Viewport node set to mask off the area of the screen you have allocated for that source. For example, in a simple two-source split, you can make one Viewport mask off the left half of the screen (dividing the *x* resolution value by 2) and have the other mask off the right half. Viewport is effectively a crop that retains the image information outside the area you've cut off, so you can reposition the source image within the cropped region further down in the compositing tree.

In case you want to do some repositioning, you can add a Move2D node *before* the Viewport nodes. If you need to reposition or scale the shot to fit in its cropped (or, technically, its Viewported) area, you can do that using these initial Move2D nodes.

Before you reposition, you'll need to create a rough comp of the shot to see the images simultaneously. Follow the Viewport nodes with a Fit node that is set to the original image size. This will expand the cropped (Viewported) images to fill the frame but will leave the crop's alpha channel intact. Follow those nodes with a Move 2D node that repositions the sources into their final split locations onscreen, each one carefully moved and scaled so that all the action can be seen clearly.

At this point, you can do a reposition to select the viewable part of each element by using the Move2D nodes you placed in front of the Viewport crops. The crops will remain unchanged, but manipulating those Move2D nodes will move the FileIn within the Viewport frame. Use whole-pixel increments in both the Viewport and Move2D nodes to maintain maximum image fidelity.

If the split screen requires the images to be scaled in any way, be careful to watch for reduced grain size and also for the black borders typical of the extreme edge of frame for most film and video sources. You'll want to crop those off and make sure they aren't seen in your composite. If degraining or regraining is necessary to return the grain to the size of the grain in the rest of the scene, perform that now. Finally, pipe all of the images into a series of Overs or an equivalent Multilayer node, and you're ready to render.

As with any composite that has some unavoidable breaks in concatenation, it's important to follow what I call the METL (for *metal*) workflow, a handy acronym that helps you remember how to generally order your trees in a node-based compositor: Masks, Effects, Transforms, and Layering. Shake will do only what you tell it to do, so it's important that you tell it to do things in the right order to avoid unnecessary processing of your images. As usual, METL is not without exception and is just a general way of thinking that is useful until you get into complex comps requiring lots of nested, precomped work or you're working in a float pipeline with a different set of rules.

If you're creating a twin shot composite on a locked-off shot, the effect is done with a carefully drawn rotoshape to layer the two shots together. Look for a logical path to slice the frame within the safe area between the separate performances so that any small variations are hidden (due to gate weave, camera bumps, slight differences in exposure, and so on). Typically, you'll choose straight lines formed by background objects like doors or windows. In the *Monkey* example above, the dividing line was the mirror frame.

Finally, if you're just creating a split screen to preview a before/after comp or two separate parts of your tree, consider using the handy macro on the FXShare site that makes a flexible "contact sheet" (to borrow a photographic term) and quickly creates a tiled preview out of as many inputs as you require. It's available for free at www.fxshare.com/shake/downloads/macros/transformations/1233.html.

Square Pixel

DEFINITION ► A pixel that has the same height as width. Computer monitors have square pixels, but NTSC and PAL video screens do not.

SEE ALSO ► pixel aspect ratio

Stabilization

DEFINITION ▶ Using tracking data to lock an object in place. That is, the process of selecting a particular region of an image, analyzing its motion over time, inverting the motion data, and applying the inverted motion to the clip, thereby causing the selected region to become stable.

For example, if an object is tracked as moving up and to the left by a certain amount, moving the footage down and to the right by the same amount will lock the object in its original position.

Clips need to be stabilized for a variety of reasons, from weave created by an unsteady camera gate, known as *gate weave*, to a shaky camera move.

SEE ALSO ▶ camera shake, smoothing and removal; hot spots, removing; tracking marker removal; Tracking Fundamentals chapter

Standard Definition

DEFINITION ▶ The term used to differentiate traditional television broadcast signals from those of new high-definition formats. Standard-definition broadcast signals are usually 720 × 486 (for NTSC) or 720 × 576 (for PAL).

Starfields, Moving

DEFINITION ▶ Moving starfields or particles without causing a twinkling effect. *Related terms:* twinkling stars, fixing

Need to move small particles or starfields without experiencing the twinkling effect? Simply scale up the original image so that no particle or star is less than 2 pixels in size, then apply the movement. The resulting subpixel motion will be smoother and less prone to twinkling. Remember to scale down to the original size after the movement. Also, don't forget to add motion blur.

NOTE ▶ Shake will concatenate scale and movement transforms, eliminating the benefit of first scaling up. To stop this, add a Reorder node between transform nodes to break the concatenation.

Stereoscopy

DEFINITION ▶ The process of creating the perception of three dimensions via a two-dimensional medium. *Related terms:* 3D glasses; 3D viewing; anaglyphs

SEE ALSO ▶ stereoscopy from 2D

Stereoscopy is the process of recording, or creating the illusion of, images in three dimensions. While the delivery methods vary, the primary concept is that two separate images are created—one to be received by a viewer's left eye, the other to be received by the right.

A stereo anaglyph of a live performance by Duran Duran with left eye information conveyed by the red channel of the image. See "Duran Duran in 3D," page 209, for the story behind this 3D concert film.

NOTE ▶ Stereoscopy differs from hologrammetry, where an observer can "look around" a scene. With stereoscopy, the illusion of 3D is created, but observers are not able to obtain new information by changing their vantage point relative to the viewing mechanism.

Stereoscopic images can be created via both physical acquisition devices (well, cameras, but *PAD*s sounds much more sophisticated) and computer-generated processes. The technique is essentially the same, with the latter being a virtual replication of what takes place in a physical setup.

Physically Generated Stereoscopy

Physical stereoscopic camera rigs comprise two identical cameras mounted to a tripod or dolly so that both cameras dolly, pan, and tilt together. If any kind of freestyle zoom is to be applied during filming, an extremely precise synchronization of zoom and focus mechanisms is required. When one camera is zoomed more than another, it will at best ruin the illusion for the audience, and at worst give them all splitting migraines—and that doesn't do so well for word-of-mouth ticket sales.

Great care must be taken to ensure the image being viewed through each camera is identical, except for the required degree of horizontal translation between the cameras. Some misalignment is inevitable, and the stereoscopic experience can be enhanced by realigning the shots in the compositing phase.

> **TIP** To correct for slight differences between the two views, follow the same method used to derive a clean plate from two adjacent frames (see **clean plates, generating**). Don't expect a perfect match, because the horizontal translation of the two cameras will result in different perspectives. If you *do* get a perfect match, something's gone wrong; the stereoscopic effect relies on the difference between the two views. Once you've corrected the two shots, separate their horizontal positions again to achieve the desired depth effect.

Say No to the Toe

One of the greatest mistakes to be made when creating stereoscopic imagery is to "toe in" the lenses. When a pair of human eyes focuses on an object, each eye angles toward the subject.

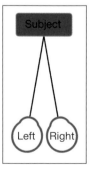

The logical conclusion some people extract from this is that stereoscopic cameras should likewise converge on their subject in order to best simulate human perception. This is a case of overthinking the problem, and is very wrong. Wrong in the way that Vegemite on ice cream is wrong. Stereoscopy is not an attempt to emulate the human visual experience;

stereoscopy creates the illusion of 3D viewing by displaying two 2D images, one to each eye. The observer is not seeing a genuine 3D scene, as with a hologram, but rather fooled into believing that the scene is 3D.

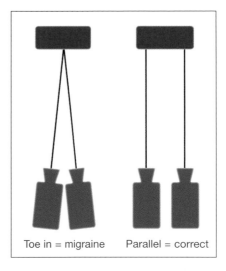

Toe in = migraine   Parallel = correct

Converging the lenses while capturing stereo image pairs results in a keystone disparity in the two images, and this is what commonly causes headaches as the brain's graphics processing unit tries to reconcile the images received from the eyes. Instead, the cameras should record the scene in parallel. That is, both camera lenses should be pointed toward the scene at the same angle.

Interocular Distance

Interocular distance is the distance between the eyes, roughly 2.4 inches from pupil to pupil. In theory, the perfect stereoscopic illusion would be created with two cameras the same distance apart, but since that's such a short distance, it allows little room for the bulky chassis of the two cameras.

Sophisticated techniques for achieving a matching interocular distance involve using angled mirrors to send the appropriately distanced image pairs back to the camera housings. While this is ideal, adequate results can be obtained even when cameras are much farther apart. The resulting image is similar to miniaturization, like a giant looking at the scene (but without all the hallucinogenic bean nonsense).

Interocular distance can be further massaged in postproduction, by reframing (usually cropping) the left and right views to adjust the distance between them.

> **NOTE** ▶ Generating stereoscopic images in the computer follows the same principles as capturing real scenes. There are two primary content-creation methods: rendering with virtual cameras from a 3D software application, or creating 3D from 2D. See **stereoscopy from 2D** for more information.

Delivery Methods

There are several ways to present stereoscopic images to an audience. These include free-form images, anaglyphs, polarized displays, and images projected by automated shutter systems. Of these, the last two are the most cost prohibitive. Polarized displays require the use of two polarized projectors as well as more expensive polarized glasses. Likewise, shutter systems require LCD shutter glasses, which are rarely practical or affordable except in controlled environments such as IMAX theaters and museum presentation areas. So for affordable mass distribution, freeform viewing and anaglyphic viewing are the reigning favorites.

Freeform Stereoscopic Viewing

By far the simplest and probably most effective 3D viewing system is freeform viewing, requiring the viewers to cross their eyes until the two images converge into a single, central stereoscopic image. Expect to see visual "ghosts" of the two images on either side of the stereo image as you view it.

Try crossing your eyes slowly while viewing the images below. Once you've locked on to the image, take some more time to allow your brain to resolve the detail. You'll notice an increased sense of depth as you continue to preview.

 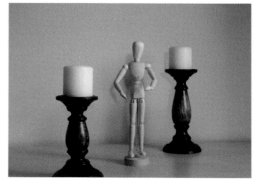

Freeform viewing takes some getting used to. It usually requires a good night's sleep. No, seriously. This method tends to be used to a limited extent, due to the training required for an audience to appreciate the effect, not to mention the obvious eye strain that results from prolonged viewing.

Anaglyphic Stereographic Viewing

The most popular form of stereoscopy, anaglyphs use cheap, colored-lens glasses to achieve their effect by tinting the two images of the stereo pair using two different colors. The glasses then filter out all but the appropriate color for a given eye.

The candlestick in front is at screen depth, causing more cyan and red separation on the other objects.

The most common scheme is to place a red filter on the left eye and a cyan filter on the right eye. The left eye view is then placed in the red channel of the image, while the right eye view occupies both the green and blue channels (green + blue = cyan).

> **TIP** It is possible to use a blue filter instead of cyan, but expect a change in image contrast as a result. Green light that would have contributed to the intensity of the image will be filtered out by the blue filter.

Creating an anaglyph is extremely simple. Just copy the red channel from the left image into the red channel of the right image, replacing the original.

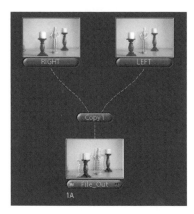

In this Shake script, the channels parameter in Copy1 is set to *r*.

While anaglyphic stereoscopy is affordable, it requires a complete or significant reduction in image saturation to preserve the color separation, and it doesn't allow for extreme depth variations for the final image.

Adjusting the Separation in Postproduction

Even after a stereo pair has been captured or rendered, it's still possible to adjust the depth of the shot. In fact, it's often necessary to compress the separation of two images to keep the illusion from breaking, which often happens with anaglyphic stereographs.

Even though the two images combined in the figure on the next page were photographed at a standard interocular distance, the spacing of the images is too extreme when they were combined to form this anaglyph. The illusion breaks, and the separation of the two views is clearly visible to the observer as ghosting.

With anaglyphs, the solution is to adjust the separation between the two images by horizontally translating (panning) one of the images relative to the other prior to copying over the red channel. Then the final image is cropped to remove any overlap at the edges.

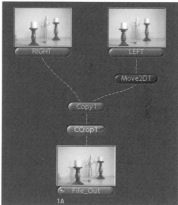

With freeform stereoscopic images, the same effect can be performed by reframing the left and right images relative to each other. For instance, you might end up trimming the edges of the first image more to the right than the other.

Stereo Depth and Screen Position

As you just learned, you can determine where objects in the scene will appear in 3D space by adjusting the separation between images. With anaglyphs, if an object appears farther to the left in the left view than it does in the right, that object will appear to reside behind the screen position. The screen position is the depth of the display device, be it a TV, computer monitor, or projector screen. So the object appears to exist behind the display.

If an object is in the identical position in both the left and right views, it will appear to be at the same depth as the screen. Finally, if an object appears farther to the right in the left view than it does in the right, it will appear to reside in front of the screen position. By moving the stereo pairs toward or away from each other, different objects in the scene will be pushed in front of or behind the screen position.

In the figure above, the candle to the right appears to be behind the screen position, the mannequin appears to be at the same depth as the screen, and the candle to the left appears to be in front of the screen.

In theory, your scene can extend in front of and behind the screen as much as you like, as long as the forward projecting objects do not touch the edges of the screen. The scene above is a perfect example of the problem, since the left candle connects with the bottom border of the image. Outside the borders of the stereograph is the real world, and the actual screen border lies at screen position, giving the brain conflicting cues: the candle looks as if it lies both in front of the screen and at the same position on the screen. As you view the figures above (as an anaglyph or a freeform image), you'll see that the left candle competes with the mannequin's position; sometimes it seems to be in front of the screen, while at other times it appears to be at the screen position along with the mannequin. Try covering your hand over the base of the left candle and you should find that the illusion instantly resolves itself and the candle clearly appears in front of the screen.

The solution is to set the left candle at screen position, and let everything else reside behind the screen, as seen in the figures below.

Reserve objects emerging out of the screen for elements that don't touch the sides—obnoxious text effects, flaming arrows, and the like.

Managing Expectations

As you negotiate with clients to create a stereoscopic production, be sure to advise them about the limitations of the process, especially in the case of anaglyphs. Also, give them an understanding of the lessening effect of 3D in motion. With stills (as displayed above), the human perceptual system can assimilate and resolve the images over time. With moving content, the impact is somewhat reduced, as the eye has less time to explore the illusion before something starts to move, be it the camera or the on-camera talent.

One way to plan for a better final show is to reduce the number of edits in the material. While modern editors like to change takes and angles every few seconds, stereoscopic content benefits from the longest takes possible in order to give the viewers' eyes plenty of time to adjust to and accept the illusion.

Stereoscopy from 2D

DEFINITION ▶ Creating a stereoscopic effect from a 2D image by using mattes and either IDisplace or virtual cameras in MultiPlane or After Effects 3D view. *Related terms:* 2.5D; planar stereoscopy

SEE ALSO ▶ stereoscopy

Stereoscopy is most authentically achieved by using two live action cameras or two virtual cameras in a 3D software package (see **stereoscopy**). However, it's also possible to generate stereoscopic images after the fact by manually extracting specific elements in a scene and setting them at different distances from the virtual camera.

Deriving stereoscopy from a 2D image can often produce more striking results than a genuine two-camera stereoscopic pair, since depth can be exaggerated for effect. The downside is that every element with a separate depth must be manually articulated. And, yes, that means rotoscoping.

The most common method for generating stereoscopy from 2D images is to separate elements onto 2D planes perpendicular to the camera. In other words, make a bunch of cardboard cutouts of the image in question and position them at different distances from the virtual camera. Backgrounds can be generated using gradient displacements, which will be discussed later in this entry.

Extracting Objects

Rotoscoping individual elements to extract them from their background can be a daunting task, especially when considering the sheer volume of roto work required for many shots. To create a convincing scene, every freestanding item in the shot must be rotoscoped separately. That could be dozens of elements.

The good news is, the specific rotoscoping required for 3D conversion can be particularly forgiving. Instead of rotoscoping the exact border around an image, the shape can usually include some background without ruining the effect. The result will be some of the background included at the same depth as the object being rotoscoped, but with moving footage, this is often unnoticed, especially if the background is a relatively homogenous texture.

It's worth experimenting with your footage first to see just how loose your roto efforts can be. When relaxing the shape, err on the side of including the background, and make sure all elements of the object are included within the shape. This is especially true of wild tufts of hair, even if it means pulling chunks of the background into the shape.

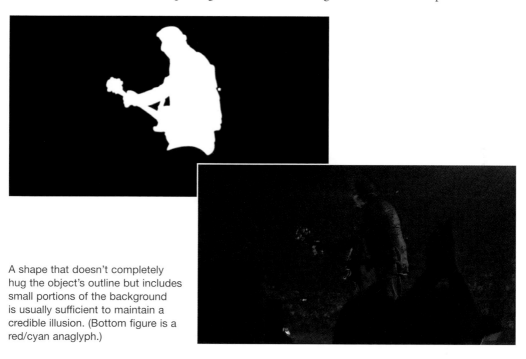

A shape that doesn't completely hug the object's outline but includes small portions of the background is usually sufficient to maintain a credible illusion. (Bottom figure is a red/cyan anaglyph.)

With still images (as opposed to motion picture or video) the mattes necessarily require greater articulation, since they'll be under closer scrutiny. The good news is that you're rotoscoping a single frame, rather than oh, say, 7,793 frames.

Creating Depth

To create the illusion of depth, objects must be translated horizontally in each of the stereo pairs (see stereoscopy). Objects intended to appear behind the display screen (computer monitor, movie screen, etc.) should be moved so that they appear farther to the left in the left view than in the right view. Objects intended to appear in front of the screen should be moved so that they appear farther to the right in the left view. Finally, objects that share the same depth as the display screen should be spaced identically in both the left and right views.

This spacing can be understood better by looking at the anaglyph below. The red coloration represents the left channel and will appear behind the screen, while the cyan coloration represents the right channel and will appear in front of the screen. If viewing the anaglyph with red/cyan glasses, give your eyes some time to resolve the image, particularly the forward-projected text.

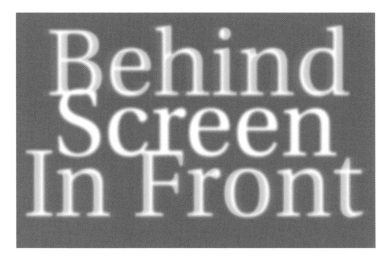

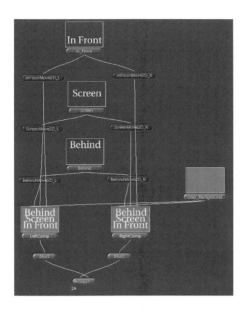

To experiment with this script, open **APTS_CycVFX/ProjectFiles/CG/Stereoscopy/ Stereoscopyfrom2DSample.shk**.

Filling In the Holes

Once an object has been extracted and moved into position, there will remain an unpleasant hole where an observer should, in theory, be able to see background. As you move your head from side to side, you'll get different vantage points from which to view the scene. Notice that the foreground objects move out of the way to expose background information you were unable to see from the initial position of your head.

The problem with moving from a 2D image to a 3D one is that the two eye views offer distinct vantage points and can see more of the scene behind foreground objects than one eye alone. So it's necessary to re-create the missing background information in order to successfully complete the shot.

Several methods exist, including the use of sophisticated pattern reconstruction plug-ins (such as The Foundry's Furnace suite). A simple and often satisfactory method is to smear portions of the adjacent background to fill in the missing information.

To experiment with this technique, use the included SideSmear macro found in **APTS_ CycVFX/ProjectFiles/CG/Stereoscopy/Macros/**. After installing the macro, insert the background in the first input and the matte used to extract an object in the second. Then adjust the smearAmount to create the effect. Adjust the falloff to vary the definition of the edge detail being smeared, and use softenBorder to smooth the smearing. The effect won't be particularly flattering, but judge the results with respect to the final stereoscopic composite, using only as much as necessary to cover the background holes in the shot.

Creating Backgrounds

Gradients can be used to vary the depth in backgrounds that recede into the distance. Simply create a gradient matching the depth of the scene, then use it as a displacement matte. Objects deeper in the scene should displace more to the left in the left view, and more to the right in the right view.

In the following figures, the displayed gradient has been used to drive a displacement on some random gray noise. The result is the appearance of a square tunnel in the random noise anaglyph.

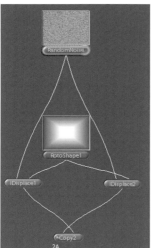

Be aware that the position of objects in the scene must match the displacement of a background at that given depth. For example, if a lamppost appears midway into a receding background, and the background at that point is being pushed apart by 5 pixels, the object must also be moved apart by 5 pixels. Otherwise the object will not lock into its natural position and may appear to float in front of or behind its correct depth.

Stop-Motion Animation

DEFINITION ▶ Creating animation from a series of still images.

SEE ALSO ▶ ramping

One of the greatest problems faced by amateur filmmakers and animators is how to create a film-quality product on a budget. One area in which this is no longer completely true is stop-motion animation.

Modern digital SLR cameras can now be purchased for well under $1000, and they possess a much greater resolution than the industry-standard film scan of 2048 × 1556. It's therefore possible to create a cinema-resolution film with one of these cameras and a *lot* of spare time.

> **TIP** ▶ Since stop-motion is so labor intensive, it's key to have good storyboards and previz before you start shooting. Eight seconds of film can take days to animate, so make sure you really want those eight seconds before you start.
>
> —Alex Suter, VFX Supervisor, *Oedipus*

Of course, there are other limitations. Stop-motion puppets like those used in *The Corpse Bride* are precision instruments and extremely expensive to make. Among the many budgetary factors are the size of the puppet and whether it is costumed. Nonetheless, clay figure animation of the *Wallace and Gromit* variety is limited only by an artist's personal talent.

Several powerful shareware applications exist to facilitate stop-motion animation, and some can remotely control the camera's shutter for shooting each individual frame. Notable software applications are Boinx Software's iStopMotion (www.boinx.com) and FrameThief (www.framethief.com).

When creating stop-motion animation, consider using optical flow retiming (see ramping). Optical flow retiming can morph extra animation frames between existing ones, smoothing some of the stuttering movement typical of stop-motion animation. It can also readjust the timing when movements between frames exceed their intended distances. Be careful not to rely too much on this process, however, or you'll end up with smudgy, unconvincing animation.

Finally, color issues and exposure changes can cause flicker when digital SLRs are used. Fortunately, these issues can usually be corrected using off-the-shelf compositing software.

A stop-motion set

Subtraction Matching

DEFINITION ▶ Aligning two images using a subtraction composite. *Related terms:* image alignment; plate alignment

SEE ALSO ▶ clean plates, generating; difference matte

It's often vital that two images be perfectly aligned for other compositing operations. You can perform this alignment very simply by subtracting the two images: Just composite one image over the other using a subtraction. In Shake, use a Move2D and an ISubA node.

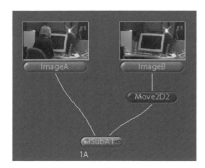

In After Effects and Motion, position one layer on top of the other and use a Difference blend mode for the uppermost layer.

The result will be a darkened image. Any portions of the image that are significantly different will show up as bright areas. Sections of the image that are similar but slightly misaligned will appear to be outlined.

Adjust the position, scale, and rotation of one of the layers until the outlining effect is minimized.

TIP ▶ In Shake's Move2D node, position the pointer over the xPan or yPan parameter slider, and then press Option and use the left and right arrow keys to nudge the image by 0.1 pixel.

When the adjustment is complete, remove the subtractive composite (delete the ISubA in Shake, or set the blend mode back to Normal in After Effects and Motion), but keep active the adjustments made to position, scale, and rotation. Your alignment is now complete.

Alternative Method

Sometimes a mix operation can be easier to judge than a subtraction operation. In this case, invert one of the images, and then blend the images equally. A pure gray indicates a perfect match between the pixels of the two layers. "Embossed" areas require additional alignment.

In Shake, use Invert and Mix nodes with the default settings.

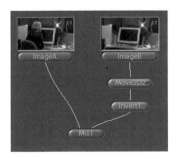

In After Effects and Motion, apply an Invert filter to the second layer and set the Opacity of that layer to 50%.

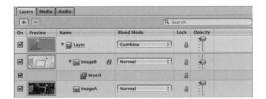

Super Black

DEFINITION ▶ A value or degree of black that is darker than the levels allowed by the CCIR 601 engineering standard for video. The CCIR 601 standard for black is 7.5 IRE in the United States and 0 IRE for PAL and NTSC in Japan.

Super White

DEFINITION ▶ A value or degree of white that is brighter than the accepted normal value of 100 IRE allowed by the CCIR 601 standard.

Surface Normal Lighting

DEFINITION ▶ Using 3D geometric surface normal information to relight objects during the compositing stage, while respecting the dimensionality of the 3D surfaces. *Related terms:* 3D lighting effect; bump map pass; normal pass; surface lighting; normals lighting

SEE ALSO ▶ "3D" Fundamentals chapter; reflections, faux

Original rendered scene

The scene after surface normal lighting is applied to simulate a light from the left of the screen

3D content is usually rendered from a 3D geometric environment into a two-dimensional image. Compositors take these two-dimensional renders and glue them together with other two-dimensional images to create the final shot. But what happens when one of the 3D elements hasn't been rendered with lighting that is appropriate for the final composite?

Usually, one (or more) of three things happens: wailing and gnashing of teeth, tedious and time-consuming re-rendering, or surface normal lighting.

Surface normal lighting is the process of color correcting a rendered image using special mattes that indicate in which direction any given pixel is facing relative to the camera.

In a typical surface normal lighting setup, the red channel of the matte image contains the horizontal angle of pixels. In the image below, a pixel with a normal that faces to the left of the camera will appear black, a pixel facing to the right of the camera will appear white, and a pixel staring straight at the camera with a death gaze appears gray.

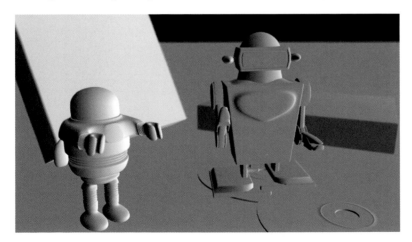

The green channel contains similar information, but describes the vertical angle of pixels from bottom to top.

By using threshold operations to isolate thin bands of these two mattes, you can establish a specific angle of dispersion for a new virtual light.

The resulting matte can be used to mask off a color correction, adding new light to the scene.

A red light coming from the left has been added using a surface normal lighting effect.

It's even possible to subtract light to subdue overblown areas of the image.

The same surface normal lighting matte can be used to darken an image at a given angle.

Creating the correctional matte from the raw red and green channels is not trivial, so we've included a sample Shake color-correction engine script that you can find on the accompanying disc as **APTS_CycVFX/ProjectFiles/CG/SurfaceNormalLighting/ Sample.shk**.

Open the parameters for CenterPoint, and then use the onscreen crosshair to adjust the angle of the lighting.

You can adjust the parameters in the node S2 to modify the properties of the light: falloffType 0 produces a quick and reasonably useful falloff, while falloffType 1 produces a more accurate but render-intensive falloff.

Limitations of Surface Normal Lighting

Surface normal lighting only goes so far before it starts to break down. Its two most significant limitations are lack of object occlusion and lack of depth attenuation.

Lack of Object Occlusion

Since surface normal lighting is a result of surface normal direction, it doesn't take into account a situation in which one object prevents light from reaching another object. That is, if one object would cast a shadow on another object, a surface normal lighting setup continues to shine light as if the occluding object weren't there. It is possible to create sophisticated solutions for this using depth mattes generated from the scene lights; but at that level of difficulty, it's probably easier just to garbage-matte out the area that should remain unaffected by the light. (Or just re-render the scene out of the 3D application.)

Lack of Depth Attenuation

Light intensity in the real world is inversely proportional to the square of its distance. In other words, light loses brightness the farther it travels. Surface normal lighting maintains a constant intensity everywhere. Additional masking of the effect is required when several objects are illuminated by the surface normal lighting.

Cameo

Van Ride Through *War of the Worlds*—Pablo Helman

THE LENGTH OF SHOT FN006 was the first thing that impressed *War of the Worlds* effects supervisor Pablo Helman (see Contributors, page iv). A standard effects shot might last five seconds, but the animatics for shot FN006 ran a full two and a half minutes.

In the shot, Tom Cruise's character and his family flee from alien tripods in a speeding van. Their previously placid world is under attack, which has caused uncontrolled panic. To convey this frenetic energy, the shot was designed as a single long, swirling move, with the camera repeatedly pushing in and pulling out of the van as it careens down a New Jersey

511

turnpike. The visual choreography had to capture a world gone mad, as well as focus in on the intimate and revealing dialogue between the principals in the vehicle.

Pablo quickly realized that there wasn't a camera rig that could do this move at 60 mph. Therefore, it was going to take a large and dedicated team of compositors to make the shot happen.

The first step was to break down the shot into manageable components. This shot had seven parts: the camera moved outside the van four times and inside the van three times. The two basic elements were the van on the freeway in New Jersey, and the van with the actors on a Los Angeles blue screen stage.

Ideally, Pablo could first shoot the actors and their dialogue to time the camera moves prior to shooting on location. Unfortunately, scheduling conflicts dictated that Pablo had to shoot the location work first. He had one day on a relatively small section of closed freeway to get the four exterior parts of the shot, as well as the backgrounds for the interior blue screen shots.

Because the blue screen shoot was tied to the timing of the dialogue, which could change, the background had to be flexible enough to accommodate alterations that occurred when shooting the actors. So a Jeep was rigged with eight cameras arranged in a circle to photograph a 360-degree view of the freeway.

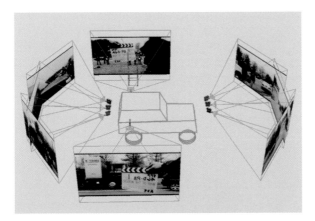

The Jeep drove a predetermined path to capture images of a fleet of stalled cars and 600 extras. To get enough footage for the full two-and-a-half-minute background plate, Pablo had to shoot four sections of freeway—moving the extras and stalled cars for each shot. The footage from the eight cameras was stitched together to create a seamless, 360-degree view of the environment. It was this full view of the background that allowed the effects team to deal with any changes that might occur during the blue screen shoot.

Prior to the Los Angeles blue screen shoot, Pablo and director Steven Spielberg rehearsed for two days, going over the hook-ups between the exteriors shot on location, and the new interior shots to be filmed on the soundstage. At the end of two days, the team felt they had a seamless blend between the different elements of the shot.

They marked the stage floor with 11 camera positions, and five crane operators had to hit those marks at just the right times to capture the actors' performances. Lighting was set to match the overcast look of the background plate, and all the windows were removed from the van.

To allow actor Tom Cruise to concentrate on his performance, his steering wheel was controlled by a second, attached steering wheel. A stunt driver turned the second wheel while watching a monitor playing footage of the van's path on location. As the stunt driver moved his steering wheel, the wheel in Cruise's hands moved accordingly. All Cruise had to do was hold on to his steering wheel and react to its movement.

The actors were available only for a half day, and only a few takes were shot of each of the three interior dialogue scenes. Knowing the complexity of the shot, Pablo asked Spielberg if he wanted to cover the shot with close-ups or cutaways. The director put his hand on Pablo's shoulder and said, no, he was confident that Pablo would assemble the elements.

Their fate sealed, Pablo led a team of compositors at Industrial Light & Magic through the difficult task of completing a polished shot. A complex matchmove took three weeks to finish. The 360-degree background required seven weeks of rotoscoping to eliminate the seams.

Several 3D CG elements were created. Since the van was shot on a blue screen stage, the wheels didn't move. CG tires and hubcaps were made to rotate at the appropriate speed. The 360-degree background didn't show the roadbed directly under the van. When the camera pulled away from the van to reveal the roadbed underneath, a CG road was added to the shot.

Since the van's windows were removed for the blue screen shoot, moving reflections had to be added with CG elements. Reflections were also added to the surface of the van to create the illusion of movement. The rearview mirror was also a CG element. And at one point, in a wide view, the stunt driver's face from the location shoot was replaced with Tom Cruise's face.

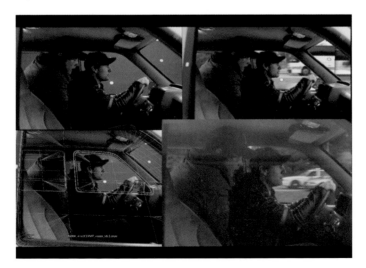

Finally, a tremendous amount of camera movement was laid on top of the original smooth photography to enhance the wild feel of a van careening through a slalom course of stalled-out vehicles and other obstacles.

The days of pre-planning and consulting time for this daunting shot were well spent, as the shot was finished as planned and as scheduled. The effort was rewarded when the shot won the Visual Effects Society award as the best composite of the year.

Tilt

DEFINITION ▶ To pivot the camera up and down, which causes the image to move down or up in the frame.

Time Remapping

DEFINITION ▶ The process of changing the playback speed of a clip over time in postproduction. The equivalent of varying the crank of a film camera.

SEE ALSO ▶ ramping

Time Slice

DEFINITION ▶ The use of multiple cameras (usually still cameras) at different physical positions recording the same moment in time. Allows a postproduction camera move that dollies around an object in a frozen moment of time. Used effectively in numerous films, perhaps best known in the *Matrix* series. *Related terms:* bullet time; frozen time

Timecode

DEFINITION ▶ A unique numbering system of electronic signals laid onto each frame of videotape that are used to identify specific frames. Each frame of video is labeled with hour, minute, second, and frame (01:00:00:00). Timecode can be drop frame, non–drop frame, time of day (TOD), or EBU (European Broadcast Union, for PAL projects).

Timecode Gap

DEFINITION ▶ An area of tape with no timecode. Timecode gaps usually signify the end of all recorded material on a tape, but they may occur due to the starting and stopping of the camera and tape deck during recording.

Title Safe

DEFINITION ▶ The part of the video image that is guaranteed to be visible on all televisions. The title safe area is the inner 80 percent of the screen. To prevent text in a video from being hidden by the edge of a TV set, any titles or text must be restricted to the title safe area.

Tracking

DEFINITION ▶ The process of identifying, analyzing, and recording the motion of specific elements within a shot. In compositing, tracking data of the background plate is typically applied to the motion of an introduced element in order to match the movement in the background plate with the movement of the introduced element. It is also used to correct frame-to-frame misalignment caused by gate weave or camera shake.

SEE ALSO ▶ camera shake, smoothing and removal; clean plates, generating; matchmoving; Tracking Fundamentals chapter; tracking marker removal

Tracking Marker Removal

DEFINITION ▶ The postproduction removal of tracking markers that were placed on a live-action set and filmed.

SEE ALSO ▶ clean plates, generating

Tracking markers are extremely useful when it comes time to stabilize or lock down a shot in post. They are small markers—often simple *X*s made with marking tape—that assist tracking engines in the absence of hard geometry in the scene. Unless you're making a film about visual effects work, those little guys need to be removed before the audience sees the film.

Most often, tracking markers can be removed using a clone tool. If the tracking markers have been locked down as part of shot stabilization, the removal of the markers by cloning is a trivial task.

When the tracking markers are moving, try using an interpolating clone brush. In Shake, use the interpolate brush mode. In After Effects, keyframe the shape parameter for the desired stroke.

Transfer Modes

SEE ▶ blend modes; skin repair (digital foundation)

Transparency, Simulating

DEFINITION ▶ The simulation of glasslike transparency in an object that was previously rendered or filmed as opaque. *Related term:* simulating glass

SEE ALSO ▶ Fresnel shading pass; reflections, faux

Before transparency simulation   After transparency simulation

Here's a sample comment representing the usual ad executive's complete misunderstanding of the complexities of rendering and compositing 3D content: "I love it. Love the entire piece. You've really captured the entire spirit of the campaign—you guys are amazing. Oh, just one other thing. The spaceman's helmet, the black one? Make it see-through for me, will you?"

Ever since the Doritos scene in *Wag the Dog*, producers and creative directors have assumed that visual effects artists have special magic on tap. It's a good thing we do.

Creating Convincing Transparency

Transparency "magic" requires a keen observation of reality. You might be tempted to make something transparent simply by fading down its alpha. That might work, but nobody will believe it. Here are a few of the factors to take into account when simulating transparency:

Transparent Things Are Usually Reflective

In the real world, most transparent or semitransparent things also reflect light at various angles. Water, glass, plastic—all reflect the surrounding environment to some degree.

To create that reflection, the best solution is to use a light probe of the current scene. In its absence, you can usually produce a decent facsimile by using a copy of the background plate as the reflection. Be sure to mash it up a little to make sure it doesn't just look like an identical copy of the actual background.

Reflectivity usually varies based on the angle of the observer to the surface. For more information, see Fresnel shading pass.

Transparent Things Are Usually Dirty

It's not enough to simulate surface reflections of a transparent object. You also need to rough it up a little. Smudges, scratches, and good ol' dirt will attenuate the strength of both reflectivity and transparency.

You Can See Stuff in the Background

Obviously, making something transparent dictates that you'll be able to see what's behind it. If the object you're converting is an element that is separate from the background, then all is well with the world. If the object and the background were filmed or rendered together, you're in for some serious cloning and background restoration.

Also, materials with a density different from air will refract light passing through them. The result is a distortion of the background seen through the object. This applies most strongly to solid objects. (An empty fish bowl, for example, distorts the background much less than a full one, since its volume is primarily air.)

Edges Are More Opaque

One of the most common mistakes made when simulating transparency is to fade down the entire object. If you look at a glass or bottle, you'll notice that the curvature of the surface produces an edge that's difficult to see through. To effectively simulate this effect, you need to make the edges of your objects less transparent than the center.

Creating a Simple Transparency

The first step in converting an object from opaque to transparent is to isolate it from the rest of the scene. In an object with varying degrees of transparency, you'll need to matte out just the section you want to convert.

NOTE ▶ To work through the following examples, use the **TransparencyStart** project file on the disc in APTS_CycVFX/ProjectFiles/CG/BotBoy.

The next step is to decide whether you anticipate a simple, subtle reflection or a strong Fresnel effect.

For a simple transparency, you'll want to create a mask for fading the object's center without significantly fading the edges.

You begin by dilating (choking) the isolation matte by a couple of pixels or more. In Shake, use the DilateErode node. In After Effects, use the Matte Choker filter. In Motion, use the Matte Magic filter.

After choking, apply a blur to soften the matte's border.

> **NOTE ▶** To exaggerate the effect, the figures that follow use the entire matte of **Botboy** instead of just the isolation matte of the helmet.

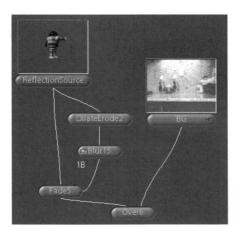

Because the matte has been shrunk and blurred, the white center of the matte will cause a full fading of the object, while the blurred edge will produce less and less fading out to the extremities.

The final step in this process is to apply a fade to the original object, and use the newly created matte to attenuate its effects. In Shake, use the Fade node. In After Effects, invert the matte and then use it as a track matte. In Motion, invert the matte and then use it as an image mask.

To "sell" the shot, grunge maps and some color correction are also necessary, but at least the fade is taken care of.

Displacing the Background

To create the illusion of light refracting as it passes through your transparent object, you need to displace (warp) the background. Background displacement is as simple as taking a copy of the background image and feeding it into a displacement filter. In Shake, use IDisplace; in After Effects, use the Displacement Map filter; and in Motion, use the Displace filter.

There are a few techniques to keep in mind when creating a displacement effect.

▶ Use the color channels as the source of the displacement rather than the alpha channel. Alpha channels tend to be flat and lack interesting contours, which creates a fairly boring displacement effect.

▶ Try using different channels for the vertical displacement and horizontal displacement. For example, use the red channel for the vertical and the green for the horizontal. This adds an extra degree of variation to the result.

▶ Pay careful attention to the edges of the displacement. You'll often find an abrupt tearing or heavy aliasing of the pixels right at the edges of the displaced area. One way to avoid this is to trim off one or two pixels from the edge of the displacement source, using an erosion process. In that way, the border of the displacement will be hidden by the semitransparent object composited over the top.

▶ In some cases, you may choose to blur the original object before using it as a displacement source. This will remove extreme displacement variation in high-contrast regions of the source image. Be sure to mask the blurred displacement source with the original object's alpha to prevent the displacement from moving beyond the object's border.

Creating Transparency with a Fresnel Reflection Effect

A more pronounced reflection on your transparent surface significantly changes the way you must approach the shot. There's no point in fussing over the fine details of edge transparency if the majority of the surface will display a reflection.

Instead of creating a matte to protect the edges from fading, create a matte that simulates the Fresnel reflection falloff around surfaces. (For more information, see Fresnel shading pass.)

Create the Fresnel matte using a radial gradient masked off by the isolation matte created earlier.

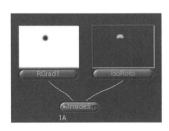 

Adding Grunge

Before you apply this matte, remember all the dirt and smudges that appear on glass surfaces. In fact, even oil residue from fingers can produce additional reflections.

To simulate these imperfections, simply use a paint tool to create the desired patterns.

These don't need to be particularly impressive to be effective.

To apply the grunge map, add it to your Fresnel matte.

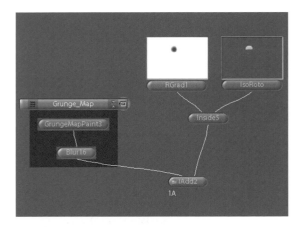

That will work for the reflections, but you need a different matte for the transparency.

Using the original isolation matte, subtract the grunge. These areas will *not* be made fully transparent, thereby creating the illusion of surface grunge that hinders the observer from completely seeing through the object.

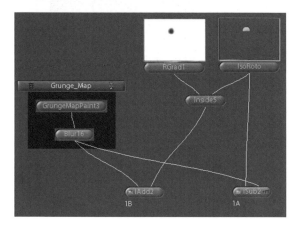

You now have two mattes: one for applying the reflection, the other for creating the transparency.

> **TIP** It's more precise to create two separate grunge maps: one to attenuate the reflection, and the other to attenuate the transparency. There may be parts of the object that lack transparency but don't reflect (such as dirt, which has a nonreflective, matte surface).

Applying the Mattes

In the case of a Fresnel simulation, the transparency matte should be applied first. Use the process outlined above for the simple transparency to fade the object using the transparency matte with its applied grunge.

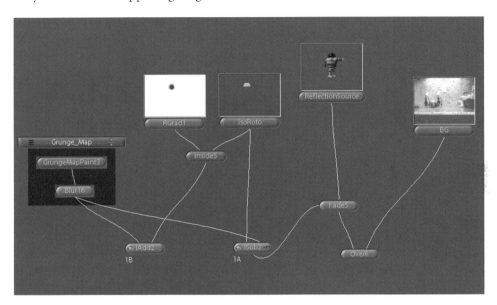

Now that the object's been made transparent, you can apply a reflection over the top. When possible, use a light probe from the scene. Otherwise, try to create a reflection from the background without revealing it as an obvious copy.

Mask off the reflection source with the Fresnel matte, and then composite it over the original object.

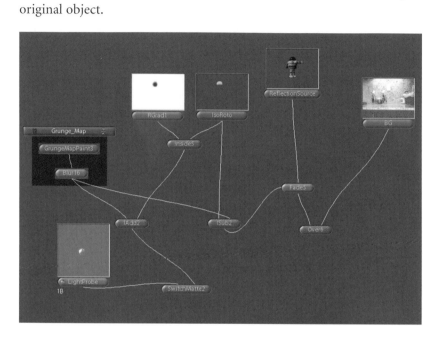

Truck

SEE ▶ dolly

Up-Conversion

DEFINITION ▶ The process of scaling standard-definition footage to high-definition and other larger formats. In effect, the process adds resolution by analyzing existing pixels and adding interpolated pixels between them. Today, adaptive upsampling is commonly used instead of traditional algorithms to selectively sharpen edge detail during the scaling. Shake includes such upsampling technology in its FileIn node. *Related term:* up-res

Vapor

SEE ▶ keying generic elements

Variable Speed

SEE ▶ ramping; time remapping

Video-in-Text Effect

DEFINITION ▶ An effect that mattes a video image inside the shapes of letters of text.

Vignette

DEFINITION ▶ A popular photographic effect in which the photo gradually darkens around the edges, usually in an oval shape. This naturally occurs due to the round nature of camera lenses, so it's sometimes useful to simulate this effect in CG content.

Warping

DEFINITION ▶ A process in which a portion of an image is deformed. The warp effect can be an animation over time or a static adjustment that occurs over the entire shot. It can be used to make animals talk, enhance facial expressions, or cause body parts to shrink or expand.

SEE ALSO ▶ lens warping; grain removal via warp

White Balancing

DEFINITION ▶ To make adjustments to a video signal while it is recorded in order to reproduce white as true white. For example, if the white in a shot is too green due to fluorescent lighting, white balancing adds enough magenta to make the white appear neutral.

White Level

DEFINITION ▶ An analog video signal's amplitude for the lightest white in a picture, represented by IRE units.

Wide-Screen Mask Filter

DEFINITION ▶ A filter that adds black bars across the top and bottom of a 4:3 image, thus cropping it to the wide-screen, 16:9 format used in movie theaters.

Wire Removal

DEFINITION ▶ Removing visible safety harnesses and stunt wires from "clean" backgrounds, angled backgrounds, and so on.

SEE ALSO ▶ clean plates, generating

Wire removal is always tricky. If you're removing wires from a green screen or blue screen, you're in luck. A simple garbage matte should suffice, along with delicate roto work wherever the wire comes into contact with a foreground subject.

More often than not, the wires are obscuring parts of the background set. In the best cases, a clean plate can be used to replace the missing background. For an example of this, see pages 181–83 of Marco Paolini's *Apple Pro Training Series: Shake 4* (Peachpit Press, 2005).

In other cases, there is no clean plate, and the background needs to be cloned in. A few other options are available here. You can use a plug-in, use Shake's AutoAlign, use a side smear, or paint out the wires with a clone brush.

The Furnace Plug-in Suite

The Foundry's Furnace plug-in suite (www.thefoundry.co.uk) is not inexpensive, but it will pay for itself many times over in a difficult wire-removal shot. It includes sophisticated tools for removing wires and creating a convincing replacement background. It's not a magic bullet—plenty of pixel grease is still required—but it will solve many problems that otherwise would be excruciatingly tedious to deal with.

If you're bidding on a wire-removal job, be sure to budget Furnace into the price.

AutoAlign

This is actually a method of creating a clean plate within Shake. The clean plate can be used to replace the wire. See clean plates, generating.

Side Smearing

If you have a reasonably homogeneous background, you might try side smearing, which smears in pixels on the sides of the wire to cover it. Side smearing works in very subtle situations. As an example, try the SideSmear macro included on the accompanying DVD.

> **NOTE** ▶ The SideSmear macro is actually designed for the repair of backgrounds when creating 3D from 2D. It's not ideal for blending the side pixels, but it gives an indication of the effect.

Note that angled wires will require a rotation of the image before smearing. To prevent sub-pixel softening, the replaced area should be composited over the original, unrotated image.

Cloning

If all else fails, reach for your favorite clone brush and go to work. Hope and pray that at least some keyframe interpolation will work for you.

X Axis

DEFINITION ▶ Refers to the *x* coordinate in Cartesian geometry. The *x* coordinate describes horizontal placement in motion effects.

Y Axis

DEFINITION ▶ Refers to the *y* coordinate in Cartesian geometry. The *y* coordinate describes vertical placement in motion effects.

YIQ

DEFINITION ▶ Shorthand term used to describe the components of an NTSC broadcast signal. *Y* refers to the luminance component, *I* and *Q* to the chrominance subcarrier signals.

YIQ is derived from RGB values using the following weights:

Y = 0.299 × R + 0.587 × G + 0.114 × B
I = 0.596 × R + −0.274 × G + −0.322 × B
Q = 0.212 × R + −0.523 × G + 0.311 × B

SEE ALSO ▶ YUV

YUV

DEFINITION ▶ Shorthand term used to describe the components of a PAL broadcast signal. *Y* refers to the luminance component, *U* and *V* to the chrominance subcarrier signals.

YUV is often incorrectly cited as a generic term referring to both NTSC and PAL broadcast components. Strictly speaking, NTSC broadcast space should be referred to as *YIQ*.

YUV is derived from RGB values using the following weights:

Y = 0.299 × R + 0.587 × G + 0.114 × B

U = −0.147 × R + −0.289 × G + 0.437 × B

V = 0.615 × R + −0.515 × G + −0.100 × B

SEE ALSO ▶ YIQ

Z Axis

DEFINITION ▶ Refers to the *z* coordinate in Cartesian geometry. The *z* coordinate describes perpendicular placement in motion effects.

Z Depth Pass

SEE ▶ depth keying

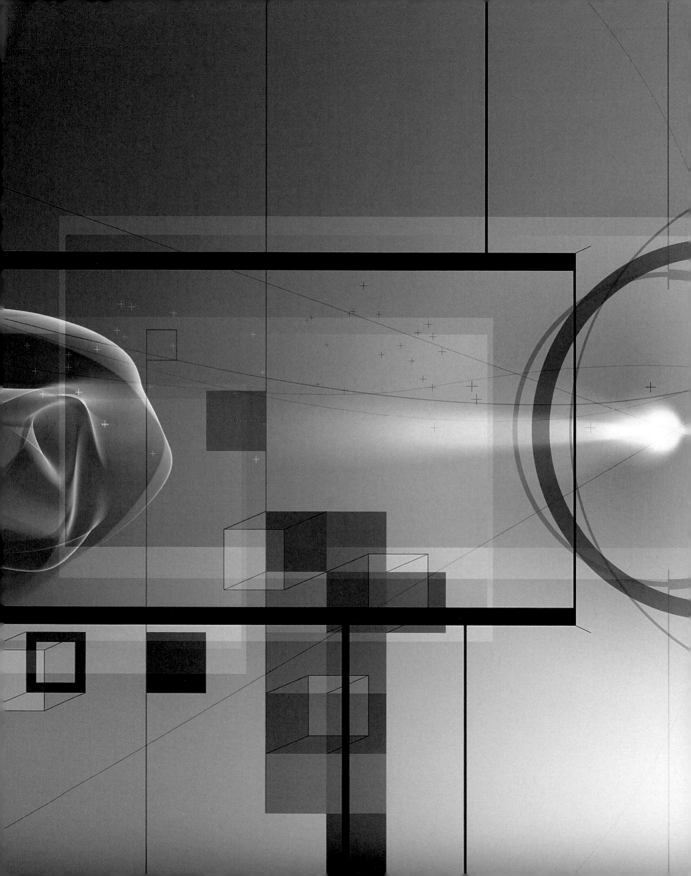

How to Install a Shake Macro

Shake has a healthy community of users who have created many, many free macros for use with Shake (check out www.fxshare.com). The biggest problem most people have is figuring out how to install them. Here's the skinny:

There are three main parts to a macro: the macro script itself, the macro's UI (user interface) script, and the icon image. More complex macros containing radio buttons and other interface elements have additional images for these elements.

> **NOTE** ▶ If you're executing Shake processes solely from the terminal, you only need the primary macro script. The other files are for the benefit of the Shake GUI.

Let's take a look at how to install a very popular fictitious macro, academyAwardGenerator.

In our fictitious scenario, once we download the academyAwardGenerator macro, we find 3 main files: academyAwardGenerator.h, academyAwardGeneratorUI.h, and Other. AcademyAwardGenerator.nri.

First we need to install the macro script, academyAwardGenerator.h. This installs in the following location:

If any of these folders don't exist (and they won't if you've never created or previously installed a macro) just right-click in the Finder window and choose "New Folder".

NOTE ▸ Shake is case-sensitive, so make sure you type the folder labels all lower-case.

Next we need to install the academyAwardGeneratorUI.h file, which is the file that tells Shake how to draw the user interface for the macro. This installs in a "ui" folder directly beneath the folder in which we just installed the main macro script.

Finally, the icon for the macro's button (which appears in the Tool Tabs) needs to be put in its proper place. Our macro "lives" in the Other tab, hence the naming convention: Other.AcademyAwardGenerator.nri.

Any images to be used for radio buttons should go in the "ux" folder inside the "icons" folder. Usually these are stored in additional subfolders; check any documentation that comes with the macro as to how these should be laid out inside "ux".

Cross your fingers, quit Shake and re-launch to discover your new macro. If it doesn't work, you most likely mistyped a folder or file name (or are trying to install a poorly written macro). You can check the Console (found in Applications/Utilities) to try to diagnose the problem.

> **TIP** You must exit Shake and re-launch in order to load the new macros into the interface. Shake only looks for the macros when the application is launched (hence the reason for putting the macros in a folder called "Startup").

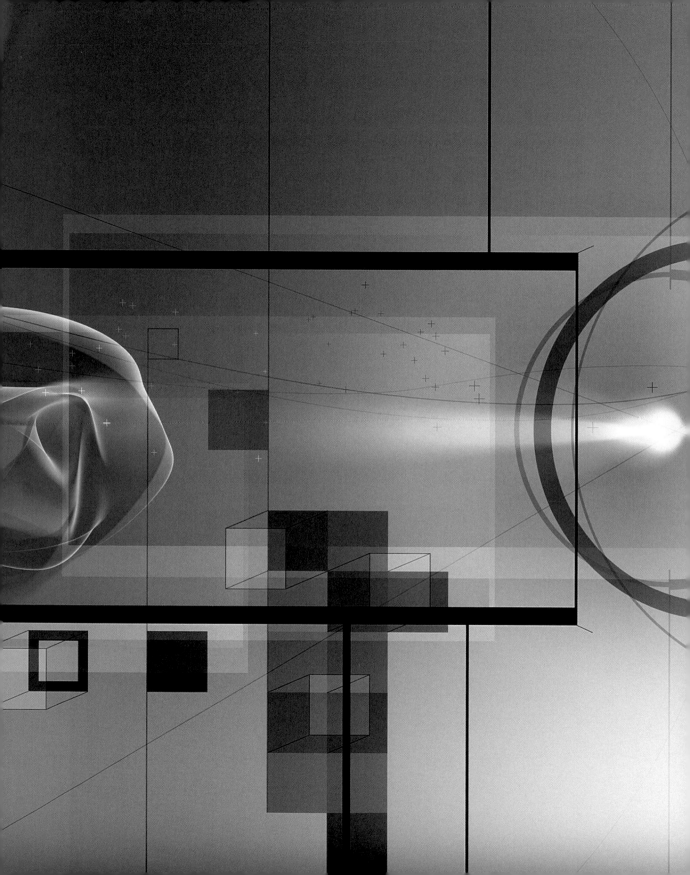

Shake in a Day

Introduction

This course is designed to get you up and running with Shake in a single day (albeit one very focused and caffeine-fueled day). It will introduce you to the fundamental principles of Shake's node-based compositing system, and familiarize you with a few of the many image-processing tools available in Shake.

Tutorial Media

We recommend storing footage on the top level of the system hard drive to simplify the process of students finding the required footage.

Folder Listings

Folders and files are denoted using the "/" subdirectory naming structure. As an example, the path to the Shake application installed on your hard drive would be written: /Applications/Shake/shake

Menu Listings

Menu selections are listed with arrows. So the ColorX selection below would be written: Tools > Color > ColorX.

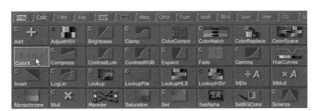

Shake Workflow

Shake uses a node-based architecture. If you're coming to Shake from timeline-based systems like Final Cut Pro, Motion, or Adobe After Effects this node-based system may seem confusing, or even counter-intuitive. It's actually the opposite; Shake's workflow is very simple and incredibly logical. Take a look.

Opening a Script

Shake works with *scripts*, which other applications sometimes refer to as *projects*. You're going to load a script that just contains images that haven't been connected to anything, yet.

1   Choose File > Open Script, or press Command-O.

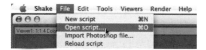

2   Navigate to APTS_CycVFX/Shake in a Day/.

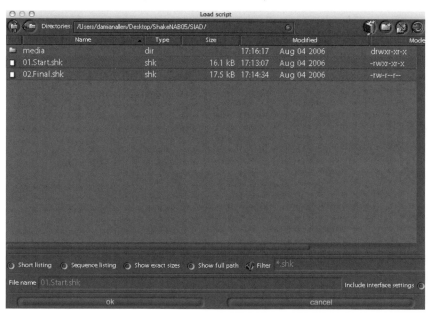

▶ The Shake Browser

Unlike most Apple software, Shake uses a UNIX-style browser. Directories (or folders) are listed down from the top of your computer's main hard drive. If you're looking for your Desktop, it's found inside the Users directory under your current login name. So, if you're logged on as Jimmy, items on the desktop will be found in /Users/Jimmy/Desktop/. This is also where you'll find your personal documents: in /Users/Jimmy/Documents/. A quick shortcut to your Users' directory, known as your *Home* folder, is to select $HOME from the directory drop-down menu in the Shake Browser.

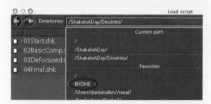

If you're looking for footage or scripts located anywhere other than your system hard drive—on a FireWire drive, a second hard drive, a DVD-ROM drive, and so on—these devices will appear on the top level of the browser directory structure in a folder called /Volumes/.

▶ Anatomy of a Browser

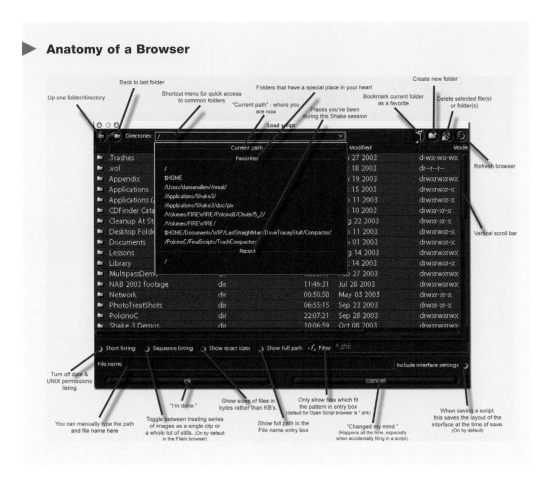

Up one folder/directory

Back to last folder

Shortcut menu for quick access to common folders

Folders that have a special place in your heart

"Current path" - where you are now

Places you've been during this Shake session

Bookmark current folder as a favorite

Create new folder

Delete selected file(s) or folder(s)

Load script

Refresh browser

Vertical scroll bar

Turn off date & UNIX permissions listing

You can manually type the path and file name here

Toggle between treating series of images as a single clip or a whole lot of stills. (On by default in the FileIn browser)

"I'm done."

Show sizes of files in bytes rather than KB's.

Show full path in the File name entry box

Only show files which fit the pattern in entry box (default for Open Script browser is *.shk)

"Changed my mind." (Happens all the time, especially when accidentally filing in a script).

When saving a script, this saves the layout of the interface at the time of save. (On by default)

3 Select **01.Start.shk** and click OK.

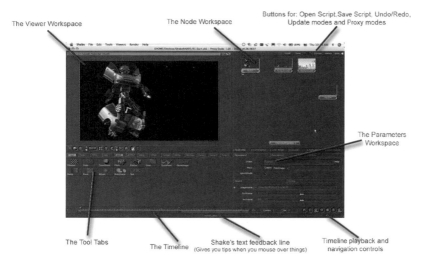

The Viewer Workspace

The Node Workspace

Buttons for: Open Script.Save Script, Undo/Redo, Update modes and Proxy modes

The Parameters Workspace

The Tool Tabs

The Timeline

Shake's text feedback line (Gives you tips when you mouse over things)

Timeline playback and navigation controls

TIP ▶ If your screen inexplicably goes blank at some time, there are several things that might cause it. One of the most common reasons is that you've accidentally moved to a frame prior to frame 1. The solution? Just drag your mouse pointer over the timeline to reposition the playhead.

You'll see you have four main areas—or quadrants—on the Shake screen. The top-right area is called the *Node Workspace* (or Node *View*). A node is one of the capsule-shaped objects in this view. What you see here is a set of clips, known in Shake as FileIn nodes. Each node is a separate image sequence or QuickTime movie being read from disk. When you opened up this script, the Viewer to the left was most likely loaded with the image from the **Robot** clip. If you click the left side of another node, say the **Foreground** clip, you can load that image into the viewer instead.

4   Click the left side of Foreground to load it into the Viewer.

If you can't see the whole image in the viewer, simply place your mouse pointer over the Viewer and press the F key for "fit". The image will now comfortably fit inside the viewer area.

Nodes all have parameters, properties that can be changed. For example, with a Blur node, one of the parameters would represent the intensity of the blur. By clicking the right side of a node, you can load these parameters into the bottom-right portion of the screen, the *Parameters workspace.*

5   Click the right side of Foreground to load its parameters into the Parameters1 tab

6   Finally, click the middle of the Foreground node to select it.

Selecting nodes is useful for editing your script. (You'll find out why in a moment.) To deselect a node, just click in the blank gray space of the node view. If you want to rearrange your nodes, just left-click and drag them around.

Oh, and one more thing: double-clicking a node does all three things at once. That is, it loads the node into the viewer, loads its parameters into the parameters tab, and selects it, all in one ninja power move.

► Anatomy of a Node

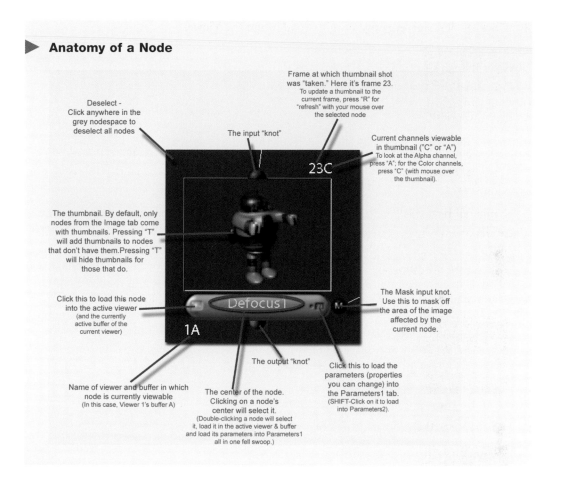

Frame at which thumbnail shot was "taken." Here it's frame 23. To update a thumbnail to the current frame, press "R" for "refresh" with your mouse over the selected node

Deselect - Click anywhere in the grey nodespace to deselect all nodes

The input "knot"

Current channels viewable in thumbnail ("C" or "A") To look at the Alpha channel, press "A"; for the Color channels, press "C" (with mouse over the thumbnail).

The thumbnail. By default, only nodes from the Image tab come with thumbnails. Pressing "T" will add thumbnails to nodes that don't have them. Pressing "T" will hide thumbnails for those that do.

Click this to load this node into the active viewer (and the currently active buffer of the current viewer)

The Mask input knot. Use this to mask off the area of the image affected by the current node.

The output "knot"

Click this to load the parameters (properties you can change) into the Parameters1 tab. (SHIFT-Click on it to load into Parameters2).

Name of viewer and buffer in which node is currently viewable (In this case, Viewer 1's buffer A)

The center of the node. Clicking on a node's center will select it. (Double-clicking a node will select it, load it in the active viewer & buffer and load its parameters into Parameters1 all in one fell swoop.)

A Basic Composite

You're now going to build a composition. You'll start by compositing the **Foreground** clip over the background clip, **Background**. If you're having problems seeing either the **Foreground** clip or the **Background** clip, you may need to pan or resize the view (see the "Shake Navigation" box below).

1 In the node view, click the middle of Foreground to select it. In the Tool Tabs in the lower-left quadrant of the screen, click the Layer tab. Click an Over node found in that tab.

The Over node instantly gets added to the Foreground node. That's because you'd earlier selected the Foreground node. The line connecting the two nodes is called a *noodle* and the noodle is running between two round dots, called *knots*. Most nodes have at least one input knot and one output knot. In the case of nodes found in the Image tab, there is usually no input knot since these nodes generate images and require no input. The FileIn node is an example of an Image node with no input knot.

2 Position your mouse just under the **Background** clip until its output knot shows up. Press the left mouse button (LMB) and drag a noodle out of the clip, connecting it to the second knot on the top of Over1, then release the mouse button.

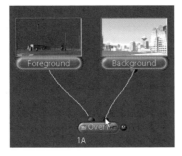

NOTE ▶ If the entire Background node moves, you've reached too far. Reposition the Background node, then position the mouse pointer directly on the center of the output knot before dragging out a noodle.

▶ **Shake Navigation**

The development team for Shake went to great pains to make sure there were as few keyboard shortcuts to learn as possible. So, the same keyboard and mouse navigation controls can be used pretty much everywhere you want to navigate around things—the Node Workspace, the Viewer Workspace, the Curve Editor, and so on. These shortcuts are *locationally sensitive*, so pressing the same key or mouse combination will affect the interface differently depending on where your mouse pointer was when you initiated the shortcut.

Here are the main ones you need to know:

LMB
(Left Mouse Button)

MMB
(Middle Mouse Button)
On a scroll wheel mouse
(shown), depress the scroll
wheel itself.

RMB
(Right Mouse Button)

To pan a view:

▶ Click and drag the middle mouse button (MMB), or

▶ Press the Option key and click and drag the left mouse button (LMB).

To scale a view in *discrete steps*:

▶ Press the Plus or Minus keys on the main keyboard.

Continues on next page

▶ **Shake Navigation** *(continued)*

To scale a view in *freeform style*:

▶ Press Control-Option and drag the LMB or MMB left and right, or

▶ Press Command-Option and drag the LMB or MMB left and right.

Press the Home key to bring the view back to a 100 percent scale

Press the F key to frame the selected nodes in the Node Workspace; or, in the Viewer Workspace, to zoom out the currently loaded image so that it fits entirely in the viewer space.

You should now see the result of the two nodes being combined in the Viewer. If not, click on the left side of the Over1 node to load it into the Viewer.

1   Click the middle of the **Robot** clip to select it. Then, in the Layer tab, click another Over node.

2   Drag a noodle out of the bottom of the Over1 node and connect it to the second input knot of Over2.

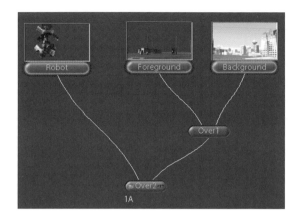

You've now composited three elements together: the **Robot** clip, the **Foreground** clip, and the **Background** clip. There's a lot more to be done for this shot; but, for now, take a look at that intuitive Shake workflow.

▶ Noodling

Is one of your noodles in the wrong place? It's easy to fix. When you mouse over the top of a noodle, it turns yellow. If you click and drag it, you can move it to another node's output knot and release it, linking the new node, and breaking the connection to the old. When you position your mouse over the bottom of a noodle, it turns red. If you click and drag the noodle, you can move it to another node's input knot and release it, linking the new node, and breaking the connection to the old.

 If you accidentally place two noodles the wrong way around going into, say, an Over node, simply drag one of the noodles into the correct knot and Shake will automatically flip the other connection.

Want to delete a noodle? It's easy. Just position your mouse over the noodle until it turns red or yellow and press the Forward Delete key. (Specifically, it's the small DEL key to the right of the main keyboard. It's Command-Delete on a laptop.)

The River Metaphor

To understand the tree structure of Shake, start by thinking of each node as a stream of water. So in our case, we have a Robot stream, a Foreground stream and a Background stream. Each of these streams flows downhill according to the effects of gravity.

At some point, these single streams connect with other streams. So, at our Over1 node, the Foreground stream has connected with the Background stream. The result is a new, single stream, which is a combination of the two streams merging into it.

1   Click the left side of the Over1 node. What you see is the single stream resulting from the combining of Foreground and Background.

This new, single stream continues to flow downhill until it connects with other streams; in our case, it connects with Robot. So at Over2 you have a new single stream combining the **Robot** clip with the single stream coming down from Over1. This could continue countless times in a large composition until the final node at the bottom of the script—the result of all the merging streams above—is attached to a FileOut node and the sequence is rendered out to disk.

2   Click the middle of Robot to select it. In the Filter tab, click a Blur node. If it's not already loaded in the Viewer, click the left side of Over2 to load it into the Viewer.

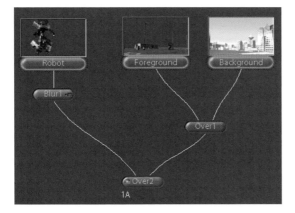

You've just added a Blur node after the **Robot** clip. Think of this as, say, a sewage processing plant that the Robot river passes through on its way to the Over2 merge point.

3 Make sure the parameters for Blur1 are loaded into Parameters1 (at the lower right of the Shake screen). If not, click the right side of the Blur1 node to load the parameters.

4 Click and drag to the right on the leftmost pixels entry box, watching the Viewer as you do so. (Alternatively, you can double-click the box and manually type a value.)

You'll see that as you adjust the value in the Blur1 parameters, the Robot part of your image starts to blur out. (By the way, that's a full Gaussian blur you're applying to the image. You can see how fast Shake renders it.) *Only* the **Robot** clip is being blurred, because it's the only thing upstream from the Blur1 processing plant. The Robot stream comes out the other end of the Blur node *blurred* and then joins at Over2 with the *unblurred* stream coming from Over2. Why is only Robot blurred? Because it's the only element upstream from the Blur1 processing plant.

5 Click the left side of Robot to load it into the Viewer.

Notice that even though you've blurred the **Robot** clip with Blur1, if you look at the clip before it reaches the Blur node, it's still intact with no blur. Obviously, that's because you're looking upstream of the Blur before it has affected the Robot stream.

This means that if at any time in your compositing you need an unblurred version of Robot for some purpose, you can simply drag a fresh noodle (think, second stream) out of the bottom of Robot and connect it wherever it's needed. You can have as many noodles coming out of one node as you want.

6   Click the middle of Blur1 to select it, then press Forward Delete key to delete it.

> **NOTE ▶** On laptops, press the Command key while pressing Forward Delete to perform a delete in Shake.

Going Further

You now want to position the robot a little further to the right of screen. In Shake you need to specify a transform node to move or scale something. Transform nodes are little "treatment plants" just like the Blur node, except that, in this case, they pan, rotate, shear, or scale the stream flowing through them.

1   Click the left side of Over2 to load it into the Viewer.

2   Click Robot to select it

3   In the Transform tab, select a Move2D node.

You've added a Move2D node to your image. There are lots of nodes in the Transform tab to apply all kinds of movements to a clip, but the Move2D node contains, in just one node, most of the transform operations you'll commonly want to apply to a piece of footage. The Move2D node can pan, rotate, scale, and shear. It's the transform node you'll be reaching for most of the time.

4   In the Move2D1 parameters, set the left of the two pan numeric entry boxes to *80*.

▶ **Anatomy of Move2D's Onscreen Controls**

Many nodes contain onscreen controls (OSC) that allow you to visually change parameters in the node by adjusting the control widgets overlaid on your screen. A node's OSC show up whenever that node's parameters are loaded into Parameters1.

Some of these control widgets can appear a little foreign at first. Here's a break-down of the Move2D node's OSC. Click and drag the indicated OSC to change that parameter.

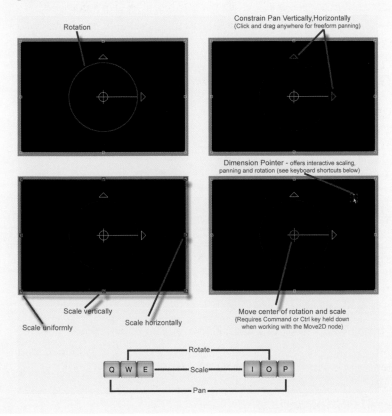

The robot is now correctly placed in the scene, but if you look at the shot, you'll notice that it's missing one of the most important visual cues: a shadow. Right now, the robot appears to be floating in space, not attached to the ground.

Fortunately, a shadow pass has been rendered that includes the robot. You can use this shadow pass to create a shadow. (You'll find the shadow pass node—labeled Shadow—just below and to the right of the Background node.)

The shadow is, of course, cast onto the background, so you'll apply a color correction to darken it down.

1   Double-click the middle of Over1 to select it and load it into the viewer.

2 In the Color tab, click a Mult node.

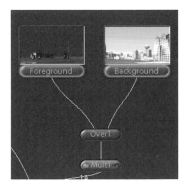

The Color tab might look more like a periodic table of elements than anything you're used for modifying color. Actually, if you've performed color correction in other software, these are all tools you've used before. They're just given names tied to the mathematical operations they perform on pixels.

A Mult node can brighten and colorize an image. There are many ways to adjust the color of the color swatch in a Mult; you'll cover a couple of different methods here.

3 Position the mouse at the center of the color swatch in the parameters for Mult1.

4 Press the L key (L for luminance) on the keyboard, and then drag the mouse pointer to the left. This will reduce the brightness of the color chosen in the color swatch. To reduce the luminance still further, release the mouse button, reposition the pointer over the swatch, and again drag to the left (still pressing the L key). Stop dragging when the three numeric entry boxes read around *0.3*. The three boxes refer to the red, green, and blue values of the color swatch, respectively.

You can also adjust the luminance by pressing the small "+" sign to the left of Color. This will expand the color controls to reveal a luminance slider.

TIP There are other keyboard shortcuts to be used like this: (R)ed, (G)reen, (B)lue, (H)ue, (S)aturation, and (V)alue. Here's another nice trick: Pressing the T key will adjust "temperature". That's artist temperature, not Kelvin. Dragging to the left will shift to warmer, red tones. Dragging to the right will shift to cooler, blue tones.

The entire stream coming from Over1 has been darkened to approximately a third of its original brightness. You've effectively plunged the entire background into shadow. Next, you'll mask off the area where the shadow will be applied.

▶ Anatomy of a Color Picker

Color swatches show up throughout Shake in color correctors, keyers, even under the Viewer (for changing the color of OSC). They all have the same basic functionality.

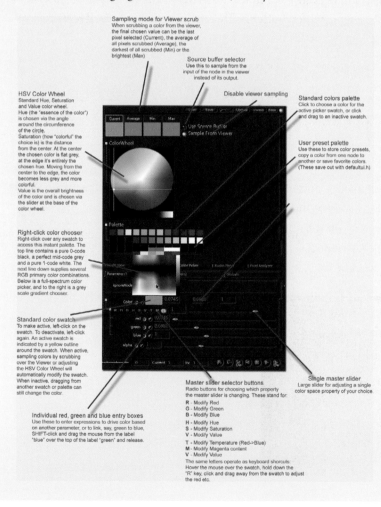

Sampling mode for Viewer scrub
When scrubbing a color from the viewer, the final chosen value can be the last pixel selected (Current), the average of all pixels scrubbed (Average), the darkest of all scrubbed (Min) or the brightest (Max)

Source buffer selector
Use this to sample from the input of the node in the viewer instead of its output.

Disable viewer sampling

Standard colors palette
Click to choose a color for the active picker swatch, or click and drag to an inactive swatch.

HSV Color Wheel
Standard Hue, Saturation and Value color wheel.
Hue (the "essence of the color") is chosen via the angle around the circumference of the circle.
Saturation (how "colorful" the choice is) is the distance from the center. At the center the chosen color is flat grey, at the edge it's entirely the chosen hue. Moving from the center to the edge, the color becomes less grey and more colorful.
Value is the overall brightness of the color and is chosen via the slider at the base of the color wheel.

User preset palette
Use these to store color presets, copy a color from one node to another or save favorite colors. (These save out with defaultui.h)

Right-click color chooser
Right-click over any swatch to access this instant palette. The top line contains a pure 0-code black, a perfect mid-code grey and a pure 1-code white. The next line down supplies several RGB primary color combinations. Below is a full-spectrum color picker, and to the right is a grey scale gradient chooser.

Standard color swatch
To make active, left-click on the swatch. To deactivate, left-click again. An active swatch is indicated by a yellow outline around the swatch. When active, sampling colors by scrubbing over the Viewer or adjusting the HSV Color Wheel will automatically modify the swatch. When inactive, dragging from another swatch or palette can still change the color.

Individual red, green and blue entry boxes
Use these to enter expressions to drive color based on another parameter, or to link, say, green to blue, SHIFT-click and drag the mouse from the label "blue" over the top of the label "green" and release.

Master slider selector buttons
Radio buttons for choosing which property the master slider is changing. These stand for:
R - Modify Red
G - Modify Green
B - Modify Blue
H - Modify Hue
S - Modify Saturation
V - Modify Value
T - Modify Temperature (Red->Blue)
M - Modify Magenta content
V - Modify Value
The same letters operate as keyboard shortcuts:
Hover the mouse over the swatch, hold down the "R" key, click and drag away from the swatch to adjust the red etc.

Single master slider
Large slider for adjusting a single color space property of your choice.

Using the Viewer

Shake allows you to create as many viewers as you want (in addition to providing external broadcast monitor support). In most circumstances, however, a single viewer is adequate. Why? Because each viewer supports two buffers, A and B.

1 In the lower left corner of the Viewer, click the Toggle Buffer button (which should read "A").

The button instantly changes to "B" and the viewer goes blank. That's because we're now looking at the second buffer, buffer B. To load an image into buffer B, simply click on its left side like normal.

2 Click the left side of Shadow. Shadow is now loaded into the viewer

3 In the lower left corner of the Viewer, click the Toggle Buffer button (which now says "B").

4 Click the left side of Mult1.

You've just loaded Shadow into buffer B and Mult1 into buffer A. Click the Toggle Buffer button to quickly switch between the two images.

Notice the letters at the bottom-left of the two nodes. Mult1 says "1A", indicating that it's currently loaded into the "A" buffer of Viewer 1. Shadow says "1B", indicating that it's loaded into the "B" buffer of Viewer 1.

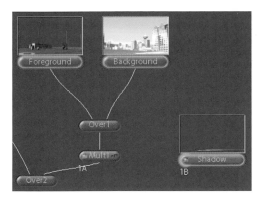

The button's nice, but you'll be fired on the first day of the job if you're caught using it. A Shake compositor worth her pay knows to use the keyboard shortcut: Simply position your mouse over the Viewer workspace and press the 1 key to quickly toggle buffers.

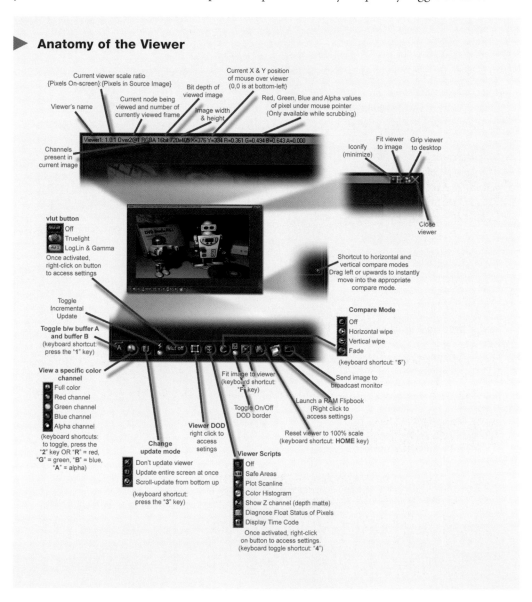

Unveiling the Mask

As you toggle between the buffers, you can see that the **Shadow** clip is white in the area where the robot would be expected to cast a shadow. We'll use this to mask the Mult1 color correction (the darkening effect you created earlier). The mask input of a node *masks off* the area of the image where the effect will be applied. If you use Shadow as a mask for Mult1, the color correction will only be applied in the white area seen in the Shadow clip.

1   Drag a noodle from the output of Shadow and bring the mouse just to the right of Mult1. As you do so, a round knot with an "M" shows up. This is the *Mask Input*.

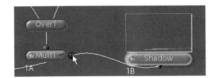

2   Release the mouse button to complete the connection.

The color correction is instantly limited to the shadow region. Do you want to compare it to the unmasked version? See how you can toggle it on and off:

3   Click the right side of Mult1 to load its parameters.

4   Click the + button to the left of Mask to open the mask parameters section

5   Click the LED to the right of enableMask to toggle on and off the effect of the mask.

You can now see the change to the coloration of the trees when you toggle on and off the enableMask parameter.

6 When you're done playing, leave the LED in the On state.

7 Click the left side of Over2 to load it into the Viewer.

Adjusting the Shadow Color

You've created a shadow, but it's not quite the correct shadow; the color is wrong. Daylight shadows are usually the result of an object blocking direct sunlight. However, the ambient blue skylight can still reach the shadowed area (since it's coming from all directions, not just the direction occluded by the shadowing object, which is the robot in this case). So, your shadow should be tinted the same color as the sky.

1 Make sure the parameters for Mult1 are still loaded into the Parameters tab. If not, click the right side of Mult1 to load them.

2 Click the center of the color swatch to see Mult1's parameters. The node view automatically jumps to the Color Picker tab, and a fine yellow border shows up around the color swatch, indicating that it's currently active and ready to edit.

3 Select the Average mode in the Color Picker. This will set your color swatch to the average value of all the pixels you scrub over with the mouse.

4 Drag the mouse pointer over the sky area, being careful not to touch any "non-sky" pixels. If you do, just lift the mouse, then drag over the sky to restart the averaging.

The shadow automatically tints to the color of the sky.

5   Click again on the swatch in Mult1's parameters to deselect it. The yellow border
should disappear.

This deactivates the swatch and prevents you from unintentionally changing the
color later.

6   Click back to the Node View tab.

You're done with the Color Picker, so there's no need to keep it open.

The shadow's a little too light, so you'll darken it using the same shortcut you used
previously.

7   Position your mouse pointer over the color swatch, press the L key, and drag to the
left until you're happy with the shadow intensity.

Notice that the hue of the shadow remains blue. The luminance adjustment you
performed by holding down the L key reduced the luminance without affecting hue
or saturation.

Adding Some Glare

It's a bright day in your scene, so you should add a little glare to the robot. Camera glare occurs on the extremely bright parts of an object. You can use a luma key to isolate just those bright parts of the robot.

1   Drag down Move2D1 a little to give you some room to work.

2   Click the middle of Robot to select it, then in the Key tab, Shift-click a LumaKey node.

Shift-clicking a button in the tool tabs *branches* the new node on a separate noodle. If you'd just used a regular click, the LumaKey would have been inserted mid-stream between Robot and Move2D1. It may look like that right now, but as you drag it out, you'll see that it has its own distinct noodle.

You can only see what the luma key is doing by looking at its alpha channel.

3   Position your mouse pointer over the Viewer and press A (for alpha).

The Viewer now displays the information contained on the alpha channel. (You can also look at the red, green, and blue channels individually by pressing R, G, and B, respectively. Pressing C (for color) will take you back to standard full color viewing.

4   In the parameters for LumaKey1, set loVal to *0.4*, and hiVal to *0.7*.

By adjusting LumaKey1, you've isolated the brightest parts of the robot.

5   With your mouse pointer positioned over the Viewer, press the C key to return to viewing the color channels.

Currently, only the alpha channel has been affected. You need to multiply the color channels using this new alpha matte to affect them, too.

6   At the bottom of the LumaKey1 parameters, click the matteMult button to activate it.

Now that the bright bits are isolated, it's time to turn them into glare.

7   Make sure LumaKey1 is still selected, and in the Filter tab, click a Blur. Set the pixels value to *140*.

You're left with a big, blurry mush.

8   With Blur1 selected, add a Screen node from the Layer tab. Drag a noodle from Robot and connect it to the second input of Screen1.

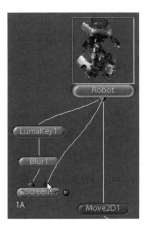

9   From the output at the bottom of Screen1, drag a noodle to the input of Move2D1. The new noodle will automatically replace the one that originally passed from Robot directly into Move2D1.

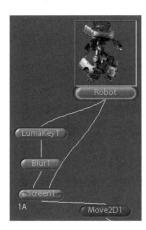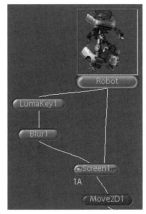

10 Click on the left side of Over2 to load it into the Viewer and preview the results.

The glare may be a touch too strong. You should fade it back a little.

11 Click the middle of Blur1 to select it.

12 In the Color tab, click a Fade node.

13 In the parameters for Fade1, drag the value slider to *0.6*.

This dials the glare back nicely. Want to compare the difference?

14 Make sure Fade1 is still selected, then position your mouse pointer over the Node view, and press the I key to ignore the node.

The glare instantly increases as Fade1 is temporarily disabled.

15 With your mouse pointer over the node view, press the I key to reactivate Fade1.

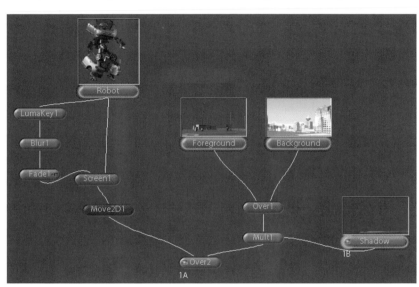

Adding a Vignette and Film Grain

A little cheating goes on in this last step. In the interests of keeping things simple, a set of nodes has been created for simulated film grain and a camera lens vignette, and then grouped together into a single item in the node view.

1 Drag up using the middle mouse button, or Option-drag up with the left mouse button upward until you can see the GrainAndVignette group node.

2 Drag a noodle from Over2 and connect it to the input of GrainAndVignette.

3 Double-click GrainAndVignette to load it into the Viewer.

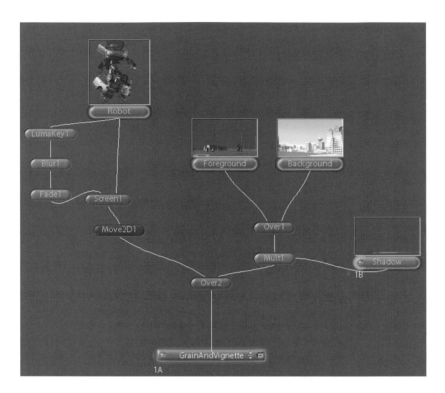

The shot is complete.

It's time to see what it all looks like with movement.

Using the Flipbook

Shake's Flipbook is an incredibly powerful RAM-based preview system. It's actually a completely separate application from Shake, which means you can continue to work in Shake while it's rendering a preview of your composite. In fact, due to the unlimited render licenses available in Mac OS X, anyone working on a Mac in your facility can access the flipbook from the terminal to preview their test renders, even if they know nothing about Shake.

Before launching the Flipbook, you need to make sure the timeRange is set correctly.

1   In the Parameters workspace, click the Globals tab.

The Globals tab is where you can make changes to general composition settings, as well as some of the interface appearance and functionality. The timeRange is the length of your composite. In this case, it's set to 1-60. For this exercise, assume you only wanted to render out the first 20 frames.

2   On the Globals tab, set timeRange to *1-20*.

3   Position your mouse pointer over the time bar at the bottom of the screen. Press the Home key.

Notice that the time bar automatically set itself to the timeRange when you pressed the Home key.

4   On the Globals tab, press the Auto button (to the right of timeRange).

You'll see the timeRange automatically sets itself back to *1-60*. When you press the Auto button, Shake sets the timeRange to the length of the longest clip in the node view, 60 frames in this case.

5   At the bottom of the screen, position your mouse pointer over the time bar. Press the Home key. Shake sets the time bar back to 1-60.

OK, without further ado, launch the Flipbook.

1   Make sure you're looking at GrainAndVignette in the Viewer.

2   Click the Flipbook icon under the Viewer, but only click once! In some cases, it may take a few seconds for the Flipbook window to appear.

Depending on the performance of your computer, this may take some time to render. If you're an impatient type, you can begin playback of the frames loaded so far by pressing the Period (.) key. (You can think of it as the Greater Than (>) key, which is the shifted version of the same key. It's supposed to look like a play-forward arrow). The flipbook will begin to play. But while it's playing, it continues to render in the background. Every time a new frame is rendered, it gets added to the playback loop. To stop the playback and give all the CPU cycles back to the job of rendering the Flipbook, press the Forward Slash (/) key.

If you want to stop rendering completely and just have Shake play back the frames it's rendered up to the current point in time, press the Spacebar, then press the Greater Than (>) key. To continue the render, press Spacebar again, then press the Forward Slash (/) key.

▶ **Anatomy of a Flipbook**

The Flipbook has no GUI control—everything's done using keyboard shortcuts. Consequently, these are some of the shortcuts you just have to learn.

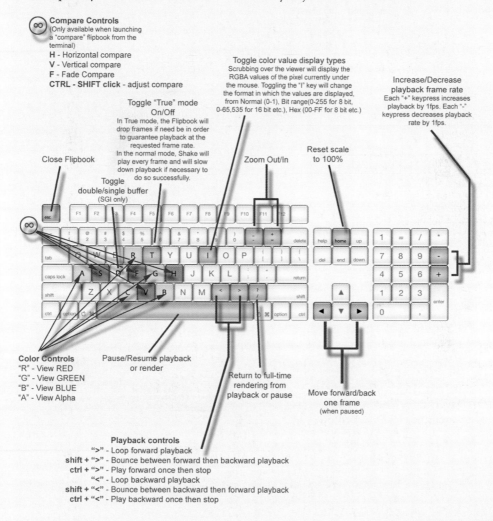

Compare Controls
(Only available when launching a "compare" flipbook from the terminal)
H - Horizontal compare
V - Vertical compare
F - Fade Compare
CTRL - SHIFT click - adjust compare

Toggle color value display types
Scrubbing over the viewer will display the RGBA values of the pixel currently under the mouse. Toggling the "I" key will change the format in which the values are displayed, from Normal (0-1), Bit range(0-255 for 8 bit, 0-65,535 for 16 bit etc.), Hex (00-FF for 8 bit etc.)

Increase/Decrease playback frame rate
Each "+" keypress increases playback by 1fps. Each "-" keypress decreases playback rate by 1fps.

Toggle "True" mode On/Off
In True mode, the Flipbook will drop frames if need be in order to guarantee playback at the requested frame rate.
In the normal mode, Shake will play every frame and will slow down playback if necessary to do so successfully.

Close Flipbook

Toggle double/single buffer
(SGI only)

Zoom Out/In

Reset scale to 100%

Color Controls
"R" - View RED
"G" - View GREEN
"B" - View BLUE
"A" - View Alpha

Pause/Resume playback or render

Return to full-time rendering from playback or pause

Move forward/back one frame
(when paused)

Playback controls
"**>**" - Loop forward playback
shift + ">" - Bounce between forward then backward playback
ctrl + ">" - Play forward once then stop
"**<**" - Loop backward playback
shift + "<" - Bounce between backward then forward playback
ctrl + "<" - Play backward once then stop

Continues on next page

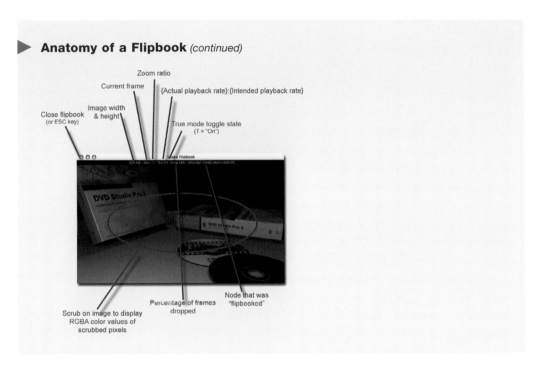

▶ Anatomy of a Flipbook (continued)

Flipbooks suck up your system RAM. They live there to give you fast, responsive interactive previews. That's your *precious* system RAM, the stuff Shake uses to manipulate images in the interface, render your final sequences, and so on. So, discard your used Flipbooks thoughtfully. With the Flipbook active, press the Escape key to close it. Because it's a separate application from Shake, clicking the main Shake interface will hide the Flipbook behind the interface but won't close it; it's still lurking in the background hoarding that RAM. So, don't be fooled. Conscientiously close all the Flipbooks when you're done with them.

RAM Flipbooks *cannot* be saved; they exist only as a temporary preview. *Disk* flipbooks—available on the Macintosh version of Shake—render to a QuickTime codec and can be saved as self-contained movies, emailed as client previews, and so on. Disk flipbooks are accessible from the Render menu.

Conclusion

This is just a basic overview of Shake. Moving forward from this basic introduction, you can discover a wealth of tools: warpers, morphers, keyers, matchmovers, image stabilizers, retimers, and color correctors, to name but a few. The Apple Pro Training Series book, *Shake 4*, written by Marco Paolini is a great way to begin to increase your knowledge of Shake.

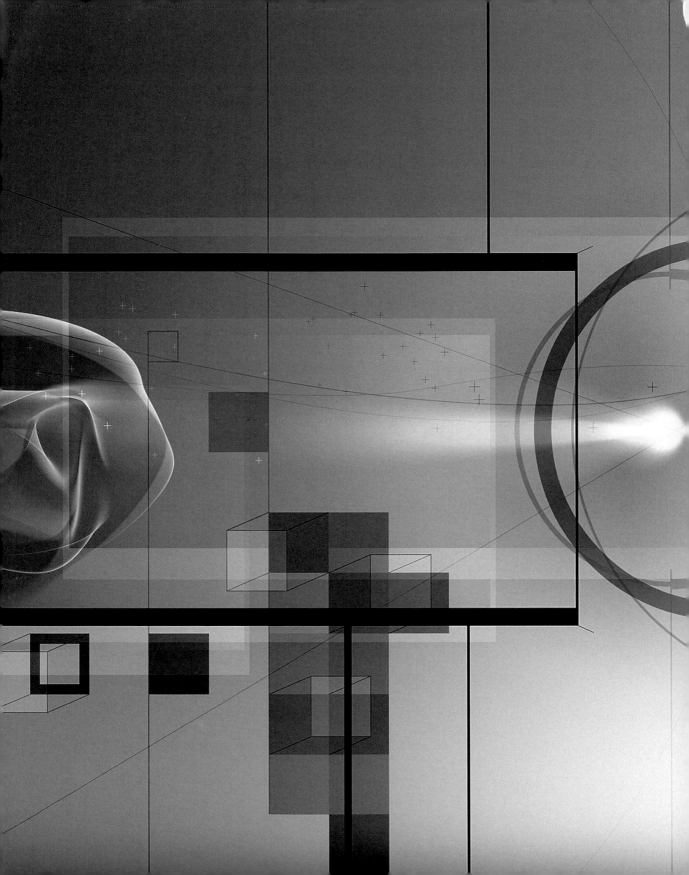

Index

silhouette + fx

silhouette roto™

Silhouette Roto is a comprehensive rotoscoping solution that's stand-alone or an After Effects compatible plug-in. Silhouette Roto allows you to quickly create sophisticated animated mattes using B-spline or Bezier shapes. Intelligent design and easy-to-use tools, such as variable edge softness on a point by point basis and realistic motion blur, assist you in creating shape animations. Integrated motion tracking can make the normally tedious task of rotoscoping a breeze.

silhouette paint™

Silhouette Paint is a high dynamic range 2D paint system designed from the ground up to handle the demands of feature film and television production. Paint and shape features are tightly integrated to form an extremely powerful shape based paint tool. Not only can paint effects be animated, but they can be combined with animated rotoshapes to take the drudgery out of everyday jobs. Whether its image restoration, dustbusting, wire and rig removal or just plain paint, Silhouette Paint provides simple and sensible tools to get the job done.

[ROTO FEATURES]
- *Unlimited number of animated B-spline or Bezier shapes*
- *Integrated Motion Tracker that can apply motion data to points or shapes*
- *Shape assisted motion tracking*
- *Move, scale, rotate, shear, and corner pin shapes and groups of shapes*
- *Point-by-Point variable edge softness*
- *Realistic motion blur*
- *Animation changes for one point or selected points across all keyframes*
- *Independent shape viewing*
- *User-definable names for each shape*
- *Preview shape animation over image*
- *Shape import and export*
- *Composite preview*

[PAINT FEATURES]
- *Includes all Silhouette Roto features*
- *Shape assisted painting*
- *Animateable paint brushes and effects*
- *Assign paint brushes to shapes and groups of shapes*
- *Sophisticated cloning interface*
- *Position, scale, rotate paint sources*
- *High dynamic range painting in Float, 16 bit and 8 bit*

silhouette+fx brings together the unbeatable combination of superior software designers and visual effects veterans. Add an Academy Award® for Scientific and Technical Achievement, 3 Emmy® Awards and experience in creating visual effects for hundreds of feature films, commercials and television shows and you have a recipe for success. Stay tuned for new products.

www.silhouettefx.com

The Apple Pro Training Series

Apple Pro Training Series: Final Cut Pro 5
0-321-33481-7

In this best-selling guide, Diana Weynand starts with basic video editing techniques and takes you all the way through Final Cut Pro's powerful advanced features. Using world-class documentary footage, you'll learn to mark and edit clips, color correct sequences, create transitions, apply filters and effects, add titles, work with audio, and more.

Apple Pro Training Series: Advanced Editing Techniques in Final Cut Pro 5
0-321-33549-X

Director and editor Michael Wohl shares must-know professional techniques for cutting dialogue scenes, action scenes, fight and chase scenes, documentaries, comedy, music videos, multi-camera projects, and more. Also covers Soundtrack Pro, audio finishing, managing clips and media, and working with film.

Apple Pro Training Series: Advanced Color Correction and Effects in Final Cut Pro 5
0-321-33548-1

This Apple-authorized guide delivers hard-to-find training in real-world color correction and effects techniques, including motion effects, keying and compositing, titling, scene-to-scene color matching, and correcting for broadcast specifications.

Apple Pro Training Series: Optimizing Your Final Cut Pro System
0-321-26871-7

Written and field-tested by industry pros Sean Cullen, Matthew Geller, Charles Roberts, and Adam Wilt, this is the ultimate guide for installing, configuring, optimizing, and trouble-shooting Final Cut Pro in real-world post-production environments.

Apple Pro Training Series: Final Cut Pro for Avid Editors
0-321-24577-6

Master trainer Diana Weynand takes you through a comprehensive "translation course" designed for professional video and film editors who already know their way around Avid nonlinear systems.

Apple Pro Training Series: Getting Started with Final Cut Studio
0-321-36991-2

This Apple-authorized guide provides newcomers with an excellent overview of all products in Final Cut Studio: Final Cut Pro 5, Motion 2, Soundtrack Pro and DVD Studio Pro 4.

Apple Pro Training Series: Final Cut Express HD
0-321-33533-3

The only Apple-authorized guide to Final Cut Express HD, this book delivers the techniques you need to make movie magic from the comfort of your Mac.

Apple Pro Training Series: Xsan 2/E
0-321-43232-0

Apple's exciting new enterprise-class file system offers high-speed access to centralized shared data. This handy booklet provides invaluable setup, configuration, and troubleshooting tips.

To order books or find out about the Apple Pro Training Series, visit: **www.peachpit.com/appleprotraining**

Apple Pro Training Series: DVD Studio Pro 4
0-321-33482-5

Learn to author professional interactive DVDs with this best-selling guide.

Apple Pro Training Series: Shake 4
0-321-25609-3

Apple-certified guide uses stunning real world sequences to reveal the wizardry of Shake 4.

Apple Pro Training Series: Shake 4 Quick Reference Guide
0-321-38246-3

Compact reference guide to Apple's leading compositing software.

Apple Pro Training Series: Getting Started with Motion
0-321-30533-7

Apple-certified guide makes sophisticated motion graphics accessible to newcomers.

Apple Pro Training Series: Motion
0-321-27826-7

Comprehensive guide to Apple's revolutionary motion graphics software.

Encyclopedia of Visual Effects
0-321-30334-2

Ultimate recipe book for visual effects artists working in Shake, Motion and Adobe After Effects.

Apple Pro Training Series: Soundtrack Pro
0-321-35757-4

Create original soundtrack's with Apple's exciting new sound design software.

Apple Pro Training Series: Logic Pro 7 and Logic Express 7
0-321-25614-X

Create, mix, and polish your musical creations using Apple's pro audio software.

Apple Pro Training Series: Advanced Logic Pro 7
0-321-25607-7

Comprehensive guide takes you through Logic's powerful advanced features.

Apple Pro Training Series: Color Management with Mac OS X
0-321-24576-8

Project-based guide shows how to set up real-world color management workflows.

Apple Pro Training Series: Getting Started with Aperture
0-321-42275-9

Introduction to Apple's revolutionary workflow tool for professional photographers.

Apple Pro Training Series: Aperture
0-321-42276-7

Comprehensive book-DVD combo takes you step by step all the way through Aperture.

The Apple Training Series

Designed for system administrators, IT professionals, AppleCare technicians, and Mac enthusiasts, the Apple Training Series is both a self-paced learning tool and the official curriculum of the Apple Training and Certification program. For more information, go to **http://train.apple.com**.

Apple Training Series: Mac OS X Support Essentials
0-321-33547-3

Apple Training Series: Mac OS X Server Essentials
0-321-35758-2

Apple Training Series: Desktop and Portable Systems, Second Edition
0-321-33546-5

Apple Training Series: iWork '06
0-321-44225-3

Apple Training Series: Mac OS X System Administration Guide, Volume 1
0-321-36984-X

Apple Training Series: Mac OS X System Administration Guide, Volume 2
0-321-42315-1

Apple Training Series: iLife '06
0-321-42164-7

Apple Training Series: GarageBand 3
0-321-42165-5